MW00878899

# Divided We Stand

ORIGINAL BOOKSWAP

Paperbacks, Trade Editions, Hardcovers & More!

316 Horsham Road
Horsham, PA 19044

# Divided We Stand

## The Forgotten War and the 181st Signal Repair Co.

Joseph W. Harding

Copyright © 2003 by Joseph W. Harding.

Library of Congress Number:     2002096584
ISBN :         Hardcover         1-4010-8769-8
               Softcover         1-4010-8768-X

All rights reserved. No part of this book may be reproduced or transmitted in any form or by any means, electronic or mechanical, including photocopying, recording, or by any information storage and retrieval system, without permission in writing from the copyright owner.

This book was printed in the United States of America.

**To order additional copies of this book, contact:**
Xlibris Corporation
1-888-795-4274
www.Xlibris.com
Orders@Xlibris.com
17428

# Contents

CHAPTER V-The Official Breakup Begins

CHAPTER VI-China (Y Force and SOS)

CHAPTER VII-Between The East And The West

CHAPTER VII-Our Final Breakup

CHAPTER IX-Eastern China

CHAPTER X-Trip Home And Separation

TO
MY WIFE RUTH
MY BEST FRIEND AND LOVER FOR FIFTY
ONE YEARS . . . AND . . . ALSO MY
PERSONAL CRITIC, WHO WAS ALWAYS
THE FIRST TO REVIEW MY EFFORTS
AT STORYTELLING AND TO
MY COMRADES FROM THE 181 ST,
TO WHOM I OWE AN UNPAYABLE DEBT
FOR THEIR MANY YEARS OF FRIENDSHIP
AND SUPPORT DURING THE WAR
AND IN RECALLING THEIR STORIES.

# FOREWARD

This effort at book writing grew out of a curiousity triggered by a chance meeting with a former army acquaintance. The sudden uprooting of a buried past and the subsequent inquiries it generated led to a series of discoveries and encounters which fanned a previously casual interest into an insatiable inquisitiveness concerning the whereabouts of my former comrades.

As they began to emerge from the misty past, reunion became a goal and eventually, in 1982, reality. Teaming with Ray Hardee of North Carolina, in launching this first effort, however, I did not anticipate the phenomenal degree of comradery that was demonstrated there by the survivors as they greeted each other. Consequently I came away from this very moving gathering with the realization that in the intensity of this common bond, combined with the experiences of these men in China, Burma and India there was a story which should be known and recorded.

While the telling of the 181ST story is intended to record events, it was motivated primarily by an almost urgent need to provide a kind of safety net to prevent, not only the unit's activities, but more importantly, the personal experiences of the men involved, from sinking silently into the inaccessible depths of eternal anonymity. I would be less than honest if I failed to include my own desire to attempt to portray the odyssey of the 181ST through the eyes of a 125 pound twenty-year-old, who was unceremoniously uprooted from a secure, ordinary, middle income home and who had never traveled more than 250 miles away from that home prior to the enactment of our story.

# INTRODUCTION

Like thousands of other army units, the contributions of the 181ST Signal Repair Company were modest, and it was destined to function in its own little niche as defined by some remote authority. It also paralleled these others in that it was comprised almost entirely of civilians, caught up in a deadly conflict about which they knew little more than what they could glean from the news media or that which the government had chosen to reveal.

The similarity with the profiles of these other army units ends at this point. Whereas the others were deployed, sometimes en masse, in the two major theaters of operation, the 181ST was, by its very purpose, shattered into sometimes minute repair teams and scattered like leaves in the most remote regions of forgotten and politically unpopular China, Burma and India. The average World War II buff's knowledge of the CBI ends with the glorious doings of Chennault's Flying Tigers, Merrill's Marauders, Stilwell's famous Chinese 22nd and 38th Divisions and the Air Corps organizations that mastered the "Hump". While some elements of the 181ST made their contributions to the activities of all of these, and others, the company is historically anonymous.

Unlike the famous combat divisions, which hailed from individual states and who, therefore, enjoyed social and political identities, the 181ST embraced a mixed bag of individuals, representative of every corner of the country. Approximately one third were drawn from Ft. Dix, New Jersey, coming from that state and neighboring New York. Another third entered the army through Ft. Bragg, North Carolina and were exclusively from that and nearby states. The remaining third, which sported longevities of six months or more over the inductees from Dix and Bragg had been collected at random from virtually every state in the country. Several had previous military experience. Some had enlisted and together with the inductees among them, they formed the cadre from which the company was spawned.

The most singular charcteristic of the 181ST was evidenced by the uniqueness of its assignments. While it was formed for the primary purpose of performing high echelon repair of army communication equipment, its pursuit of this charge in the primitive remoteness of the China, Burma, India region ordained for it a much less regimented existence than the one for which it was trained. Depending on the size, nationality and location of the various military units it serviced during its two years in Asia, the company was repeatedly fragmented into varied-sized teams, ranging from platoon strength down to one—man assignments. As a result, its members frequently found themselves so immersed in the situation confronting them that "signal repair" sometimes became a distant, even non-existent, employment.

After its formation at Camp Crowder, Missouri, at the height of the North African campaign, it was dispatched to California to suffer in the 120 plus degree summer heat of the Mojave Desert. As the North African war wound down, it did not, however, find itself in a desert scenario to which it had finally become acclimated. Instead the sadistic tour guide had elected to lead it to upper Assam in the rain forests of northeastern India.

Its arrival there in late 1943 was followed by a period of several weeks during which it was to enjoy its last experience as a complete military unit and its last chance for togetherness as a social entity. Within weeks of arriving in Ledo, from which building of the Stilwell Road had already begun, the permanent breakup of our military family started and for the next two years, we wandered the mysterious trails and roadways of India, Burma and China. By war's end the handful of men who had started as a unit three years earlier in Missouri, found itself spread over three countries, a distance of no less than 1000 miles.

Formal dismantling of the company began in September of 1944 when the Fifth Repair Team was spun off to father the 223rd Signal Depot Company. Two months later fragmentation of the Third Team began, eventually ending in its becoming part of the new 191st Signal Repair Company and the 3199th Signal Service Battalian. Then, as though to ensure its permanent dissolution, Major General Claire Chennault, in an order dated March 20, 1945, decreed officially that the 181ST no longer existed and was thereafter combined with other units to become the 4011th Signal Service Battalion.

Although the continual dispersal of the unit persisted right up to war's end and through the returning-home process, the survivors became aware of the presence of a surprisingly strong inner gravitational force. A force which, just as persistently, reversed the destructive direction of events following our arrival at Ledo and which also revealed a heretofore unperceived but very deep sense of common kinship.

While the accomplishments of the 181ST will be recorded in history as having made little, if any, difference in the final outcome of the conflict, to its members, these accomplishments, however miniscule, will always represent the results of their contribution of a three or four year segment of their lives. This time would have been spent, otherwise, in starting families, continuing educations, solidifying job positions or establishing viable farms. The reader, therefore, will gain a greater appreciation of our story if he or she does not lose sight of these truisms, for they were behind the manner in which we coped with our privations.

To these men and comrades I dedicate my effort. I regret that it took fifty plus years for this story to be told, because too many of its participants have already passed on to their rewards. I also regret that over such a long period much of the story has faded in the memories of the survivors and is eternally lost. Very few of the events are based on cold facts, mined from official records. They are, instead, reconstructed primarily from the memories of the participants and whatever personal records they kept. To assist the reader in following the chronology of the 181ST and to establish a framework within which our activities took place, occasional references have been made to major events as they occurred in the China, Burma, India theater.

I must acknowledge the assistance, encouragement and information received from my comrades. Special thanks is due Ben Tillman from whose diary I was able to find critical dates and to Dr. Bernard Silverman, who gratiously proof-read my manuscript, correcting my grammatical errors and smoothing out several rough spots. A large debt is owed to Bob Callinan, who had the foresight, during our overseas voyage, to secure a list of names and addresses of most of the men . . . and to Bill Wraspir who turned up a company roster which had been compiled as we prepared to leave for Staten Island and our "mystery voyage". These lists, more than any single factor have made possible a post-war life for the 181ST as a unit and the triggering of events through which the unrelenting dispersal processes of wartime have finally been reversed.

I wish, also, to thank Luke Strass and Ray Bumgardner who took the time to record on audio tape valuable, personal contributions to our story . . . . and several others whose letters were so very informative.

My very special friend, Mary Hitchcock Fuges, acquiescing to my desire to emphasize those geographical features most pertinent to our story, created the maps of the CBI, India-Burma and China Theaters.

Last, but not least, I owe much to my grandson, Jim Harding, my personal computer guru, who guided me through that mysterious world and who collaborated with me in designing the book's jacket, using a photo taken by me so many years ago in Kunming.

# PROLOGUE

For those who may not be familiar with the scenario within which the story of the 181st occurred, a brief glimpse into the conflict on the Southeast Asian continent may be helpful. As our story began, Chiang Kai-shek was the leader of China, a China which was still in the throes of its recent efforts at unification. It had been invaded by Japan, which was nibbling away territory as the impoverished Chinese yielded it, sometimes with a fight and just as often without. Great Britain had lost much of its empire to the Japanese and was attempting to quell the tides of nationalism in India, while, at home, it faced the real threat of extermination at the hands of the Nazis. In the United States, isolationism by many was suddenly dealt a telling blow by the events at Pearl Harbor, which laid bare the state of our material and psychological unpreparedness for war.

Events then had conspired to create a convocation of Allies, each of whom was struggling for survival with the barest means at hand for ensuring it. Though their interests in Asia were important to them, they nevertheless were forced by circumstances to assign them last priority . . . economically and militarily. Each, at one time or another, conceded that they were fighting a "cheap war" in the C.B.I. Theater.

The following quote from "Life's Picture History of World War II" (1950) is representative of the nature of that war and the political climate of the theater:

> C.B.I. stood for China-Burma-India, but the initials
> might very well have meant "constant bickering inside."

No other theater of war produced more recrimination. The disagreement started at the top: Roosevelt insisted that China's half-billion people could contribute much to victory; Churchill refused to be impressed by numbers and turned his share of the campaign toward recapturing Singapore, Hong Kong and Rangoon for the empire. In 1944 cooperation reached a wartime low and the theater was split: India-Burma and China. Dissension was even sharper among Americans. General Stilwell wanted to fight overland; Major General Claire Chennault, the air commander, had such exaggerated faith in combat aviation that he promised Roosevelt in 1942 to "accomplish the downfall of Japan" if given 147 planes. Chennault and Stilwell despised each other. Stilwell also hated the British and Generalissimo Chiang Kai-shek (whose chief of staff he was); Chennault liked Chiang but he had contempt for his own superiors. For seven months of 1944-45 the B-29's attempted to bomb Japan but the distance was too great to make the raids effective. But if the C.B.I. produced many failures, it had one notable success: the Hump airlift which kept China in the war during the long months the Burma and Ledo roads were building."

In this writer's opinion, the lone figure who emerges from this political morass, boasting the most consistent record of honest, unswerving resolve in conducting a war to defeat the hated enemy is General Joseph W. Stilwell. Although excessive in his criticism of our political allies; prone to overplaying the role of the ordinary soldier's general; and apparently naive in expecting his West Point-trained subordinates to understand his brand of overly-simplistic Sino-American military administrative methods, he nevertheless stands head and shoulders above any of the principals mentioned above, in espousing and attempting to effect a swift and real end to the war in the C. B. I.

I believe that his greatest transgression was his failure to practice mature objectivity regarding the arrival of, deployment of, and medical, material and moral support of the officers and enlisted men of the 5307th Composite Unit (Provisional), (Merrill's Marauders). Without the unswerving determination that they demonstrated in the face of unbelievable sufferings from nature, the Japanese and, unfortunately, theater personnel, it is unlikely that his goal, of taking Myitkyina, in the face of overwhelming international opinion that he could not do it, would have been possible.

Nevertheless, the failure of our politicians to stand behind him in his most critical hour, when his visions of victory were finally beginning to approach fruition stands out, in my opinion, as one of the most sordid performances of recent history.

The real tragedy is that, while we have adulated men like Patton and Mac Arthur, who wallowed in their own self-esteem, we allowed a truly worthy man to slip into history without ever acknowledging his heroic accomplishments in an environment in which no ordinary man could have survived.

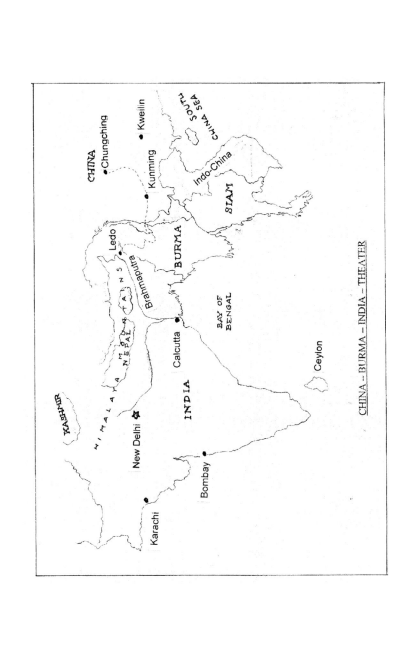

CHINA – BURMA – INDIA – THEATER

# CHAPTER I

# The Company Is Formed

## COOKS, BAKERS,
## AND WHO KNOWS WHAT

Immediately following our wholly unexpected and traumatic military setbacks at the hands of the Japanese in the Pacific and while the British were being driven across North Africa by Field Marshall Rommel, the "Desert Fox", events were occurring in Burma which would subsequently produce the scenario from which the very reason for the existence of the 181st Signal Repair Company would emerge. In January of 1942 the Japanese had overrun Rangoon in Burma and were heading north for the eventual occupation of the entire country. In the meantime, the Allied Command in India, anticipating the probable isolation of China, had already approved a plan to construct a road, capable of handling jeep traffic into northern Burma via Pangsau Pass in the Patkai Mountains. On the other side of Burma, the Chinese were hailing America's entry into the War as the spelling of certain doom for the Japanese. At the same time Chiang-Kai-shek was demanding American troops, supplies, planes and money in exchange for China's continued active participation in the war . . . a promise on which he spent the rest of the war trying to renege.

Back in the United States our personal response to these momentous events had already started . . . . the process of forming the 181ST had begun. Lt. John Petri from Cooperstown, N.Y. had set up shop at Camp Crowder, in southwestern Missouri and was proceeding to collect a cadre. His goal was to field an organization boasting five teams, capable of performing the highest echelon of repair on all types of field radio, teletype, telephone and telegraph equipment used by the army. The company, which would also include a Headquarters Platoon to supply administrative, transportation, food and materiel support, would have a total strength of about 180 men and seven officers. The unit would also have to qualify as a military entity, achieving certain minimum skills in the use of firearms and the other tools of war. The extent to which this all was accomplished was attested to eventually by the performance of the company in the truly extraordinary assignments it received and the manner in which it carried them out.

The secret to this success was, of course, the personnel who found their way to the 181ST. In early 1942, the call went out for a nucleus of about sixty men and seven officers. These were to become the skeleton, which would be filled out with draftees from Forts Bragg and Dix. Since the writer was one of the latter lucky souls, he was not a witness to the events covered by this chapter. Those who were party to this "birthing" process were the "older" fellows, with a little less recall power, at this time, than those who were to come later.

Consequently the details covering this early formative period are less distinct than subsequent events. Varner Shippy tells of there being only eight or nine men when he and Jimmy Jones reported in from not-to-distant Holden, Missouri. Besides Lt. Petri this group included big Joe Hardwick (first sergeant), Sergeants Gil Carlson, Arley (regular army) Palmer, Joe Cheeseman and Carl Clampett. William H. Stull, from Binghamton, New York, who had been recruited directly from an automobile firm and given a buck sergeant rating, was the boss down at the motor pool where Matt Fassio, Bob Jones and Octavius Bottary were struggling to make the engines "clean enough to eat off of". It's not clear what Felix Orsini's (New Orleans) job was. Let's just say he was part "expediter" and "social director" dividing his time, when not abroad on some special errand, between the mailroom and the day room.

Robert E. Walker, Houston, Texas was inducted February 19, 1942 and found his way to Camp Crowder on the twenty-sixth. He, Johnnie Roberts, Skiatook, Oklahoma . . . and several others arrived, eventually, at the 181ST from the camp's "Cooks and Bakers School", signaling the prospects of having our own mess hall. Percy T. Olson, from Commerce, Oklahoma recalled that after being inducted at Camp Grant, Illinois, he was sent to Camp Crowder. Following the completion of basic—training, he and several others were escorted by Stull and Hardwick to the other side of the camp to join in the activation of the 181ST. He also recalled that the early members of the company took their meals at another company's mess hall.

Percy was soon followed by Charlie Boyd, who arrived from Detroit, Michigan via Ft. Leonard Wood, Missouri.

Like most of the camps rushing to mobilize, Crowder was, as John Omer, Tabor, Iowa, described it, "a sea of mud, without sidewalks". When he wasn't sweating as a barracks orderly, fighting to keep these elements outside, he attended radio school in Kansas City.

From all accounts March and possibly April of 1942 stand out as the months during which most of the cadre found their "home away from home" in Crowder. Some of these were Ed Rozmerski (Chicago), Charlie Matthews (Connecticut), Al Kljun (Ohio) and Willis (Willie) Dengler (Iowa). As they arrived, they were either assigned to the camp's Central Signal Corps School, spirited off to classes at Kansas City or plugged into the motor pool or other HQ jobs. Dengler replaced the company clerk, Corporal Counts, for whom the army had other plans.

April was significant for another and more menacing reason. The world was presented the numbing news that the Japanese had closed the Burma Road, China's lifeline from the west. Not privy to the desperate squabbling over military priorities in the region, which was to become the hallmark of British, Chinese and Washington behavior throughout the war, we were yet to learn of the real gravity of these ominous tidings and what they portended for us.

By July 1942 the head count in the 181ST had reached 44 and the time had arrived for a field test of the unit. At 6:30 on the morning of August 30th, a repair team, probably about 30 men and Lt. Petri, headed east through Independence, Mo., their destination . . . the Nashville, Tenn. fairgrounds. First Sgt. Hardwick, with his key right hand, Dengler, stayed behind to mind the store, providing a homing point for those still arriving, those who were still in school and the HQ team. By now the Missouri mud had turned to dust and the holes had all been neatly filled by the "strawberry picking" details.

The events in Tennessee have been the most difficult to reconstruct. We do know from Al Kljun's very brief diary that the wire squad (telephone, telegraph and teletype) was separated from the rest of the team. This group, which included Milton Herman, Bob Finkel, Sam Monteleone, Bernard Metz and Joe Cheeseman were stationed near the little town of Wartrace, about 50 miles southeast of Nashville. Al's diary also recounts his learning, on September 2, that he was the father of his first child, an eight-pound baby boy. We also know, from first hand accounts that Matt Fassio was credited by Bob Finkel with saving his life by braving, if not enemy, at least disciplinary fire, by infiltrating the local drug store and securing a precious medicinal cure for the very uncomfortable and much too common "GI's", a malady akin to dysentery, with which we were all to suffer too often before returning to the civilian world.

Signal Repair Bus Bodies In Convoy

Sightseeing In Tennessee

Lt. John Petri and Private Alvin Kljun

With maneuvers over and the team back at Crowder, the shaking down process accelerated. Organizationally the biggest news was the arrival of the new CO, Captain Robert C. Scott, an Army Reserve Officer, from Ft. Leonard Wood. During the summer and fall of 1942 the full officer complement was realized in the persons of Lt. Gonski (Camden, N.J.), James Mc Veigh (N.J.) and George Holmes Wilson (R.I.) from Ft. Monmouth and Kermit Swanson (Ill.). These and Lt. Petri would subsequently command the five repair teams in the summer maneuvers (1943) in the Mojave Desert

For those who were seeking to improve their ranks and, therefore their personal living privileges, attention was focused on the unfilled positions in the Table of Organization (T.O.). The contest was on among those who had arrived originally already sporting stripes, those bucking for some recognition of real or imagined accomplishments demonstrated in Tennessee and finally those who, in the interim, had slipped into camp, already carrying some rank. Bill Hasse was one of these, having accompanied Capt. Scott from Wyoming, at the latter's request. Another was William H. Stull, who was recruited directly from

General Motors and who arrived with a Regular Army sergeant's rank. As events progressed, it became evident that many of the expected promotions would not occur until we reached California and maneuvers at full company strength.

The stage was now set for starting preparation for the arrival of sufficient flesh from Forts Dix and Bragg for filling out the company skeleton to the required 180 enlisted men. The officers and cadre were now faced with the dubious task of performing the minor miracle of transforming 120 civilians into functioning military individuals. This had to be accomplished in such a way that, not only the basics of military knowledge were acquired but, in the process, these individuals from such diverse geographical and cultural roots had to perceive themselves as members of a new identity, namely the "181ST". The degree to which the cadre was successful in achieving the first can probably be measured by the absence, with one exception, of any major disciplinary breakdowns, especially overseas. As for the second objective, the very fact that the survivors today, after forty years, and in the face of repeated scatterings and even the official dissolution of the Unit, still see themselves as a family, does indeed attest to its realization.

On the other side of the globe, the Japanese had soundly beaten the British and Chinese, cutting China off from its Allies. The Air Transport Command (ATC) had started flying supplies from Dinjan and Tinsukia, in Assam, to Kunming, China over the 20,000-foot high Himalayan Mountains (The Hump). Ledo, in Assam, was officially designated "Base Section 3" and as President Roosevelt inked his OK to kick off the start of construction of the "Ledo Road", the most momentous event of the war occurred . . . . this writer reported to Fort Dix.

## THE INVITED

To those of you who have been through the process, please bear with us as we dwell briefly on the impact dealt by the short note many of us received from our president. In every major conflict joined by the U. S., plain Joe Civilian has been made to carry the main load. For the enlightenment of those whose role spared them the receipt of this life-altering communication, we're going to pause here to try to describe some of the trauma experienced by these citizens before, during and after their transition from free men to prisoners. I feel that it is only appropriate since it is germane to our story inasmuch as it describes how over 150 men were initiated into the beloved army, their first step toward joining the 181ST.

I feel that I can do this best by telling a little of my own story since it is cruelly typical of what the others experienced. I seemed to feel then, that because of world events, I was perched on an irresistible treadmill, from which there was no exit. It seemed to be propelling me toward a life style, which I had not previously anticipated. From the moment of registering for the draft, life shifted into a sort of state of suspended animation, wherein planning stopped, ambition lost direction and all of my activities were pursued for the day-to-day value or enjoyment they produced. I began to realize that I was possibly faced with a very dangerous experience, which could result in considerable pain, even death. Although I had serious doubts as to what a 125-pound male, such as I, could contribute to the war effort, envisioning myself confronted by 200-pound German storm troopers, I elected to save fear for its appropriate time. In looking back, I suppose I was protected by the optimism of youth.

The older men, who were to receive the same summons, although subject to similar apprehensions, probably knew that their contributions were going to be much more difficult to make. With the knowledge that only comes from age and experience, while probably less fearful of their immediate danger, they knew that they had much more to lose. For several of them, these concerns proved to be unnecessary. The extent of their aggravations were limited, eventually, to the physical indignities inflicted on them only during the induction process and basic training, since upon reaching the age of thirty-eight they were returned to civilian life.

Whether young or old, approximately sixty men each from Ft. Dix in New Jersey and Ft. Bragg in North Carolina, along with many from locations scattered across the country, did indeed receive their invitations from the president to report for induction. These sobering "greetings" abruptly transformed their apprehensions into inescapable reality and were, then, the instruments by which the next step in the 181ST growth process occurred. These men were to be joined by a handful who had decided not to wait for induction but taking advantage of the opportunity to select their preferred arm of the service, had volunteered for the signal corps. Ray Bumgardner, from North Carolina, was one of these.

Webster defines induction as the process by which civilians are inaugurated into the military. In the opinion of this writer, Webster has given us only one half of the real meaning of the word. There is no question that when the often humiliating and brutally impersonal ritual is complete, the main actor is indeed "in" the military. What Webster has failed to include in his definition is the very real fact that the process not only projects the hapless citizen into a new lifestyle, but most unceremoniously plucks him "out" of a heretofore, normal, democratic environment and brings to a cruel halt all of his plans, aspirations and everyday pleasures. He is, instead, confronted with the psychological task of adapting himself, whether or not he has yet accepted his new lot, to a Spartan routine, founded on an alien totalitarian concept. He learns immediately that there are two ways to do things, the right way and the Army way.

The "plucking out" proved to be, not only emotionally difficult, but in some instances, it resulted in considerable material loss. A very real example of this occurred in the 181ST when one of the men, who was a tenant farmer, was forced to sell his equipment at below-value prices prior to the army reporting date, or face the inevitability of its deterioration or theft while he was away. I am sure that there were many other forms of material sacrifices made, possibly one for each inductee. We do not know how many new or pregnant wives or small children were deprived of their husbands or fathers. Although young and single and not subject to either of these losses, my test consisted in having to leave a very seriously ill mother. Who knows the extent of the total sacrifices made by the millions who served? To their credit, after the initial shock of induction began to abate, most of the men of the 181ST accepted their changes in fortune and soon confined their complaints to the scores of minor discomforts they endured and the seemingly endless illogical demands made of them.

We are not going to dwell too long here on the classical series of inconveniences; pain, indignities and overt humiliations piled onto the newcomers at the reception centers at Dix, Bragg and elsewhere. That story is not peculiar to the 181ST. Suffice it to say here that we experienced all of the above and when finally paroled from the prison camp atmosphere of these centers, had learned our first lessons in soldiering, that of keeping our mouths shut and volunteering for nothing. We also learned that there really was no curved inoculation needle, referred to sadistically by our tormentors as the "hook".

This, however, is the story of the 181ST and, as such, must include some examples of the processes by which 150 plus unsuspecting citizens were systematically introduced to a heretofore romanticized form of life. I have always pondered the origin of the title "Private", which defines the lowest form of army life. Of all the personal amenities denied the recruits, the most obvious was certainly privacy. Fortunately the human animal has demonstrated its capability for adapting to some very extreme situations. We were no exceptions. This writer, who was raised in a normal Christian home, where modesty was always expected, soon adjusted to freezing latrines and showers inhabited by dozens of naked men of all shapes and ages. They ranged all the way from rugged, hairy and obscene incorrigibles to beardless clean-skinned youths. Needless to say, the first days were a little frightening and certainly sobering.

As is often the case, adversity sometimes breeds its own brand of humor. Rumor had many of us convinced that, to suppress sexual appetites, the army had laced our meals with saltpeter. Whether the psychology of the rumor, the extreme cold, or the actual consumption of saltpeter seasoned food was in fact responsible, on the first bleak freezing mornings at Ft. Dix, that appendage of the male anatomy through which early morning fluid relief was achieved, seemed unduly shrunken. This prompted one enterprising inmate to comment that he was going to start tying a string to it when retiring at night so that he could find it in the morning.

The short time I spent in Dix, with the real pain and discomfort attendant to multiple medical injections, was made much worse by the weather and backbreaking work details. Arriving December 5, 1942, I was assigned to Company "M", of the 1229th Reception Center, which unhappily happened to be quartered in a tent area. The individual six-man pyramidal tents were equipped with pot-bellied coal stoves. These had one very annoying shortcoming; they had to be refilled in the middle of the night. This, of course, was seldom done by the weary, temporary inhabitants who instead attempted to keep warm by sleeping in all or most of the strange-fitting clothes that they had just been issued. Matters were not improved at all when Mother Nature chose my very first night as the government's guest to drop four inches of snow. In all of my years on the planet I have never seen a more forlorn half dozen individuals than those who shared my first reveille, before daylight of course.

The camp's complement had some very clever and innovative techniques for assigning men to the various details necessary for operating a military establishment. One group, whose task was to be one of ditch digging and wheelbarrow pushing, was recruited through the apparently innocent query of "Who of you have driver's licenses?" Although I never volunteered, having been forewarned, I caught a detail for "battalion headquarters". It certainly wasn't a typing job. Instead it turned out to be a morning atop of a garbage truck and an afternoon on the same vehicle shoveling coal into the bins serving the entire battalion, of which Company "M" was a part. A disturbing discovery made during this assignment was that most of the other inductees were living in wooden barracks. Upon returning one midnight from an all day tour of KP, I checked the bulletin board, as we had been admonished to do, to discover that in four hours hence I was scheduled for a repeat performance. It was at this point, in real desperation, that I approached the omnipotent orderly room to question the physical wisdom of such an assignment. To my surprise, I was informed by the sergeant-in charge that I was excused. After surveying my drooping 120-pound countenance, he decided, out loud, that "We better leave something for the enemy". This courageous act bought me about a four-hour respite the following day, the rest of which was spent loading 200-pound field kitchens into trucks.

Eventually, however, the ordeal finally came to an end, when my name appeared mercifully on a list of people shipping out. I wasn't to know it at the time, but it also contained the names of 59 other future members of the 181ST. My recollection of the procedures that immediately followed the knowledge of our reprieve, are very dim at this time. The morning of December 12, 1942, the day of liberation, was probably taken up with the usual processing activities. This conclusion follows from the assumption that our embarkation by rail occurred in late afternoon, since the first leg of our trip was accomplished in darkness. At this point it must be noted that we did not know to which part of the army we had been assigned. Consequently we had no clue as to where our midnight junket was taking us. Just before total darkness engulfed us we had glimpses of small hillside towns and endless, drab, gray, leafless tree-covered mountains. Based on our eventual destination, Camp Crowder, near Joplin, Missouri, the route could have been through any combination of Pennsylvania, Maryland, West Virginia, Kentucky, Ohio, Indiana or Illinois. In any event, morning found us stranded and unhooked from our engine, the only source of heat, in the remote recesses of a railroad yard in a very large city, probably St. Louis. After several very cold hours and just about the time several of the group had decided to seek out more comfortable accommodations, we were reconnected to an engine and were again on our way.

Several days later, a similar band of assorted civilians entrained from FT. Bragg, North Carolina. Their induction ordeal was identical to that of the Dix captives except that their tormentors voiced their threats in southern drawls. Mute testimony that the draft boards were beginning to hit bottom in some small communities was confirmed by the presence among this contingent of one lad who could not bend one of his knees. On the whole, though, these fellows mirrored the social cross section of their northern compatriots. Their economic profile did, however, reflect the more rural nature of their state. Hamp Mc Bride, a lumberman from Asheboro, recalled that the train ride was long and uncomfortable, made more so by the development of a "hot box" on one of the car wheels. He remembered that it put out a nerve-wracking banging all night long, making the already inadequate sleeping arrangements agonizing.

Like the Dix excursion, the "Ft. Bragg Limited" was delayed at a large city, while the faulty wheel was attended to. Their subsequent arrival at Camp Crowder occurred within days of their "Yankee" cousins and the stage was set for our mutual integration. Actually the process had already begun in the commonality of our adventures since reporting to our draft boards.

## CROWDER

My recollections of our first weeks in Camp Crowder do not generate reassuring vibrations. Maybe it is because they conjure up the icy blasts of the Missouri winter, which was worst than New Jersey's. Maybe it's because they bring back the nightmare of the ill effects of the medical shots, souvenirs of the reception center and the agonizing cold as we stood in line outdoors for additional series of the same. I recall very vividly one of the new arrivals fainting dead away and falling into a snowdrift, while waiting his turn. Maybe it's because the recollection triggers memories of being feverish, either from the shots or from an extremely persistent bronchial disorder, known unaffectionately as the "Crowder Croup". Maybe I was never successful in comprehending or appreciating the apparent callousness of the Post Medics toward our plight. By design or otherwise they confined surprisingly few of us to the warmth of the barracks. They might have become conditioned to the belief that of the people who reported for "sick call" (the sick, lame and lazy) most were of the latter persuasion. At any rate I credit my own survival of this period, not to their ministrations, but to the timely receipt from home of an old favorite family cough remedy.

In looking beyond this unfortunate period, I must concede, however, that the cadre had done a pretty good job of getting things ready for our arrival. Evidence that they viewed us as more than faceless fillers surfaced in the form of a Christmas show and dinner. It was well done and very timely in that it gave us a brief glimpse of what army life would be like once we got past our then-current problems. Credit for it was shared by Bob Finkel, Joe Cheeseman, Al Kljun, Arley Palmer, Jimmy Jones, James Beck, G. Bennett and Clyde Oie. Its production was approved and probably dictated by Captain Scott who included the following message in the program which was distributed:

TO THE MEN OF THE 181st

THIS CHRISTMAS DAY FINDS YOU ALL FAR FROM YOUR HOMES AND LOVED ONES. ALSO SUCH IS THE EXERIENCE OF MILLIONS OF OTHERS SCATTERED OVER THE ENTIRE WORLD. THERE IS A DEFINITE REASON FOR YOU BEING HERE. THERE IS A JOB TO BE DONE. YOUR COOPERATION IN THIS GIGANTIC UNDERTAKING HAS A DIRECT BEARING ON WHETHER OR NOT THE OBJECTIVE CAN BE ACCOMPLISHED. THE SOONER WE REALIZE OUR OBLIGATIONS TO OUR FAMILIES AND COUNTRY, THE SOONER WE WILL SPEND OUR CHRISTMAS DAY AT HOME WITH OUR LOVED ONES. MAY EVERY MAN IN THIS ORGANIZATION REALIZE HIS RESPONSIBILITIES EARLY AND STRIVE TO ACCOMPLISH THE MISSION.

ROBERT C. SCOTT
CAPT. 181st SIG. REP. CO.
COMMANDING.

Considering the fact that the Dix and Bragg contingents were in Camp Crowder for less than two weeks, that they were still smarting from the army's reception techniques and had not yet begun to break down some very old north-south cultural barriers, the party succeeded in setting the tone for the relationship which endures today.

. . . .

Up to this point the reader has probably deduced that our primary preoccupation was with the individual agonies caused by entry into this frustrating and threatening existence. We soon had several other distractions toward which we could direct some of our apprehensions, anger and hate. Of these, first place had to go to Friday nights, which appeared to have been created for the singular purpose of terrorizing the recent civilian arrivals. Friday . . . . preceded Saturday morning, an interval after which Captain Scott and First Sergeant Joe Hardwick inspected the mess hall, the barracks and the inhabitants therein. The scrubbing of floors, walls and windows in sub-freezing weather and the post mid-night ritual performed by the poor devils who had caught KP on Friday, of carrying a half dozen garbage cans filled to the brim with kitchen slop seventy five yards to the barracks furnace rooms to prevent them from freezing, pretty much sums up my recollection of this weekly event.

Another daily routine, which evoked a colorful chorus of sarcasm, was the early (pre-dawn) search for old cigarette butts, matches and other miscellaneous trash. This activity, officially called "policing the area", required the participants to assume a bent-over stance with their faces close to the ground. I can still hear Bill Hasse shouting irreverently "I don't want to see anything but asses and elbows".

As far as soldiering goes, neither the Ft. Dix nor the Ft. Bragg contingents had a monopoly on sad sacks. The many hours spent on the drill field, in the hope of acquiring the talent of marching in cadence, had no effect whatsoever on several poor souls, who really never got around to joining the war. Maybe they were the smart ones. The rest of us humored the sergeants and to our surprise, mastered the "close order drill" thing so well that, after several weeks, we were summoned to parade before General Ben "Yoo Hoo" Lear, the corps commander. With a live band to perk us up, I believe we actually enjoyed it, getting our first military goose pimples.

Reflecting the urgency of the national mobilization effort, the decision had been made earlier to have basic training of the new recruits conducted by the cadre. Thus our first lessons in soldiering began. Sergeant Willis Nichols, assisted by Al Kljun handled the task of teaching us how to keep from shooting ourselves with the deadly weapons we were to be trusted with later. I believe Varner Shippy taught us first aid; while some of the others, including Sam Monteleone filled our heads with military courtesy, military discipline, map reading and aircraft identification. We learned the eleven "General Orders" which we could mumble as we walked fire guard in various sections of the camp, having been warned that the Officer of the Day (OD) would execute us on the spot if we couldn't rattle them off when asked. I remember one that went something like (To salute all colors and officers not cased) whatever that was. This duty was performed with empty rifles, causing those of us, who had never before been assigned the task of protecting our fellow man, to wonder just what we could have accomplished had we been called on to do so.

Who can ever forget our first encounter with the firing range? If it had not been so painful and pathetic, one might have considered the day's efforts humorous. The fact that some of the fellows actually hit the targets with enough regularity to win medals is still, to me, truly amazing. First, I could hardly lift my Enfield rifle. Secondly, I was shivering so badly from inoculations and the cruel Missouri cold that when I did get the rifle on the target, there was absolutely no way that I could keep it there. Lastly, when trigger-pulling time came, all of my attention was focused on trying to keep the gun from breaking my shoulder and/or cheekbone. As things turned out, I did manage to wind up with a fat lip. In spite of all of this, I only missed a "marksman" medal by a couple of points.

As if the agony of firing wasn't enough, we discovered that we had to take our turns at operating, marking (the shots scored) and repairing the targets. This was done from a trench about eight feet wide by ten feet deep, called the "pits", from which the targets could be lowered and serviced. While approaching the target area from the firing line, I was struck by the bizarre sight, behind the targets, of an entire forest of mature trees, which had been literally chewed down to six-foot stumps. To a young city boy, the sound of the bullets whining overhead and the ear shattering "crack" of low shots hitting stones was a little terrifying.

It has often been said, "The army made strange bedfellows". This session at the firing range was a classic example, when it contrived to place Harry Prince, from New York City, who I am sure never held a gun before, next to a Lumbie Indian, named Locklear from North Carolina. When their turn at the targets was over, it was discovered that Locklear, who was believed to be completely illiterate, had been firing at Prince's target whose bull's eye was demolished. Harry, not surprisingly, was not awarded a medal.

On one of the most brutally cold Missouri nights I can recall, we were trucked out to a remote, Godforsaken, piece of countryside. We soon discovered that our instruction in map reading and the use of the compass was to be finished off with a typical army "hands on" version of the well-known Friday night quiz. In describing it best, the key words are "exposure" and "night". We were split up into groups of six or eight, given a compass, a flashlight, a set of coordinates to follow and then dropped at intervals along a dirt road. The name of the game was, of course, find our way back to our tormentors, the hard way.

Since we would have frozen to death standing in the roadway, we grumbled, shrugged our shoulders and plunged into the heavy woods. As chance would have it, the group I was with did not know each other at all and there were probably only three or four who had more than a passing interest in what we were about to attempt. At first no one would take the lead so the interpretation of the first coordinates was pretty hit or miss. As the situation became more uncomfortable, we began to realize that, unless we got serious we might spend the whole night wandering aimlessly. During the process we found out who had been paying attention in class and subsequent decisions were arrived at by consensus. By this time, also, I had volunteered to serve, on hands and knees, so my back could be used as a flat area from which to read and adjust the compass.

It was fortunate that we had organized our resources because we discovered that our instructors had found the worst locale in all of Missouri. The entire area was nothing more than a series of gullies, hills, and small streams interlaced with countless barbed wire fences. This was all covered with endless patches of thorny berry bushes. As a matter of fact I learned from Matt Fassio that this was the very area where the charter members of the 181ST had gathered the stones, etc. for filling the holes back at camp. We know now why Charlie Matthews referred to those details as "strawberry pickers".

For what seemed like hours we climbed or crawled under barbed wire and stumbled and cursed our way through the underbrush. Our extremities had become numb and just about the time we figured we had been wandering in a circle, we popped out of the woods onto a road, probably the same one from which we started. Our keepers had deduced, very wisely, that by then we would be out of gas and in need of some heat. So it was with enormous relief that we welcomed the sight of the truck, which soon deposited us in front of a roaring bonfire. Others were not so fortunate. Ray Bumgardner reported that his group had to leg it all the way back to the lifesaving heat.

Of all the methods employed by the cadre in instructing us in the basic mechanics of soldiering, the most sadistic exercise was our graduation ceremony from poison gas school. Conducted by Joe Cheeseman and Ed Rozmerski, this consisted in the placing of ten or twelve unsuspecting victims in a small wooden building with their gas masks tucked away in their pouches. One of the conspirators then tossed in a tear gas canister, as an incentive for us to don our masks ASAP. Rest assured this method was very effective and we all passed the course, subject more or less to severe burns on our unprotected necks.

. . . .

The assignments to technical schools, started when basics were completed, reflected previous schooling, civilian occupations and were probably influenced by the Army General Classification Tests administered in the reception centers. Sometimes we wondered what they used for logic. For example, Bob Callinan, who was a draftsman for the Signal Corps at Ft. Monmouth before being drafted, was told that he should be an armored vehicle mechanic. Fortunately for him and the 181ST he carried a letter from a colonel, his employer, recommending him for the Signal Corps. Cal was one of those who came to the 181ST with previous schooling (six months at Ft. Monmouth). He, along with about half of the company spent eight or nine weeks at the Central Signal Corps School at Crowder.

This was a typical G.I. establishment . . . . wooden buildings, soldier instructors and military discipline. The courses were excellent for the quick preparation of the students for very specific technical skills. The warmth of the buildings, however, together with the monotonous drone of the instructors created an environment, which was conducive only for sleeping. Many succumbed and were duly punished. The standard penalty . . . . scrubbing the middle aisle of the classroom. One could truly eat from the floor of the building I occupied.

It might be pertinent to our story to include here the fact that we were still pulling twelve-hour guard duty (from supper until dawn) and were given no time to rest before attending school.

Those men who were destined to repair more sophisticated radio and electronic equipment were sent to several private schools. One group from Midland Radio School in Kansas City included Howard Speake, Stan Greggo, Charlie Matthews, Frank Downing, Carl Clampett and Sam Kraft. There were many others, of course.

. . . .

Our several months together during which we adjusted to our new environment and each other was, as you can imagine, replete with disciplinary incidents. Willie Dengler recalled Ossie Brandsdorfer's too frequent audiences with Captain Scott because of altercations while on KP. On one such occasion, the good Captain, in a fit of frustration, was heard to say "Ossie, I'm getting damn sick and tired of you coming in here every other day to see me". To which Ossie, in his inimitable way, was heard to reply, "You're getting tired? Hell I'm doing all of the work".

It wasn't too long after this that Willie surrendered his comfortable "company clerk" job, along with his corporal stripes for a two week furnace-tending stint at the officers' barracks . . . a job he had been admonished by Scott not to foul up on, since he was an inhabitant therein. It seems that Dengler had made the mistake of objecting too strenuously when the MP's woke him, with some difficulty, at the bus station in Joplin. Willie compounded his status when a pile of hot coals, he had stacked near a coal bin started a fire, while he was asleep inside. It was about this time that George Cole, from the Dix contingent took over as company clerk.

One of the more severe forms of company punishment was the digging in the unyielding, stone-filled Missouri earth of a hole measuring four feet by four feet by four feet. Rene Sandoz from Palmyra, New Jersey was one of the unfortunates who paid this price for one very brief moment of vocal freedom. Another was Eugene Gilbert, also from that area in Jersey. At his request, he was transferred to the 180th Signal Repair Company, which shared our camp area.

Their training was farther along than ours and as chance would have it, they were destined to serve later in North Africa and to suffer almost total annihilation. When they left Camp Crowder for desert maneuvers, we moved into their barracks, named "Shrewsbury" and "Red Bank" after two towns in the vicinity of Ft. Monmouth, the eastern version of Crowder.

By now we were becoming accustomed to our new life style which, from up close, seemed to be a career dedicated to being on time for formations. There was one to check that you were out of bed in the morning. There was one after breakfast, one after lunch and whenever the brain trusts in the orderly room decided on some entertainment, there was another. Prior to supper each evening, we donned our dress uniforms, and with our trusty Enfields, formed up for "Retreat". This one always impressed me, with the entire camp observing the lowering of the colors to the strains of the national anthem. It also came with inspection built in. During the first of these, Captain Scott, Joe Hardwick and my platoon sergeant learned that the army did not make a web belt to fit my twenty-eight inch waist. We had the choice of it hanging down either in front or in back. My ego received a giant boost at this time also, when I was told to shave.

All marching lessons were started from formations. These, of course, were the most frequent. On one of these, Sergeant Arley Palmer suddenly produced a record player, a loud speaker and two Soussa marches for our inspiration and the preservation of his vocal chords. Arley was a career soldier, regular army (RA), who operated a mini-extortion program with the recruits. A negative response to his solicitation of a fifty-cent "loan" earned the subject a graphic description of the various dirty details he might otherwise incur.

. . . .

From the time that we had surrendered ourselves to the reception centers, we had been incessantly reminded that we were no longer free to come and go as we pleased but were the property of Uncle Sam. By the time that we had finally resigned ourselves to this sobering reality and were well along to having adjusted our living habits accordingly, we were informed that we could again mingle with the civilian population.

This writer was still only a very young twenty year old at the time and I can still remember my first pass to Joplin, the most populated city in that part of Missouri. Despite its size (today 38,000 plus) it was inundated by GI's from Crowder, one of three major Signal Corps camps in the country. Accordingly, even though its population must have understood the military necessity of our existence, and as I recall were reasonably civil to us, we were treated as anything but fellow civilians, temporarily under arms. Instead it was evident that, to them, we were something different, to be avoided but tolerated. My first day in Joplin was my last. For those of us who did not have relatives or friends near the camp, the city was nothing more than a momentary change of scenery and maybe a source of passing enjoyment. Sensing that our stay in Missouri was coming to an end and not in desperate need of a diversion, I felt more comfortable taking advantage of the Sunday break in our routine back in camp.

This, of course, did not hold for the others, some with wives or sweethearts off post and most whose tolerance for army restrictions had passed the saturation point. One newly formed alliance, Hugh "Hoot" Gibson and Reese Bailey, both from the western North Carolina hills made full use of their new liberty, which included a ritualistic stop at the twenty-five cent photo booth before returning to camp from each escapade. Unfortunately for me, Hoot would almost always wake me for my critique of his latest likeness. After several such intrusions, I finally acquired a copy of one, which I still possess.

· · · ·

As you might have deduced from this, the historical barrier between the "blue bellies" and the "rebels" our sad inheritance from the Civil War was crumbling. A rare opportunity had come to us from left field and most of us grasped it with pleasing results.

There was also another and much more subtle change which was occurring in our lifestyle. Whatever feelings we had experienced in our first separations from civilian life, whether they were homesickness, anger, frustration or fear, they were gradually being pre-empted by a strange new bond, born of our common lot. This manifested itself in many ways. One was the appearance of a company newspaper, "The 8 Ball", edited by Bob Finkel, Bill Snider, Preston Selz, Al Stursberg and Stanley Greggo. Other forms of this phenomenon ranged from sessions of common griping to the countless incidents involving the sharing of material and spiritual encouragement with each other. Considered at that time to be temporary, a natural product of our extraordinary status, it is quite possible that it was during this period that the seeds of brotherhood were sown, which grew and flourished into the permanent relationship that endures today.

. . . .

As the bitter Missouri winter relaxed its icy grip on the inhabitants of Red Bank and Shrewsbury, much of the pressure built up during our struggles with basic training and the technical schools began to abate. The personalities and talents of both the newcomers from the draft boards and those of the cadre had surfaced to the extent that certain individuals rose to claim their places of fame or notoriety among the 181ST population.

One ensemble of yard birds from Dix and Bragg responded to the relaxed climate by opting to reciprocate to the Finkel-lead Thespian performance at Christmas. This stellar group included New Yorkers Bill Friedman, Ossie Brandsdorfer, and Luke Strass, accompanied by North Carolinians Don Sanders, on the harmonica and Bill Snider on piano. The antics of this foolhardy group were alternately enjoyed or tolerated, depending on one's personal need for spiritual uplift. While Sanders gave a truly professional performance, Snider encountered some difficulty when an encore was demanded after his rendition of "Night and Day", since it constituted his entire repertoire.

The production took on a controversial complexion when the skit called for the tossing of water-filled eggs into the audience, which, as chance would have it, included Captain Scott and several officers. The idea, which was hatched when Bill Friedman suggested that the insides could be easily sucked from the eggs, bought the entourage several days of KP duty. Needless to say, this initial, impromptu theatrical offering was their last.

. . . .

By March 18, 1943 we had reached the level of training where it was now time to find out what kind of soldiers we were or could be in a more war-like environment. Again, remember, where we were headed was, as always, a mystery to most of us. Just the knowledge that we were about to take the next step toward the real war had, on the writer at least, a sobering impact. While learning to perform guard duty, one activity upon which much emphasis had been placed was the correct manner for challenging any interloper encountered, including the Officer of the Day (O.D.). Being shy by nature, I had felt fortunate up to this point, in never having had to put these instructions to the test. This soon changed when several unexpected events occurred which, together, made my first test . . . . very interesting. We were informed that, while we had been languishing in signal school, our keepers, the cadre and Sergeant Stull's motor pool gang had loaded and secured all of our vehicles aboard railroad flatcars and also equipped a baggage car as a rolling field kitchen. I learned, also, that I was part of the guard detail assigned to the rail yard and upon reporting was further surprised when we were issued live ammunition. Gradually the significance of this began to sink in. Soldiering had now reached a point where there was a possibility; very remote I was sure but nevertheless real, that I could be faced with the necessity of having to shoot someone.

Thus sometime during the chilly dead of night, I found myself alone with a string of railroad cars. Either because my body would rather have been back in the warm bunk or because of the anticipation of what lay ahead of us, I had a good case of the shivers. In the fictional media guards are often portrayed as sleepy dullards not prone to the exercise of much independent thought. Well I assure you . . . . that was certainly not true on this occasion. If anything, I had too much time to think. This frame of mind and the vulnerability incurred while clamoring over the couplings, so as to cover both sides of the train, had aroused my senses to their optimum functioning capability. Suddenly, immediately after passing a junction between two cars, I was stunned when the fool who was acting as O.D. decided to test me by leaping to the ground behind me. Well . . . . I did not shoot him, obviously, but he did not ask me to recite any of the "general orders" either, so we were even. My challenge was letter perfect and earned me a compliment from him. This experience was the last that I can recall of Camp Crowder and we were soon on our way to "somewhere?"

. . . .

## SOLDIERS ?

March 18, 1943, the day we boarded the train from Crowder for the next episode in our adventure, was also the day that the spring monsoons started in Assam, India, and our eventual destination. From the beginning of the year the 823rd African-American Engineers, starting at Ledo, had hacked their way through 34.5 miles of the twisting, jungle-covered foothills to reach Hellgate, a spot on this earth that Al Kljun and I would get to know intimately. From there they were poised for the month long attack on the final eight miles, which would be sliced out of the sides of cliffs leading to Pangsau Pass and the Burma border. The composition of these cliffs made them so prone to erosion and landslides that they were referred to by the natives as the "Mountain That Moves". An ominous indication of what lay ahead, not only for the 823rd, but any American luckless enough to be assigned to this piece of the war, then occurred. Accomplished in spite of huge leeches, malaria and the initial wrath of the monsoon, the completion of this last link to the border had required every resource they could muster. As they settled back to gather strength for their next effort, however, they were forced to watch helplessly as the mules of the Chinese 38th Division, in their struggle to reach the Pass, churned the new road into a quagmire, impassable to any motor vehicle.

. . . .

At that moment, however, we were off to California, our new home and still blissfully ignorant of a place called Ledo. I for one was too busy marveling at the monotony of Kansas and complaining about my Pullman bunkmate, a gawky, redheaded country boy from North Carolina, named Yates, who had fourteen elbows and twenty-six knees. I managed more sleep on my guard tour in the cab of one of the six-by-six trucks than I could accomplish with Yates' contortions. In contrast, my partner in the truck, who eventually surfaced as one of the 181ST's most popular citizens, James Henry Hopper from Somerset, Kentucky, was a pleasure to be with. Our version of the "Arkansas Traveler", Henry was about ten years my senior and filled the empty hours as we sped across the plains with an endless stream of his priceless folklore.

Food came from the improvised kitchen fashioned from a baggage car where Kermit Swanson was mess officer, Henry

Cieszykoski mess sergeant and the cook complement consisted of George A. Henze, Percy T. Olson (Commerce, Oklahoma), Johnnie D. Roberts (Skiatook, Oklahoma), Oscar L. Goss (North Carolina), Renfrow, Weinberg and Thomas. The latter three were not destined to join us on our subsequent ocean voyage.

Lt. Kermit Swanson with cooks:
Percy Olson, George A. Henze
Johnnie Roberts, Oscar Goss
Mess Sgt. Henry T. Cieszykoski
Renfrow, Weinberg, Thomas

During the scheduled stops, seldom near population centers, everyone deboarded for calisthenics. At one of these, Hoisington, a small obscure whistle stop on the plains of Kansas, the handful of inhabitants who watched our antics were afforded mute testimony that the country was indeed in a war. From their pensive expressions it seemed that they were mildly surprised to discover that their army was such a conglomeration of strange shapes and faces.

Loosening up at Hoisington, KS

Cook—Dominic D. Hruby, NE

The train followed the Arkansas River from Ford, Kansas to Leadville, Colorado. When we reached the Rockies, our trip took on a menacing quality for anyone assigned to the unheated truck cabs. March in the high passes that year was bitter cold and was delivering heavy snows. Henry and I wrapped our calves and ankles in newspapers and kept moving our limbs throughout our guard stint. Others actually started fires in the cabs and several were subsequently treated for severe frostbite.

A misunderstanding, occurring as we paused momentarily before traversing Tennessee Pass, at 10,426 feet, and about ten miles north of Leadville, cost us one of our people. It had been agreed that the guards on the flatcars would be changed at the second stop of the day. When this short, unscheduled halt was misinterpreted, an abortive attempt to change the guards wound up with a rather robust fellow named Shankman falling while trying to clamber aboard the train, as it started moving. For his effort he suffered a broken leg and was attended to temporarily by Arley Palmer who jumped from the train to assist him. Palmer carried him a mile or so until the train crew was alerted by shots fired over their cab by several of the fellows guarding vehicles on the flat cars. After backing up to retrieve our two comrades, the train then proceeded to the next town having the necessary medical facilities. For his part, Palmer received a vivid welt across the back of his neck, caused by his steel helmet as he rolled down the embankment after jumping. This incident turned out to be Shankman's permanent separation from the 181ST.

At this writing we know that our move also took us through Wichita, Dodge City, Pueblo, Canon City, Grand Junction and Provo. After skirting the south shore of the Salt Lake, we turned abruptly to the southwest, passing through Tooele and Milford in Utah, Caliente and Las Vegas in Nevada and into California and the desert at Kelso. From there we covered the last leg of our trip to San Bernardino via Barstow and Victorville coming to a final halt at a siding named "Ono" just north of the town.

. . . .

What a different world California presented to just about all of the company. With desert sand, cactus, palm trees, gorgeous sunrises and sunsets and soothing dry heat, our first impressions, both on and off duty were radically changed from those experienced in Missouri. Just to start with the bitter winter was ended for us. San Bernardino was close to many picturesque Southern California towns and only about an hour from Los Angeles and Hollywood by car, train or thumb. Suddenly our uniforms, which had been liabilities, somewhat, in places like Joplin, had become objects of respect and much civilian consideration. Hitchhiking was a pretty efficient mode of transportation and every town had its own version of a U.S.O. club.

We were to discover that many Californians had an acute sense of reality about the war, with some even anticipating Japanese landings on the coast. The most glaring but unforgivable demonstration of their paranoia was the totally unconstitutional, indiscriminate, confinement of the entire west coast Japanese-American population. The state, which was host to several major military establishments had suddenly become home to the fearfully, apprehensive families of those men who had been thrown into the breach at places like Wake Island, Midway, The Philippines and the Solomons.

There is the story of Harry Koch (NYC) and John Omer, our favorite Iowa farmer, who had acquired a part time job and a car, riding around one of the small towns when rumor or fact had the natives up tight about an alleged U-Boat attack. Upon stopping for a little liquid refreshment our unsuspecting heroes found themselves the center of attention, treated as erstwhile protectors whose money was less than worthless, a situation often fantasized by many of us. There were many other instances, of course, when the good people of the region exhibited their feelings for the servicemen.

Every barroom story wasn't as serene as the foregoing, however. An eyewitness described a scene where a fight between the army and navy broke out in a San Bernardino establishment and in which Fred Linton, a very robust ex-boxer from Memphis felt he had an obligation to participate. He was described as charging through the swinging doors and before they had stopped swinging was seen exiting with a bar stool over his head.

Most of us did manage to get to Los Angeles and Hollywood, although not as often as we would have liked. Several made friends with some of the more prominent citizens and were treated accordingly. The writer, who had a long lost uncle working in a Los Angeles funeral parlor, visited him twice and on both occasions had the questionable distinction of sleeping under the same roof as the less fortunate inhabitants. Dick Wells from New Jersey was with me on one of these trips and had to be literally dragged into our host's quarters.

With passes now available to everyone who had managed to avoid antagonizing the front office, the Dix and Bragg inductees began to feel and behave like old timers. The usual allocation of ducats for a given weekend or otherwise was enhanced somewhat once George Cole became proficient at forging Captain Scott's John Hancock

As you probably suspect, however, everything was not all fun and games. The army was still in one great hurry to get their moneys' worth out of us and did not waste any time getting to it. Naturally we arrived at Ono Siding just before night and during a drenching downpour. By now we were almost expecting this kind of misfortune. In the rain and the darkness confusion reigned supreme, as we went about the job of setting up our six-man pyramidal tents. The situation became really frustrating when many of us discovered that the reconditioned canvas cots were defective refusing to open wide enough to permit the two supporting wooden ends to snap into place. In the dark we were forced to try to use them as is, spending what remained of the night half in and half out of them . . . . our first but not our last exposure to defense contractors. When the first reveille jolted us out of our new torture racks, however, the sun was almost up and the contrast from Camp Crowder was striking; a sea of olive green tents against a background of sand, cactus and mountains.

We had arrived at one of the army's standard desert-type camping areas. In our nocturnal confusion, we had somehow managed to set the tents up in two rows about fifty feet apart. At the foot of this "street" was a plain, type lean-to latrine (without running water). At the other end, under one roof was the enclosed kitchen with a serving counter, resembling a booth at the county fair. It faced inward to a space open on three sides and occupied by picnic tables and benches. KP here was a bear. First it was hot in this country. Secondly the main chore was to scrub and shine, like a mirror, three garbage cans which were lined up after each meal, full of boiling water (one with soap and two clear) for each man to scrub and rinse his mess kit, knife, fork, spoon, and canteen cup.

These kits were another commodity with which our patriotic defense contractors had supplied us. The new ones were stamped from sheet metal and coated with a rust proofing finish. The old ones, many of which I'm sure had been gathered up from the battlefield at Verdun, were aluminum and, though not much to look at, did not rust. To survive the 181ST inspection, however, one was instructed to steel wool either type or face the consequences. I discovered, the hard way, that steelwooling the new ones only removed their rust prevention coating with equally disastrous consequences. I was eventually forced to augment mine with a small aluminum basin purchased from a Hindu at the bazaar in Ledo.

The area beyond the mess hall was virgin desert and had to be cleared to accommodate the motor pool. Many large needle-bearing bushes and other types of foliage were uprooted either by pick and shovel or by pulling them out with the trucks. During this action one of the groups unearthed a huge rattlesnake. Although my first, it was to be the biggest I have yet to see, and as fat around as a man's forearm. While we were successful in depriving these natives of their home-sites, we certainly didn't drive them completely from the neighborhood. Walking guard duty in that motor pool in the dead of night was not a restful experience. When relieving big Tom Williams of North Carolina one night, he advised me not to stop moving for too long inasmuch as when he had done so just prior to my arrival, something had slithered over his foot.

The camp had a Post Exchange (PX) where, among other items, one could get a half-pint of ice cream for a pittance, an almost daily ritual for yours truly who had been denied such an opportunity during the depression years. A stage was located near the center of the camp, where there were weekly shows presented by volunteers from that section of California. On several occasions Jimmy Jones, a short 130-pounder from Missouri and Fred Linton, from Memphis, Tennessee who tipped the scales at about 280 pounds would stage a wrestling match, with Jones tossing Linton around with apparent ease. Our company had its share of athletes and competed with moderate success in a base softball league. There were also other unrehearsed contests, usually following excessive sampling of "the sauce", between individuals who were out to prove their physical prowess.

Our stay in this camp which served as "Base General Depot" for the maneuvers about to start in the Mojave Desert, lasted from March 22, 1943 until August 30th when we left for the east coast and the port of embarkation. We took our turns, along with other organizations in camp, in guarding various post establishments such as the finance office, warehouses and the guardhouse. In the latter, we had our first experiences with holding a loaded rifle on our fellow man. Even though they had broken some army laws, who knew how serious, to this day I do not know whether I could have fired on any one of them, had he attempted escape, despite the threat by the O.D. and sergeant of the guard that I would have to serve the remainder of his term, if he did. The guard tour covered twenty-four hours, starting at 8AM, with the following day free for recuperating. Most knew better than to stay in camp, knowing the army's penchant for unpleasant surprises and elected, instead, to spend the day in town.

A standard problem at any army establishment is keeping the men busy. To do so required an ingenious and sometimes devious game plan. The strategists in our think tank decided that one project which would keep us out of their hair was to fashion paths around some of the HQ tents near the mess hall. This meant that work parties had to be dispatched by truck out into the surrounding countryside in search of rocks and stones, etc. You can be sure that they found much more than that. Willie Dengler told about one such safari, which just happened to pass a ripe orange grove. Just about the time that a goodly supply of the fruit had been requisitioned by the group the owner appeared. Not knowing that he had already been robbed, he insisted on giving them more oranges and by so doing put a large dent in the exhilaration they had gotten from their adventure.

While at Camp Ono, we learned a little more about soldiering. We were issued the firearms we were to carry for the next two and a half years . . . learned how to crawl up to a live machine gun under barbed wire without getting sand in our rifles . . . and given a short familiarization course in the use of the Chicago gangster-type sub-machine gun. The latter exercise produced a short but exciting moment of deadly humor.

Set up among some sand dunes, the course called for an individual to expend two clips, of ten rounds each at pop-up, silhouette targets. He did this by firing ten single shots from a low platform, with the weapon set on semi-automatic. The targets were operated by a sergeant from behind and below the platform. After the first clip was empty the individual had to replace the clip with a fresh one, race forward into a prone position, switch the weapon to full automatic and fire short bursts at multiple targets as they appeared. Things went along reasonably well until a young fellow named Nissenbaum came up to bat. His first mistake was in failing to check that the empty gun was set for semi-automatic (single) firing. Not having done this, when pressing the trigger after loading the first clip the results he got were truly sensational. It seems that, if a very firm grip and a downward pressure are not exerted on the barrel when firing a long burst with this weapon, it will climb up and to the right scribing a deadly arc in the air. Fortunately for Captain Scott, who was standing to the right of the platform, ten rounds was not sufficient to cause a completion of the arc and the clip was expended very rapidly. Naturally, we all hit the ground as soon as the burst started and I, for one, did not get to see the expression on our captain's face. I don't even recall what his official response was but I do know that Nissenbaum was not on the ship when we left New York harbor.

By April we were ready to take on the desert (we thought) and the five repair teams were named. There were, of course the usual last minute changes. Some of the men had reached age thirty-eight and were sent home. Some, like Nissenbaum, disappeared for other reasons. These were eventually replaced, some before we left for the desert and some joining us out there. One notable change occurred in Lt. George Wilson's team when he discovered John "Blackie" Omer, who was on sick call, and Matt Fassio, one of our more skillful foragers, with a case of beer. They were transferred to Lt. John Petri's team. It was about this time that the only real breakdown in our organization occurred. We had with us a fellow from New York City who appeared to be a person that society had shoved aside. Unpleasant to look at, bordering on being ugly, he was dubbed "Angel" after "The Swedish Angel", a ghoulish-looking professional wrestler of the time. A loner, he was constantly guilty of breaking some company regulation, for which he eventually became the permanent latrine-orderly. Several times he took off and, while awaiting a more severe, official punishment by the army, was finally assigned a permanent armed guard to ensure that he stayed put. When my turn came to guard him, it just happened to be the night when we experienced our first California earth tremor. I stuck to my post even though the single light bulb in the tent was dancing erratically. "The Angel", bless his heart never even awoke. By the time that we had returned from maneuvers and had been alerted to go overseas, he solved the army's problem his own way by deserting permanently. Many years later he was confronted by Harry Koch, in a New York subway and to Harry's question answered that he had never been caught.

The earth tremor, probably considered mild by the natives,

was a new experience for us easterners. It was violent enough, however, to pitch Sabatino Gentile from his cot. He came up fighting, assuming that someone was making sport at his expense. At the movie in town, it caused quite a furor. According to Ray Bumgardner, who was enjoying "This Land is Mine", starring Charles Laughton and Maureen O'Hara, the house lights went on revealing spinning and swaying chandeliers. With the shouts of the people drowning out the sound track, the theatre emptied quickly.

. . . .

Our introduction to San Bernardino and its social amenities, however, had just about run its course and the time had come for us to get back to the business that had brought us to this beautiful country. It was also time to start wondering what the desert was really like. About a week before we headed out on the first of two exercises, there was a sudden flurry of activity behind a hedgerow that bordered the back of the motor pool. Almost overnight a gigantic hospital tent was erected and truckloads of GI's with no insignia on their uniforms were rapidly filling it. The word soon got around that these men were not the usual run of hospital patients but had all cracked up on the desert, presumably from the heat and other hazards encountered. This discovery added a bit of apprehension to our wondering and, if nothing else, caused us to pay a little more attention to any instructions received thereafter.

. . . .

Before the men of the 181ST sallied forth, however, a very important change was made in our middle management. With the company now at full strength, Captain Scott had been able to make a successful case for the addition of a warrant officer. First Sergeant Joe Hardwick was awarded the honor, leaving his job open and in contention. As an interim measure Tech Sergeant Joe

Cheeseman was named temporary first sergeant. With his length of service he was considered a logical successor to Hardwick. Thus it was with some surprise, when the smoke had cleared, that T4 Harold Hess was subsequently announced as the new first sergeant. Now the army is certainly not known to be without differences of opinion and the 181ST not-so-recent civilians were no exceptions. Most of us had enjoyed the brief respite, under Cheeseman, from Joe Hardwick's overbearing ministrations and with no ill feeling towards Hess, were sorry to see Cheeseman replaced. Some gave voice to a popular opinion that Cheeseman had just not been "chicken" enough. As things turned out, once we became accustomed to seeing Hess's rather slight figure in front of the morning formations, he was accepted without any rancor. Prior to his good fortune, he had been known to most of us as just a pretty good shortstop on the company softball team. This writer never found cause to dispute the Captain's decision and Harold served the company well for as long as it existed.

It was about this time, also, that we received a visit from a lieutenant, allegedly the only survivor of the 180TH Signal Repair Company, whose barracks we had inherited in Camp Crowder. It had found its way to North Africa and, as the story goes, had paid the ultimate price for inadequately camouflaging its area from enemy bombardiers.

. . . .

By late April or early May (1943) we loaded our equipment and personal gear onto the trucks and turned our faces south, preparing to take on the infamous desert. Any apprehensions we had at the time could probably have been reduced somewhat if we had been paying better attention to the war news . . . . as we mounted up and headed for our rendezvous with the fighting units we were to service, the British had stopped Rommel & Co. at El Alamein and the Allies were about to deliver the coup de grace to the entire Afrika Corps. The colossal irony of that news was that our upcoming ordeal, during the scorching summer months, was to prove to be of limited value.

In the process of researching the history of the China, Burma, India Theatre, I found out that, after much disagreement among the Allies, a unanimous decision had finally been reached to initiate an offensive in November 1943 from Southwest China's Yunnan Province aimed at reopening the Burma Road. Events subsequently included two of our five repair teams in that effort. One wonders if the army knew, before we were committed to the maneuvers in the Mojave Desert, that we had already been earmarked for the CBI, not Africa. We, nevertheless, did receive training on how to function as a signal repair company, needing only our Yankee ingenuities with which to adapt to the jungle and mountainous environments we eventually encountered in the C.B.I.

Base General Depot
San Bernardino, CA

Webster (NC), Harding (NJ)
Hopper (KY), F. Brown (MO)

Wingler (IL), Firman (IL)
E. Clark (NC), Koch (NY)
Bennett (NJ), Shippy (MO)

R & R At Lake Arrowhead

Tech. Sgt. William Wraspir (ID)

# INTO THE OVEN

Mere survival in the desert required the maintaining of a healthy respect for the two powerful forces at work there. The first of these was nature itself. During the summer, especially, life depended almost entirely on sustaining minimum fluid levels in the body. One had to eat, of course, and be adequately protected from the blistering sun by day and the severe cold at night . . . . but obtaining regular water rations and using them prudently were musts if one expected to last for weeks and avoid the mysterious hospital tent in San Bernardino . . . . or worse.

The second threat lay in the dangers inherent in the maneuvers themselves. From bitter experience, the army had promulgated several ground rules, which if followed, would improve the odds for survival. One of the most critical, but unfortunately the most violated was the edict that, because of the presence of several armored divisions . . . . (1) vehicles traveling cross country after dark had to be preceded by someone on foot with a flashlight . . . . and . . . . (2) anyone sleeping out in the open had to fence their location with white streamers. Infractions of either or both of the above were reported to have generated some grisly statistics. One infantry platoon, which had become lost, instead of staying put and waiting for help, made the fatal mistake of miscalculating the distance across the desert, of a mountain range they tried to reach. The entire group died of dehydration. There were many accidental fatalities. One occurred near Camp Granite my team's first assignment, when a P-38 fighter plane hit a sudden down draft while buzzing some troops. We were to hear afterwards that the maneuvers had chalked up ninety fatalities.

So it appears, in retrospect, that any misgivings we had as our convoy threaded its way south and then eastward, over the route now occupied by Interstate 10, were well founded. As we proceeded, the temperature began to edge upward until we reached Indio. There the individual teams started breaking from the convoy and heading off in search of their repair customers.

Into The Oven

Luke Strass recalls that his team stayed in Indio and of sleeping "on top of the canvas of the 6X6 (trucks) between the bows." He was almost as skinny as I and could accomplish this without falling. It was the best spot to pick up any breezes that might happen along. Luke also tells of him and Jim Beck almost stepping on a rattlesnake in the chow line.

At Indio our team took a left over a railroad track, followed an "S" curve through a cut between some arid, rock formations and were met head on by a blast-furnace gust of air. I remember the distinct sensation of having slipped into a huge oven. We probed our way along the two lane macadam roads, surrounded by boundless desert, until we reached Camp Young the "Desert Training Center", from which General Patton had directed earlier maneuvers. Bill Hasse, our platoon leader, soon came bounding out of one of the low wooden buildings and we were off again in search of Camp Granite.

This camp was entertaining a field artillery brigade whose people were practicing setting up and firing their 105 howitzers and 155 rifles for record, moving to new locations and repeating the process over and over. Apparently the army was very successful in fine-tuning this maneuver and later received an interesting testimonial from German Field Marshall Kesselring, when at his surrender in Italy he asked to be shown our "repeating" cannon, which had given his troops no rest.

It took only one night for this remote desert scenario to reveal its personality. The setting sun was breathtaking and after it had slipped behind the granite hills far to the west the days heat immediately began to abate. At first this came as a blessed relief. Falling asleep came easily but sometime after midnight I discovered that I was chilled to the bone. It was then that I conceded the army some foresight in having issued us two woolen blankets. I soon devised a simple method for adjusting to the nocturnal temperature drop. Spreading the blankets fully opened, one on the other and folding them once gave me four thicknesses. From then on it was a matter of deciding how many layers I required over me to keep warm and making the necessary adjustments throughout the night.

( Standing) James Henry Hopper (KY),
Horace Gooding (NC), Jater Lee (NC,
(Kneeling) Joseph W. Harding (NJ,
Edgar O. Clark (NC)

Daybreak started out pleasant enough, except that Hasse insisted on us getting our physical exercise . . . by the numbers. With the sun came the brutal heat, however, and we began to learn how to cope with it. In addition to the 6X6 trucks and a jeep, each team had a mobile repair shop built into a bus body, similar to that in which a roving knife sharpener used to ply his neighborhood trade back home. Usually it remained stationary and served as the center for repair of telephone and radio equipment brought to us by the people in the brigade. By noon the temperature was near or above 100 degrees and if business was slow we would burrow underneath the bus body, scooping out sand until we could sit.

Unfortunately we had few opportunities to try our repair skills at this camp. Some time was spent trying to adjust mobile transmitters and receivers, carried in the jeeps of the artillery teams. The only telephone related repair, I can recall, was to a small six-circuit switchboard, which had been dragged about a mile over the desert during one of the battery's moves. They suggested that it be junked but we weren't missing the chance to do our thing and Forest Brown and (James) Henry Hopper were able to convert the box full of smashed parts, which were delivered, into a working switchboard.

Forrest Brown (MO), Jater Lee (NC)

It began to seem that our apprehensions over desert conditions had been premature until we tried to refill our canteens. We soon discovered that we would be allowed only two canteens of water per day, which had to accommodate our drinking, shaving and washing needs. We also found that we had better be on hand when the lister bag was filled (with boiling chlorinated water) or stand a good chance of facing a very dry day. It was a new experience, washing in the same water you had just used for shaving. We also learned to use soap sparingly during our weekly community shower, because there was no warning given before the water was turned off.

On weekends some of the Hollywood notables would come out to entertain us. We saw Carole Landis, Kay Francis, Dennis Morgan, Frank Mc Hugh, Maury Amsterdam and other less famous performers. On one occasion Joe Louis brought a stable of fighters. These people were truly amazing since they had to contend with the 100 plus degree heat.

In another part of the desert Lt. Petri's gallant crew was heading for Thermal, California when the lead vehicle went off the road. As Bill Wraspir describes it they "were suddenly following the leader off the pavement, and driving out thru the sand dunes up to our axles, and still within a matter of about 100 yards" of the highway. Some time later they overtook an entire battalion of black GI's marching four abreast and thanked their good fortune in being motorized.

At their camp in the vicinity of Thermal, they had to learn to dig their own latrines and chlorinate water. Here also they encountered another army regulation, which stated that shirts had to be worn at all times while the sun was up. One exception was that they need not be worn while working inside the bus body but they were still to be within easy reach and to be used for even the shortest errand outside. Unfortunately a couple of Bill's boys decided for a quick, short sneak and were caught by "Captain Boots", a regular army officer from a neighboring unit. What followed was a very one-sided tongue-lashing during which Bill was reminded in no uncertain terms of his sacred responsibility to seeing that orders were obeyed and of his own vulnerability to disciplinary action. Bill's contribution to the conversation was a long series of intermittent "Yes Sirs".

. . . .

In yet another desert vacation spot Charlie Matthews drew the job of installing a transmitter/receiver in an artillery, piper cub, spotter plane. He also had to don a parachute and fly with the pilot, while facing backwards to test his work. Charlie reported that on the last day at this location he and others were stricken with food poisoning and hospitalized.

. . . .

At this point I must explain that our desert story has two parts. The foregoing activities were preliminary exercises, preceding the main maneuvers which would pit the red and blue armies against each other subject to the rulings of a third force of umpires. As these preliminaries ended, the 181ST repair teams headed back to San Bernardino where additional personnel and material changes were made.

. . . .

By July 1, the main show had begun on the Mojave and we were again deployed among the antagonists, with one significant exception. Our team, again led by Lt. Gonski and Bill Hasse, reported to the Umpires at Desert Center. Lt. James Mc Veigh's team, with Gil Carlson as sergeant was operating in the desert outside of Needles, California, while this time Lt. Petri & Co. were over in Arizona, east of Blythe. The others we cannot place at this writing.

. . . .

In Desert Center the sand seemed to be deeper and the temperature hotter (it reached 120 degrees by 2:00PM just about every day). The snakes were more colorful but the water just as scarce. The cook who served his fare a good half mile away, had a penchant for hot chili, which my tender stomach still has trouble with. This assignment was very uncomfortable and even eating lunch was a chore as the area was cursed with scores of twisting whirlwinds, sometimes called "wind devils". These invariably presented themselves just as we assumed a cross-legged position on the sand, with our mess kits perched precariously between our knees, and proceeded to salt everything in sight with flying sand.

Desert Center with the maneuver umpires

From Desert Center, General Leslie Mc Nair and the other "Brass" commanded an expansive view of the maneuver exercises from the top of a rocky elevation, called "Alligator Hill" because of its unique shape. The Umpires traveled in command cars, which had link radios mounted behind the back seats. Maintaining these in working order was the main source of activity for our radio people but here; again telephone repair was a losing occupation.

At this point we added two radio repairmen to our contingent, Quentin Brandt from Wisconsin and Charles "Chuck" Cortwright from the flat, delta country of southern Mississippi.

Chuck was one of those youngsters who had been raised in a radio-oriented environment. His Dad had been a "Ham" Operator at a young age, an appliance dealer and, working for Westinghouse in Pittsburgh, had helped put station KDKA on the air. After the depression and the cold Pennsylvania climate, the family wound up in Florida. From Key West Chuck enlisted in the Signal Corps Reserve, taking an electronics course at The University of Alabama and a pre-radar course at Georgia Tech. Eventually active duty put him in Camp Crowder for basic training and a 90-day stint at the Advanced Student Training Program at The University of Wyoming. Here he received his assignment to the 181ST and, leaving from the Laramie railroad station headed for San Bernardino. After three days of searching, found us at Desert Center.

The maneuver finally ended about July 17th. We were acutely aware that it was winding down when a continuous stream of tracked vehicles roared all night past our repair station in headlong retreat. Shortly thereafter our little contingent was picking its way across some really wild country. We stopped overnight at a huge Air Corps base, possibly Blythe. This stop was impressive for two reasons. First we got a peek at an Air Corps PX, which looked like the largest 7-Eleven ever built with beer lockers extending from floor to ceiling. The other event, which left its impression on me, was Fred Linton winning ten dollars by lifting the back wheel of a command car high enough for the loser of the bet to slip a newspaper under it.

But our goal was Niland, California, where we joined Lt. Swanson's team and other elements of the 181ST, which rumor held, had been bombed into oblivion and who were waiting out the cessation of hostilities. Whatever the reason for their being there, they took full advantage of the area's opportunities. John Omer and Harry Koch went right into their act. While on a detail to get water, they spotted a small chicken farm. They then convinced the woman proprietor to, not only kill, but also to cook two of the chickens. While polishing them off in the cab of the truck, they marveled at the deftness with which she had snapped the two from the flock with a whip made out of string, after the boys had selected their victims. On another occasion they employed their innate entrepreneurial skills after a trip to Brawley to pick up honeydew melons for the troops in Niland. After distribution was completed they still had a half truckload of melons, which they and Sam Firman promptly traded to the local market for beer. Some of the fellows visited the bars in Mexicali, and on one occasion Willie Dengler and Sergeant Stull had to go into Mexico to persuade several of the boys to come home.

The final straw, which resulted in the company being invited to leave town was when they ate all of the steaks in the local restaurant and were caught swimming in the town's drinking water. The latter offense was easily understandable. The water in question traveled via small concrete aqueducts across the desert from the Colorado River. The temperature was a little warm but after two and a half months of two canteens a day it was too great a temptation for all of us, including the writer.

Niland, CA water supply from the Colorado river

The Mc Veigh team's client was an armored division that was maneuvering in western Arizona. One weekend a contingent from the team borrowed a truck and headed off over 100 miles for a weekend of R & R at Las Vegas. They were so successful in their efforts to wash the desert sand from their throats that by Sunday evening no one was sober enough to drive the truck . . . . except for a teetotaler, Bill Wilkerson. Unfortunately Bill had never had an opportunity to drive a 6X6 truck and could not solve the complicated gear locations. The result is that he got them home all right, but did so by driving the entire distance in one of the low gears. Charlie Boyd recalled that on another occasion he and the Lieutenant traveled all the way to Phoenix, where they languished in hotel rooms for three nights.

Varner Shippy checks out his client's equipment

Koch supervises while Fichter and Shippy
Check out a 6-circuit BD 71 switch;board

. . . .

While these teams were exercising their ingenuities in search
of ways to overcome the uncompromising discomforts of Mother
Nature, Lt. John Petri's caravan had crossed the Colorado and
worked its way, through the vicinity of Yuma, to an area on the
Gila River. Here they joined with their client, the 8th Infantry
Division. As was the case with the rest of us, they did not get
much opportunity to put their newfound repair skills to work. All
was not lost, however, for in a week after their arrival, they
demonstrated one of the 181ST's finest talents. Invited to
participate in a beer party, given for the company to which they
were attached, the men of the Petri platoon upheld the best
traditions of the signal repair fraternity. Even those who abhorred
the evils of alcohol were not to be outdone. Ray Bumgardner
recalled that he was so dry from the rigors of the hot, rocky, arid
environment that he consumed no less than two grape sodas and
seven cokes. He stopped there, even though he was still

dehydrated because, as he says, "I didn't want to make a pig out of myself."

Shortly after their arrival, they also were entertained by the same group of Hollywood stars, with several new faces, that I had seen in Camp Granite. Again these folks performed out in the searing desert sun. Here Dan Chesser learned the hard way that a suntan overseas cap was no substitute for a helmet liner as protection from sunburn.

During their free moments they discovered a dam on the Gila River, several miles north of the encampment. Just below the dam was a washed out area with a most welcome swimming hole. The Gila was not wide, by eastern standards at least, and had they thought about fishing, our comrades would not have anticipated the next event. During one of their bathing details, they witnessed several fellows from the 8th Division pulling in, from their favorite water hole, six or eight giant catfish which measured from four to five feet. They were given the smallest, which they delivered to the cooks, but not until they had taken a picture of it held by Jimmy Jones. The team's preoccupation with the natural wonders of the area, however, was finally brought to a sudden halt when it was announced that they were to take on the infantry infiltration course. This was similar to the one described earlier but was made more realistic by the random detonation of charges in shell holes. The course was entered and exited via two parallel trenches and required the candidates to crawl under barbed wire, with strict warnings to stay clear of the shell holes. The temperature was brutally hot and as they struggled with the wire and through the powder-like soil they sweated profusely. As a result they emerged from the exit trench covered with mud, looking as though they had just traversed a swamp instead of a choking dry desert. Although none of them had witnessed it, they were told that two men had been killed earlier when one became frightened and crawled into one of the shell holes just before its charge was exploded . . . and the other had stood up for some reason and been struck by the machine gun bullets which were firing over their heads.

During the four weeks that the team was with the 8th Division they were plagued by regular weekend dust storms. Escaping their fury was almost impossible, with the best refuge being inside of the bus body repair vehicles. Even with the pyramidal tents tightly laced up, bedrolls were still covered with an inch of the choking dust. There was no venturing outside without goggles and dust respirators. Whenever the opportunities presented themselves, our valiant group headed for the nearest town, which sometime was more than fifty miles away. As in other parts of the Mojave, temperatures often reached 130 degrees during the day and plummeted at night. Even without any physical activity, perspiration seldom reached liquid form but showed up as salt granules on the fatigue uniforms.

Jeffrey A. Bennett (NJ) finds the only shade around

From their assignment with the 8th the Petri Team traveled next to Camp Hyder and the 77th Division and then into the maneuvers as part of the Red Army. Here they were knee deep in the war games and experienced aerial bombardment. This they proudly survived, possibly in deference to the fateful lesson learned at the expense of the 180th in Africa. The Red Army was supported by A20 attack bombers, which treated the boys to some real dog fighting. They put on a spectacular show as they flew low over the desert, zigzagging to elude the faster fighter planes of the Blue Army. As before, the signal repair business was very lean and the daily routine was one of following behind the Red Army as it advanced. When it stopped, they stopped, spread out and sought cover until nightfall, when they would gather together. During one of the daytime stops, Ray Bumgardner was instructed by Lt. Petri to camouflage his jeep. Ray accomplished this by simply driving it into a clump of brush, which completely hid it from view. The team then went into its dispersing routine placing it some distance from where the jeep was hidden. As dusk approached, Petri told Ray that he could not find it and asked him to retrieve it. This turned out to be more difficult than expected, with Ray having to go back a mile or more searching the clumps of brush which began to look all alike. It was by sheer luck that he finally managed to locate it.

Hamp Mc Bride (NC) with his camouflaged jeep

While the platoon was camped in a dry wash, one of the men, whose description fits George Loftus of San Antonio, Texas, killed a six-foot rattlesnake. He skinned it and said that he was going to make it into a hatband. We do not know if he ever did.

Kermit Clark (NC) with unwelcome native

There is no doubt that, on the desert, water was by far the most precious, sought-after commodity. This was especially true during the maneuvers where one canteen a day was often the standard ration and bathing was out of the question. As the dirt and grime became mixed with the body's salt, and caked on the uniforms, living with ones self became most difficult. In the four or five weeks that the Petri Association followed the Red Army, they had one five-minute shower break . . . and had to travel twenty miles to get it. At the four-minute mark, a bell rang warning our frolickers that they had better stop soaping up. Then it was back on the truck and another hot, dusty twenty miles back to the action. When this was over they were as dirty as when they left but, as one fellow explained, "The water had felt so good and . . . after all . . . it was new dirt."

By mid July the battles were over and the Petri ensemble were ordered home. En-route they passed through Buckeye, crossed over into California at Blythe, and proceeded to join their contemporaries from the Hasse and Swanson platoons near Niland on the Salton Sea. While there, a truckload of our valiant warriors was spirited to San Bernardino for a little R & R, with instructions that they be back aboard by 11:00PM, Sunday. In the interim the team had received orders to proceed to Needles, Arizona, where Lt. James Robb, who had filled a gap created by the departure of Lt. Gonski, replaced Lt. Petri. They packed up their camp at Niland and retraced their path to Blythe. There they turned north and followed the Colorado to Needles, where they spent several more days. Bill Wraspir recalls that when they arrived they were overcome by thirst. In his own words (and Bill was never known as a drinking man) "That was the best beer I have ever tasted". The combination of the air-conditioned bar, the beer and the sudden exposure to the heat outside took their toll on our dehydrated heroes, however, making maneuvering momentarily difficult. After Needles they were informed that they were finally heading back to San Bernardino, which they subsequently reached via Victorville.

. . . .

In the meantime a very strong rumor was about to the effect that furloughs were being awarded. The thought of getting home to our families added an entirely new dimension to our existence and we waited, not so patiently for some confirmation of this news.

. . . .

As for our team . . . we were now made to pay for our good fortune in being assigned to the umpires rather than the "fighting forces". Our arrival back at San Berdoo was delayed for a week while we stopped at Palm Desert, which turned out to be hotter than any location we had been at. I personally saw a thermometer outside of the mess tent at noon, which read 150 degrees. We worked hard at the job of removing those same link radios from the command cars, which had been used by the umpires. The work was very hazardous. You could not leave any tools in the direct sun, and had to wear gloves most of the day, nor could you kneel anywhere on the outside of the vehicle without suffering at least a second-degree burn.

The only good feature about the place was the availability of a public swimming pool, which got much use after supper. One of the fellows also met a wealthy date grower who invited us to his oasis nearby. This pleasant interlude put a very nice ending on our desert experience, marred only when Frank McCraw, in a fit of uncontrolled exuberance broke the diving board in the owner's Hollywood-like swimming pool.

# CHAPTER II

# Off To The War

## NOW WHAT?

Upon arriving back at San Bernardino, we learned, happily, that the furlough rumor was indeed true and some of the fellows had already left for home. Another very sobering announcement was awaiting us also. I was to learn of it the hard way, however.

The local attitude toward the armed forces, at that time, was still favorable and was visible in the operation of several U.S.O. type activities by volunteers in some of the surrounding communities. One, which was patronized weekly by the 181 ST heroes, was located in the neighboring town of Ontario. It was small, compared to similar establishments in the larger cities. Consequently, the young ladies who entertained us became very familiar with the organizations and locations their patrons came from.

This was brought home to me very bluntly one Friday, as I marked time, waiting my turn to head east on my own furlough. In the middle of a romantic Glen Miller rendition, while trying to generate some interesting small talk, my partner inquired as to which unit I was from. Knowing that she was a secretary with one of the many army logistical units in the vicinity, I took the chance of exposing my comrades to the fifth column and divulged my only consciously known military secret. The response was nothing less than earth shaking as I stared with open mouth as this lovely, sweet, little blonde purred "Oh that's the outfit that's been alerted for overseas". I learned later that some of the other boys had been delivered of the same bombshell in similar settings.

Before the next week was over, we had been notified officially of this new development. I also was given a ten-day furlough, with which I had to get to New Jersey and back (traveling time by the Santa Fe was three and one half days, each way). In questioning whether the two announcements were possibly contradictory, I was assured that I would have at least three full days at home. For me and for several others, this turned out to be a typical army assessment.

The events from this point until we headed for the docks in Staten Island in New York graphically demonstrate the value of knowing what is really going on. Most of us took the words we heard as gospel and dutifully bought our tickets, boarded the trains and headed home. A much smaller, but wiser group, managed to elicit from someone in company headquarters the fact that our Port of Embarkation was to be New York (about an hour from my home in Newark, N.J.). This latter gang, upon reaching home, and being summoned almost immediately to return to California, formulated what has to be considered some of the most unique and original alibis for not being able to accede to orders. The least original of these, however, has to be the one about having broken a leg. In reporting this most inopportune occurrence, the informant also advised that he expected to be O.K. in about two weeks.

Two of the fellows didn't try to con anyone but just took off, with the intention of never coming back. "The Angel", whom I had guarded in his tent as he slept blissfully during an earthquake, never did come back. The other fell victim to poor planning, insufficient funds and a very patriotic father.

He was one of those colorful individuals who had a penchant for surfacing in unusual and bizarre circumstances. At age thirteen he had convinced his mother to authorize his induction into the Civilian Conservation Corps. Although he assured her that he would be stationed in nearby Jackson, Tennessee (his home was in Memphis), he emerged in Yosemite, California. He was rotund, belying his age and, to hear him tell it, became quite a boxer.

True to form, after deciding that he had had enough of the army, he headed straight for home. His funds, however, ran out in Little Rock, Arkansas, from where he called home for more. After listening to him, his father wired him enough to get home. Without telling him, however, his dad, a veteran of World War I called Captain Scott, informing him of his son's whereabouts and getting a clarification of his actual status. When he finally arrived home, our miscreant received a blistering lecture on the gravity of desertion in wartime, was given a suit of suntans procured from the local army-navy store and directed to Camp Shanks post haste.

The saga does not end at that point, however. Consistent with his other escapades, the lucky star that he operated under again rescued him from the fruits of his misbehavior. As punishment for his current transgression he was subsequently assigned permanent KP duty aboard ship . . . . the net result being that he ate three meals a day for the thirty-two it took us from New York to Bombay . . . . while the rest of us had to settle for two.

As he was making his round-about way to a rendezvous with the company at New York, many of us were enduring the confusion and discomforts of transcontinental rail coach travel in order to spend what we knew would be our last brief moments with our families. After three and one half days of breathing soot and dust and trying to survive on over-priced, dried—out Fred Harvey sandwiches, Jim Hoff, Ray Fichter and I arrived at our respective destinations in New Jersey.

I do not know why, but home was not as I had been remembering it during the previous nine months. My city street seemed to be devoid of people. Most of my friends had joined in the war. My family, however, was still intact, with the exception of an older brother, who was temporarily in Fort Monmouth in Officer's Candidate School, but who managed to get home for my benefit. Naturally I was served a meal fit for a king and treated accordingly. My only wish had been that my mother could see that I was well and had even gained some much-needed weight, before she had to give me up again "for the duration" . . . This hope, at least, was realized.

Any thoughts I may have had of spending any real time at home were dispelled within twelve hours of my arrival, however, when the phone rang with orders to return immediately to California. By morning of the following day, my traveling companions and I were retracing our paths to the west. We had managed to salvage only two nights and a day from our ten-day furloughs.

Some of the fellows, however, did not get any furloughs. Two of these had especially urgent reasons to get home. One, who had planned to get married during his furlough, was subsequently dealt a particularly cruel blow by the fortunes of war, when his betrothed died, without him ever seeing her again, while he was overseas. An example of the bond that had formed between many of us was discovered by the writer, when a third man just recently confided that, upon returning from his furlough and discovering the predicaments of the above fellows, actually agonized for a long time over the fact that he could have given his furlough to one of them, since his was virtually meaningless to him.

 . . . .

August 1943 was a pivotal month for the 181st. Our stay in the United States was about over. The reality of the furloughs, the packing of our equipment and supplies for shipment overseas and the completion of final organizational changes emphasized this fact. Most of those who had been excused from the 181st's war, for age, physical, psychological or other reasons, disappeared from the roster, to be replaced by other healthy "less fortunate". Among those leaving was Lt. Gonski, who was probably too close to the maximum age limit.

On July 22nd ten men left Camp Crowder for Pomona, California and then on to the Base General Depot on August 2nd to cast their lot with the 181ST. This group included Millard Sturgell, George Simon, Salvatore Corritore, Lloyd Teske, Phil Thompson, Leonard Tridico, James Spaulding, Thomas Shown and Harold Webb. They joined other newcomers, Lt. James H. Robb (an English teacher), Arthur Follett, Isidore Kishner, Spencer Ogden, Richard Williams, Roy T. Murphy, Meyer Berger, Lorin Bolin, Robert Gunning, Fred Linton, James Moulder, Charles Nolan, Deward "DB" Russell, Harold West, Quentin Brandt, Milton W. Mc Donald, George Raabe, Ernie Gioia, Chuck Cortwright, Bill Mercer, Elbert Escherich, Jim "Red" Hale, Tony Benanti, and Dick Donoway.

With the influx of newcomers, the disappearance of others and reflecting evaluations of individuals on the desert, wholesale changes were made in the team complements. Lt. Petri's platoon, now Lt. Robb's and Sgt. Joe Cheeseman's, received many of the new men, including Leo Tridico, Tom Shown, Chuck Cortwright, Elbert Escherich, "Red" Hale, Tony Benanti, Spencer Ogden, James Moulder, and Dick Donoway. The team, now designated the "Fifth", was also split, with several going to Bill Hasse's platoon which Lt. Petri took over.

This was designated the "First". It included this writer and was totally reorganized, picking up men from most of the other teams as well as newcomers George Raabe, Phil Thompson, Arthur Follett, Isidore Kishner, George Simon, Richard Williams, James Spalding, and Lloyd Teske.

The "Second Team" was under Lt. Jim Mc Veigh and Sgt. Gil Carlson; the "Third" led by Lt. George Wilson and Sgt. Willis Nichols; and the "Fourth" by Lt. Kermit Swanson and Sgt. Varner Shippy.

While the reorganization was in process, another piece of business had to be attended to. Apparently the army had decreed that, before the 181st could take its place in the overseas conflict, its proficiency on the rifle range had to be measurably improved. Some of the fellows were sent out to the range several times until the requirements were eventually met. The writer does not recall being part of this effort; possibly it occurred while our team was delayed at Palm Desert, following the maneuvers. I did participate in, what I was informed, was a familiarization firing of my newly won weapon, the carbine and managed to achieve a minimum score, but received no medals. Maybe I misunderstood the purpose of the exercise.

Regardless of whether I did or did not, we no doubt satisfied Washington's criteria, because on August 30th we boarded the train for the trip back to the east coast, from which several of us had just come. Our objective . . . Camp Shanks for final processing before boarding ship for . . . many presumed . . . North Africa, for which we had just completed training.

About the same time, and unknown to almost everyone, Lt. Robb left from Wilmington, California to deliver our equipment via the Pacific.

All packed for shipment overseas

In the CBI, August was also a special time for the Allies, who finally suppressed their venomous political infighting long enough to face reality and decide on some real goals, (at least for India and Burma). Recognizing that, with the Burma Road now closed, with HUMP tonnage the only means of supplying Chennault's air force and the Chinese ground troops, previously made plans for retaking Burma could not be supported and were moved to the back burner. So on August 1st, 1944, at the Quebec (QUADRANT) Conference, six objectives for India were agreed to, one of which was that a road capable of handling the delivery of 30,000 tons per month would be built to Kunming by January, 1945

# CAMP SHANKS

Three days and two nights aboard a speeding train can seem like either an eternity or a mere blink in time, depending on your viewpoint. Some fellows soon became bored with the motion and sound as we rolled monotonously through state after state.

To those who could not generate the degree of concentration required for gambling or reading, the trip was just another version of the all-too-common army hurry-up-and-wait game. The only diversions occurred when some poor soul went into conniptions as we passed too close to his hometown. Matt Fassio had to be restrained when we hit Aurora, Illinois, twenty-miles from his home in Joliet. In between these occasional outbursts the men were left with nothing much to do but think . . . about what lay ahead . . . or what our army tour had thus far produced.

To others, the indomitable ones, who always managed to live for the moment, time was seldom a factor, especially if there was a poker or crap game handy. I expect that there was yet another group, whose size one can only guess at, who had no stomach for Africa or any other place where there was shooting going on, and who felt that time was flying all too quickly.

Within the first group were several men who were taking stock of the 181st. They were particularly concerned about its role in the desert and what they perceived to have been an apparent disinterest on the part of Captain Scott in the operation. My own recollection of the Captain was of an older man whose reserve commission had been won during peacetime, when a popular diversion from military routine was found in wining, dining and general hell raising. The fact that, under his leadership, the new recruits were ably schooled in basic military concepts, however, comprises a valid argument for affirming his competence as a soldier. Nevertheless, at the time, this writer shared with several others the feeling that the Captain overdid the part, failing to demonstrate enough identification with or camaraderie towards the company as a whole.

Whether his military talents or psychological posture were tuned to the critical period the country was struggling through, I am not qualified to judge. An interesting yardstick one might employ for measuring the Captain's stewardship might be the responsibilities of the Signal Repair Company's commander as defined in the Signal Corps Field Manual (June 12, 1941). It states that the Company is under the control of the signal officer of the unit to which it is attached (Army GHQ, Division HQ, or Signal Battalion) and if possible, it is to work in consort with a Signal Depot Company. The responsibilities of the Signal Repair Company Commander are:

> The company commander advises the signal officer or signal depot commander concerning the operations of his company. He supervises the establishment and operation of the repair sections (squads) and determines the priority of repairs within limits prescribed by the signal officer or signal depot commander. He will require each repair section to keep such records as may be necessary to enable it to take timely steps to replace consumed spare parts and repair materials and to keep him informed of work that is being done, of abuses to equipment which, have been discovered, and of faults which have developed in equipment. He renders the

necessary reports and recommends to higher authority action to be taken for the conservation of signal equipment. He develops standard practices for repairs and suitable spare parts lists for his sections, and arranges for the distribution of technical manuals and instruction books.

I can only imagine the chuckles escaping from my comrades, who spent the war following rag-tag Chinese and their mules in the mountains around the Salween River, as they read, what to them must appear as a ludicrous assignment. The reader must remember that the above assumed that we would have been operating in conjunction with large units of troops, which we did on the Mojave Desert. In light of this fact, the Captain's performance—vs—Washington's ground rules might very well be questioned.

One who was sincerely concerned, particularly over the lack of direction from San Bernardino during maneuvers, however, was Bob Finkel (then a Technical Sergeant). Serving with a transportation unit, he reported originally to a supply depot at Banning and then to Camp Onofrio. Having been in a better position than most, for witnessing first hand some of the aforementioned problems as they were experienced by Lt. Petri, he soon became aware of an apparent absence of any visible communication link with company headquarters during maneuvers. He was also convinced, after watching our equipment being packed, that we were short many critical items. Knowing of his concerns, several of the officers came to him and urged him to effect a meeting with the Inspector General. They agreed with Bob's position, adding the opinion that they didn't think we had received enough training. Since it was the understanding of army regulations that only enlisted men could take such an action, they explained that he would have to go it alone. They agreed, however, to support him in the meeting with the I.G.

I suppose deep down in the depths of army records there is an account of the subsequent hearing at Camp Shanks, and a list of those in attendance. In retrospect, after having had a chance to dwell on the subsequent performances of a couple of our officers overseas, I think that we can imagine who they were and picture them recanting their purported support when confronted by some real authority. As you may have already anticipated, Bob found out that he was indeed alone. It seems that it suddenly dawned on his would-be supporters that to have accused the Captain they would, technically, have been accusing themselves, since they had a share in the responsibility for directing the company.

Even at this writing, Bob recalled that in spite of his courageous attempt to do right by the company, he regretted ever trying, not only because he paid for it many times over, and had really expected the officers to live up to their words but also because of its utter futility.

Although our memories of Camp Shanks have dimmed with the passing of time, some remember a possible second meeting . . . . this time with the chaplain. Here again allegations of drunkenness, etc. were made against the captain by one of the officers who, it was suspected, would have succeeded Scott as company commander. It was recalled that, while the officer was voicing his reasons why we should have a change in command, the man who had just returned from his aborted attempt at desertion, spoke up in the captain's defense. He suggested that Scott should be present to answer his accusers in person. After several warnings that he was out of order, he managed to get himself ejected from the meeting and immediately sought out Scott to apprise him of what was occurring.

It is reported that, to the surprise of several there, the captain was not only cold sober but gave an eloquent dissertation on his military philosophy and his understanding of the company's impending role. It was also reported that, when he finished, the chaplain stated unequivocally that he would have no compunctions at serving under the captain, the would-be deserter's action on behalf of Scott probably won him the lesser punishment of KP aboard ship, rather than a much more drastic sentence consistent with his attempted desertion. Camp Shanks was many things to many people. To the New Yorkers and Jerseyites it was another chance to get home. As things go, it just so happened that one of the fellows' Dads worked on the Post. Each night he would hide in the back of his Dad's truck, under some canvas and return the next morning. After one of these excursions he arrived to find that we had sailed without him. The army quickly made arrangements for him to fly and he was waiting for us when we hit Bombay.

Another, who was attending a course in teletype repair at Chicago and who was fortunately spared the experience of the ocean voyage on which we were about to embark, was Dan Russo from New York City. He joined us eventually overseas, traveling by air.

My parting had been so painful for my mother, after my furlough expired, that I made no attempt to get home again, nor even let her know that I was nearby.

Technically we were confined to the company area and, at one point, to the barracks . . . under guard by some of our non-Easterners. At a recent reunion of the survivors, Jimmy Jones, who functions as our unofficial chaplain, recalled how he and Sam Firman, who hailed from Chicago, conveniently turned their backs as the New Yorkers made their nightly visits home.

On the morning of September 8th, 1943 our processing had been completed and we prepared to take our leave. In so doing we were afforded another opportunity to observe our comrades-in-arms performing under a little duress. On previous moves many of our personal possessions had been committed to trucks etc. for transportation to our various destinations. These items included two barracks bags, a gas mask, web belt with ammo clips, a canteen and medicine packet, a weapon, a full backpack with horseshoe blanket roll and a steel helmet. On this exercise we discovered that we had to carry all of the above. Our route was first to train side where we struggled with our assortment of goodies. This we managed with some difficulty but nothing unexpected. The next step was detraining at the Weehawken Railroad Station.

Here the fun began. Some of us had experimented before we left camp until we devised a method for carrying all of this paraphernalia. After slipping into our packs, to which the bedrolls were attached, and carrying our rifles slung over a shoulder, we found that we could toss one of the barracks bags crosswise over our backpack and bedroll. We also found that, with care, we could then toss the other bag across the first. To move with this load, without dropping it required all of the agility and concentration one could muster.

At this point two factors came into play that led to one of the most pathetic yet humorous scenes I have ever been part of. Along the Hudson River none of the train stations run parallel to the river. All are perpendicular, with the train engine usually pointing toward the river. The result is that those alighting from the rear cars had to travel the entire length of the platform before reaching the ferry slip where our next mode of travel awaited. The other factor was the critical timing required in loading several thousand troops onto a ship as large as the Mariposa, our home-to-be for the next month. Thus once we started moving there was little margin for delay if we were to arrive at dockside for ushering up the gangplank in our assigned order. Our sergeants were responsible for keeping us moving and they did it with a vengeance.

At the Weehawken station we scrambled from the train and attempted to form a column of sorts. Before we had time to arrange our equipment, however, the order "Move out!!" was delivered followed by a virtual melee as some tried to hoist their gear onto their backs. I immediately went into my juggling act but only succeeded in getting the first bag into place. While being literally prodded by one of our non-coms, my effort to swing the other bag over my head proved absolutely fruitless and I had to settle for hugging it lovingly to my chest with one hand, while hanging onto the rest of my possessions with the other. Even my rifle refused to cooperate and kept slipping off of my shoulder and down the arm holding the second bag.

Some of those indomitable ones, who live only for the moment, however, were worse off than I was. Not having approached this vexing, logistical problem scientifically as others and I had done, they made weak attempts at imitating us but, not having rehearsed beforehand, never had a prayer at mastering such an intricate maneuver. They took the obvious and more simple course and unceremoniously dragged both their "A" and the "B" bags the entire length of the station . . . wearing gaping holes in their bottoms. I was thankful that any civilians, who certainly would have experienced concern that their very existence depended on this band of stalwarts, did not witness our antics. The entire episode bore mute testimony to the indisputable fact that the United States was truly not a militaristic nation.

My next recollection is of crouching, with my compatriots in the bow of the ferry as it nudged out into the river current, as though we were about to mount an amphibious attack on Staten Island, our next objective. Here it was my turn to experience concern. We soon learned that the type of pack issued to non-combat troops, such as we, were not designed for carrying heavy loads. Because the carrying straps were narrow, they failed to protect the shoulders from any load larger than could be accommodated by a musette bag (similar to a small ruck sack). When a load as large as the one we were carrying was added, the metal clips, which attached the musette bag to the harness cut deeply into the shoulders. In time these could wear their way through the skin unless some object, as a glove, was used as protection. Being one of the skinniest members of the 181st, I always assumed that, when the chips were down, my survival would be a little more assured if I stayed close to some of the bigger fellows. In this instance I watched in disgust and disbelief as some of my would-be protectors paled under the pain, complaining almost to the shedding of tears.

Of course we survived the ordeal and in a short time were struggling up the gangplank, after having responded with our first names when the G.I. tour guide, stationed at its foot called off our last names.

My first impression of the ship was its enormity. The next was to prove very disarming when I found myself in a neat stateroom, on "B" deck, with only Clyde Oie, from Ironwood, Michigan and Frank Mc Craw from Hendersonville, N.C. as roomies. We even had a private shower. "Maybe", I thought, "this isn't going to be so bad, after all".

# THE MARIPOSA

Ten o'clock, the next morning September 9. 1943, the S.S.Mariposa edged its way out into Upper Raritan Bay between Staten Island and Brooklyn, pointed its bow due south and slipped through "The Narrows" into the Lower Bay. Within minutes, it seemed, we were skirting the tip of Sandy Hook and preparing to take our chances with the mighty Atlantic.

To me, personally, this moment was especially meaningful. The water we were then traversing had been the scene of many family-fishing adventures. On one occasion, it had almost cost some of us, including my mother, our lives when we were surprised by a tremendous storm which threatened to overturn our small boat and blow us out to sea in the process. With a sinking feeling, I pointed out to those with me at the railing, each familiar detail of the area, including the point of Sandy Hook and the distant lighthouse on the beach in Leonardo. It was from there that the family had embarked on each trip across that part of the bay. This small town, tucked into a corner of the bay, had been my summer home ever since my first steps were taken on its sandy beach.

As we worked our way out into the regular shipping lanes, I was thankful that we had left during the daylight. Not only did it give me an opportunity for a last look at the "Hook" but, having lived on the coast, I knew also that the threat from U-boats was less than at night. Despite all efforts to black out the coastal cities and towns, to eliminate a backdrop against which targets could be silhouetted by the German subs, the land still gave off a faint glow.

Our attention now, however, centered on investigating our new surroundings and we began to discover the immensity of the S.S. Mariposa. This ship was the 19,000-ton Pacific queen of the

Matson Lines. She was 632 feet long, had a beam of 79 feet and, in normal times could accommodate up to 700 passengers. After modification for military use, she was able to carry six times that many. While this was an obvious asset in the struggle to move large numbers of troops, logistically, it created a whole new series of problems, all related to food, water and protection for its new class of passengers.

The first two we found out about immediately. In solving the problem of feeding four thousand GI's with the available mess facilities, the answer arrived at was to eliminate one daily meal. Thus our first discovery came with the receipt of meal tickets, which reflected this fact and informed us of the meals schedule. As if to add insult to injury, we were then to discover that what we anticipated as meals and what we were subsequently served were not even close. For thirty-two days we learned to contend with various combinations of hard-boiled eggs, boiled potatoes, mutton and stew . . . . for which we had to stand in line for an hour . . . down in the odoriferous, steaming, heat of "D" deck.

From the graffiti over my bunk I learned that this was not the Mariposa's first voyage as a troopship. It soon became apparent that the U.S.Army personnel, who were permanent party on the ship and members of a military transportation organization, were prepared for the reaction of their guests to the meager fare. This was demonstrated very emphatically by the presence of armed guards at the mess hall exit. Their job was to ensure that no food was smuggled out of the facility. Despite their hard-nosed vigilance, they were beaten by at least one of our hungry southerners, who discovered, that by stuffing the baggy side pockets of his fatigue trousers with handkerchiefs, he could conceal an apple or orange successfully . . . food for his ego as well as his stomach.

Many of the men could not tolerate the poorly prepared food and the sickening smells which had to be endured while standing in line. The movement of the ship, of course, did not help the resulting effect on appetites. Gradually the patronage of the mess fell off as the fellows turned to some emergency rations (about eight days worth) which, we had been issued before boarding.

Yankee ingenuity and growling stomachs also led many to the ship's PX. I do not remember what they were able to obtain there. I do remember that whatever it was, it did not last very long. Myer (Herman) Berger, who shared a stateroom with Harold Hess, our first sergeant, remembers the latter paying a crewman ten dollars for a can of sardines and one onion. Someone claimed later that our fare was part of a contract struck between the US government and the agency (British), which was providing our passage, probably on a "reverse lend-lease" basis. At any rate, the case for improved Anglo-American relations was dealt a telling blow by the time we reached India.

Next we learned, the hard way of course, that there was a limitation on fresh water use. While availing myself of the pleasure of our private shower in our classy "B" deck compartment, and just about the time that I had gotten thoroughly soaped up, somewhere in the bowels of the ship, someone turned a valve which switched my shower from fresh to salt water. Take my word for it . . . Lux soap does not dissolve in salt water. A paint scraper would have better served me. Naturally, I discovered, after the supply had been depleted, that the PX had carried special salt-water soap.

Upon visiting some of my fellow travelers, however, I soon appreciated the advantages of my accommodations. Some of the fellows were jammed into staterooms or stacked like cordwood on tiers of canvas bunks, which filled converted dance floors. There must have been smaller staterooms than mine as Millard Sturgell, Arley Palmer and Salvatore Corritore shared one that Sturgell described as being so small occupants were like "sardines in a can". He also had problems with boils . . . one, which the ship's doctor removed from very close to his eye, and another on his arm that had to wait until we arrived in India.

Another patient of the ship's doctor was Ernie Gioia, who had developed a high fever and was confined by the former to his bunk. Ernie was one of those who had joined us just as we left California for the Port of Embarkation and was consequently not familiar to his platoon officer, Lt. George Holmes Wilson. When the latter visited him, accompanied by the First Sergeant

Harold Hess and apparently assuming that Ernie was taking undue advantage of the doctor's diagnosis, ordered him up on deck to participate in exercises. Upon doing so, Ernie promptly collapsed. About two days later our company commander, Capt. Scott was informed of the incident and after discussing it with Gioia, proceed to chew the lieutenant out. The result, of course, was that for many months thereafter Ernie was fair game for Wilson. In due time, however, and after Wilson had finally realized his error, he was man enough to compliment him for having stood up for his rights.

Ray Bumgardner related that he shared a small U-shaped cubicle with eight others, including Tom Shown, Ray Altenbach and a master sergeant. The bunks were in three tiers with the most favorable being the top, center one, under the only air vent. The master sergeant, of course, claimed this one, which increased in value with each mile that we came closer to the equator. His smugness over his underhanded triumph blinded him to the vengeful enterprise of his cabin mates, however, for when he went to sleep, which was usually early, Tom Shown and Bumgardner who had the other two upper bunks, would tie a pair of trousers over the air vent with each of them having a pant leg through which they enjoyed the diverted air. When the sergeant awoke sweating, they yanked the trousers down and secretly enjoyed, with the rest of their mates, his wondering, aloud, why it was so hot, even with the air vent.

Despite the aggravations of the food and water situation, the fascination by most of us at being on an ocean voyage was very real. Once we had resigned ourselves to the fact that we could do nothing about the possibility of falling victim to an attack, we began to enjoy some of the wonders of the ocean. Our route was southeast and as we encountered warmer waters, we began to see flying fish, dolphins, and several species of sharks and at night the luminescent phosphorous as we churned through the dark seas. The majesty of the Mariposa was dramatically manifested by the manner in which she gracefully dipped her bow to acknowledge the equally awesome royalty of King Neptune's mountainous swells.

Several concessions were made however . . . to the menacing intruder who cruised below these swells. Because of her better-than-adequate speed, the Mariposa was unescorted by any Naval vessels. To disrupt the timing required by any submarine in the process of aiming and launching torpedoes, our course was altered every few minutes. We literally zigzagged across the ocean. In the event that this maneuver was unsuccessful or for some other reason we failed to evade the German menace, however, we also began lifeboat drills.

Another grim reminder of our status came with the sudden crash of a five-inch gun, mounted aft, as it tossed a shell into the air. As it exploded, the small puff of smoke it created was then used as a target by several twin-barreled forty-millimeter "Bofors" anti-aircraft guns.

After nine days we had earned the title of "Shellbacks" and were so enrolled in His Majesty's nautical kingdom as we crossed the Equator in the Caribbean. Three days later, September 21st, we dropped anchor in Rio de Janeiro harbor. For one poignant evening we were witness to the distant splendor of the nightlife along the beaches of Rio's Riviera. Remaining in this beautiful, natural harbor only long enough for a select few to go ashore and arrange for additional supplies, we again turned our bow toward the menacing Atlantic. As the famous Sugarloaf slipped by on our starboard, it seemed to me to be a strangely bizarre set of circumstances in which to be viewing, for the first time, this impressive landmark that was such a standard in so many American geography classes.

. . . .

It soon appeared that re-entering the Atlantic had more ominous ramifications than when we had left New York. As we threaded our way through the waterways leading from the harbor, some of us noticed that we had acquired a blimp and airplane escort.

Several days out of Rio, word came up from the ship's hospital that a couple of volunteers were needed to clean up a room in which one of the passengers had died from spinal meningitis. Someone in the 181st front office supplied the name of one of my Fort Dix compatriots, Earl Troy as our "volunteer". Earl was one of the smallest members of the company and, to my memory never boasted of being a hero or of even being brave. He related later that he was indeed extremely apprehensive, maybe frightened at the prospect. Nevertheless he had no say in the matter and was ordered to perform the dangerous assignment. Some of us wonder, to this day, how his name was selected for such a hazardous job.

When we arrived in Rio many had begun to doubt that our destination was indeed North Africa. Some logical alternatives were the South Pacific, New Zealand or Australia, the latter of these becoming the front-runner in the rumor race. This gained some credence when, after observing the stars one evening, Bill "Junior" Wilkerson announced that "We are in the South Atlantic" and "That constellation, there is the Southern Cross." Bill, who made no claims at being athletic, had acquired his dubious nickname during the first days in Camp Crowder, when he was unable to pull his plump body above the chinning bar even once. With his dramatic demonstration of astronomical knowledge, he put to rest any ideas that physical strength was the only measure of one's maturity. By his very simple pronouncement he acquired much, well-deserved respect and a small following to boot.

As we headed due east, a rumor surfaced to the effect that one of the crew had reported that we had picked up a U-Boat tail ever since leaving Rio. This disquieting news flash persisted all the way to the tip of South Africa. Another incident, which gave us additional cause for concern occurred when one of our folks dropped his life preserver overboard and watched it sink out of sight like a rock. The crew, we observed, had a different type, which probably floated.

Standard practice for ships plying this route was to put in at one of the South African ports for material and morale purposes. Whether that had been the game plan for the Mariposa, we'll never know. About the time that we would have been altering our course toward land, someone announced that a Marine had spotted a periscope. As a result, we spent a couple of nights sleeping in life jackets and shoes. Consequently our total African experience was in catching a minute, almost fleeting glimpse of the Cape of Good Hope. We then plunged headlong into the Indian Ocean.

It was now September 30th and we had been out exactly three weeks. With little to occupy our time and with several fighting seasickness, the sea had lost most, if not all, of its appeal. Still much time was spent at the railings for the simple lack of anything better to do. During one of these moments Tom Stephenson, from Selma, North Carolina, and one of the Ft. Bragg draftees was heard to utter, in disgust, "We aren't ever going to get back." When asked why he felt that way, he replied simply "The distance has got us." Now we had been together as a complete family for ten months and some individuals had become notable for having demonstrated certain dubious talents. Among these was Ray Hardee, another draftee, from Clayton, North Carolina, not too far from Stephenson's hometown. Ray had acquired a talent for assigning nicknames to particular individuals and, before Tom had completed his remarks, he had been christened "Distance", a name that he had to contend with for many months afterwards.

At one point, during our voyage, the monotony of the unchanging horizon; the growing intolerance with the food menu; the shortening of patience and heightening of apprehensions over our elusive destination had eroded the morale to its lowest point. To combat this, an event was staged on the open portion of the upper deck, an area where church services were regularly conducted. This particular distraction took the form of a staged wrestling match between 280 pound Fred Linton and diminutive Jimmy Jones, from Missouri, who tipped the scales in the 120 to 130 pound range. The contest featured Jimmy tossing the robust Linton over his head and other equally amazing revelations of extraordinary, hidden strength. A better pair could not have been selected for the performance. Fred was always a colorful, controversial but good-natured hulk of a man and Jimmy was and still is the personification of country wit and wisdom and a truly religious person.

On October 8th we had again crossed the Equator, going the other way this time and after having passed through the Straits of Madagascar. We were in our twenty-ninth day since leaving New York, during which we had traveled through all four seasons of the year . . . . we had left during the summer; crossed the equator in the Atlantic into Southern Hemisphere winter; which shortly thereafter turned into spring and were now back in the Northern Hemisphere, which was by then experiencing autumn. Two days later the announcement came over the ship's speakers that our destination was India. This surprising development was punctuated by the distribution of Indian guidebooks and supplemented by additional instructions via the PA system.

The reactions ranged all the way from relief and curiosity to . . . ."Who cares as long as we get off of this _ _ tub"? One notable outburst came from Troy who pointed out with some alarm that India had many jungles, which were inhabited by such things as tigers and huge snakes. For this unthinking observation, Hardee immediately dubbed him "Jungle", a nickname he was never able to shed.

The anticipation that we were finally going to land somewhere and put our feet on solid ground was without question the predominant reaction to the news. It was therefore with more than casual interest that we observed our first glimpses of life in our new home. It was as though we had been suddenly placed into the center of a far-eastern travelogue. The strangeness of the small sailboats, with their curved, slanted sails and their pilots' slippers placed neatly beside the boats' cabin doors; the sights and sounds that grew more audible as we approached the mysterious city of Bombay and the smells that reached out into the harbor were all so unreal to our parochial senses.

But it was indeed real and on October 12th (Columbus Day) we worked our way past a long line of vessels, which were at anchor along our path to Ballard Pier. As we drifted quietly by their sterns, a portent of things to come, and a direct result of what we perceived to have been our treatment at the hands of our recent British hosts, suddenly surfaced. When a group of very young seamen on the stern of an English warship, in an obvious attempt at camaraderie, shouted "Hi Yanks", the instant response was loud, ugly, obscene, apparently unanimous and certainly spontaneous. To a few of us it was grossly unfair, immature and unwise. It was over as quickly as it had started however, and in minutes we were at dockside.

For two more nights the Mariposa was to remain our home. During the trip over, Captain Scott had volunteered us for KP duty, knowing that we would get an extra daily meal. Our offer, however, was not acted upon until we had tied up at the dock. We then discovered that, instead of going ashore, as we had anticipated, we were put to work in the galley. During this period, however, we learned firsthand of how desperately the Indians needed food and of the extremes to which they would go to obtain anything that was edible. In our haste to demonstrate our inherent generosity as Americans, we took great delight in tossing coins into the harbor and watching the natives retrieve them. One of the fellows, obviously very moved by the scene before him, folded up a rupee note and dropped it into one of the many small boats milling below. The slender occupant reacted as though he had just been delivered into the hands of the almighty. He probably survived an entire month on this piece of good fortune. Bob Callinan related how he watched with amusement and some wonder as an armada of small boats jockeyed for position whenever the cooks dumped garbage overboard. The objective was to be in position, just below the kitchen so that the falling debris landed in the boat, often times on the occupant's head. As this manna cascaded on them they would keep repeating "Tek hai sahib" (teek high sob) "Very good sir".

While waiting our turn to go ashore, we feasted on the spectacle of frenzied activity erupting below us on the two-storied pier. When a two hundred pound, florid-faced Englishman began abusing a puny little Hindu who was too slow in hefting a bundle larger than himself onto his head, a mighty roar went up from the Americans lining the rail. He was booed and berated loudly and invited to try the same on some of those on board. The memory of the endless meals of mutton was still fresh in their minds. The roar attracted most of those still on board to the dockside of the ship. This created a sizeable list to that side, which prompted a frantic announcement from the bridge to "knock it off".

Permission was finally given for one half of each organization to go ashore for the day. When our turns came we paraded down the gangplank with our guidebooks in our pockets and a whole list of do's and don'ts in our heads.

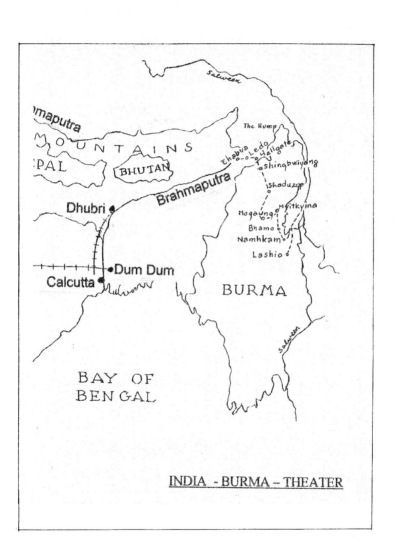

INDIA - BURMA - THEATER

# CHAPTER III

# India

## SO MUCH FOR LOGIC

But what kind of world were we walking into? Was our hit-and-miss desert training going to be of any use to us in a jungle environment? Were we really supposed to be in India or, as some jokingly suggested, had someone merely misspelled Indio (California) when they cut our orders? What was the state of the war here and what would we be expected to contribute? To get a feel for what the answers to these questions would eventually be, let's take a quick look at our new environment.

The history of the CBI, up to this point, had been one of defeat, frustration and dangerous political uncertainty. In China, Chiang's erratic resistance to the ever-pressing Japanese in the east and the ambitious Communists in the north was being conducted from a tenuous power base held together by the muck of self-serving cronyism and corruption. His strategy for the war was to let the United States win it for him, while he and his friends became fat on our Lend Lease supplies.

The British had their hands full with Indian demands for immediate independence. The will to resist the inevitable invasion by the Japanese from their new bases in Burma had been critically weakened by a growing defeatism within the army. This reflected the reluctance, by many of the men, to serve again under officers who had too often abandoned them in the retreat in Burma. It also was based on a prevailing belief that the Japanese were invincible, particularly in jungle warfare.

Top British brass, including Churchill, had made it clear that they wanted to bypass Burma completely and had made no real plans to fulfill their repeated commitments to liberate it.

Against this scenario Stilwell, backed by the War Department; and Chennault, with Chiang and FDR in his corner, were espousing two opposite game plans for besting the Japanese.

Chennault, whose motives were seated in personal aggrandizement for him and air warfare generally, espoused an exclusively aerial conquest of Japan. He refused to acknowledge the abject state of the Chinese armies, which would have to protect his air bases from Japanese counterattack, choosing to believe Chiang's boasts that it could be done. A long-time veteran of China, his professional American Volunteer Group (AVG) had racked up spectacular victories in the losing Burmese campaign, during which he held the rank of colonel in the Chinese Air Force

He strongly resisted the induction of his organization into the U.S. Army Air Corps and showed little respect for his superior officers, including Stilwell. He demonstrated this repeatedly by deliberately bypassing Stilwell, General Marshall, the Joint Chiefs of Staff)(JCS) and Secretary of War, Stimson. On one occasion he even gave a letter, for Roosevelt, to Wendell Wilkie, who delivered it personally to the president. Chennault played heavily on FDR's pressing, political desire for some positive headlines from the China front and had won the president's support for his air plan against the advise of the JCS and Stilwell, who was the Theater Commander.

General Stilwell was the complete opposite of Chennault in every way except his personal tenacity and his fierce hate for the Japanese. General Marshall had selected "Vinegar Joe" early in

1942, in response to a request by the Generalissimo for an American Chief of Staff for the Chinese Army. He had many other charges given to him before he left for China. One was to control the distribution of Lend Lease supplies to the Chinese and another, which was to eventually bring about his recall to the States, was to "IMPROVE THE EFFICIENCY OF THE CHINESE ARMY". This latter he religiously believed could be done. It was a charge that had been approved by both the JCS and the president.

Stilwell's motives were much different than Chennault's. By nature he was a very simple and humble man. As a typical West Point graduate, he was totally committed to the values of army discipline and had an outstanding career record. He unselfishly gave up the opportunity to lead the African campaign, a right he had won by his earlier performance in the same desert we had experienced. Like Chennault, he had a long tour in China before World War II.

Unlike Chennault's, however, his methods were straightforward, often tactless but totally dedicated to accomplishing his almost impossible mission. After his dramatic walk out of Burma, there was no doubt that his desire to beat the Japanese was more than professional. He believed that the Air Corps was just another weapon for use in supporting the ground troops, although a very important one. When the 181st arrived on the scene, he had no less than three different bosses, Chiang Kai-shek, Lord Louis Mountbatten and General Marshall . . . and . . . twice as many titles.

By this time, also, politics and military materiel realities had reduced his call for an all-out effort in Burma to the reopening of a land route to China. This was to be accomplished by mounting offenses from India into Northern Burma (by X Force) and from Southwestern China (by Y Force). These two forces would then unite with another being trained in the east and (as Z Force) drive to open a seaport.

The battle between this concept and that of all-out aerial warfare had finally been resolved at the Quebec (QUADRANT)

Conference, held during August just before the 181st left California to seek its fortune elsewhere. The irony of the decisions finally reached at the conference was that they were based on the discovery that neither of the competing plans could be implemented until the supply lines, starting at the Calcutta docks, were improved considerably.

Earlier meetings of the Allies had repeatedly produced agreements for the Y-Force participation in the Stilwell plan. The timetable for its start, however, had been revised several times. As we arrived in Bombay, the standing plan called for the Chinese Y-Force armies to cross the Salween River in the fall of 1943, or about the time we left New York. (The discovery of this during the writer's research efforts, plus the immediate assignment of our second and fourth teams to YFOS, raises the question that, since these plans predated the start of desert maneuvers, and the fall of Rommel in May of 1943, why the 181st was subjected to the desert at all).

So much for logic . . . the reality was that we were there "for the duration" and our immediate futures had just been predicted by the decisions reached at Quebec. These plans and those made at earlier meetings were to become patterns for dictating our life styles for the next two years. In addition to the "Y Force" effort in China, plans now called for improvement in the supply lines to Assam. These included increased emphasis on completing the Ledo Road, Americanization of the railroads and the Brahmaputra barge line, and the installation of pipelines to Assam and Kunming.

So . . . although the CBI had been designated a war theater since July 16, 1942, there really hadn't been too much actual war going on. Except for the occasional fluctuating activities of the antagonists in northern and eastern China, the contest was being conducted almost exclusively by the Fourteenth and Tenth Air Forces and the Air Transport Command (ATC). With the completion of the Quebec Conference, which also created the Southeast Asia Command (SEAC), the stage had finally been set for the serious start of ground activities and our unsuspecting heroes had arrived to become bit players in the acts that were to follow.

For the moment, Stilwell had given up his efforts to get Y-Force (YOKE) off of dead center and had returned to India to personally direct the activities in Northern Burma. The summer monsoons had ended and things were about to start happening on the Ledo Road. As we debarked from the Mariposa, the American malaria rate was being reported at 955 hospital admissions per 1000 troops per year (including readmissions) and Lord Louis Mountbatten, of commando fame and the Supreme Commander-elect of SEAC was presenting his credentials to Chinese Supreme Commander Chiang Kai-shek.

# TOURISTS

Among the many "don'ts" we were reminded of aboard ship, a little extra emphasis seemed to have been put on the fact that the natives did not like to be touched. We were told that, to them, we were spiritually unclean, and they would, therefore, be greatly offended if we so much as brushed against them. It was with more than a little confusion then that we reacted to the scene just outside of the gates to Ballard Pier. Here we were beset upon by the sorriest array of beggars and peddlers. As we tried to work our way clear of them, a diminutive shoeshine boy attached himself to Willie Wingler's leg by sitting astride his foot, while keeping up a verbal stream of "Shoeshine Joe?". Willie's only comment was "How do I get this little—off without touching him? So we learned right off that we could have left the pocket guides behind.

The stench and the poverty were overwhelming. We learned immediately that the word "baksheesh", which sounded like "boxies" meant alms and what sounded like "sob" was really "sahib" or "sir". With only seven hours allowed before they were due back at the Mariposa, the men headed for those parts of the city that most interested them. There was some souvenir hunting, but I believe that most just wandered about taking in the strange newness of this fabled land.

Some of the indomitable group managed to locate the red light district, only to find its presentation of its wares to be unbelievably bizarre. They reported later that one could literally window shop as the prostitutes were publicly displayed in storefronts and in cages. The discovery of this sordid treatment of "the oldest profession in the world" had a lasting impact on this group of warriors and probably was more effective than any of the subsequent army lectures in alerting them to the heavy medical prices to be paid for sampling the ladies' wares.

As we wandered through the downtown area of the city, we were at once struck by the stark contrast between the imposing, affluent, dignity of the government or commercial buildings and the unsightly dwelling hovels, which reeked with the sickening odors of abject poverty.

The path of the folks I was with eventually stopped in Churchgate Street, in front of an establishment named "The Coffee Club" which advertised itself as "The House for Service to the Services". It reminded us that we were hungry and, besides, had not been able to select our own menus for many weeks. A modest restaurant, it included, in addition to good food, an orchestra composed entirely of English matrons, who filled our time with conservative ditties and popular patriotic tunes. After eating and drinking our fills and after parting with a good portion of the new and strange money we had been given aboard ship, we stumbled outside to find ourselves in a darkened city.

Some decided to continue their tour of romantic Bombay but I and a companion directed our efforts toward trying to find the Mariposa. This turned out to be more difficult than had been expected, as that part of the city was a series of park-like traffic circles. In the course of taking a short cut through one of these, we discovered that it was the sleeping place for several of the "Untouchables", those impoverished unfortunates who were outside of the caste system and analogous to our homeless. In our semi-inebriated state and the total darkness between the trees and shrubs, we managed to stumble over several of the sleeping forms, causing considerable uproar and prompting us to break into a sprint until we had reached the street on the other side.

Deciding that we might never find our way back, we opted for some transportation in the form of a gharrie. This is a horse-drawn carriage, with two leather, upholstered seats facing each other. We paid the driver and had gone less than a block, when a large English policeman emerged from the darkness and asked what we had paid "the blighter". When we obliged him, he suddenly broke into a tirade at our driver in Hindustani. Our unspoken question was answered when the driver turned to us and sheepishly handed back about half of what we had given him. We were grateful but also annoyed at this intrusion into what we thought to be our personal business. We were soon to learn, however, of the economic impact that we affluent Americans were having in the marketplace, previously dominated by the poorer paid Britishers.

. . . .

On October 14th the 181ST left the Mariposa and boarded a train for a British camp in Deolali, about seventy-five miles north of Bombay. Behind us lay the interminable ordeal of the endless days of watching the ocean horizon for a destination that no one had been able to predict. Any misconceptions that we had brought with us of mysterious India had been rudely altered by our brief glimpses of Bombay and the dock area. It was with much curiosity, then, that we anticipated what rural India would have for us.

Our arrival at Deolali was very military. Dismounting from the train, we disdained the use of truck transportation, choosing instead to make our entrance as the warriors that we were, on foot. It was grand indeed, as, in columns of threes we stepped out to "Elmer's Tune" which poured forth from Al Kljun's harmonica. My recollection is of marching about a mile or so and, as I record this, I am also reminded that it was the very last time that the 181ST had the opportunity to do so as a complete unit.

Our barracks area was located at the edge of the camp, resembling nothing that we had seen back home. It was remarkable in several ways and right out of Kipling. Our American military standards for camp hygiene were missing in almost every critical area. To start with the latrine was at the top of a hill. It was a series of dry holes perched over a concrete base with outlets behind each, leading to a common ditch which eventually found its way downhill toward a nearby stream. Responding to the many horror stories with which we had been deluged regarding the many evils attendant to toilet seats, we conducted our business there from the squatting position. Here again American humor demonstrated its superiority over adversity. Standing on the seat one was treated to the usual collection of art and wit. In addition to the message that Kilroy had preceded us to the camp, was a rhyme that said "It does no good to stand on the seat, the—crabs can jump ten feet"; a prediction of things to come.

At the base of the hill was the building that served as a mess hall, a definite "no, no". Along the stream the local women could usually be seen beating the dirt (and buttons) from our clothes on the rocks.

Deolali, which still today functions as a military establishment for the Indian Army, was probably a staging area for newly arriving troops. To us it was a rest camp, where thankfully, we had only to share gate guard duty with the British. The food, still British, was better than the fare on the Mariposa with the emphasis on Australian mutton and canned corned beef. One very pleasant exception, at least to my personal taste, was coarse, locally baked bread and a cheese-like sweet butter.

The word was out by now, of course, about the loose-spending proclivities of the American sahibs and we were soon the objects of various vendors. The most celebrated of these was one who showed up with a sack in one hand and a ferret-like animal on a length of string in the other. It was no time at all before his cries of "Watch the mongoose kill the cobra" had attracted an excited audience. He made the rounds of the encircling spectators several times, persisting until he either had a large enough "take" or until the crowd's impatience was about to get out of hand. Finally he stepped back into the center of the circle. Here . . . . at last . . . . we were about to witness, first-hand, one of the fabled activities of the mysterious east. The bag was dropped and out tumbled a half-dead, punch-drunk snake. No one was expert enough to identify it as a cobra or any other reptile. The Hindu then approached with the mongoose, allowing it just enough slack so as to reach the hapless snake. The animal was indeed swift and deadly and could have dispatched the snake in a flash had it been permitted. This, however, was not about to happen. Instead the mongoose struck the snake only once and, almost as quickly, the latter was back in the sack and our vendor was on his way up the road shouting "See the mongoose kill the cobra" . . . . Score one for the vendors!

Another wandered between the barracks shouting what sounded like "Pull", which was really "Phal", the Hindu word for fruit.

One custom, which did conform to earlier accounts of British behavior, was the religious-like pause in the conduct of world events for the partaking of tea. During my sole assignment as gate guard, I teamed up with two long-term Englishmen who were almost twice my age. Sure enough, at exactly three in the afternoon, they produced three agate cups and the war stopped for tea. Tea was also peddled in camp by an imaginative vendor to the tune of "Tea walla, get your lovely; lovely, Charlie Chaplin tea!" He was asked, on one occasion if it was lousy tea, which he assured the inquirer it most definitely was. In the spirit of the true entrepreneur, he then responded to what he deduced to be a key element of market demand and was thereafter heard proclaiming loudly "Get your lousy, lousy tea! . . . . Score this one for the 181ST and the "Ugly Americans."

In addition to experiencing the military atmosphere of an Anglo-Indian camp, our two weeks in Deolali gave us an opportunity to explore the nearby village and its surroundings.

In camp we learned to sleep on the crisscrossed rope springs of the Hindu chapoy and to slip into a mosquito bar (netting) without attracting any unwanted companions. We watched with some amazement, the striding antics of an English sentry as he gyrated through an endless series of lefts, rights and about-faces in the doorway of a stucco building. We witnessed the full-dress rehearsal of a Sikh bagpipe band as it maneuvered under the arrogant orders of a florid-faced Englishman in shorts and knee socks. I was stunned by the bloody savagery of an alcohol-fueled football (soccer) match between the crew from an English ship and its Marine contingent. We also tasted warm British beer for the first time at their non-com club, again causing some friction with our free-spending ways. There I received a bit of a disappointment when I attempted a conversation with a fellow from Manchester, England . . . only to discover that I could barely penetrate his accent and that he wasn't the least bit interested in the fact that my dad, an English native, had served in the British army.

In town we were introduced to fish and chips and banana fritters as we tried to make up for the shortfall of the mess hall. Here we had another opportunity to wrestle with the arithmetic of rupees and annas.

It was at this point that the team of Harry Koch and Blackie (John) Omer, always on the alert for opportunities to fine-tune their entrepreneurial skills, discovered one at the town well. They observed that the water was drawn from the well by a turnstile-like device, made of crossed poles propelled by small donkeys. They also noted that several of the workstations were without their four-legged components . . . and promptly contracted with the proprietor to supply the missing parts. Having made a mental note earlier, of several donkeys grazing near our sleeping quarters, our ambitious twosome quickly added two to their inventory and with the animals in tow headed back to town to close the deal. En route they encountered an officer, whose nationality has faded with time, but who challenged our heroes for not having saluted. They explained very soberly that the donkeys were easily excited and might have bolted if any hands had been raised, even to salute. This dubious explanation served its purpose and they proceeded to town and closed the deal. As Harry related the story, they then blew all of their ill-gotten earnings at the local Chinese restaurant.

I believe that most of the 181ST memories of Deolali are favorable, aided no doubt by the fact that many of us received promotions in rank while we were there. Your writer ceased to be a private, rising to Technician Fifth Grade (T/5), earning him the title of "Corporal". We were able to put the Mariposa behind us for good and did receive some rest and fresh air. It was fortunate that we did because the next four days were to find us being propelled from the sublime to the ridiculous.

. . . .

As mentioned earlier, the brain trusts that were charged with conducting the war in this part of the world had conceded that communication and transportation facilities in India were woefully inadequate for supporting both the Hump and the Ledo Road. We discovered, firsthand, that they hadn't overstated the case regarding the railway system as; on October 27th we packed our gear and boarded a train for Calcutta, twelve hundred and twenty-three miles away.

The cars to which we were assigned, proudly stenciled the "Greater Indian Peninsula Railway", consisted of compartments, which were equipped with park-like benches, stacked four high. A sign in each compartment announced its capacity of "12 Europeans or 40 Indians". In their own incongruous fashion, they were the equivalent of the Pullmans we had recently taken from California to New York. The incredible contrasts between the two, however, dramatically portrayed the great gulf between the American and Indian standards of living. We were soon to learn that living in this strange country was going to be more than just different . . . . it was going to be uncomfortable, at best. On the train washing and shaving facilities were extremely limited, as was water itself.

The latrine accommodations, however, were unbelievable.

Located on the end platforms, they consisted of nothing more than rectangular holes in the floor, with footprints indicating where one should squat and with a handle on the wall to hold onto. It does not require too much imagination to envisage the state of this lavatory, considering the difficulty in always hitting the hole as the train rocked violently from side to side. The net result was revolting, except to the swarm of cockroaches, which feasted there.

Sleeping on the bench-like pallets was another test of our abilities to adapt, with only our woolen blankets between the wooden slats and us. Bob Callinan recalled that the ride was so rough at times that he literally tied himself in, since he had one of the upper bunks.

Train travel in India, at that time, was not a smoothly coordinated event. Continual stopping and starting punctuated the journey, as though the crew were lost or navigating by the seat of their pants. We were fed a combination of American and British rations, whenever one of the stops was of sufficient duration to permit it. During one of these, someone discovered that the cooks were getting hot water from the engine and we were all soon drinking "locomotive tea".

As uncomfortable as the ride was, it was priceless in its never-ending revelations of Indian rural and urban lifestyles. We were fascinated by the steaming poverty of the industrialized cities with their ever-present multitudes of emaciated cripples and beggars, clamoring for "baksheesh". We were equally impressed by the peaceful huts of the rural villages and hamlets. Manure appeared to have many uses, including fuel. What caught our attention, and was seen repeatedly, were manure patties about the size of a large "Aunt Jemima" pancake slapped onto the walls of the huts to dry, with the handprint of the lady of the house plainly imprinted in their centers.

But tourists or soldiers that we were, we could not remain detached from the horrible suffering and sights of the pitiless famine which gripped the country that fall. Our reactions, generated by our deep, national traditions of compassion against pain and suffering, were spontaneous, if sometimes understandably naive. One instance, which brought home most graphically how much we had to learn about this strange country, occurred when we offered almost ten pounds of corned beef to an emaciated man carrying a starving child, whose stomach, was enormously distended. Instead of grasping at it, to the amazement of those watching, he nudged it hesitatingly with his toe, then refused it completely. A Hindu, he held the cow . . . . for which there was one for every two persons in the country . . . . to be sacred and never to be killed. We discovered that what he and the others were after were the hard, round biscuits, which were included in army "C" rations.

As we passed through the vast expanses of jungle and farmland that separated the cities, I was struck by the occasional appearance of raised platforms in the fields, far from any habitation. Often a lone individual could be seen perched thereon, presumably to warn off stray animals, domestic or wild. I assumed that they were raised, not only to afford a broad view of the crops but also as a means of protection against those too large or vicious to be warned off.

The trip, however, tried one's patience. Arriving in Calcutta on November 1st, some four and one half days from leaving Deolali, a simple computation tells us that we averaged between eleven and twelve miles per hour, a record worse even than anything I experienced in thirteen years of commuting to New York City.

Our destination, outside of Calcutta, turned out to be the town of Dum Dum. I also recall it being referred to as "Dum Dum Orphanage".

Here, after erecting six-man pyramidal tents, we proceeded to belabor a Gurkha sentry until he unsheathed his fabled, curved, triangular-shaped knife (khukri) and stared in wondered disbelief as he ceremoniously inflicted the back of his hand with a neat little cut, before replacing the weapon in its foot-long scabbard fastened behind his neck. We were informed shortly thereafter that upon its formal presentation to him during a solemn ceremony, he had sworn never to remove this deadly instrument without drawing blood. Many months later I was to hear an account by a British major of a grisly Gurkha ambush of a Japanese patrol during the tragic retreat over the jungle trails of Malaysia. He alleged to have been witness to the stealthy, silent, systematic beheading of the trailing members of the patrol as the Gurkhas launched their deadly knives, boomerang-fashion from the cover of the shoulder-high elephant grass.

The Gurkhas, who had acquired well-deserved reputations for ferocity, are small men, about five and a half feet and weigh in the neighborhood of 150 pounds. Natives of Nepal, they were totally loyal to the British and because of their love of combat had to be ordered home at regular intervals to ensure the continuation of their race.

When eventually learning of all of the above, I wondered how these quiet and retiring warriors perceived us and also at the politeness and restraint with which they had accommodated our intrusive inquiries.

. . . .

Some of the 181ST found that, at Dum Dum, they had to sleep outdoors, with only their mosquito nettings between them and the sky. As many will recall, during the night, the condensation of the humid air formed small puddles, precariously suspended in the tops of the nettings. Thus, unless one was extremely careful in extricating himself from the folds of his blankets, he received a wet, chilling welcome to the new day. This afforded a wonderful opportunity to early-rising practical jokers to run around shaking mosquito nettings.

Our stay at Dum Dum lasted only three days. Arriving on November 1, 1943, we left on the 4th. During that time we were allowed to visit Calcutta. For those who elected to forego the opportunity, however, several films were shown in camp. Those readers, who are trivia addicts, might be interested to know that one of these was "The Glass Key", starring Alan Ladd and Sheldon Leonard.

Those who went into Calcutta found that, like Bombay, it was another example of unashamed British affluence in the midst of untold squalor and abject suffering. Having been admonished not to allow ourselves to become involved in the incomprehensible complexities of this colonial morass, we confined our roles to those of typical tourists, enjoying such luxuries as the Grand Hotel's liquid and culinary offerings and making good use of picturesque two-passenger rickshaws as we probed the depths of the city. The experiences of our gallant group, as they allowed their wanderings to follow their individual inclinations and curiosities could indeed supply ample material for another volume, which would, I suspect, cover the entire gamut of literary classification from travelogue to high adventure. Such was the cross section of the 181ST population.

. . . .

In their inimitable fashions, however, they all managed to be on hand when we loaded onto the trucks, which took us to the railroad station at Howrah, a separate city, connected with downtown Calcutta by an impressive steel girder bridge spanning the Hooghly River. Thus began the final phase of our trek across India and heralded the approaching end of our role as tourists.

The station was much like those in our own large cities, with several broad-gauge tracks leading north from a platform seething with humanity. The differences, of course, were in the unique makeup of the crowd, with the ever-present, pitiful beggars and the milling mob of white-clad Hindus and Moslems. By now we were beginning to accept the odor of India so the greasy smells of overly spiced cooking, with which the air reeked, went largely unnoticed.

Like the train that took us from Camp Crowder to California, this one was also equipped with field kitchens, which occupied one or several smallish freight cars. Although I do not recall the sleeping arrangements, I am fairly certain that we were not blessed with the four-tiered park bench accommodations, which we shared from Deolali.

The first leg of our journey, which took us across the legendary Ganges River to Parbatipur, where we switched from broad-gauge-track to the narrower meter-gauge was truly interesting.

One event happened with a suddenness none of us were ready for. At a meal stop at Santahar, we alighted from the train and lined up in good old mess-line fashion as the cooks prepared to dish out the delicacy of the day. Charlie Matthews, from Connecticut had somehow managed to beat Millard "Jesse" Owens, from New Jersey, who held the uncontested position of the number one chow-hound of the company, to the front of the line. He received his food and stepped away, balancing it in his standard G.I. mess kit. With one eye on the long line of ragged children who had positioned themselves to receive his leftovers and looking for a spot to settle in, he was suddenly attacked by a small flock of dive-bombing hawks, called kites. They struck his mess kit like a hammer, sending it spinning and scattering the food in every direction. As he jumped backwards, not realizing what had occurred, the youngsters dove into the dirt to salvage whatever they could.

These children could tear at your heart and behaved like the starved animals they had become. Most held out U.S. Army one gallon #10 ration cans. I approached the smallest one in the line and proceeded to dump my offering. As I turned to leave, he clutched my sleeve, motioning me that he wanted the tea remaining in my canteen cup also. When I asked him where he wanted it, he held out the same #10 can into which I hesitatingly poured what was left.

. . . .

We had left Howrah on November 4, 1943, at least two months before the first American Railway Battalions were to arrive in India. Therefore our train was operated under control of the highly inefficient Indian Civil Railway Administration, which was biased towards the British. (In December, reports by the U. S. Army showed that the British had deliberately welshed on high-level agreements to share the rail facilities equally with us. Of the tonnage allocated for the month, the British lost only 723 tons while the U. S. lost 14,981 tons. It took direct action between Roosevelt and Churchill to correct the situation.) For whatever reason, our train experienced many stops and delays.

At these we learned, first hand of the rigid separation between the Hindus and Moslems. We observed the separate toilet and water facilities in the stations . . . watched in fascination as the women bathed, fully clothed at the public water taps without revealing a thing. We observed our first leper, a woman who had half of her face eaten away and who, by the way was given a wide berth on one of the station platforms. We continued to see the hopeless beggars, many of them cripples. I know most of the men will remember one in particular whose legs were deformed in such a way that he walked on all fours, like an animal.

"Baksheesh Sahib"

Despite their failure to fulfill performance agreements made at the Quebec Quandrant Conference, the Indian and British authorities were pushing construction on the system, evidenced by numerous excavations along the right of way. The Hindu laborers had an intriguing custom of leaving narrow, cone-like formations standing in the empty pits. Some of us theorized that these were left as proof of the quantity of soil that had been removed. I have learned since that these pits were known as "borrowing pits" and that the formations were left to please the spirits who, it was believed, lived therein.

Two days on the broad-gauge brought us to Parbatipur where it was everybody and everything off of the train and then back onto the narrower meter-gauge. On November 7th we reached a riverboat dock at Dhubri on the banks of the mighty Brahmaputra River. As we struggled with our belongings across an open area, toward a vessel reminiscent of one of those that must have plied the Mississippi around Mark Twain's day, we were confronted with a large, ominous sign, which informed us that we were entering Assam. The part of the message it delivered which raised the hair on the back of ones neck, however, was a chilling warning that we were entering malaria country.

Riverboat at Dhubri—entering Assam

From the moment of reporting to Ft. Dix for induction, all of my attention had been divided between apprehension about my physical ability to "hack it" with the other, more mature men; learning the fundamentals of becoming a soldier; coping with army aggravations and indignities; and marveling, much as a tourist, at the wondrous world we occupied.

To me at least, and I suspect to some of the others, the warning lettered on the Dhubri sign, redirected that attention to the cold fact that we were about to be ordered to do what we had been inducted for in the first place, put our lives on the line for the good old USA. It also signaled an end to our role of tourists.

## NON-TOURISTS

Our Odyssey as a military unit, starting when we boarded the train at Camp Crowder for our trek to San Bernardino, had developed an identity comparable to a "mystery bus ride". Resigned to the prospect of having to endure an unknown period of months or even years of whatever army life had in store, we had, by now, become inured to the succession of unpredictable scenarios into which we had been injected. So it came as no great surprise that our next mode of transportation should be a riverboat. Why not???

It was with a sort of expectancy, then, that we filed aboard, found sleeping spaces on deck and turned our attentions toward our next destination . . . whatever it was to be.

· · · ·

I doubt that any of our illustrious group had ever heard of Assam before reading the imposing sign at our embarkation point on the bank. Not so the folks in Britain. With tea being to them what coffee (and Brazil) was to Americans, Assam was well known as its source and, therefore, of vital concern to them and to British commercial and political interests.

We were learning, the hard way, that Assam was also at the end of the longest supply line in the world. Before coming up the rail line, which we had just traveled, everything required to build the Ledo Road and to support the air and ground war efforts had to be transported 14,000 miles from the United States to Calcutta.

The summer monsoon, which, in Assam and Burma lasts from May until October and drops in excess of 200 inches of rain, had just ended. If one wanted to be extra charitable, he might suggest that the army had actually had the foresight to schedule our sailing and arrival dates so that we would miss this logistically difficult period.

Whatever the circumstances were that caused it to be, mercifully, the rains had stopped by the time we boarded the "Buzzard". This paddle wheeler was another example of a typical Indian passenger conveyance. It was a far cry from those that carried commuters in the "States" but certainly up to the task of battling the muddy, debris-strewn, rain-swollen Brahmaputra. It was plain, dirty and one step above a cattle boat, which it smelled like.

We headed out into the current and turned upstream . . . our goal . . . Dibrugarh, two days distant. They turned out to be a difficult two days. Living conditions were worse than Spartan. Sanitary facilities were obviously not designed for the number of troops on board and the crowding itself was aggravating.

Nevertheless, like most of our other adventures, the ride on the "Buzzard" added to our growing list of novel experiences. As we watched the flat expanses of what is now known as Bangladesh give way to the higher ground of Assam, with its distant hills, our attention was suddenly drawn back to the river by the sighting of a passing corpse. This grisly symbol of the fragile quality of Indian life was only the first of several that we were to observe. But the mighty river was full of surprises. On one occasion a school of dolphins appeared, playing "follow the leader" as they led our barque, some 500 miles up stream from their customary home in the Indian Ocean.

Many years later, John P. (Jack) Hale, one of the men from Lt. Wilson's 3RD Team penned the following in a letter to the Ex-

CBI ROUNDUP in which he described his recollections of the river boat experience.

> We transferred to the river boat after a day or two and we were ordered to help transfer the contents of our boxcars to the boat. We had an old regular Army officer who stood at the gangway and as each of us approached with a box on our shoulder, he quietly asked what it was. If it was canned fruit or another delicacy, it went on the pile of cargo traveling with our unit. If it was Spam or some other undesirable, it went with the cargo of the other companies traveling with us.
>
> He later advised us that he was simply re-routing since we were all in the same Army. That sounded reasonable to me and we were well equipped with dessert for quite a while.
>
> We slept on the deck of the stern-wheeler and I recall one of the officers had a serious attack of nerves since it sure did appear we were heading for desolation as we plowed up the Brahmaputra and watched bodies floating down stream. I thought it was grand to experience what life had been for Mark Twain on the Mississippi.

The routine activities of everyday life along the Brahmaputra, like living pages out of National Geographic, gradually drew our attention away from our floating discomforts. On the shore we saw youngsters washing their elephants and bullocks, while their mothers and sisters beat clothing on the nearby rocks. The landscape started to give up its small farms and gardens and the occasional town or village to be replaced by stretches of undisturbed wilderness interrupted by large British tea plantations.

Dibrugarh, on November 9th, was another surprise. The unloading facilities, while probably adequate for serving seasonal tea plantation requirements, were not designed for their new task of supporting a war. They consisted of a series of shed-like buildings standing on pilings about twenty-five yards out from the riverbank, to accommodate the draft of the paddle wheeler. The only connection with the bank was over a series of planks, supported about every fifteen feet by pilings driven into the river mud. Navigating these with all of one's equipment, including a barracks bag was a hair-raising test of balance as he struggled to keep from being pitched off into the mud below by the springboard action of the planks as he crossed each fifteen—foot span.

With the recent deterioration of both the quality and the size of meal portions, the usual level of bitching had started to increase. Some of the men were showing signs of apprehension as a result of the miserable conditions we had had to contend with since leaving the "States". As I stepped off of the last plank and started to breath again, Jesse Owens followed close on my heals, carrying a full case of Australian corned beef (later dubbed "corn willy") in his barracks bag. I was never able to learn from him what he had done with its previous contents.

. . . .

Waiting for us was another, narrow meter-gauge train, which we piled into. This, we were assured, was the last lap of our surprising expedition. The announcement was received with the usual mix of individual emotional retorts. Like a child on Christmas Eve, however, I found the next few hours to be interminable. Riding upright in coaches with wooden seats, this stretch was the worst of the entire journey. For some unknown reason, I had anticipated an hour or two on the train. Instead we traveled throughout the night and did not arrive at Baragoli, Ledo until the sun had come up. It was November 10, 1943 and it had been no less than two months and two days since we made our way up the gangplank at Staten Island, New York.

# WHERE ARE THE JAPS ?

Ledo, then, was to be the new home of the 181ST . . . . a remote railhead which, prior to the war had only served a nearby colliery, a brickyard and a few tea plantations. It derived its name from the bazaar to which the local Indian workers came to buy goods brought in from the outside. It was also a place where the least-hostile Naga headhunters could exchange poultry for some of "civilization's" exotic goodies such as salt. Before hostilities started, its only visitors were gem traders and big game hunters. These had to obtain special permits to enter the jungle and also to waive all official liability for their safety. Soon after our arrival, a rumor surfaced to the effect that this was the very place from which the famous wild animal collector, Frank Buck, had operated.

The unhurried pace of this remote outpost had been shattered, however, in early 1942 when the refugees from the Burma defeat started arriving. The local British officials estimated that of about 30,000 who attempted to reach Assam over, what became known as the "refugee trail", only 23, 000 succeeded. Things must have really become interesting in May, 1942, when the main body of the Chinese 38TH Division flooded the area. One of the first refugees had informed the Governor of Assam that the Chinese were a "mere rabble" and should be disarmed upon arrival. The tea planters were especially cool to them and were relieved when their main body was relocated to Ramgarh, northwest of Calcutta. During July and August the survivors of the Chinese 22ND Division, in much worse shape than their compatriots in the 38TH, repeated the scene at Ledo.

The coveted privacy of the tea planters was permanently disrupted, finally, in November 1942, when Ledo was designated Base Section #3 by the Allies and the following month the first Americans arrived, African-American troops and white officers of the 45TH and 823RD Engineers. The building of the road was handed over to the 823RD and the 45TH won the job of preparing areas for warehouses, housing and hospitals; and cutting additional roads to accommodate the military buildup, which was to follow.

Now, just about a year later, we and other units who would support the efforts of the combat troops responsible for clearing the Japanese from the road trace were making our appearances. Implementation of the plans agreed to at the Quebec Conference had begun and we were going to make our modest contribution toward their success.

Our company was assigned to an area carved out of very heavy jungle. About twenty bamboo barracks with thatched roofs, called bashas, plus a day room, kitchen, supply room, shower, latrines and mess hall were waiting for us. All of these were to be interconnected by raised paths lined with lengths of four-inch wide bamboo.

Our new home for two years

The bashas were indeed made completely of bamboo, starting with the frame, which utilized larger diameter sections for rafters and wall studs . . . all tied together with thin strips . . . also bamboo. Woven mats, fashioned from long slices and fastened to the studs formed the exterior walls. These also covered doorframes and shutters that opened upward and outward from the windows. Horizontal members, tied across the rafters supported the thatching, which was the happy home of many small rats and similar rodents. While lying in bed, Luke Strass recalled observing them often-frolicking overhead.

"Home-Sweet Home" 10 man basha

Ledo was the topographical opposite of our San Bernardino desert home, where the 181ST front office had had to invent work details to keep us out of trouble. Because it was in such a primitive state, our new scenario offered a plethora of opportunities for management to keep us busy. Having been given the minimum treatment possible by the heavy engineering equipment, it was starkly evident that this piece of real estate was going to require much additional work to bring it up to a level of comfort that we could tolerate.

This project was our own, of course, and using shovels, axes and pick axes (appropriately called "pioneer tools" by the army) . . . a plentiful supply of Yankee ingenuity and sweat . . . some occasional four letter words . . . and . . . a steady stream of materials unearthed by some of the best foragers in the U.S. Army . . . . we set about converting the 181St encampment into a virtual "bedroom community" . . . . with slit trenches.

"Steel Helmet" washroom

Motor Pool Operators (partial)
Kennedy (NE), Stephenson (NC), Anderson (NYC)
Zace (IL), E. Clark (NC), M. Jones (IA), Bottary (IL)

Motor Pool Garage & Co.

"What's Cookin' ?"
Shirley (NC), Follett (KS),
Omer (IA) Wagler (IA)

Knowing that we had a home again, even though it was within striking distance of the Japanese, did much for morale. This received a very decided boost the day after arrival, also, when we discovered that our mail had caught up with us. Among the many news flashes from home was one from Bill Hasse's wife informing him that he had become the father of a daughter the day before we docked in Bombay. It would be over a year and a half and she would be already walking before he would finally get a chance to hold her.

Life in our new community was indeed different than that expected in the usual army camp. So that the reader does not get the wrong impression, we must point out that facilities were still primitive. For the first time since leaving the "States", however, we controlled their condition. Nevertheless, we were still using pit latrines; sleeping on rope beds (chapoys); eating "corn willy" and Spam; shaving and washing from our steel helmets and, for the first time in our army careers, some of us were doing our own laundry in large cans over open fires. Sensing an opportunity to make a little extra spending money, Louis Reams (North Carolina) set up what developed into a very successful hair-cutting enterprise.

Two pits were dug . . . one next to the mess hall, in which golf ball-size potatoes were kept . . . (the writer caught KP only once here and thought that the cooks were kidding when they insisted that these be peeled). The other pit was much larger and was our answer to the local waste-disposal problem. At regular intervals a little gasoline was tossed into the pit and its contents was burned off. At one of these well-attended performances one of our more prominent non-coms, who shall remain anonymous, in investigating why ignition had not occurred after a match had been thrown in, wound up with a beautiful case of singed eyebrows.

In the meantime the battle to carve an acceptable camp out of the jungle was still in progress. For those in the 181ST whose repair skills were not yet in demand, continuing the landscaping of our new community became their unfortunate lot. Part of their efforts was utilized in collecting bamboo for the natives who were employed in completing our walkways. This was cut from a patch of jungle about five miles up the Road. The writer joined in this venture for one day only. For days, work details had been hacking their way into the area searching for acceptable product with which to enhance our recent real estate acquisition. In hunting for specimens of consistent diameter, they had managed to litter the entire jungle floor with a two-foot layer of discarded bamboo. As a result, standing upright had become an almost impossible achievement and the entire project took on the appearance of a drunken ballet performed on a roller-bearing-like stage. When someone mentioned that bamboo was a favorite habitat of the Indian cobra, however, the task lost some of its festive character.

The other half of the walkway project required the hauling and application of truckloads of ashes, gravel and a curious variety of other types of aggregate that had been bird-dogged by our ace company foragers, led by the army's best, Matt Fassio from Joliet, Illinois.

Speake (DC), Fassio (IL)
Buy a wild pig

Some of the task was given to Lt. Robb's 5TH Team, while it awaited his arrival with our repair tools and vehicles. The job of hauling ashes for the inter-connecting pathways was given to Ray Bumgardner, who commanded a working crew and a truck. Now any of our readers who have had the good fortune to be part of an army work detail know that job preservation is essential. With this in mind, they had arrived at a delivery objective of one truckload in the morning and one in the afternoon. This plan went well until the front office discovered it and opted for a doubling of the production objective. They also replaced Ray with Carl Clampett who readily "inspired" the group to meet management's new bogey . . . almost "ruining the detail".

Ray joined the attack on the undergrowth, a job, which was made unexpectedly difficult by the large number of leeches present. Avoiding them was impossible and long-sleeved fatigue shirts were a must. At regular intervals work had to be suspended while the men scraped the tenacious, bloodsucking parasites from each others' uniforms.

While struggling with the landscaping project one crew leveled what appeared to be an abandoned anthill, which measured fifteen feet across and eight feet high from behind the officers bashas.

Another project, which addressed itself to the early morning crush at the latrines, was the construction of outdoor urinals, utilizing an exclusive 181ST design. A large pit was dug and about a dozen hollowed out bamboo poles were set at angles in the pit. The latter was then filled with gravel and covered with soil. What this nature-like facility lacked in privacy it made up for with its utility and individual accessibility.

. . . .

With the war in Europe and the South Pacific monopolizing material and troops, the CBI continued to be critically wanting in provisions and American personnel. One remedy for this situation was the supplying of food, material and native labor by the Indian government. The 181ST's share of these was represented by more

Australian "corned willy" and other food, (ie: the miniature spuds) and the assignment to us of native bearers or "basha boys". These latter, who came from Bengal and other provinces, were chaperoned (rather severely) by overseers who controlled their civil and religious behavior.

One was assigned to each basha and was responsible for keeping it looking neat and picked-up. Crude native brooms were their most conspicuous implements. They became our personal contacts with India and received our exclusive, American brand of treatment. Their reaction to the generosity and kindness of the American "sahibs", many of whom met them as equals rather than colonial serfs, was interesting and gratifying. Unfortunately they also had to contend with our American brand of humor and occasional practical jokes.

Two quick stories come to mind. . . . While showering, one of the men noticed that the basha boy cleaning the adjacent stall was sneaking a few curious peeks at our bather. With a twinkle in his eye and for pure devilment, the latter suddenly lunged at the boy. Thinking the worst, the boy fled out into the company area with our nude signal-repairman in hot pursuit. Up and down the bamboo-lined paths they went to the great amusement of everyone . . . until . . . as Bill Wraspir, a Tech Sergeant from Idaho, related, "Wiser heads came to the rescue." It suddenly occurred to some that the entire episode could be interpreted entirely different and Bill, who just happened to be the nearest senior non-com, and also enjoying the scene, was subsequently so advised . . . officially . . . by some of the officers.

Another bit of activity centered on the native custom of carrying a small-necked bottle of water with which to clean themselves after defecating in the nearby bushes. Our next-door neighbors were one of the radio repair squads and listed Ray Hardee, "Blackie Omer" and several other culprits among their membership. Another was a distinguished-looking North Carolinian, named Colden Daniel Chesser, who could easily have passed as a prominent politician or bank executive. He belonged to that exclusive group who, no matter what the circumstances, always managed to appear in well-pressed uniforms and was always tonsorial immaculate. He and others had been given regular work assignments in nearby signal operations and supply installations. Returning late one afternoon he was stunned when he observed "Charlie", their basha boy, coming out of the bushes with Chesser's canteen. The ensuing roar was probably heard across the border in Burma and as he charged the boy to mete out the appropriate punishment, his ever-loving roomies interceded to save their unsuspecting servant, who had been the unwitting tool of their sordid humor. It took some fast-talking to convince Chesser that his canteen had not been used for the purpose he had deduced.

Charlie was well liked by the members of the Hardee-Omer Association, a condition which earned him an invitation to participate in some liquid celebration during one of our holidays. In his eagerness to please the generous strangers from far-off America, he committed the deadly error of overindulging in the festivities and eventually succumbed to the magic of the "sauce". This unfortunate transgression of the religious rules imposed by the leaders to whom he was answerable, earned him severe physical punishment. To their credit, his employers never allowed him to repeat the mistake.

As a whole, these bearers were trustworthy. Like any human contingent, however, they had their miscreants, one or more of which managed to pilfer what Luke Strass had thought was a well-hidden cache of sardines.

Among the bearers serving the 5TH Team was one known as "Hobby", a corruption of his Indian name. He was very efficient at shining shoes, washing clothes and other chores and so pleased by the treatment he received, that he followed the team when it was ordered later to Chabua, where he attended to the wants of seventeen men for the rest of the war.

· · · ·

The neighborhood was alive with wildlife ranging from ground monkeys and turkey buzzards to jungle cats and large apes. En-route to the mess hall early one morning I glanced upward to the top of a tall tree that somehow had become isolated during the ground clearing process. Staring at me, straight down the trunk of the tree, from its perch about forty feet up was an ape as large as I. The telephone and telegraph repair squad that I was a member of occupied a basha on the perimeter of the company area, about thirty yards from the jungle wall. My bunk was next to an open door, which faced toward that same jungle. Fortunately, because of the malaria-bearing mosquitoes, netting protected the bunk. Waking on another morning, I was informed by several of my compadres that in the dead of the night we had had a visit by a very large cat . . . which had made the rounds of the entire basha, starting with yours truly, sniffing each bunk, but apparently either not hungry enough or confused by the mosquito bars.

In the bashas, which accommodated ten men, five on a side, the center aisle was lined with two strands of telephone field wire from which one end of each man's mosquito bar was suspended. One of the other squads, which had acquired a small ground monkey as a pet returned on one occasion to find that their diminutive charge had spent the day running along the field wire strands and diving headlong into their mosquito nettings tearing them to shreds.

Sergeant William H. Stull had a baby monkey, which he allowed to roam free. At night it would slip into bed with whoever was nearby. When the occupant finally awoke, and jumped on discovering the unknown intruder, the equally startled monkey urinated on him with spectacular results. In time some of the men became accustomed to the little menace and learned to evict him without the uncomfortable consequences.

Chuck Cortwright had acquired a full grown and ferocious-looking monkey, which he kept on a leash. Someone else on the 5TH Team had a small mischievous monkey, which received much attention and affection from the occupants of its owner's basha. The diminutive devil also enjoyed unlimited freedom of the premises . . . . until the following incident occurred. It had become standard practice for Roy Murphy, Jimmy Jones and others to bring tidbits back with them from the mess hall and to signal that it was monkey mealtime by jangling an empty mess kit. As soon as the puny primate heard this music he would race for the basha to await his feast. To afford him access when the doors and window shutters were closed, a small opening had been cut in the wall, near the floor, and a rubber flap attached to allow the animal to come and go as it pleased. On one occasion, after rattling the mess kit and observing that their little charge had darted into the basha, the men entered to find that the playful prankster had discovered a roll of film, which had been left out and had managed to unroll it, destroying its usefulness.

Film being very hard to come by, and deciding that some control over the animal's access to the unoccupied basha had to be exercised, Jones placed a wooden box just inside the animal's private entrance the next time that the group left for the mess hall. After the meal, they performed the monkey chow-call routine and then watched in disbelief, as the inevitable, humorous, but for the monkey, near-disastrous occurred. As expected, the unsuspecting rascal raced to the basha, dove at its private entrance, struck the wooden obstacle behind the rubber flap and recoiled into a pathetic heap on the ground outside. Not having anticipated such a dramatic result, with sincere concern they worked over the fallen beast in an attempt to revive it. With no immediate success they finally opted to bring their little patient to the dispensary, where with some smelling salts and tender loving care, they succeeded in restoring their pet to consciousness. From then on the minute monster always tested the opening with its hand before entering.

On occasion, the folks assigned to brush clearing would tire of the sport and slip away into the jungle for a sightseeing constitutional. Ray Bumgardner and Jimmy Jones utilized this diversion several times. On one of these, our heroes were strolling down an abandoned road, en-route to Ledo for a noontime snack, when they came to a clearing in which there were two or three hundred chattering monkeys blocking the path. Upon sighting the men, the long-tailed primates became ominously silent. With some apprehension, Ray and Jimmy approached the herd, which watched them closely but made no threats to their progress. The distant goal of lunch at one of the Chinese restaurants in Ledo was then accomplished, followed by a short ride on the shuttle truck back to the company area in time for the next formation.

Different though it was, life in Ledo soon fell into a more-or-less routine pattern, interrupted by an occasional air raid alert or when some careless smoker contrived to burn down one of the latrines, which were treated with used diesel oil to keep down the mosquito population.

We lost no time in casing the bazaar and became accommodatingly proficient at haggling with the Indian merchants, who evidenced considerable consternation in the beginning, when some of us paid them the first price they quoted for an item. Their upset stemmed from the fact that these Americans were breaking the ground rules by failing to enter into the age-old bargaining game.

The bazaar offered us our first long-term opportunity to observe an Indian community, albeit one on the very edge of civilization and one beset by an alien military presence. Besides the permanent stalls of the Hindu merchants, the bazaar was host to the Chinese United Restaurant and several Chinese dentists. The latter serviced the Chinese troops who by now had returned to the area, although most were deployed near the point of the Ledo Road. These dentists drilled holes into which they would then drive tapered, golden spikes.

Ledo Bazaar

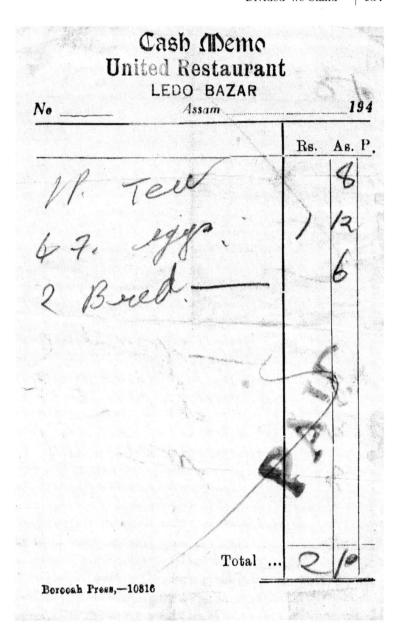

Check from the Chinese United Restaurant

The bazaar was also the "jumping off place" for the Ledo Road and was only a couple of miles short of the end of the railroad. It was at a point where the road turned right, crossed the tracks, made a left, passed another Chinese restaurant (the Kon Ming), which advertised itself as being at Nadua Siding . . . and headed eastward towards Pangsau Pass and Burma, 43.2 miles away.

While there were other army units adjacent to ours and in the immediate vicinity, the buildup for the oncoming offensive had not yet started. It would not be possible until the communication links . . . the airfields, railroads, roads and Brahmaputra barge line were overhauled. Not only Ledo, but all of the areas stretching back to our debarkation point at Dibrugarh would be involved. Some of these were Chabua, Digboi, Dinjan, Dikom, Tinsukia, Likhapani and Margherita.

The latter was the home of the 20TH General Hospital and a large bamboo chapel. A particularly quaint town, a little closer to civilization, it had a larger bazaar than the one at Ledo. This was located at a point where the road and railroad crossed a river over a common bridge. It was so constructed that only one or the other could use it at one time. As some of the 181ST survivors will no doubt recall, the inevitable happened one day when a truck trying to beat a train coming from the other direction had to settle for a tie . . . . with very grisly consequences. Bill Hasse recalled that bodies and the engine from the truck were strewn in the stream below the bridge and that parts of bodies were draped grotesquely all over the structure.

A more pleasant and even humorous recollection of Margherita comes from Joe Shirley (from North Carolina) and Bob Callanan. With army chow being what it was, everyone operated their own personal snack bars, subject to their particular monetary situations. Joe and Cal, who by the way, were also part of the Hardee-Omer Association, uncovered a can of milk on one of their shopping forays, which had taken them to Margherita. Now this was a real find and it was with great anticipation that they returned to Ledo expecting to enjoy a rare change from the usual fare. Deciding to examine their precious acquisition a little closer, they proceeded to read the fine print on the label . . . . only to discover that the contents was actually mothers milk . . . . That night they drank their coffee black.

Margherita was the location of the only Red Cross establishment in the area. Ray Bumgardner, who made regular use of it recalled spending much of his spare time there, utilizing its fine library. He also joined John Haisel, from Long Island, N. Y., and others in some pretty intense ping pong matches. Another memory, triggered by the mention of Margherita is of obtaining short lengths of sugar cane somewhere in the vicinity. These were an interesting substitute for candy when chewed.

Looking back, it is difficult to recall the degree of apprehension we had over the fact that we had finally reached the place where our contact with the enemy, if any, would occur. Possibly our preoccupation with more immediate, practical matters distracted us from such profound contemplations. Had we known the facts as they existed the moment we arrived in Ledo, however, I am certain that the answer to the question, "Where are the Japs?" would have generated much more concern than it did at the time.

Just before we arrived in Ledo, Stilwell had decided to turn the Chinese 38TH Division loose . . . the objective . . . have the Road through to Shingbwiyang (103 miles from Ledo) by December 31 (1943). With division headquarters near Tagap (73 miles from Ledo), three battalions from the 112TH Regiment started over three parallel routes through the mountainous jungle. Their job was to dislodge the Japanese from supposedly lightly held outposts along the Tarung and Tanai Rivers, just beyond Shingbwiyang. The attempts were disastrous, with one of the Chinese companies being completely annihilated, two battalions cut off and regimental headquarters of the 112TH overrun. The remaining Chinese immediately dug in and even with re-enforcements could not be prodded from their holes to counterattack. What had really occurred was that the Chinese patrols had failed to discover that the Japanese crack 18TH Division had taken up positions just south of the scene of the current fighting. The entire area had been reconnoitered personally by their commander, General Tanaka in preparation for an exercise which, as he himslf later declared, would, " . . . . destroy the American and Chinese forces which would advance in a long column through the tortuous Ledo Road in India." As things eventually turned out, (fortunately for the 181ST) Stilwell, who had been at the Cairo "Sextant" Conference with Roosevelt, during the foregoing, returned hurriedly to convince Lt. General Sun Li-jen, the 38TH commander, that instead of retreating, which Sun wanted to do, the whole 38TH should be committed. This was done and a major battle at a place called Yupbang Ga, on the Tarung River ensued, which the Chinese won . . . . to their own amazement.

We had arrived, however, at the precise moment when the Chinese were experiencing their worst reverses and waited, deep in their foxholes, for the certain annihilation they had become accustomed to at the hands of the Japanese "supermen".

# THE ROAD

After the smoke had cleared, following the British defeat in 1942, only one outpost . . . Ft. Hertz, in Burma . . . remained in their hands. It was located northeast of Ledo but on the other side of the Patkai Mountains. In February, before the Japanese had overrun the country, an attempt had been made by the British to build a road to this remote settlement. It was soon abandoned and when, in November of that year the Americans took over the job at Hellgate, 34 miles from Ledo, the British predicted that they would fail. This was enough reason, of course, to convince us to go ahead.

By November the eastern terminus of the road had also been changed from Ft. Hertz to Kunming in China, and it was now needed to replace the Burma Road. It is interesting that this decision had been reached as a result of an agreement between the Chinese and Indian governments in January of 1942, five and half months before the Burma Road was closed. The decision did not become fact, however, until Washington, which was trying desperately to do something for the Chinese, agreed to supply the required lend-lease supplies. Thus the groundwork had been laid for a road, which would ultimately bear his name, long before Stilwell ever got to see it.

As a matter of fact, his solution to reopening the supply route to China was not a road in Northern Burma at all. His plan was to retake Rangoon and drive the Japanese clear out of Burma. For political and military reasons, that we will not discuss here, his plan never got off of the ground and he had to settle for the Chinese alternative.

. . . .

As for the Japanese posture on the road, following on the heels of the last refugees, they had gotten as far as Tagap, a village occupied by the Kachins, who were not known for their cordiality to strangers, particularly Japanese. Being quite aware of the Kachins' attitude toward intruders, during the night, the native porters and the elephant contractors accompanying them remembered that they had some pressing business back home and elected to disappear. This forced their recent employers to withdraw to Shingbwiyang at the eastern edge of the Patkais, where they set up a supply depot. Thus the stage was set . . . . the Japanese in Shingbwiyang . . . the British assuring us that we would fail . . . . enter . . . . Uncle Sam!

. . . .

As mentioned earlier, on November 7th, 1942 Ledo was designated Base Section #3 in anticipation of its coming importance as the supply point for the Road. Colonel John C. Arrowsmith arrived to begin reconnaissance of the area, the road trace and the Ledo base . . . . the ball was rolling in earnest. His task, however, was not an easy one. No one had ever done any surveying in this Godforsaken corner of the world and to demonstrate how difficult it really was, one of his crews underestimated the distance to Shingbwiyang by 42 miles. The jungle, itself, with its medical hazards proved to be an awesome adversary. Its malaria-bearing mosquitoes, typhus-carrying mites and leeches (three kinds) . . . its dangerous pests, such as ticks, wasps, hornets, scorpions, ants, flies and hundreds of others had killed 600 British coolies in April of 1942.

As the survey teams floundered about in the Patkais trying to find the best route for the Road, the 823RD's engineers attacked the mountains between Hellgate and Pangsau Pass . . . . eight miles of lofty, slippery Hell. While stationed at Hellgate during the winter of 1943-1944, I had an opportunity to travel over the finished product. To this city boy, it was a frightening experience. That these men, all second-class citizens, with a minimum amount of the necessary equipment, and after the British failure . . . were able to carve a two-lane roadway around the precipitous cliffs of "The Mountain That Moves", as the natives called it, was, in my opinion just short of miraculous. The occasional view of trucks, jeeps and construction vehicles lying, like abandoned "match box" toys, on the distant floor of the valley below, was mute testimony to what must have been a terrifying assignment. Add to this the fact that their only protection from Japanese patrols was the insecure Chinese and their own rifles . . . and you have the perfect reason for requesting a furlough to Calcutta.

Looking down from Pangsau Pass toward Hellgate and the road on the "Mountain That Moves"

Nevertheless, it was done . . . . and at exactly 1706 hours (5:06PM for you civilians) on February 28th, 1943, Colonel Ferdinand J. Tate; the battalion commander fired his pistol as the lead bulldozer crossed over the Pass into Burma, 43.2 miles from Ledo. This, however, was about as far as the Road would get. By May 11th, the monsoon hit, stopping all forward progress at mile mark 47. From then until September an even more difficult battle was fought to keep the Road open, as the rains (clocked at 14 inches in 24 hours) washed away section after section of their hard-earned prize.

Pangsau Pass (Burma Border) looking west toward the Himalayan Mtns.

Little progress, if any, was made on the road during the monsoon. Much of the equipment was inoperative due to either lack of replacement parts or being mired in the mud. An alarmingly large percentage of the men were hospitalized by injuries, malaria, dysentery and other jungle-wrought maladies. On the advance sections of the road, traffic stopped completely. The 38TH was supplied by airdrops, weather permitting, and from the end of March until the middle of August 1943 the road head moved only three miles, from mile 47.3 to mile 50.7.

Returning from Quebec in August, Stilwell inspected the entire Assam area, reviewing the progress, or better still, the lack of it on the road. Although sincerely sympathetic to the conditions under which the troops were struggling, he still thought that more could have been accomplished. Fearing for the very success of the entire Northern Burma Project, code-named SAUCY, he promptly relieved Arrowsmith, who he described as, " . . . a sulky, indifferent bird . . . ." "You wouldn't catch him out in the mud, pushing. No, he's the Big shot at the base . . ."

Colonel Lewis A. Pick, an engineer who had developed the "Pick Plan of Missouri River" flood control, replaced him on October 17, 1943. With the monsoon ending, Pick immediately initiated round-the-clock operations on the road, moved his headquarters to the point, at mile 48 and assured Stilwell that the road would be in Shingbwiyang by New Years. On November 30th the lead bulldozer had reached Nathkaw, mile mark 92 and on December 27th the men made good on Pick's promise. Right behind them was a convoy of fifty-five trucks carrying Chinese combat troops, the first to enter North Burma by motor vehicle . . . . the same troops who would taste their first victory at Yupbang Ga.

History has now recorded the amazing feats of the international team that went on to beat both the jungle and the Japanese in extending the road to Kunming. Therefore we are not going to attempt to duplicate that account here. To help our readers get an appreciation for the size of the job, which was accomplished . . . it was reported by Tillman Durdin in the New York Times, that 13,500,000 cubic yards of earth were moved in the construction . . . . enough to build a solid dirt wall three feet wide and ten feet high from New York to San Francisco.

In early 1945, after the road was completed, the writer and Jeff Bennett were selected to serve as part of an honor guard, with four Chinese soldiers, at a solemn requiem mass held in Kunming, to remember the men who had died during the road's construction.

After its completion, the Ledo Road or Pick's Pike as it was called by some, was officially renamed the Stilwell Road. It was truly appropriate that it be named thus, but it sticks deep in this writer's craw, that it was suggested by Chiang Kai-shek who had personally caused Stilwell's recall, depriving him of the opportunity to enjoy the fruits of his excruciating labor on behalf of the war and the Chinese soldier . . . . and whose back-stabbing duplicity throughout Stilwell's tenure as his Chief of Staff, is now a matter of record.

# CHAPTER IV

# The Scattering Starts

## WE GO TO WORK

But it was November1943 and our personal war was just beginning. We were to find out very quickly that the role, which had been written for us by someone in the War Department, and for which we had trained was going to be quite different from the one we eventually played. Our combined Army job descriptions made us one of the most skilled signal repair organizations in the military. Our role, one of servicing large troop concentrations, as those in Europe, was quickly rewritten by the scarcity of personnel available to meet the entire gamut of signal needs in the CBI. Finding ways to compensate for this lack of talent had been a never-ending series of frustrations for the Theater Signal Headquarters.

Upon our arrival at Ledo the Lion's share of the load for meeting all Army Ground Force communication needs had rested squarely on the shoulders of the 835th Signal Service Battalion. Starting from seven radio teams and a handful of other survivors of an ill-fated convoy trying to reach India in the spring of 1942, the 835th, by the end of that year, was maintaining and operating a signal network out of New Delhi that extended from Karachi to Chungking. It also operated the theater radio station in New Delhi, which, through a relay installation at Asmara, East Africa, was linked to WAR, the U.S. Army station in Washington, D.C.

The first thirty-seven miles of pole line construction on the Ledo Road had been started in mid-1943 by a group of quartermaster troops, using Indian Pioneer Labor and British materials. Near the end of 1943 the (African-American) 430th Air Force Heavy Signal Construction Battalion picked up from there and extended the line over Pangsau Pass into Burma. Operation of the stations at Ledo and Hellgate, and supervision of the pioneer troops were then taken over by the 835th.

As we took up residence in our jungle setting, the 835th's tenure in the CBI was passing the year and a half mark. Their efforts in Ledo and along the road had been adequate for the slow pace of the war up to that point but complete revamping of the communication supply, construction and operations responsibilities was about to start and most of what the 835th and the 430th had been doing was to be taken over by others.

Just when it appeared that the Theater was about to receive some much-needed relief in pole line construction, however, an event off the coast of Algiers added yet another to its long list of frustrations. Two signal battalions, the 31st and 96th, left North Africa for India, with elements of each distributed among several ships. The official version of the incident states that, as the convoy passed Algiers, it was attacked by German bombers, with the loss of the H.M.S. Rohna. Months later one of those fellows who was forced to witness his friends plunging into the water as the Rohna was going down, described to the writer how the torpedoes, launched from the bombers by what was then considered a secret weapon, after first missing the target, turned about and finally found their marks. The net result of the enemy action was that the 96th, whose cadre was made up of men from the Bell System and was destined to play a major part on the road, was delayed in reaching Ledo.

. . . .

The rapidity with which the next chain of events occurred forms a magnificent blur in our collective memories. Adding to this mental cloud is the fact that our repair teams had been restructured as we left the desert on furlough and throughout all of the traveling, many never got a chance to know who their team-mates were. Some could not even tell you who their platoon officer was.

One fact does stand out loud and clear . . . what we had learned in the Mojave desert was to have limited value in the roles to which we were assigned in the C.B.I. There we were signal repairmen only, and worked with large army units. The nature of the war in the C.B.I., however, required that we operate stationary shops; follow various sized units, sometimes by mule; contend with jungle conditions; and perform assignments not related to signal repair at all.

· · · ·

The failure of the 96th to arrive in Ledo as expected unfortunately coincided with the kickoff of the offensive from Tagap. With the 835th already stretched too thin, support and extension of communications on the road, as the point moved deeper into Burma required desperate measures. One of the few left to the brass was to draft the 181ST to plug some of the holes, which were already appearing. What happened next resembled a police raid on a speakeasy during prohibition . . . . with people scattering in every direction.

In retrospect this unexpected call to action was probably the best thing that could have happened to us. It not only gave us a legitimate reason for being there, but it also afforded us a chance to reveal the wealth of talent that we had been hiding.

· · · ·

One of the first to go to work was Charlie Wilson, who was assigned immediately as a switchboard operator at Base Section

#3 Headquarters. One of his memories is of being on duty at 2 AM when saboteurs set a massive fire at the gasoline tank farm in Digboi.

Within a week of our arrival in Ledo Sergeant Joe Cheeseman led a contingent from his 5th Team wire squad forty-eight miles up the Road to Loglai, in Burma. In the group were Jimmy Jones, William Wasco, Al Zilian and Bill Fitzgerald. Also with them was Ben Tillman and James "Red" Hale, both Teletype repairmen.

Their stay at Loglai, where Colonel Pick had just assumed command of the road-building effort and had set up his headquarters, was short-lived. After leaving Wasco to do some clerking for the local forces, they headed for Tagap, another thirty miles into Burma and the base for the Chinese 38th Division. En-route they got a taste of what the engineers were contending with in trying to convert the road trace into a bona-fide roadway. The short journey took them no less than three days, due largely to the fact that the hairpin turns they had to negotiate, while climbing to the 4600 foot elevation on which Tagap perched, required several passes and hair-raising backing-up maneuvers while nursing their trucks around each bend.

At Tagap they found themselves so close to the fighting that they could hear the noises of the battles. The three battalions from the 112th Chinese Regiment were catching hell from the supposedly lightly held Japanese positions beyond Shingbwiyang. Rumors, proven later to be fact, were that the Chinese had dug in, refusing to advance and that the American advisors were seriously concerned with the general situation. Two weeks earlier they had lost chief liaison officer Lt. Col. Douglas G. Gilbert, who was captured when the command post of the 112th Regiment was overrun. Desperate attempts at reinforcement were being thrown back and the fates of the 112th battalions were in question.

In Tagap Cheeseman's telephone men went to work, dividing their efforts between operating the switchboard and maintaining telephone lines in the area.

Here another example of the latent talent of the 181st revealed itself when an attempted airdrop of a Teletype machine went awry.

Striking the ground harder than had been planned for, the glass on the machine shattered into hundreds of small pieces, which fell through and under the keyboard, completely jamming the mechanism. "Red" Hale jumped in and, on an army blanket, disassembled and spread out most of the parts of the very complicated machine. He then reassembled them and soon had the vitally needed instrument ready for use again.

The Cheeseman squad spent Christmas on the Road, remaining there through the New Year and well into 1944. They eventually returned to Ledo, after being relieved by the 96th.

With their team officer shepherding our equipment across the Pacific and their team sergeant and wire squad keeping busy at Tagap, the remainder of the Fifth Team took their orders from Lt. Petri. One of these directed T/3 "Chuck" Cortwright to report to an Office of War Information contingent, nearby. He spent ninety days on the assignment where he set up recording equipment for intercepting Japanese transmissions.

. . . .

Charlie Boyd was another who was put to work early, when he was grabbed by the 835th folks operating a radio station on top of a mountain about an hour's ride from Ledo. Also carrying the rank of Technician Third Grade (T/3), he bought the job of supervising the men on one of the operating shifts who lived at the station, which was supposed to go on the air about 8AM each morning. He soon began to suspect that his charges on the hill were slacking off but was unsuccessful in all of his efforts to catch them at it. To get to the station he was given a big Harley Davidson motorcycle, which was a little unwieldy for Charlie, who was short and tipped the scales at only about 135 pounds.

Abandoning his efforts to surprise his little group, he concentrated, instead, on trying to conquer his recalcitrant vehicle. One morning, as he approached the station, the big Harley started slipping in the sandy silt near the edge of the road and when he tried to gun it, it reared up tossing him into the ditch with the cycle on top of him. Although unhurt, he discovered, to his dismay that he was trapped under the monster, which was still idling. As he struggled to extricate himself, worrying about the possibility of a gasoline leak and its fiery consequences, a convoy of trucks carrying a unit of one of the engineering battalions happened by. Just about the time that he was convinced they had not spotted him, two men in the very last truck did and pounded on the roof of the cab until the driver stopped.

After acquiescing to his request to, "Get this damn thing off of me," one of them asked if he could try the cycle out. Charlie alleges that he told the G.I. to, "Keep it!" and never saw it again.

During the short time he was with his rescuers, Charlie got a chance to exchange some minor "war stories". He couldn't outdo these boys, though. One related an incident that occurred while he was operating a bulldozer. He told of being jumped by a Japanese soldier, wielding a knife and who was probably cut off and lost from a patrol. As the big African-American G.I. explained how he quickly dispatched the Jap with a wrench, he smiled and chuckled as he asked Charlie, "Can you imagine that guy thinking that he could take one of us with a blade?"

"Lady luck" sometimes has a way of evening things up. After some hassling, Charlie was given a weapons carrier to replace the Harley. On one of his next trips to the station, he surprised the whole crew in the act of feeding rations to the monkeys who, he swears, were battling over them with clubs. The station was filthy and littered and after a session of chewing out, he asked the group why he had never been able to catch them before. The answer was simple . . . they had always been able to hear him coming with the Harley in time to get their act together.

He soon left Ledo for China with Lt. Jim McVeigh's Second Team, but before doing so received painful injuries when there was an explosion where he was working. It blew his glasses off, cutting his face and shoulder, earning him a session in the 20th General Hospital.

Some radio repair activity was also done by Bob Gallagher and Millard Sturgell, who marveled at the former's talent for improvisation. After learning how to use a jeep battery as an electric source for soldering connections and the uses that the carbon rod from a dead dry "D" cell could be put to, Sturgell then accompanied Bob into Burma to deliver the fruits of their labor. Also from the 2ND Team, they joined Boyd during the trip over the "Hump" to Kunming.

. . . .

Ed Rozmerski (now Ross) was put in charge of a crew at a signal supply depot at Likhapani. Many of the others in the company, including the radio repair squads from our First Team were also assigned to signal supply depots. For one day only I was stuck on a detail trucking coils of #8 open copper wire from Tinsukia to Ledo. Weighing only 130 pounds, at the time, this was probably the worst physical task I ever encountered in my three-year tour. I recall that the coils were so heavy that I could not raise them high enough to get my fingers under them. It took two and sometimes three of us to get them over the tailgate.

. . . .

Harry Koch, who after the war operated a small telephone company in New York City, brainstormed the revamping and expansion of the switchboards at both Ledo Army Headquarters and the 20th General. He was assisted by several fellows, including Jeff Bennett, who, as an AT&T Long Lines splicer had participated in installing the first transcontinental cable across the U.S.A. Harry, a lowly T5, soon emerged as the best telephone man in Ledo and was repeatedly rewarded with additional stripes as he completed job after job. Each promotion had to be properly celebrated, however, and in such grand style that after each he was similarly demoted and relieved of his chevrons before he ever got a chance to sew them on. His reputation, however, was never in question, either as a technician or party lover.

. . . .

The writer, whose background in civilian life, was as a telephone central office installer for the Western Electric Company, spent about a week on the 20th General job but was pulled away and reassigned, along with Al Kljun to the communication center at Hellgate. Al carried the rank of T3 and, after Bill Hasse who was also the platoon leader, was senior non-com on our First Team telephone squad. Not knowing where the front lines were and with my apprehensions increased, somewhat, when we were issued live ammunition, Al and I climbed aboard a weapons carrier and headed into our next adventure.

I do not know, at this writing, what thoughts Al had regarding our immediate future. I do recall that outwardly he exhibited a sense of satisfaction and excited interest that we were finally getting down to the serious business of winning the war. His attitude was contagious and helped allay my own concerns about the possible dangers we might have to cope with.

Hindsight now tells me that these concerns were groundless and typical of those haunting the uninitiated. Nevertheless after we left "X Force" headquarters, several miles beyond the bazaar, the jungle seemed to become closer and more menacing with each mile. When we boarded the vehicle the only seat left for yours truly was on the compartment outside of the front seat, where mud chains were stored. Perched there with my feet on the running board, I felt like one of the ducks at an amusement park shooting gallery. As mentioned before, Hellgate was thirty-four miles from Ledo over a bumpy, dusty roadway cut out of the raw jungle hills. We made half a dozen stops; dropping folks at several engineering, truck ordnance and quartermaster camps along the way. The largest camp, at Namchik, was the 14th Evacuation Hospital, which was receiving wounded Chinese from the front.

Our assignment to Hellgate was the end of our role as reserve troops. It also turned out to be the severing of our physical association with many of our friends in the 181st, whom we would never see again.

. . . .

Two other men, Al Stursberg and Mert Kallman, both from New Jersey, were also assigned to switchboards on the Road. Al won a job in Namyang, beyond the Pass in a very wild and rugged location in Burma. Mert's assignment was the exact opposite of Al's, at army headquarters just outside of "metropolitan" Ledo. Here he operated the switchboard that Harry and his associates were expanding.

. . . .

In the first chapter, when we were discussing the formation of the company at Camp Crowder, mention was made of the extensive training Bob Callinan had received at Fort Monmouth, before joining the 181st. While he was one of our leading radio repairmen, his talents included most Signal Corps occupations, including all aspects of telephone communication. When it was discovered that he was also a qualified draftsman, he was dispatched to Stilwell's headquarters, and those of the Chinese Expeditionary Forces in Northern Burma (the Chih Hui Pu . . . later the Northern Combat Area Command . . . NCAC), where Al Kljun and I had picked up our ride to Hellgate.

"Vinegar Joe" had just arrived from Chungking, where he had become convinced that Chiang was not going to permit "Y" FORCE to attack across the Salween in the fall of 1943, as he had agreed. Stilwell had finally tired of waiting, had decided not to waste the dry season and proceeded to start the Northern Burma campaign (SAUCY) with the Chinese 38th and 22nd Divisions ("X" FORCE). Brigadier General Haydon L. Boatner was Chief of Staff of Chih Hui Pu, which was under the command of the Northern Combat Area Command. It was to this organization that Bob reported. He recalled that after checking in at Headquarters:

> A colonel and a major wanted to talk to me about an
> assignment. First, they said their records showed I had

worked at the Ft. Monmouth Labs and had a TOP SECRET clearance. I said this was so. Then they gave me a room to work in equipped with a drawing board, drawing supplies, etc. The major gave me my first job. He plopped down a Western Electric book in front of me. Then he told me to study the book thoroughly. He said I was to draw up sets of the wire transpositions that would be needed for the sixteen wires going from Ledo to Kunming. Whew! I thought—here I am planning a communications line! The book was invaluable though and after a couple of days of study I managed to plan a 100-mile segment and draw that up and it was repeated ten times for the 1000 miles to Kunming. As I recall, each pole was numbered and had two crosspieces with eight wires over eight, all numbered 1 to 16. Transposing is done to cancel out capacitive and inductive ground effects upon the wires, thus eliminating cross-talk at the destination. (I got a kick later, when we were in China, that it worked great.)

The next job he was given was the mapping out of all the W110 telephone wires going out south of the Ledo Headquarters. Surveying and recording the line facilities was a different task entirely. It meant that he had to get out and physically inspect what was out there, much of which was not recorded anywhere . . . . not surprising when considering how thinly the 835th had been spread. This job proved to be hard work but when he told his friends of the new assignment, he was chided for the soft job he had inherited at Headquarters. In his own words he recalled:

> I got ribbed a lot at having this soft job at headquarters but I could never say anything at that time. This "soft" job consisted of walking and mapping these lines about five hours a day, then going back to the drafting room and putting everything on a master map, which really got to look like a rat's nest. Once the major

told me that General Stilwell had looked at it different times.

This was about the time that the Japs had penetrated 50 or 60 miles into India. If no pressure was brought . . . by the British around Manipur, I guess General Stilwell wanted to see what communications lines were in place for outposts. (if) The Japs would start heading for Ledo.

Thank God that Roosevelt was able to get Churchill to listen.

Mapping these wires was a very lonesome job, I'd be walking in a jungle path and all of a sudden I would come to a very large open space consisting of a tea plantation. The cottages, most deserted on these properties all seemed to be hooked up to the hqs switchboard. One day I was tracking a set of wires going along a jungle path when all of a sudden 6 or 8 shots rang out and leaves started falling down around my head followed by a bunch of shooting. A soldier appeared and motioned for me to put my hands up.

He directed (me) over to someone who looked like the CO. It was a mess, no one knew what the other was saying. After about a half hour, which seemed like an eternity, they let me go. They had studied my fatigues and their fatigues and realized that we were allies. This was a company of Chinese who were being trained by the US Army. When I finished the mapping job they gave me another consisting of making drawings of buildings to depict how Americans could or would make buildings using only bamboo and leaves. Soon after completing the gem we were scheduled for China.

. . . .

Shortly after our arrival at Ledo Robert (Roby) Robertson (Riverton, NJ) and Bill Snider (from near Winston-Salem, NC), from Lt. Wilson's 4TH Team, were also summoned to Headquarters to perform some clerical work, associated with signal supplies. They evidently impressed their new bosses because after several weeks they were transferred back to Chabua, where for the duration of the war they continued to apply their talents with a signal supply organization.

. . . .

As the battle with the jungle in the company area wound down, the gallant men of the 5th Team were assigned the more constructive task of digging holes for a pole line, which started above Ledo and continued past Margherita. Two-men teams leapfrogged along the route as they completed each previously marked hole. They used three tools . . . a sort of long-handled shovel for digging; a crescent-shaped right angled scoop for removing the soil; and a round plate, which they attached to a pole and which served as a template to check that the specified diameter had been maintained. This project employed a sizeable crew, which completed the entire job in about two weeks. Compared to their earlier task of jungle-clearing this constructive assignment was much easier to tolerate.

The repair teams were not the only people put to work, of course. The skills of the 181st truck drivers were probably more valuable than those of us who were filling in here and there. Signal supplies had not only to be received and warehoused but they also had to be carried into Burma. On one of these errands, Mickey Zace and Hamp Mc Bride were traveling the Road inside of Burma, when they encountered a young, African-American GI running toward them, waving wildly and shouting that the Japanese were bombing just ahead. After delivering his urgent warning he continued his racing and soon disappeared in the direction of Ledo. After waiting a short time, and with no little amount of apprehension and much curiosity, they started forward, watching for signs of the attackers and the GI's truck. Expecting to find the truck just over the rise where its recent driver had indicated it was, they traveled three miles before they came upon it, unharmed and deserted in the middle of the Road.

. . . .

While the repairmen and the personnel from the motor pool probed the mysteries of the region, the folks in Headquarters had the trying jobs of maintaining all of their services to the men of the company. With supplies, such as extra shoes and clothing at a premium and food quality leaving much to be desired, material things which had been taken for granted in the "States" now required all of the talents of First Sergeant Harold Hess and his gang in the orderly and supply bashas. Vehicle Maintenance became especially critical, with the condition of the roads in the area and the serious shortages of spare parts.

For a while Roy Murphy, from Ft. Mill, S.C., tried his hand at driving the Road in a jeep as a courier, delivering mail, PX rations, small parts, medical supplies or anything else that needed transporting and was small enough to be carried. He had a new story to tell after negotiating each round trip to the front.

. . . .

With SAUCY just getting off the mark, activity in Ledo and on the Road was still very limited . . . Colonel Pick's recent arrival had not yet triggered the acceleration in construction that was about to occur. The Chinese 22nd Division was still in Ramgarh and the only Americans involved in the actual fighting at the front were General Boatner's advisers with the 38th Division.

. . . .

Now that we were halfway around the world and away from the rigid, garrison lifestyles of our previous encampments, military customs in Ledo were a bit more relaxed. The pretense of projecting the appearance of spit and polish had become a thing of the past. The struggle to maintain healthy and comfortable living standards negated any need to invent work details, for there were too many real jobs to be done to sustain a unit of our size. While this laid-back atmosphere and the relaxation of military discipline was good for morale, regular morning and afternoon formations enabled Sergeant Hess to keep track of where everyone was or was supposed to be. Events were happening at an ever-increasing rate, however, and it was not to be much longer before each of us in the company would find his niche in this far-flung theater.

## WE TAKE ON THE HUMP

As some of the company was dispersing to take on various jobs around Ledo and on the Road, a conference, called "SEXTANT" was convening in Cairo, attended by Churchill, Roosevelt and Chiang Kai shek and their CBI commanders.

Two facts which emerged, unknown to the Chinese, were that the American Joint Chiefs of Staff had convinced FDR that, with the increasing successes of the Marines in the Pacific; the initial failure of the American-trained Chinese in Burma; and the growing consensus that Chiang was indeed a "Reluctant Dragon" . . . China was no longer considered a critical jumping off place for the invasion of Japan. Because of earlier diplomatic promises to Chiang that the Allies would contribute their efforts towards opening a land route to China, however, the campaign to complete the Ledo Road would continue. At the same time, agreement had again been wrung from Chiang to dispatch troops to Yunnan to fulfill the long-promised commitment to YOKE Force and to coordinate their attack across the Salween River with "X" Force's drive through Northern Burma.

. . . .

To the 181st this meant that two of our teams, the Second and Fourth, were ordered to China. The scattering of our gallant band, then, was about to accelerate.

. . . .

For two and a half years following the closing of the Burma Road by the Japanese, the only way into China was through the air. On January 31, 1942, when airway alternatives were being discussed, T.V.Soong, Madame Chiang's American-educated brother and Minister of Foreign Affairs stated, in a memo to FDR, that a 700 mile route from Sadiya to Kunming was already available and that fortunately it was over "comparatively level" terrain. Soong, who eventually became a permanent knife between Stilwell's shoulder blades, failed to mention that the route was also over some of the most treacherous mountains in the world. The route finally selected traversed 550 miles, from upper Assam to Kunming over the eastern spurs of the Himalayas, which reached heights of up to 15,000 feet.

To clear these it was necessary to fly at, what was then twice normal altitudes, of up to 20,000 feet, sometimes through turbulence capable of tearing an aircraft apart. In their book, "Thunder Out of China", Theodore H. White and Annalee Jacoby reported that,

> . . . the Hump drove men mad, killed them, sent them back to America wasted with tropical fevers and broken for the rest of their lives. Some of the boys called it the Skyway to Hell; it was certainly the most dangerous, terrifying, barbarous aerial transport run in the world. Unarmed cargo carriers crossed 500 miles of uncharted mountains and jungles at 20,000 feet in spite of the Japanese air force, tropical monsoons, and Tibetan ice. In some months the Hump command lost more planes and personnel than the combat outfit, the Fourteenth Air Force, that it supplied.

In the beginning the only planes available were C47's, the military version of the commercial DC3. These were too old, with many grounded for lack of parts. Although useful workhorses, their contributions to Hump tonnage deliveries were severely limited due to their cargo capacities. When the Chinese discovered that Curtis Wright was making a larger C46, Madame Chiang put so much heat on FDR that he ordered their immediate delivery to India even though they had not yet undergone performance tests.

The results were lethal. Introduced in April of 1943, their bugs were immediately evident, one of the worst being the fatal freezing up of carburetors. Some planes arrived with whole sections of rivets missing from wings and fuselages. Ground personnel were neither trained nor available in sufficient numbers required for safe maintenance. Again spare parts were scarce. In the three years of their use 468 planes were lost, an average of thirteen a month.

The effect on Air Transport Command crew morale was devastating. Hearing that the Chinese were not using the material they were risking and losing their lives for, they became rebellious, sometimes refusing to fly if the weather was at all threatening and if their cargoes were not ticketed for the 14th Air Force. They often bailed out as soon as trouble started, too often with disastrous results. Less than half of those who chose this option lived to tell about it. Although many were found and guided out by Kachin patrols working for OSS (Office of Strategic Services, forerunner of the CIA), most succumbed to the jungle or were captured. Some were stranded in the trees and their bodies were later found, still suspended and ravaged by ants.

· · · ·

Fortunately for the 181st, by November of 1943, most of the C46 bugs had been taken care of, the monsoon was over and the weather over the Hump had likewise improved. The route, however, was still over the worst of the mountains and the Japanese had been building up for an attack on India.

. . . .

With his Second Team slated to leave first, Lieutenant Jim McVeigh flew alone to Kunming, probably to make arrangements for bed and board for his people. As a grim reminder that, despite the improvements accomplished during 1943, the Hump crossing was still wrought with danger, the plane which took him to China, crashed on its return trip, killing everyone on board. After flights were halted for about a week, Mc Veigh and his team said their "goodbyes" to their friends in Ledo and at 3AM, December 7th departed for Chabua . . . and China . . . leaving behind one of their fellows, Hamp Mc Bride, who was nursing a chronic back problem at the 20th General Hospital at Margherita.

Charlie Boyd described the ensuing flight. Prior to takeoff all of the passengers were given parachutes, instructed in their use and shown how to adjust all of the straps so as to prevent injury in the event they were put to use. Then, true to the military logic to which we had become accustomed, these same parachutes were then collected and piled in the rear of the plane to balance the load from front to rear. After a short lecture on what to do if they found themselves lost in the Burmese jungles, including the proper social amenities to be observed in the company of the Naga headhunters, the gallant men of the Second Team boarded and were on their way. It might be interesting to note, here, that very few of us in the 181st had ever been on an airplane before.

The plane, designed for hauling cargo, was not pressurized and had only rope bucket seats along the sides for passenger use. Mounted on the rear of the flight crew compartment were two lamps, green and red, which the crew chief explained instructed the passengers to "put on oxygen masks" or "jump" respectively.

As the plane gained altitude approaching the Hump and the air became thinner, Charlie began to doze. Suddenly they hit an air pocket, dropping rapidly and jolting Charlie from his sleep. Looking out of a window, he saw that the engines, whose superchargers were engaged to cope with the altitude, appeared to be on fire as their tail pipes glowed red. At that moment, the crew chief, in error, activated the red "jump" lamp instead of the green "oxygen" lamp. With everyone else, Charlie dove for the pile of parachutes, creating a radical imbalance in the airplane. As the tail dipped and the pilot fought furiously with the controls, the crew chief appeared, sliding down the cargo floor, frantically explaining the error, while attempting to project an air of humor into the situation. The sudden, chilling fear of not being able to find a parachute that would fit his very small frame well enough to prevent him from being castrated or falling completely out of it, left neither Charlie nor the others in a very jocular frame of mind. For the moment they had much darker intentions regarding their military flight attendant. Nerves were so tight that, when the landing gear was dropped during the Kunming approach, panic almost broke out again.

The following day, on December 13th, Lieutenant Kermit Swanson's Fourth Team followed the Second. They too left a man at the 20th General, Varner Shippy, their platoon sergeant. The flight was described, by Bob Gunning Sacramento, California, as "scary". Aside from the sudden drop in temperature as the plane rose to clear the Hump, however, it was uneventful.

# HELLGATE

As the 2nd and 4th Teams adjusted to their new Chinese environments, activity back on the Road and in and around Ledo began to pick up. The "Race to Shingbwiyang" as Leslie Anders entitled it in his book, THE LEDO ROAD, was on in earnest.

For Al Kljun and me, who had just arrived at Hellgate, it meant that we were going to be, if not where the action was, at least eyewitnesses to its progress. It also meant that we were free from all of the mundane routines of the Ledo encampment and that we had been thrust into an environment in which we, like many of the 181ST after us, were to become our own masters. It was a good feeling to know that we had finally become functioning parts in the local war machine. We received little, if any contact from our headquarters, with the receipt of mail the only evidence that the folks in the front office knew where we were.

In the short history of the Road, Hellgate, in the shadow of Pangsau Pass, had been forward headquarters to Stilwell; the site of Dr. Gordon Seagraves's hospital for the Chinese troops; and base camp for the 823rd Engineers and other units.

The message center was located in heavy jungle on a knoll about 50 yards above the Road and a mile this side of Hellgate Headquarters, where the Road crossed a small mountain stream before ascending eight miles to the Pass. From the air, the building appeared as just another basha among about a dozen others, all empty when we arrived. It was, however, fitted with wooden doors, had no windows and had a corrugated metal roof constructed under the thatch. Communication gear consisted of a transmitter/receiver, a Teletype machine and a switchboard, which I believe was a BD 96 with automatic Tele-ring. As a reminder that the Japanese had recently roamed the jungle just over the Pass, the center was also equipped with a Thompson sub-machine gun, which hung just inside one of two doors.

On the Road to Hellgate

Steps on left lead up to Hellgate message center

Shippy (MO) and Wagler (IA) above
Hellgate message center

Now unless the reader has been a long-time city resident, who for some reason was suddenly transplanted into a remote rain forest, inhabited by some of the largest, stealthiest and fiercest creatures on the face of the earth, he might not be able to appreciate the following. Upon arriving, we were shown where to erect our folding canvas and wooden cots in a basha across a small clearing from the message center. Thus, for the first two weeks we made occasional trips between them. Now this, by itself, is hardly worth mentioning here. But to make this little trip, of no more than fifty feet, in the ominous opaqueness of a moonless night, when the use of flashlights was forbidden was, at first, no small chore for this writer. Stepping out into the pitch black my first night, and not being able to see where I was walking, I was suddenly struck with the realization that I was trespassing in one of Mother Nature's remotest sanctuaries. The roof of the basha was barely visible and on nights when there was some moon, I was convinced that I could see my feline neighbors' eyes reflected from the shadows. That I was literally afraid to cross that open space was both astonishing to me and certainly embarrassing. The human animal, however, has amazing adaptability capabilities. I was no exception and in a matter of days the fear had become nothing more than the caution warranted when being introduced into such an unfamiliar environment.

Half-dozen men from the 835th were running the station under the command of a sergeant who used a World War I helmet as a washbasin. I believe it was actually his and that he was one of the original members of the veteran battalion. In addition to operating the station, the group supervised the squad of Indian pioneer (labor) troops, who performed much of the "grunt" work required in maintaining the lines along that section of the Road. These Indians were all from the "dhobi" or laundrymen caste and were not bashful about demonstrating their craft . . . so we always had clean clothes.

Less than two weeks after our arrival, the effects of the renewed pressure to reach Shingbwiyang were felt, when the 835th folks started to move forward. First we lost the teletypewriter and when our telephone customers began to take their business into Burma, our BD96 became a local-battery, twelve-circuit BD72. After the Chinese success at Yupbang Ga and the establishing of Shingbwiyang as a major supply depot and Stilwell's Command Post, we lost the radio and its operator.

By now we were only three . . . Al, I, and a lad named Joe, about my age, from Youngstown, Ohio. We welcomed being on our own but sorely missed the radio, since it had brought us all the latest music (and laughable propaganda) via Tokyo Rose. It soon became apparent that Hellgate had become just another repeater point in the scheme of things. This was driven home when they came and took away our BD72, leaving in its place a humble six-circuit BD71.

With the departure of the 835th and the radio we had indeed been put on our own in what had become a pretty lonely jungle outpost. Taking advantage of our new freedom we soon found a multitude of diversions. Leaving one man to watch the switchboard (how much business can you get from less than six customers?) we tried our hand at hiking some of the trails which led to the Naga villages, but making sure that we turned back before reaching them. We also took a stab at some big-game hunting, but elected to beat hasty retreats on two occasions, when the sounds from our would-be prey convinced us that we were over-matched. On Sundays we hitchhiked twenty miles back to Namchik and Mass at the army chapel at the 14th Evacuation Hospital. On one of these hitch-hiking escapades with a Chinese, who did not know that it was impossible to down-shift while racing down an incline and who only succeeded in getting his six-by-six out of gear, we came to within a whisker of being pitched into the valley far below.

Upon returning from one of our exploration forays, I stepped through the door of the message center to the following scene. Al was seated with his back to the door and in the act of making a connection for one of our exclusive telephone clientele. Standing right behind him and watching with rapt curiosity was a native Kachin boy, about fourteen or fifteen years old, with a long knife, resembling a machete, hanging across the front of him. It was quite apparent that Al was totally unaware of the boy's presence. The boy, in turn was so engrossed in the American who was "talking to a box" that he did not hear me. Not knowing what to expect, but tempted beyond any power to resist, I said as quietly and matter-of-factly as I could, "Hey Al, turn around." The result was everything that the reader can imagine. When Al recovered, he smiled at the youngster and blurted out "Hello" in English and Hindustani. Probably not understanding either, the boy responded in turn to Al's smile and 14,000 miles were spanned in an instant. Like any self-respecting native, the youngster wanted to trade. I do not know what Al gave him, maybe only a cigarette, but in return, he gave Al a small necklace of beads, which were similar to those strung on Christmas tree garlands. He had them on a piece of string with a loop on one end and a simple shirt button on the other.

Food, as usual was a problem. At first we dined with a band of hell-raising MP's at Hellgate, who were guarding an ammunition dump. The food was poorly prepared, probably because they did not have a cook and when the 835th left, taking their vehicles with them, the mile walk in the heat and dust of the Road became most unappetizing. Now just across the road from the MP's was a small Quartermaster unit that, miraculously it seemed, baked bread daily. Fortunately for us, they were repeatedly running out of flashlight batteries, which we just happened to have access to. Thus in the spirit of Omer and Koch, we activated the market mechanism, thereby gradually amassing a neat pile of rations in the corner of the message center, which by now was also our living quarters. Utilizing a stove, which someone had fashioned from an empty fifty-gallon drum, we then began to cook for ourselves. Subsequently a wandering lieutenant, who after seeing our food hoard and having to be convinced that we were not drawing rations, made arrangements for us to mess with a nearby 115th (truck) Ordnance Company, one of our few telephone customers. These folks had been around so long that they had corralled a veritable herd of wild razorback hogs, which eventually became a very delicious and welcome roast pork Christmas dinner.

The folks from the 115th were also a "wild and wooly bunch" who apparently were not averse to firing their weapons. While trudging the hot and dusty mile back from breakfast with the MP's one morning Al and I heard a sudden outbreak of rifle fire ahead of us on the Road. We continued, not too concerned, since occasional firing, although illegal, was not unusual in that out-of-the-way valley. But the firing did not stop and at times became so loud and rapid that we finally conceded that something significant must have been happening, though we doubted that any Japanese could be in the area. We reached the message center and the firing continued for some time and then ceased. Now it was time to venture out to solve the mystery. As we reached the Road, two 115th "Great White Hunters" emerged over a rise carrying what appeared to be a wildcat. They had chased it all over the local jungle before finally bagging it.

When New Year's Eve arrived, the whole battalion, it seemed took a hand in reminding us that we were non-paying guests at their mess hall by firing into the trees over our cozy establishment, as we quietly welcomed in 1944.

In the meantime we had somehow inherited a bootlegging business from one of the 835th characters. We were pleasantly surprised one day to discover that our own Roy Murphy, from South Carolina was not only a road courier, but that he also kept us supplied with Bullfight Brandy, Fighter Brand Whiskey and gin. Naturally we did not advertise our wares but there was no doubt that our predecessors had done a brisk business in earlier times as we entertained many itinerant customers, mostly black. Meeting them and hearing their stories about the Road and home was a warm and truly educational experience. I remember visiting an African-American buck sergeant, from the 823rd, to pick up some pipe tobacco and who had converted a basha into a private, sheikh-like salon, with carpeting and bamboo furniture. I am surprised that someone has not written of the experiences of those men, who spent so many months in India.

. . . .

Our tour in Hellgate lasted through most of the winter of 1943-1944. During that period the only formal entertainment we enjoyed was an occasional traveling outdoor movie, which defied blackout regulations.

One memorable diversion from this routine was the appearance of film star Joe E. Brown at the 14TH Evacuation Hospital at Namchik. Two of us hitched a ride so as to arrive early, assuring us good seats. Just before the show was about to start, however, a Lt. Colonel announced that anyone sitting in front of a rope, delineating a section reserved for officers, would have to vacate their seats. With loud protests, we and many others, grudgingly complied, in true army manner. Finally, when everyone had settled down again, Joe E. Brown took the microphone from the colonel and similarly announced that there would be no show until everyone had resumed his original positions. This caused another round of confusion punctuated by loud cheers from the enlisted men.

Then the show proceeded . . . almost. Up to this point, the only Chinese we had encountered were those we were foolish enough to hitchhike rides from. There were many in the hospital and those that could walk were in attendance. One group, arriving late, congregated to one side of the stage, which had a bamboo wall impeding their vision. As their frustration mounted, their chattering and bustling about, as they strained to see, began to drown out the performers and in a short time they literally tore the wall down . . . . to the great amusement of Joe E. Brown. He was superb, not only in his performance, which naturally included his famous baseball windup, but in the manner in which he addressed all of us. He had lost a son in the South Pacific and I imagine he saw some of him in each of the bedraggled-looking, fatigue-cladded GIs before him.

. . . .

From the creation of the Southeast Asia Command (SEAC) and the ever-increasing signs of buildup in Assam, the Japanese correctly deduced that a major Allied offensive was imminent. In late 1943, therefore they increased their air activity in the Ledo area and over the HUMP airfields. In Hellgate this kept us busy relaying "red" air alerts to Ledo as well as passing the warning along to our few subscribers.

It was also becoming evident, judging by the increasing rate of truck traffic through Hellgate, that things were going our way beyond Shingbwiyang. Had we known more about this part of the war, we could have deduced that the Chinese 22nd Division had arrived on the Road, since they wore American style uniforms, including helmets, while the 38th Division wore British uniforms. By the end of January these divisions had moved beyond Yupbang Ga allowing the conversion of Shingbwiyang into a major depot with its own airstrip.

The famed Merrill's Marauders had arrived in Ledo and on January 14th reached Pangsau Pass, having slipped by Kljun and me at Hellgate, without us knowing they were passing.

While all of this was taking place, the 96th Signal Construction Battalion, whose cadre came from the Bell System, reached Assam . . . . and our very interesting assignment to Hellgate was fast coming to its conclusion.

## THE SHOW GETS GOING ON THE ROAD

Back in Ledo several significant things had occurred. The nagging question of how long the mail would take to reach us in that Godforsaken corner of the world was answered when the Christmas packages arrived on January 23RD. Since most of the folks back home had mailed them in September and October, one could not rightly characterize this performance as qualifying it for the label "express mail".

On January 28th Lt. Petri, platoon officer for the 1ST Team (the writer's), was traded to New Delhi in a straight player deal, which brought Bernie Silverman to the 181ST. Bernie, who had become tired of rear echelon life, wanted to see some of the war.

For this unthinking failure to accept New Delhi mores, he was banished to Ledo and the 181ST. At the same time, a Colonel Dale A. Newlin, who knew Petri in his permanent regular army rank of Master Sergeant, thought that the transfer to Delhi might help his career.

Bernie recalled that he ". . . reported to the orderly room and after the usual exchange of niceties, Captain Scott . . . suggested that I inspect my detachment." Now, as reported earlier, because this was considered a combat zone and military discipline had been reduced to a minimum, the men had become accustomed to an unregimented way of life. Why the good captain exposed Bernie to a situation, which was certain to get him off on the wrong foot with men that he would spend the rest of the war with, is a question. One can conjecture that Scott did so because he was miffed over Petri being given the opportunity that Scott thought was rightfully his. Having witnessed Scott's "Old Army" hard-drinking, rough and tumble ways, one could also theorize that he made the suggestion out of personal dislike for this "Twenty-one year-old ROTC, college-bred shave tail" or just for the pure sport of it.

Regardless of the captain's reason, Bernie related that "I told Sgt. Bill Hasse that I wanted to inspect the detachment that afternoon. Hasse turned out the men in suntans and I inspected everyone's carbine and asked their names just like it is done in ROTC at VPI." It was not long thereafter that Bernie discovered how wrong he had been in following Scott's advise. On the same morning that he received it, Junior Warrant Officer Joe Hardwick also suggested that Bernie relieve him of the job of censoring the mail. Since he was now the newest officer he accepted the job and, as he remembers, "For a week I read the enlisted men's outrage at the young chicken lieutenant who had just arrived and inspected the troops; something that had never happened before. I wondered about the motives of Captain Scott."

But Bernie's education regarding the captain had only begun. Some time later, after the sight of "Corn Willy and Spam" had begun to wear awfully thin, and the repeated sight of potential steaks, hamburger and other American favorites wandering through the camp area, a "SWAT Team", led by "Blackie" Omer planned and executed the entrapment, drawing and quartering of two sacred cows. Knowing the taboo on such carryings-on, everyone was sworn to the utmost secrecy. Whether such a bizarre act could ever have been kept from the front office, we will never know . . . for someone thoughtlessly attempted to borrow a carving knife from Mess Sergeant Cieszykoski. He, in turn, made the implement available . . . but only after he, literally, received his pound of sacred flesh. Shortly thereafter, while censoring Omer's mail, Bernie suddenly found himself staring in disbelief at a photo of "Blackie" standing with a foot on one of the fallen beasts and his arm raised aloft holding his rifle in a grand victory gesture. Fearing the international repercussions that could result if this photographic evidence of such a monumental sacrilege became public, Bernie showed it to the captain . . . whose only comment was, "What is that, a reindeer?". Many years later Bernie recalled that, "We officers were served steaks so were implicated also."

. . . .

The Japanese response to the buildup in and around Ledo was felt directly by the 181ST folks stationed there. For a period of time the air raid sirens went off every day during the noon meal, chasing everyone to the slit trenches with their half-eaten meals not too appetizing after the "all clear" had sounded.

One raid occurred during Joe E. Brown's evening show in Ledo and sent everyone scurrying while he was on stage. Obviously perturbed by the interruption, Brown was reluctant to leave the area, with some of the calmer heads seizing the opportunity to get his autograph. A line formed and as he completed each signing, he urged the recipient to go to the slit trenches. Through all of this, General Pick calmly held a flashlight for Brown to write by. Charlie Matthews, from the 5th Team, related how, after getting knocked down in the initial rush, he asked Brown to autograph a five-rupee bill, which he did. Many years later, after attending one of Brown's shows on Broadway, Charlie worked his way back stage and presented the bill for another signing. He reported that Brown remembered vividly that evening in Ledo.

The air attacks continued with varying frequency and intensity through the winter, culminating in one on March 27th, which, for the Japanese was a minor disaster. It consisted of nine heavy bombers, escorted by sixty fighters. Met by the fighters of the Eastern Air Command, eight of the bombers were shot down and the ninth made a forced landing. Ray Bumgardner recalled that during the raids on Ledo, oftentimes he and the other fellows from the 181ST, in spite of Mr. Hardwick's urgings to the contrary, would sit on the edges of the trenches and occasionally be treated to an aerial dogfight. On the March 27th raid or a similar one, they watched a P51 Mustang shoot down a bomber, which crashed on a hill nearby. Shortly thereafter Ray, Jimmy Jones and several others hiked to the spot where it had fallen, bringing back pieces of metal, which they fashioned into bracelets and other souvenirs, for sending home.

But air battles were still not the only cause for plane crashes. As former members of the Air Transport Command will readily agree, I am sure, weather, topography and the step-child status of the CBI, itself, decreed a continuation of the hazards of flying in that corner of the world. Luke Strass recalled that, while reading in his bunk one evening in Ledo, "I heard this airplane all of a sudden gunning its engines (and) seemed to be in some kind of trouble. Next thing I heard was a loud crash and explosion. (I) jumped out of my sack and ran outside along with a couple of others in my basha. We could see a huge fire in the hill across from our compound. The next day we found out that a C47 was trying to make an emergency landing at the Ledo strip, didn't make it and slammed into the mountain across the valley. No survivors were found" . . . Such was life in Ledo at the beginning of 1944.

Acceleration of the war also picked up about then. Signal construction activity took a giant step forward when the 96TH finally got its act together and took over on the Road. Fighting increased also as the Chinese 22ND Division joined the fray, causing the Japanese General Tanaka to decide to fight a withdrawal campaign in the Hukawng Valley. For the Americans, however, the big news was the arrival of the 5307TH Composite Unit (Provisional), better known as "Merrill's Marauders".

. . . .

Like so many others made by the Allies, the decision to create and deploy the Marauders was not finalized until their use had been thoroughly fought over first. As early as May 25, 1942, only weeks after his grueling walk out of Burma, "Vinegar Joe" had asked General Marshall and Secretary of War Henry Stimson for "one or more" U. S. divisions to join with the Chinese and British as part of a plan to drive the Japanese out of both Burma and Thailand. As we already know he did not get an opportunity to try his plan, for reasons which would fill another book. Later . . . on February 18, 1943, Brigadier Orde Charles Wingate, famous for his knowledge of guerilla tactics, perfected in Palestine and Ethiopia led a special British Long Range Penetration brigade behind Jap lines in Burma. Although it was later estimated that the damage they did could have been done more cheaply by aerial bombardment, the Chindit's exploits were heralded in the free world and he became the darling of the Prime Minister. At the August, 1943 QUADRANT Conference, in Quebec, Churchill convinced the Allies to allow the reinforcement of the Chindits and the addition of an American contingent to their force. When Stilwell learned of this, he blew his top and reminded Marshall and the War Department of his earlier request, which had been denied for several reasons, one being that the U. S. had vowed not to use American troops to help regain any part of the British Empire and another being that our main purpose in Burma had been limited in Cairo to one of opening a land route to China.

The British, in the meantime had been busy lining up American support for the Chindit project, with the result that mobilization of sufficient veterans of jungle warfare had been completed and the group, all volunteers, was already enroute to India. The writer, discussing this subject with one of the "volunteers" was told that he expected to receive his furlough in California. Instead, upon reaching California from Panama, he was confined to a staging area and subsequently shipped out.

The furloughs never materialized. In his very excellent book, WRATH IN BURMA, Fred Eldridge described the reaction to this army oversight.

> However every Marauder knew he had been promised an Indian furlough, and in typical GI manner started rectifying the discrepancy when the furloughs were not forthcoming.
>
> Training, of course, was in the technique of long-range- penetration. Marauder teams developed an odd habit of going out on their exercises and penetrating to Bombay.
>
> Soon they started penetrating all over India, until more than 300 of the total strength of 3,000 were AWOL.

Originally intended for deployment in Central Burma, as part of a plan to be coordinated with the start of YOKE Force in Yunnan, the Marauder's mission was scratched when Chiang decided not to cross the Salween and they were assigned to Stilwell, over Wingate's bitter objections.

Now also known officially as GALAHAD, they had arrived in Margherita and on February 9th started hiking the 125 miles to Shingbwiyang. General Merrill, ignoring the advise of our OSS folks, who had become experts on the jungle's impact on stamina and survival, had decided that the walk could help toughen them up for the oncoming offensive. Subsequent events were to prove him fatally wrong. The Marauders' reactions to having to walk where everyone else was riding were explosive. There were rumors of them shooting holes in the pipeline and of other extraordinary acts of inventive vandalism. Marking their path, there appeared a long trail of discarded personal belongings and equipment.

Matt Fassio told of one of his friends finding a valuable camera that had been left just outside of Ledo. By February 21st they were assembled at Ningbyen, just east of Shingbwiyang, preparing to take part in the attacks on Maingkwan and Walawbum.

In the action that followed, Maingkwan fell to units of the Chinese 38TH Division, which inflicted a heavy toll on the Japanese. One shallow mass grave, discovered later was found to hold 200 bodies. The capture of Maingkwan was significant because it was the first major settlement to be recovered in North Burma. The Marauders' attentions were focused on Walawbum, which they took after a very grueling, but spectacular, sweeping flanking maneuver via the Kumon Mountains. They inflicted heavy casualties on the enemy. Estimates were that 2000 Japanese had been killed in the two engagements . . . ."Saucy" was off and running!

. . . .

For the 181ST, these developments meant that we were finally going to do what we had been created for, what seemed like ages ago . . . . that was to "repair signal equipment."

For the storyteller the task now becomes rather complicated. Up to now we have been able to follow the fortunes of the 181ST as an integral unit. With the dispatching of the 2ND and 4TH Teams to China just after we arrived at Ledo, and the events that were now about to take place, our story becomes six stories, one for each of the five repair teams and one for the Headquarters contingent. Like a deck of cards, we were soon to be shuffled, cut, and dealt summarily to the four corners of the CBI.

. . . .

Following the departure of the 2ND and 4TH, the next to leave in search of their World War II fortunes were the men of John Banks' squad, from the 3RD Team. After them Lt. Jim Robb's

5TH and Lt. Bernie Silverman's 1ST Team, within a month of each other, headed in opposite directions . . . . the 1ST flying to China, while the 5TH retraced some of its steps toward the Brahmaputra, stopping at Dikom. Remaining in Ledo were two squads from Lt. Wilson's 3RD Team and the men of the company headquarters platoon.

## SUPPORTING THE ROAD

In the latter part of February 1944, a call from the Northern Area Combat Command (NCAC) for a signal repair unit sent Lt. G. Holmes Wilson and Tech. Sgt. John Banks' squad scrambling to pack their personal gear and repair equipment. In the squad were Eddie Blake, Len Ebert, George Henze, George Loftus, Henry Frank, Dick Wells, Warren Pienack, Ludwig "Luke" Strass, Sam Monteleone and Hugh "Hoot" Gibson.

Early morning found them pulling out of Ledo . . . their transportation . . . a jeep; a six-by-six truck towing a trailer mounted with a gasoline generator; and a bus-body truck, fully equipped with workbenches, spare parts and the tools of their trade. The little convoy made good time until the latter part of the day, just as the sun began to set. By then they were well inside Burma and had been abruptly halted by a long line of army vehicles. Having no alternative, they joined the eternal army game of "hurry up and wait" and took their places in line. When it became apparent that the delay was going to be a long one, the energetic Wilson, frustrated by this unexpected obstacle to his joining the war, ordered his driver into the oncoming lane and, with Luke Strass aboard, raced forward to determine the cause of the holdup.

Although the spring monsoon was still some weeks distant, our heroes discovered that an itinerant downpour had washed a thousand yard section of the Road into the canyon far below. By now it was dark and the engineers, by the light of huge spotlights were doggedly carving a new roadway out of the mountainside, bypassing the collapsed section.

Strass recalled that, at the time, he marveled at what an outstanding target the illuminated scene afforded to enemy bombers, had they been in the vicinity. He was also anticipating the appearance of a Japanese photo-reconnaissance plane which came over each evening just as the sun set, and of the excellent eight-by-ten glossies it could have gotten. Because of the peculiar sound of its engine, this nightly intruder was officially dubbed "Washing Machine Charlie". Fortunately this was not his night, though, and the repairs were made with the only loss being one of time suffered by the people trying to reach various objectives in Burma.

Wilson's entourage continued, stopping only when held up by Road traffic or to allow time to take care of some of nature's demands, such as food and sleep. The journey lasted about forty-eight hours. Just before reaching Shingbwiyang, they overtook the last elements of the Marauders, still struggling with the energy-sapping heat and humidity of the Burmese rain forest and the acrid dust stirred up by the continuous parade of grinding vehicles.

Once in Shingbwiyang, the Banks squad set about the business of establishing a bonafide repair identity. While their primary task was to service NCAC headquarters, they also wanted to establish a reputation that would attract anyone else in the area with signal equipment problems.

Since the Japanese had only been evicted from the neighborhood less than two weeks earlier, and with a continuous flow of men, vehicles and materials pouring off of the Road, personal facilities were at a premium and those, which were there, were more primitive than what we had found when we first arrived at Ledo. Picking a spot from which they would conduct business they set up camp around the bus body repair truck and several lean-to type tents, which served as living quarters. With the spring monsoon not too distant, a water cistern was fashioned from a fifty-gallon drum to catch the rain and an added touch was applied when a five gallon can, acquired from the mess kitchen was converted into a shower head by punching holes in it and tying it to a tree. Arrangements were then made for the Banks squad to take their meals at a mess operated by the 96TH Signal construction Battalion, which had arrived earlier.

PX rations were still distributed through company headquarters in Ledo, however, and on March 1st, about a week after the Banks unit had left, Bernie Silverman was ordered by Scott to deliver the squad's PX rations and payroll to them at Shingbwiyang. Payment was in Indian rupees ($.32) and annas ($ .02).

Shingbwiyang                      2 March 44

Received from Lt. Silverman the following
amounts as indicated for pay for the month
of February 1944.

Rs 110,12as     7/sgt John R Banks
Rs 284/13       T/3 Leonard T. Ebert
Rs 267/3        7/4 Henry J. Frank
Rs 296-12       T/4 George a. George
Rs 287/13       T/4 Richard O. Wells
Rs. 187/6       Pvt. Hugh C. Gibson
Rs 104/1        Pvt. Ludwig Straus
Rs 227/12       T/5 Warren C Piercook
Rs 151/1        T/5 Sam Monteleone
Rs 275/12       T/5 George R Loftus
Rs 943/11       T/4 Elbert L Enderich

Lt Wilson's pay  570/11

. . . .

After a short wait for assignment to a convoy, he and a driver started out in a weapons carrier. To control and expedite it, Road traffic was being incorporated into convoy units, which would be assisted, if necessary, through known road hazards by engineering units. As an example, at a particularly muddy spot, a bulldozer would be prepared to spread additional gravel and physically push any vehicles that became stuck, thereby keeping traffic moving. Thus, by day's end Bernie had reached Shingbwiyang.

While he was at breakfast the following morning, General Pick came in. Having only received his promotion one week earlier, Pick, a grandfatherly figure liked to eat with the junior officers. He obviously enjoyed their company and it also gave him an opportunity to keep in touch with things. A rather humorous situation occurred when Pick asked one of the native boys, who waited on the tables, for some pepper. When the lad hesitated with a questioning look, the general repeated, "Pepper . . . pepper, pepper!". Finally the boy got the message and ran out, returning shortly thereafter . . . with a role of toilet paper . . . obviously in need of some additional English lessons.

After completing their mission, Bernie and his companion started back towards Ledo. En-route they passed many black engineers at work on the Road and at one point picked up one who was hitchhiking. When asked where he was going, he replied that he had a three-day pass and was on his way to Ledo. The elation with which he related his good fortune impressed Bernie with the incongruity of the fact that the miserable living and working conditions of the engineers could cause time in Ledo to be looked upon with such excited anticipation.

Back in Shingbwiyang Wilson and his little band began to adjust to their new environment. While acquainting themselves with the other military units in the area, they were reminded regularly that they were close to the fighting by the distant thunder of the 105's as the Chinese and the Marauders smashed into Maingkwan and Walawbum . . . Maingkwan falling to the Chinese

38TH on March 5th, just three days after Bernie had paid Banks' squad.

They soon discovered, however, that Mother Nature was for them a more immediate problem than the Japanese. Within weeks the spring monsoon began and quickly transformed the Road into an oozing, ankle-deep quagmire. In some of the worst stretches, where the trucks invariably became bogged down, logs were cut and placed to form a corduroy road. This remedy could not be utilized everywhere, however, with the only alternative being the application of the age-old "shoulder-to-the-wheel" practice with some well-chosen four-letter words thrown in for good measure.

The health hazards, which abounded in the Burmese jungles, especially during the rainy season eventually struck our small contingent, when Luke Strass came down with a case of amoebic dysentery. He was moved to a nearby hospital unit, where he remained for three or four days. During his stay he occupied a bed next to a black truck driver from an ordnance company, who proudly displayed a jar of gold teeth that he had collected from the battlefields. His object was to accumulate enough of them to go home a rich man.

As had happened in previous monsoons, traffic on the Road was reduced significantly, making normal support of the increased number of troops now in the Hukawng Valley impossible. PX rations stopped completely, piling up back in Ledo and vitally needed food, and other supplies, along with spare parts and ammunition had to be air-dropped by the C-47s.

The war continued, however, as Stilwell pressed General Tanaka's 18TH Division. Several attempts to outflank it and trap it in the valley almost succeeded, thwarted only by the inexperience and poor leadership of the Chinese divisions. As they became learned in Stilwell's brand of war and after some adjustments in command assignments, the Chinese proceeded to confirm in some measure, his belief that, if properly fed, armed and trained, they could make a positive contribution to the war. While the Chinese improved, the Marauders added to their list of amazing exploits and the war shifted from the Hukawng Valley south into the Mogaung Valley.

Sometime in April, Stilwell moved his headquarters from Shingbwiyang eighty miles down the Road to Shadazup, at about the 185-mile mark. From here he engineered the drive for the much sought-after Myitkyina, the main Japanese base from which they had been attacking the Hump. If it could be taken, the route to China would not only be shortened but it would be south of the worst of the Himalayas, allowing a much-needed increase in Hump tonnage.

During the final drive to Myitkyina, the Marauders executed another, but much more physically costly, outflanking maneuver. It was dramatically successful but it was to be their last hurrah. As predicted by Lt. Col. William R. Peers of OSS Detachment 101, who had warned Merrill before GALAHAD started out from Margherita, the brutal march and the sharp but brief battle on May 17th, which gained the vital airfield, brought them to the end of their endurance and combat usefulness.

The following day an opportunity for a quick victory in the lightly held town, itself, was tragically lost by the inexperienced Chinese of the 150TH Regiment of the brand new 50TH Division, which had been flown into a new airstrip a Maingkwan. While approaching the town from opposite sides, they encountered several Japanese snipers near the railroad station, who began picking off Chinese from both sides. The result was devastating as the 150TH troops opened up on each other and before they could be stopped, had inflicted so much damage they had to be replaced, giving the enemy just enough time to bring in reserves. In the interim the summer monsoon struck with a vengeance and eventual victory was not achieved until August 3rd, with the loss of eleven weeks and many more men than necessary.

. . . .

In June, NCAC Headquarters followed Stilwell to Shadazaup and with them Wilson's little unit. The process of setting up personal accommodations and the repair shop was repeated, after which business was conducted as usual, while outside the monsoon wrapped the war in a mantle of muck and mire.

Shortly after their arrival in Shadazup, about seven in the evening, a considerable amount of firing was heard, coming from about a half-mile downhill from where the 181ST was camped. While the area was considered to be secure, speculation nevertheless arose over the possibility of a Jap patrol having infiltrated. While it gave most of the fellows a scare, they managed to keep their cool. As the firing continued, however, it began to wear down some of their resolve. Warren Pienack, another New York boy, became very apprehensive, convinced that they were under attack. Strass, Frank and Sam Monteleone, from Kansas City came to his aid, trying to reassure him and finally quieting him by warning that if they were being attacked they would be better served if they remained quiet. This helped to calm him somewhat and the whole affair soon passed without further incident. Several inquiries were made the following day but nothing was ever learned about the cause of the disturbance.

Not long after that, during a break in the monsoon, anti-aircraft cannon and machinegun fire broke out about 6AM, just as the men were climbing out of their cots. There was a scramble for the slit trenches as two Japanese, two-engine "Betty" bombers were completing a run on General Stilwell's headquarters up the mountain from the 181ST. After sweeping low over the valley, the planes turned south toward Myitkyina, which was still in Japanese hands. Within five or ten minutes a flight of four P-51 Mustang fighters streaked by, disappearing down the valley after them.

· · · ·

Early in March, 1944, while our gallant band was still in Shingbwiyang, General Wingate's Chindits, airlifted by Colonel Philip "Flip" Cochran's transports and gliders, dropped into an area between Indaw and Mogaung, cutting Tanaka's supply lines.

They managed to hold their positions through the months of April and May but, like the Marauders, their mission was planned to last only ninety days, after which past experience had revealed they would be physically and psychologically unfit for combat. During their three-month stint, General Wingate was killed in an air accident and in June, his successor, over the protests of Stilwell, ordered the Chindits back to India. Two brigades were airlifted to Assam, but the third, the 77TH was ordered north, by foot to Mogaung.

Desperately in need of supplies and some way to evacuate their wounded, they elected to build a temporary airstrip at Pinbaw, also south of Mogaung. Four gliders were loaded with engineering equipment and flown to the site, named Clydeside. The following day first one and then two more, carrying additional engineering equipment and an armored car were sent. Shortly thereafter, the 77TH then proceeded north to Mogaung, where they participated in its capture on June 26th.

But what does all of this have to do with the 181ST? Not long after the incident when the Japanese "Bettys" tried to take out NCAC headquarters in Shadazup, the roar of airplane motors was heard again . . . but this time without any response from our anti-aircraft batteries. This signaled that they must be friendly, prompting some of the 181ST to stand and observe them. Eventually the flight appeared over the edge of the jungle, revealing half dozen or so C47s towing gliders. Luke Strass headed immediately for the NCAC folks up the hill, inquiring about the mysterious air activity. His persistence was finally rewarded when a lieutenant informed him that their destination was a unit of Chindits who had been assigned the job of joining the Chinese in the taking of Mogaung. Thus our small band of signal repairmen were afforded a unique opportunity to witness one of the rarest moments in CBI history, the American Air Commandos delivery of much-needed supplies to a celebrated British unit, which would join with the Chinese in an operation heralding the beginning of the end for the Japanese blockade of China.

186 JOSEPH W. HARDING

While it is true that, ". . . all good things eventually come to
an end . . ." the same holds for bad, including the miserable
monsoon. When it finally loosened its stranglehold on the activities
in North Burma, overland supply returned to normal . . . and our
little band received their PX rations. For the benefit of any
civilians, who might be following the 181ST's exploits, we should
point out that, even in this out-of-the-way combat zone, PX
supplies were not free but only available for purchase. Unless
one is a dedicated gambler, money has very limited use in the
deep jungle. So when this long-awaited opportunity to again
partake of some of America's luxuries, such as beer, cigarettes,
candy and nuts appeared, it found the boys "well healed." To
prevent any of their collective rations from being lost to other
organizations, a solemn agreement was reached that obligated
each person to purchase his share, whether he planned to
consume it or not. As a result, some individuals were able to
enjoy more than their allotted quota of their favorite goodies and
when negotiations were over everyone had broken even.

. . . .

In the military, which, it must be remembered was not a
democratic institution, rank had its privileges, and whenever
possible, this included access to the best food that was attainable.
Another, unwritten edict was that opportunities to eat better, when
presented to those with no or little rank, should always be taken
immediate advantage of. One such piece of good fortune befell
Strass one night while walking guard. As he strolled along,
wondering what was playing at the "Paramount", back in Times
Square, a six-by-six rolled into the compound. The driver, who
was beat from fighting the ruts and dust, inquired as to where he
could find suitable lodging for the night. Taking compassion on
him, Luke disclosed the location of a vacant cot and directed the
weary traveler toward it. As he continued walking his tour, Luke,

who readily acknowledged his obligation towards improvement of the culinary habits of the squad, succumbed to a fit of curiosity and, about 3AM, sidled over to the truck and lifted one corner of the tarp covering its contents. To his amazement, he discovered that the truck was loaded with food. After quelling the inner excitement of such a find in this land of misery and enlisted men's' hunger, and closing his mind to the knowledge that there had to be an army regulation covering what he was about to do, he deftly plucked a case of canned peaches from under the tarp. Were it possible, I am certain that he would have received a medal from his contemporaries. As it was, he could only bask in the grateful looks he received from them as they partook of the fruits of his enterprise.

Shadazup is located on the Mogaung Hka (River), which flows almost due north, eventually joining the mighty Irrawaddy south of Myitkyina. While it served the many needs of the Burmese natives in the area, its primary value to the Banks squad was as a means of washing their clothes. Considered women's work by most of the men in the squad, it nevertheless was one of those chores that fell to each individual to accomplish. As time passed, Strass began to notice that Hugh Gibson, known better as Zeke or Hoot, after the famous movie cowboy, always seemed to have clean clothes though he was never seen down on his knees at the river rocks. When his inquisitiveness could no longer be restrained, Strass cornered Hoot, insisting on knowing where he was getting his laundry done.

Despite the fact that they came from totally diverse backgrounds . . . Luke from a predominantly Jewish neighborhood on the lower eastside of Manhattan, and Hoot from near Asheville in the western hills of North Carolina . . . their common lot in the 181ST and the war had caused them to become very close friends. Nevertheless it took much persuasion from Luke before Hoot, who had acquired more than just a passing knowledge of spoken Chinese, divulged that he had made friends with a Chinese soldier, who he had nicknamed "Hatchetface" because his countenance looked as though it had been hit with the flat side of an axe. For a price, he had contracted to take care of Hoot's laundry. After much urging and after Luke had been duly sworn to secrecy, Hoot agreed to include Luke's soiled clothes in future bundles delivered to Hatchetface.

Several of Hugh Gibson's Chinese friends

. . . .

The valley through which the Mogaung River flowed was covered with dense jungle, inhabited by some very spectacular animals. On one occasion, several Chinese soldiers were seen lugging a twenty-four foot python, estimated to be about six inches in girth . . . an interesting supplement to their basic rice diet. The 181ST contingent also received a visit from a four-foot long lizard, which they were prevented from shooting at by Lt. Wilson . . . who suggested that any firing might be misinterpreted as indicative of enemy activity. The Lieutenant demonstrated an interesting phenomenon for the squad, one day, when he put to sleep a six-foot snake that George Loftus had captured. The snake was taken into the bus body and held so that its mouth could be pried open . . . whereupon Wilson unscrewed the stem of his pipe, thrust the end holding the filter into the snake's mouth and then clamped it shut. To the astonishment of those looking on, in two or three minutes the reptile was asleep.

On another occasion, the Lieutenant again provided the squad with some entertainment, although it was totally unplanned. Wilson . . . who was known better as "G.I." to those of us in the company, because of his uncompromising behavior on soldiering during our early training in Missouri and California . . . was an excellent technician. While working on a radio in the bus body, however, he proved the hard way that electricity respected no one, regardless of their talent. In making a test, probably in the plate circuit, he accidentally came in contact with 440 volts which literally blew him bodily out the door of the bus body, clearing the three steps there and depositing him on his back on the ground. By sheer luck he was not seriously injured, suffering only a sore back and a pair of blackened hands.

. . . .

The Banks squad remained in Shadazup from June until late October, a period of about three and a half months. With the passing of time, the war moved away from them and Myitkyina, which fell in August and became the terminus for ATC activity as well as the Allied base for the drive to link up with the Chinese in Yunnan. Air superiority had now shifted definitely to the Allies although the Japanese air force was still a threat.

Shadazup was becoming just another spot on the Road and the area command decided that the time had come to set up an outdoor movie. A hillside was cleared off and a screen erected at its foot. Intended for the entertainment of the American troops from the NCAC units in the area, the novelty of such a modern phenomena in the midst of the remoteness of Shadazup immediately attracted several other viewers. Paramount among these was our overly inquisitive neighbors from the Chinese 22ND Division. Once they became familiar with the schedules they made a point of arriving long before showing time, while most of the Americans were still working, and proceeded to fill up the entire seating area. This, of course was not considered "cricket" and a proclamation went out banning our "pushy" allies' attendance altogether. Now anyone who has had any dealings with the ordinary Chinese soldier, knows what came next . . . they simply ignored the announcement completely and continued to show up as usual. When the Americans asked them to leave, several refused and scattered fighting ensued. This was soon brought under control when the Chinese military police arrived on the scene. With the exception of some belated stone throwing, our unwelcome allies were convinced to leave and peace again reigned. Although it was a false assumption to believe that none would return, most did not. From then on, the few that did contented themselves with positions in the rear or on the edges of the audience.

A rare treat was enjoyed when a bit of Hollywood appeared in the person of movie stars Paulette Goddard, Ben Blue and several professional dancers as part of a U.S.O. troupe. Their show was reminiscent of those popular at the time in the Times Square area and in major theatres across the U.S.A. Like the Joe E. Brown aggregation, they deserved considerable credit for voluntarily visiting a region that was so rampant with dysentery and dangerous insect-borne diseases. They were a real tonic for the men, many of who were embarking on their second year away from the "States".

Sometime before they left Shadazup, the Banks team made their own personal contribution to the local theater, when Luke Strass allowed himself to be coerced into performing a seductive dance, dressed as a voluptuous blonde . . . in a stage show produced by a Special Service unit.

WHEN LUKE (Ludwig) Strass volunteered for "a job at Signal Center" in Shadazup in 1944, he didn't know he was going on the stage. But here he is, dressed in a chute and with a couple of baseballs to improve his figure, a lot of makeup and a blonde wig.

. . . .

As time, in the remote area of Shadazup began to weigh heavily on our little group, Lt. Wilson revealed a side of him that the men had not hitherto seen. Maybe the G.I. way of doing things had elements that we had not considered before . . . like the old adage that all work and no play makes Jack, etc . . . At any rate he designed work schedules, which deliberately allowed free time for the fellows to use as they chose. During one of these recesses, Strass, Loftus and another

192 | JOSEPH W. HARDING

New Yorker, Henry Frank, decided to try their hands at a little big-game hunting.

During my brief abortive attempt at the sport in Hellgate, I discovered that, despite the proliferation of animals in the Burmese rain forests, unless you are a legitimate hunter you are not likely to see many of them. So it was not surprising, that our ambitious trio encountered the same frustration. Setting out, armed with a submachine gun, two carbines, food and water they opted to follow the river, theorizing that they might spot some game in the act of drinking. After about two and a half hours of scrambling through and over ravines and under bushes, the only wildlife they had come close to were scores of leeches, which they had to pick off of each other every fifteen or twenty minutes. They tried tucking their pant legs into their socks but the persistent parasites dropping from the trees, found their way down the men's necks and up the sleeves of their jackets.

Thinking that they might find more game on the other side of the river they decided to find a narrow spot to ford. Stripping completely, they bundled their clothes and weapons on their heads and proceeded across. Before they reached the other side they were in chin-high, swift-running water and sweating out potholes.

Hunting on the other side of the river proved to be no better. In their wandering, however, they stumbled upon a small pond away from the stream, which abounded with fish. Like Dillinger taking a Chicago bank, they opened up on the pond with all of their fire power . . . the result was a very impressive string of eight or ten beauties over fourteen inches, which they proudly presented to the cooks back in camp, who by the way were also with the 96TH Signal Construction Battalion.

The new work schedules, with the built-in time for leisure pursuits that they provided, were not wasted on our hard-working group. In true 181ST fashion they sallied forth to ascertain what was happening in the area and up and down the Road. On one of his jaunts, Luke Strass wandered down to the airstrip, which had been built to handle C46s, C47s and L4 and L5 liaison planes. The latter were piloted by sergeants and used for running a host of errands, ranging from bringing in spare parts, medical supplies and ammunition . . . to taking out the wounded or sick to the 20TH General Base Hospital in Margherita.

In picking the airstrip, Luke had nothing more in mind than to get away from camp and thought that he would just see what was happening there. Like most inner city dwellers, he considered flying to be an activity reserved for the wealthy or a certain class of adventurers . . . an experience in which he did not expect to have an opportunity to participate. So it came as an unexpected surprise that, after striking up a conversation with one of the pilots, during which he voiced his desire to someday get a chance to fly, he found himself climbing into the back seat of one of the L5s. The pilot had explained that he had to pick up supplies at Warazup, about fifteen miles south and deliver them to Maingkwn, which was north and that Luke was welcome to tag along.

Having given no thought at all to the logistics of the venture, as they lifted off the end of the runway, Luke prepared to revel in the anticipated pleasure of his first flight. As they leveled off at about 4000 feet, his sweeping gaze took in the breathtaking panorama of the plush jungle below. Once Shadazup disappeared behind them, however, he was gradually struck with the realization that, if the valiant little engine that was pulling them along should quit, there was absolutely no opening in the mass of green foliage where they could effect any kind of landing and that if they crashed, the little plane would certainly be swallowed by the jungle and they would probably never be found. Once his mind began to contemplate some of the less-than-ecstatic aspects of his position, the thought then occurred to him, that there were still occasional Japanese planes about and should they encounter one, it could dispatch them without much difficulty. These misgivings then triggered the realization that, in his eagerness and joy in accepting his host's offer, he had given no thought what-so-ever to the real dangers it entailed.

Thus it was with unquestioned relief that he welcomed the landing in Warazup and breathed an inward sigh of thanksgiving.

In response to his benefactor's inquiry regarding his continuing the flight to Maingkwan, Luke thanked him for the offer but explained that, reluctantly, he felt that he had to forego the pleasure and try to find ground transportation back to Shadazup.

. . . .

In time the word came down that furloughs were to be had and were awarded to two men at a time. Transportation was provided back to Ledo or another location on the railroad, from which the lucky ones traveled to Calcutta. Quarters for two weeks or ten days were made available at a girls' college in Dum Dum, where it was discovered that members of Lt. Jim Robb's team were also enjoying a breather.

When everyone had taken their turns at Dum Dum, the Wilson entourage pulled up stakes at Shadazup and headed down the Road to Myitkyina. While en-route, the ever-active Lieutenant insisted that they call a halt to investigate the scene of one of the major battles in the area (possibly Mogaung). They had gone only a short distance from where they had parked their little convoy, when the odor of decaying corpses became intense. The scene was apparently the location of a hastily fashioned mass grave, probably accomplished with bulldozers. It was so shallow that arms, legs and parts of bodies and uniforms were protruding above the ground. With the exception of the really curious and the souvenir-seekers, the visit for most of the men was a very short one.

. . . .

Their arrival in Myitkyina, in mid-October of 1944 coincided, unhappily with the tragic recall of General Stilwell to the States and the splitting of the theater into the India-Burma and the China Theaters. The activation of a new 191ST Signal Repair Company, for India-Burma had been decided and the Banks squad was ordered back to Ledo. For their part in the drive to Myitkyina they received the following commendation:

HEADQUARTERS
NORTHERN COMBAT AREA COMMAND
OFFICE OF THE SIGNAL OFFICER
A.P.O. 218

GFM/EWS
28 OCTOBER 1944

SUBJECT: COMMENDATION FOR DETACHMENT
181ST SIGNAL REPAIR CO.

TO : COMMANDING OFFICER, 181ST SIGNAL
REPAIR CO.

1. TO LT. GEORGE WILSON AND TO EACH OF
THE MEN OF HIS REPAIR TEAM LISTED BELOW, I
WISH TO EXPRESS MY SINCERE APPRECIATION
FOR THEIR SERVICES RENDERED WHILE
ATTACHED TO THIS COMMAND.

T/SGT JOHN R. BANKS
T/3 EDWARD C. BLAKE
T/3 LEONARD T. EBERT
T/4 GEORGE A. HENZE
T/4 GEORGE R. LOFTUS
T/4 HENRY S. FRANK
T/4 RICHARD O. WELLS
T/5 WARREN C. PIENACK
T/5 LUDWIG STRASS
T/5 SAM MONTELEONE
PVT HUGH C. GIBSON

2. THEIR ABILITY AND MANNER OF
PERFORMANCE HAS BEEN COMMENDABLE; THEIR
ATTITUDE AND CONDUCT, EXEMPLARY; THEIR

COOPERATION, EXCELLENT, AT ALL TIMES. IT BRINGS A FEELING OF REGRET TO HAVE THESE MEN TAKEN FROM THIS COMMAND; THEIR LOSS WILL BE NOTICED, FOR THEY HAVE CONTRIBUTED MATERIALLY TO THE HIGH EFFICIENCY IN REPAIRING, TESTING, MAINTAINING, AND SERVICING OF OUR SIGNAL EQUIPMENT.

2. MY THANKS AND APPRECIATION TO EACH OF THESE MEN FOR A JOB WELL DONE.

GEORGE F. MOYNAHAN, JR.
LT. COL., SIGNAL CORPS
SIGNAL OFFICER

(Standing) Wells (NJ)—(Back Row) Henze (IA)
Banks (IL)(squad leader), Blake (CA)
Frank (NYC)—(Front Row) Loftus (TX)
Strass (NYC), Ebert (NJ) Monteleone (MO)
Pienack (NY)

As though in recognition of their contributions to the success of the Myitkyina campaign, some of them were flown back to Ledo, rather than have to endure the discomforts of the Road. Several others, including Len Ebert and Eddie Blake remained, reporting to an officer not with the 181ST. Their vehicles, including the fully equipped bus body were left behind for use by their replacements. Len recalled that he and Eddie did eventually return to Ledo and subsequently became part of the 191ST.

The sight of the familiar faces of the Headquarters folks, after nine long months of jungle and monsoon was most welcome. Bank's band lost no time in getting replacements for their worn and missing clothing and equipment from their favorite haberdashery run by H. Maurice Lichty and Morris Hollander at the supply basha.

In a matter of a week or ten days (in mid-November) some of them and several others from the Wilson Team received orders to report to Chabua. After receiving instructions on how to survive in the jungle with the equipment and weapon, which allegedly were packed in their parachute seats, they, like those before them from the 181ST flew to Kunming, China. Although they were still required to use oxygen when clearing the Hump, thanks to the fact that Myitkyina was no longer in Japanese hands, their route was much safer and farther south than their predecessors', taking them between several of the tallest peaks, rather than over them.

They remained in Kunming only about two weeks. During that short time, Luke Strass, who had raised pigeons in lower Manhattan, met an Army pigeonaire sergeant, who made him a gift of two birds and five pounds of feed. Luke remembered the expression on Lieutenant Wilson's face when he boarded the C46 for Yunnanyi with the two, new, feathered members of the 181ST.

For Luke and the others, their arrival at Yunnanyi had a pleasantly surprising aspect. Here they found themselves reunited with some of their compatriots from the company, whom they had not seen for up to a year from arriving in Ledo. Among these were Bill Friedman, Salvatore Corritore, Paul Mrogenski, Jim Beck and Sabatino Gentile and, of course, others whose names can no longer be recalled.

The men who had seen nine rugged months in Burma with Wilson and Banks were now faced with an entirely new scenario, peculiar only to China.

# LEDO 1944

In the army's grand scheme of things, Signal Corps organizations did not usually report to other units of less than division level. In the case of the Banks' squad, they were working for the NCAC, which commanded the Chinese 22nd, 30th, 38th and 50th Divisions and Galahad. Subject to the needs of the NCAC signal officer, if so ordered, our comrades could have found that their work locations were anywhere within the NCAC jurisdiction, including the front lines.

In China some of the repairmen received similar work assignments with Chinese Army Groups, Armies and Divisions, under the same conditions.

Our people in Ledo, however, found that their roles were to be much less romantic even though, at times, they were indirectly related to the actual conflict that was raging in Burma. With the arrival of Colonel Pick and in conjunction with major organizational changes in Services of Supply (SOS), Stilwell had drawn an imaginary demarcation line at about the five-mile mark on the Ledo Road, at which SOS authority stopped and NCAC's began. Reflecting this, the 181st repair and headquarters teams, at Ledo were consequently placed under the command of the Base Section #3 Signal Officer, rather than an army or division.

. . . .

Responsibility for setting up a repair shop in Ledo fell, naturally, to Lieutenant George Wilson's team, under the direction of Sergeant Willis Nichols. From the memories of those who shared this effort, the shop was temporarily housed in a basha, which was empty and waiting for us when we arrived. It was located in the company area, between the officers' and mess bashas. After Lt. Jim Robb arrived from his lonely errand in the Pacific Ocean with the company's vehicles and tools, a new permanent shop was occupied with benches, testing facilities and all of the other features, peculiar to a commercial repair establishment. There were also two repair bus bodies, which, during the hot weather, forced the occupants to strip down to shorts.

Sgt. Nichols' repair team at Ledo

Following the departure of Lieutenant Wilson and the John Banks' squad to Shingbwiyang, the two remaining squads concentrated on handling the business coming from the many units in and around Ledo. Harry Koch and the other telephone repairmen continued caring for the facilities at the 20th General Hospital, which occupied the Margherita polo field. Its business was always expanding to service the personnel buildup in the region as well as the increases in wounded, flown in from Burma. The telephone and Teletype folks also received and serviced equipment brought to the shop by the many units stationed in the vicinity who supported the Road.

Despite Stilwell's demarcation line, the 181ST was also needed to attend to repair and miscellaneous communication requirements along the Road from Ledo to Shingbwiyang. When the Banks squad followed NCAC headquarters to Shadazup, the void they left was filled by our folks in Ledo.

Responding to this need on one occasion, Koch accompanied a contingent of natives who were clearing brush along the Road as far as Tagap. In recounting the trip, Harry described the assent around the precipitous curves that the Cheeseman squad had negotiated in 1943, as "going up, up, up through the clouds . . . like you were in an airplane". His impression of Tagap was that it would have been an excellent spot for a vacation resort.

Back in Ledo, Quentin Brandt, who was in charge of a radio squad, recalled working on hospital equipment such as photo-flourometers and electro-cardiographs. His team also repaired F.M Tranceivers for a Chinese Tank Unit and some Air Corps communication equipment. He found that, "The Chinese had a theory that if they discreetly cut out a suspected bad part, that would fix things. Then when the unit still didn't work they would bring the radios to us to repair." His squad had the responsibility for setting frequency channels for units leaving for Burma. After changing frequency on a couple of armored scout cars, they tested their range by taking them for a spin up the Ledo Road.

He was confronted with a real challenge when, working with Platoon Sergeant Willis Nichols, they received some units with mercury-filled rectifier tubes that had been broken in transit. There were no replacement tubes, so Nichols devised a circuit to do the job, while Brandt cleaned the mercury out of the units. He found that, "Trying to get parts that were out of the ordinary was a problem when we were doing first to fifth echelon repair." He also remembered, "Another tricky item were units that had explosive charges to destroy them. Was the explosive (that was) in and armed causing some anxious moments!"?

Time was found, of course, for the practice of our special brand of private entrepreneurship, so essential to the enhancement of the still miserable living conditions in Ledo, particularly during the monsoon. Brandt recalled repairing other units' dayroom radios and some belonging to officers and receiving canned turkey or liquor in return. He and several other sergeants, including Harold Webb and platoon sergeant Willis Nichols, managed some relief from the monsoon, constructing a building from materials acquired by "midnight requisition" from the supply depots at Margherita. He remembered that, "It had a concrete floor with rugged, waist-high burlap walls and mosquito netting above. (The) roof was a double canvas of British style with canvas drop outer walls . . . ." They also discovered that by converting the dynamotors that worked off the direct current from truck batteries, by rewiring them in series, they could be used to operate fans.

Another group that included Bob Finkel and Herman Berger, the latter assistant to George Cole the company clerk, and two fellows named Marino and Bateman (not familiar to the writer and probably from the 191st Signal Repair Company which was being formed) also built a house, thus escaping much of the discomfort of the monsoon rains. Berger remembered a native bootlegger, near the camp, who filled orders when his customers held up one or two fingers, designating that they wanted "Bullfight" brandy or "Fighter Brand" whiskey.

At this writing, accounts of the experiences of the men in the motor pool and headquarters are very few. Although both groups' everyday routines did not make for exciting, romantic episodes, performing these duties under the conditions that existed contained the elements of many colorful tales.

Several recollections are from Octavious Bottary, who succeeded Bill Stull as motor pool sergeant. On several occasions he personally drove Captain Scott up the Road on deer-hunting ventures. The captain used a silver-plated rifle that he had brought with him from Wyoming, when he reported to the 181ST in the fall of 1942.

In August Bottary and Warren Diesel, also a sergeant in the motor pool, drove Scott and several repairmen to Shingbwiyang. Like the Banks squad six months before them, they had with them a jeep, six-by-six truck and a bus body repair vehicle. At Shingbwiyang Scott tried his hand again at hunting. Having no success, he returned the next day to Ledo.

The group stayed on in Shingbwiyang for about a month, during which they received an air-raid alert and had to utilize one of the slit trenches. As they clambered into the trench, they found the floor completely covered with beer cans . . . . truly an American facility. The subsequent trip back to Ledo proved to be too much for the bus body and its motor gave up the ghost en-route.

. . . .

Shortly after the fall of Myitkyina Warrant Officer Joe Hardwick was told to fly a payroll to a group that was operating a repair shop there. He was a very large man and, as first sergeant in Camp Crowder had reveled in his role of the tough, blustering, tyrant . . . especially to the recruits from Dix and Bragg. When it became obvious that our stay in India and Burma was going to be a long one and when his "Articles of War" security blanket which had protected him in the "States" began to show a few holes with the "every man for himself" atmosphere of Ledo and the Road, a marked change was detected in his attitude toward his 181ST associates . . . . of all ranks. To some, "Big Joe" appeared to have suddenly taken stock of his real situation and had wisely elected to begin working hard at becoming everybody's friend.

When he received the order to fly to Myitkyina, he became visibly shaken at the prospect of performing the dangerous assignment and quickly pawned it off on Warren Diesel.

Now Warren was the very antithesis of Hardwick. He was not only an excellent auto mechanic but was the type of real soldier of which there were so many in the North Burma Campaign. He was one of those who cursed the impossible elements but then went ahead and found some way to get the job done.

He packed the necessary personal gear . . . . and . . . . taking no chances, armed himself with a '45 sidearm and, for good measure, shouldered a Thompson submachine gun . . . picked up the payroll . . . . and reported to the Ledo airfield.

When he saw the beat-up condition of the C-47 that was to be his transportation, he asked the pilot and co-pilot where his parachute was. They responded that they had none for him and smugly pointed to two stored overhead that belonged to them. When the cocky airmen started to reach for them, however, Warren quietly drew his '45 and suggested that the chutes be left where they were.

He reported that the crew did an excellent job of transporting him to Myitkyina, that the payroll was delivered without fanfare and that in due time he was back in Ledo.

About the same time, Bottary again drove Scott up the Road, this time to Myitkyina. After the captain's business was completed with one of the Signal Corps commanders there, they headed back towards Ledo. At the scene of one of the many battles, they pulled well off of the Road, and keeping a respectful distance enjoyed a session of detonating unexploded mortar shells . . . . Scott, with his prize rifle and Bottary, with his carbine. This event may have been Scott's "last hurrah" with the 181ST.

During the late summer of 1944, Paul Mrogenski, a teletype repairman (Brookfield, Missouri) and Evan Evans, a radio repairman (Brainard, Minnesota) spent several days at Shingbwiyang. Paul recalled that, shortly after their return to

Ledo, he, Evans and about six others took their turn at flying the Hump. At the parachute briefing, Evan insisted that, should the need arise; he knew that he would not be able to jump from the plane. Paul told him not to worry; that he, Paul, would accommodatingly shove him out. Evan's concerns were not diminished any when the plane, after taking off, found that the landing gear would not retract, necessitating their return to Chabua and an additional landing and takeoff.

. . . .

As we approached the first anniversary of our embarkation from Staten Island, events were developing in the CBI which would not only accelerate our dispersal but would also ultimately decree an official end to the 181ST. These events were the culmination of Stilwell's many disagreements with Mountbatten, Chennault, and Chiang during his two and one half year assignment. The result would be his eventual recall to the "States" and the division of the CBI into two separate theaters.

With the latter occurring, the role of the 181ST was to be redefined, along with a decision to activate another repair company. As we now know, this turned out to be the 191st. Based on several documents received from Bob Finkel and Bernie Ring, this writer estimates that, following the victory at Myitkyina, orders affecting the 181ST, as a direct result of the decision to split the CBI, were cut sometime in August.

One unconfirmed fact is that Captain Scott was transferred to the 835th Signal Service Battalion. Three other changes in the organization are documented in a brief history of the Fifth Team, written by Lt. Jim Robb and a letter from Lt. Petri to CBI Headquarters recommending Bob Finkel's promotion to lieutenant.

In his account of the Fifth's accomplishments, Jim Robb (by then a captain) stated that the team was transferred to the 223rd on August 30, 1944.

Support for the theory that the Captain Scott transfer and his replacement by Lt. Petri, upon the latter's return to the company

from New Delhi occurred about Septembe
in the content of Petri's letter, dated Septe
   In his letter, which he signed as comma
as an argument for the immediate commiss
fact that:

> "One (1) officer and thirty-one (31) rep
> transferred . . . . to cadre a newly activated col       , . . . ."

(presumably the 223rd). It might also be worth noting that the incident in which the captain and Bottary shot up the unexploded mortar rounds could not have happened until after the fall of the Myitkyina airfield in June. This would have limited his departure from the 181ST and his replacement by Petri to have occurred between the fall of Myitkyina and September 15th, the date of the Petri letter.

Although we have been unable to establish the precise time frames during which they occurred, several accounts, received from the men from Lt. Wilson's Third Team, include references to working and living with people from the 191st cadre. Since half of the team stayed in Burma and India with the 191st, we can logically assume that the orders for activation of the new repair company might also have been cut during August (1944).

This theory receives some support from the fact that, on November 1st, one week after the splitting of the CBI Theater (October 24, 1944), Platoon Sergeant Willis F. Nichols (OH) took a squad to Myitkyina to establish a permanent repair shop. Besides Nichols, in the group were Octave Bottary (IL), Warren Diesel (East St. Louis, IL), George Loftus (TX), Ernie Gioia (NJ), Jack Hale (NY), Harold Webb (Norfolk, VA), Hugh Gibson (Asheville, NC), Sam Monteleone (Kansas City, MO) and a John Clark, who was not a member of the 181ST when it first reached Ledo. Sharing the same tent were Hale, Monteleone, Gibson and Platoon Sergeant Nichols (Ohio). He recalled the excellent job that Clark had done in wiring the repair shop.

with the 181ST, the Nichols contingent was attached to 199TH Signal Service Battalion. In return for taking their meals with the 96th Signal Battalion, they had to share KP and guard responsibilities. Eventually they were transferred into the newly formed 191ST Signal Repair Company, functioning for several months without an officer.

In his letter to THE Ex-CBI ROUNDUP (see Chapter 3), Jack Hale also described the arrival of the squad in Myitkyina:

. . . . I wound up flying into Myitkyina in Burma, which wasn't bad duty since the fighting had ended by the time I arrived. The only disadvantage was that we were behind the Jap lines with very limited use of motor vehicles until the engineers were able to push the Ledo Road through to our location.

The adventure continued with many of our fellows adopting Burmese children orphaned by the battle.

When things settled down, the civilian government took the children away, much to our regret since they were beautiful kids who in short order had been fitted with cut down army uniforms. They had quickly learned passable English (not all of it suitable for the drawing room). I fear some had also learned to smoke. but, I give a passing grade to GIs as foster parents.

With the children gone, dogs became the pets of choice and at sick call the Medics insisted that those with human ailments be seen first. The Medics were then willing to venture an opinion on dogs and monkeys.

One of the problems with my pet dog was that he kept bringing home bones, sometimes still inserted in a rotting shoe. The area abounded with bodies of Chinese and Japanese infantry. Our graves registration units had given priority to our fallen GIs.

. . . .

Harold Webb explained that, since there was little for Gibson to do around the repair shop, he was loaned to the Chinese who employed him as a jeep driver for one of their colonels. An interesting by product of this assignment was that Gibson became very fluent in spoken Chinese and also gained the personal friendship of the colonel. Ernie Gioia told the story of having attended a show with Gibson and the Colonel, an Ohio State graduate, and of joining them at a meal in which they had to use chopsticks.

The entrepreneur spirit, always present in the 181ST psyche, manifested itself when Gioia and others were assigned the mundane task of testing flashlight batteries. The criteria for determining the serviceability of a case of batteries dictated that if more than five were defective the remainder were placed in salvage and as Ernie recalled, "were traded for ice cream, meat, etc.".

A chance assignment to join five others who were selected by Captain Scott for a detail to travel to Calcutta to procure ammunition, and the good services of the Red Cross afforded Ernie an opportunity to meet his younger brother, who was in the 31ST Signal Construction Battalion. He was to meet him once more in Myitkyina, before he was sent to China. Ernie related that his brother contracted dengue fever while in the CBI. He died years later at home.

. . . .

On January 17, 1945, Bob Finkel finally received his commission as a Second Lieutenant. Captain Scott first recommended him for the promotion on August 30, 1942. Following the session with the Inspector General in Camp Shanks, however, at least three attempts by Bob in Ledo, to get any action from the captain were unsuccessful. There is some suspicion that Mr. Hardwick, who, as far back as Camp Crowder, had made little effort to hide his personal dislike for Finkel, filed his applications in the waste can.

Knowing that he was leaving the company, the Captain, on August 18, 1944, (just about two years after first doing so) again signed his name to a recommendation for Bob's promotion. We can only guess at his reason for so doing. Maybe he felt that he had gotten sufficient revenge for Camp Shanks; or that he knew Petri would certainly expedite the application anyway; or he, Scott, would look bad, when Finkel had received recommendations from Lt. Wilson, his Team Officer and Lt. W. J. Smith, the Ledo Base Wire Officer.

At any rate Bob became the Third Team Officer, replacing Wilson who had flown to Kunming in mid-November of 1944. One of his first actions as an officer was to exact a salute from Hardwick.

In March of 1945 a radio message, ordering some of the 181ST men to return to Ledo, was received at Myitkyina, relayed through the 96th. Bottary recalled that when they finally reached Ledo, they found the entire 181ST headquarters contingent and what remained of the 3rd Repair Team, formed into a convoy . . . . and about to start the grueling trip to Kunming.

# CHAPTER V

# The Official Breakup Begins

## THE WAR PICKS UP—
## THE FIRST GOES TO CHINA

Beginning with the buildup of Service troops in Assam and the start of serious offensive activity in Northern Burma, the events of early 1944 signified a marked escalation of the war in India and Burma. Even the British, who politically had no stomach for an all out Burmese offensive, did eventually mount a limited undertaking into the Arakan area of Burma, bordering the Indian Ocean. Stilwell's Chinese and Merrill's Marauders, in the meantime, were driving the vaunted Japanese 18TH Division out of the Hukawng Valley and Wingate's Chindits were raising havoc south of Myitkyina. Having anticipated that such offensives would be forthcoming, the Japanese high command decided to activate a defense plan, which had been devised to counter such threats to their recent conquests in Burma.

Their plan, called "Operation U" was to invade India and secure the area of Assam in and around Imphal. A preliminary to the main event was launched on February 4th by their 55TH Division against the British units in the Arakan . . . . their objective . . . to lure reserves away from Imphal. The tactic worked and by March 15th they were threatening both Imphal and Kohima. The latter, to the north was less than fifty miles from Dimapur on the Bengal-Assam railway. This was the vital lifeline, which sustained Stilwell's troops in Northern Burma, the airfields from which supplies were flown to China and all of the service forces in the area. Unfortunately, 181ST HQ and the 3RD and 5TH Teams were part of the latter.

The Japanese drive was devastatingly successful and both Imphal and Kohima were soon surrounded and fighting desperately for survival.

Logistically the Japanese who were punishing Kohima were now only forty-six miles from Dimapur and the railroad. Thanks to the pig-headed inflexibility of their high command back in Burma, however, they refused to divert any of their troops from the original target, probably denying the 181ST in India an opportunity to share some of the glory of combat duty.

While this comment is made in jest, such an eventuality could have actually occurred. To cope with the potent threat to his supply line, Stilwell, at a meeting in Jorhat with his British counterpart, Lieutenant General William J. Slim accepted responsibility for the defense of the area, which extended north from Nazira (headquarters of the OSS) to Tinsukia. This was to be accomplished by the accelerated on-the-job combat training of Service of Supply (SOS) troops and the creation of a special GASPAR FORCE, comprised of some units from the new Chinese 30TH Division.

. . . .

Just about the same time, FDR had finally concurred with Stilwell's oft-repeated contention that, if we were to get any action out of the Chinese on the Salween, some heat had to be put on Chiang. On April 3rd Roosevelt informed the Generalissimo that, since everyone was fighting but his Salween army, maybe there was no reason for continuing to provide him with American aid.

This sober message finally got his attention and Brigadier General Frank Dorn, who commanded the Americans attached to the Chinese "Y" Forces, reported that the long-awaited attack across the Salween would be made by May.

Apparently American brass had anticipated FDR's action and Chiang's response, because things began to happen, not only in China but in Ledo also. On March 23rd, eight days after the Japanese launched their main attacks on Imphal and Kohima, Bernie Silverman's 1ST Team (including this writer) was ordered to Chabua for transportation to China. This move put us in Chabua during the mobilization of the SOS and Gaspar Force for the defense of the vital railway and the area between it and the Japanese.

. . . .

The wait for an available plane to transport us over the feared HUMP into China lasted eighteen days. During that time several momentous events occurred. Historically General Wingate, the driving force behind the British Chindits was killed in a plane crash while returning from Burma. Another event was the massive, but (for the Japanese) costly air raid against Ledo and Tinsukia, mentioned earlier in our story.

For the men of the First Team, it was a period of waiting for something to happen, an activity at which we had, by now, become quite proficient. Those of us who fancied ourselves as somewhat athletes were administered a potent serving of humble pie by a group of air force officers in a touch-tackle football game. Like us they were also transients awaiting passage to other parts of the CBI. Unlike us, however, they played football as though they had all done so previously in the "Big Ten".

Some other forms of entertainment in the area also provided diversion for Silverman's stalwarts. The most memorable of these was the appearance of Paulette Goddard and her troupe at a nearby post. Some time was also killed at the evening movies, one of which featured the song, "My Shining Hour". During all of the ensuing years, just hearing the song has always rekindled vivid recollections of our brief stay at Chabua.

In our battle with the monotony of waiting for, what was for most of us, our first airplane flight, a few of us visited a nearby P-51 fighter strip. There we were treated to the exciting return of a flight of four "mustangs" from a sortie. One of them executed a victory roll, announcing the fact that he had downed an enemy plane . . . . possibly one of those from the Tinsukia raid. This experience was capped off when I and a companion chanced to hitch-hike a jeep ride with several of the same pilots, who bounced over the dirt road back to Chabua as though they were still dog-fighting Japanese.

Back in camp I met a buck sergeant who alleged to have been in the party with the famous newsman, Eric Severeid, who had been forced to bail out over the HUMP and who had been hosted by Naga headhunters. Of course the good sergeant wasn't about to waste the opportunity to intimidate this young city boy and painted a nerve-wracking scenario of the entire party on the brink of being slaughtered by the Nagas, seconds before the arrival of a native runner delivering a life-saving ransom. The true story, learned forty years later was much different, with the Nagas succoring the Severeid party until a British rescue team reached them.

Some of us "lower grades" were made to serve a tour as KP's in the transient mess kitchen. Aside from recalling that a can of peaches, which I managed to abscond with, and which turned out to be very sour grapefruit juice, the most stirring memory of that assignment is of suddenly encountering one of the cooks emerging from the mess hall with his '03 rifle slung over his shoulder and with a sagging web belt full of ammunition. Now this fellow was upper middle-aged, portly in stature and would have looked more in place at a shuffleboard in an Irish bar in New York City. To my automatic inquiry, he replied that he was going on patrol duty against the possible infiltration of Japanese into the area. Not having known anything about the events, which were occurring to the south in Kohima, I was stunned by the sobering news.

Shortly thereafter the team was assigned to a plane and, in the early hours of April 10th, the day after Easter and following a delay caused by a flat tire on the C-46, we took off for China and Kunming. The briefing and the fitting of parachutes was identical to that received by the teams that had left in the fall of 1943. I recall that we kept our parachutes on during the flight, that we had been instructed which foot to leave the plane with, if we had to jump and that the emergency supplies in the seat of the chutes would probably be missing several items, especially the '45 automatic that was supposed to be there.

Flying above the clouds, in one of the last flights to leave Assam before the monsoon hit, we caught only brief glimpses of the Burmese jungles, saw none of the Himalayas, but thought that we would freeze to death as we lifted to clear them. As we landed in Kunming, we left behind us the memories of India and the battles raging fiercely for Imphal and Kohima.

## DIKOM, CHABUA AND THE FIFTH

But the 181ST was not to be left out of these conflicts. On April 8th, two days before Silverman's First Team left Chabua for China, Lieutenant James Robb's Fifth left Ledo to report to Captain Herman O. Voight, the Signal Supply Officer for Advance Section #2, located at Dikom, not too far from Chabua.

Like the First, Second and Fourth Teams before them, they voiced their final farewells to the ever-decreasing contingent at Ledo. Like the others, also, they were not to know that, for most of them, it would be the last time that they would ever see their friends in what remained of the Third Team . . . . the John Banks squad at that very moment operating a repair shop in Shingbwiyang, 102 miles from Ledo, beyond the Patkai Hills.

As the Robb vehicles, with all of their equipment, passed through Chabua, their occupants were greeted by stark evidence of the devastation wrought by the recent Japanese air attacks.

Matt Fassio recalled that as they passed the railway freight station, whose walls were riddled with shrapnel holes, "It looked like some kind of battle had taken place there".

Their immediate destination was a large tea plantation in Dikom, which was to be their home for more than four months. Here they were neighbors to the 219th Signal Depot Company, which had shared the same officer's mess at Crowder; had been at Niland, California with part of the 181ST, where their Lt. Bill Miller had joined Captain Scott in many beer-drinking and dice-throwing sessions; and finally had been our ocean-going, traveling companions on the Mariposa.

The accommodations at Dikom were the very practical and comfortable English tents (four men to a tent). These all had either cement or wooden floors and featured the patented double roof, with an effective insulating air space between the layers.

For the lower ranks, the misery of KP was now a thing of the past. Here another and most favorable aspect of reverse lend-lease came to their rescue in the form of Indian labor.

The first task for the team was the conversion of an empty 60' by 20' warehouse, with a cement floor, into a repair shop. This required that partitions be erected to separate the stock room and office from the repair area, which had to be equipped with benches, shelves . . . etc. Charlie Wilson, a refugee from a New Jersey utility company, wired the entire layout, including each bench, for AC. By April 15th, exactly one week after their arrival, the Fifth had completed the warehouse's face-lift . . . . and were open for business. Bernie Ring, from New York City, who, it was discovered could type, was assigned as clerk in the repair office taking on the job of traffic cop for the flood of activity that followed.

The Team was made up of two radio repair sections headed by Technicians Third Grade (T/3's) Carlyle Biggs and Charlie Matthews, and a wire repair section under Technical Sergeant Joe Cheeseman, who was also platoon leader under Lt. Robb. As explained in Chapter 1, when Lt. Petri was forming the company, its responsibility was for the highest echelon of repair of army communication equipment. Here then, one of our teams was finally about to perform the function for which it had been created.

With the trouble brewing south of them at Imphal and Kohima, a call for their services came immediately from Gaspar Combat Headquarters, commanded by Brigadier General Joseph A. Cranston. The first order of business was the checking of all new equipment before it was issued to the Chinese, British and American troops. As the campaign progressed and extensive patrol activity increased, calls were received for the services of our heroes in the field. Like their counterparts in John Banks' squad in Burma, Robb's fellows discovered that their front line was wherever their repair chores took them. When the equipment being used by Gaspar Forces was not repaired on the spot, it was returned to the shop at Dikom. As sober proof that they were now part of the real war, one of the first repair jobs that came in was a British army radio with a very conspicuous bullet hole in it.

Although not deployed in direct support of troops engaged in a major offensive action, because of the close proximity of their establishment to the area which Gaspar was patrolling, our gallant band of repairmen, nevertheless, found themselves doing guard duty with live ammunition against the threat of Japanese infiltration.

Along with the attendant uncertainties and apprehensions created by their predicament came the inevitable flood of rumors. One of these was that the Japanese had cut the rail line. Ray Bumgardner recalled hearing this one and also that all rail traffic had been stopped. Although this writer could find no historical confirmation that the Japs had reached the railroad, several of the men vividly recalled that some supplies were being received by air.

As the Japanese threat to the railroad and the units stationed north of it was escalating, the possibility of the need to evacuate the area was foreseen. Thus it came as no surprise to the Team that they received instructions on how to demolish the repair shop they had just worked so hard to establish. Although they were prepared to execute the order when it came, fortune was in their favor and their lessons were never put to the test. The threat of encirclement, however, was very real and Sergeant Joe Cheeseman began to hold daily classes in combat training. At one point, someone suggested, whether seriously or in jest, that they should attempt to break out of the Jap trap. He was told that, if the British failed, it would be up to the Chinese to take on the Japanese, not the Americans since, as one of our uncharitable comrades put it; one American was worth 1000 Chinese.

The Fifth watched as Chinese from the 30TH Division, fresh from their training in Ramgarh, passed through, some riding in trucks and jeeps and, as Carlyle Biggs recalled, "Hooting and hollering and holding up their fingers in the "V" for victory salute." The joke going about then was that the British were too busy having tea three times a day to fight the war and that the Chinese would stop the Japanese. The facts were just the opposite, with the British engaging in extraordinary feats of heroism in the face of overwhelming odds, with too little water and food.

Another rumor that caused considerable concern was that Japs had been discovered in some of the chow lines. Several of the men recalled having seen some infiltrators, who had dressed themselves in native Indian garb, being detected and herded at bayonet point by Chinese troops from the GASPAR Force.

Attesting to their proximity to the conflict was the appearance of numerous troops from the British colonies. They ranged all the way from ebony-skinned West Africans to the diminutive but deadly Gurkhas.

In an attempt to assuage the concerns of the Americans caught up in these events, Lord Louis Mountbatten decided to tour the areas occupied by the noncombatant SOS troops. Our men at Ledo heard him close up. As he spoke, he displayed uneasiness, probably triggered by his fear of our obvious lack of respect for his royal position. Paul Mrogenski, who sat only ten feet from him, was struck by the SEAC commander's constant fidgeting with his uniform during his speech.

Later Mountbatten repeated his appearance at Dikom, where Lieutenant Robb's "Fearless Fifth" listened attentively. As he shook hands with each of our stalwarts, he assured them that there was nothing to fear and that the British had deliberately withdrawn so as to bring the Japanese out of the jungles where they could be dealt with. History has accurately recorded that had the Americans not diverted much of the HUMP traffic for air-dropping duty to sustain the desperately beleaguered contingents trapped in Imphal and Kohima, the British "alleged" strategy might very well have had the same result as that of Custer's at the Little Bighorn.

With the aid of the American airlift, which bought the British the necessary time to bring up reserves, they were able to relieve their heroic forces. In the meantime, Japanese supplies ran out and the monsoon destroyed the jungle trails over which any help might have come. On July 5th they broke off the attack and attempted to withdraw via these same trails into Burma. The results were tragic indeed. Of the original 155,000 troops that began the attack, 65,000 perished.

As the British gained control of the conflict at Imphal and Kohima and the need for Gaspar ebbed, the bulk of repair demands began to come from the Northern Burma campaign. Working with the Galahad rear echelon headquarters, the Fifth Team, not only rigidly pre-checked and supervised the packing of all of their signal equipment, but also stayed with it, flying in the air-dropping planes until it was out the door and on its way to the Marauders on the ground. Leonard (Leo) Tridico, from Metairie, Louisiana, was one of those who made the hazardous flights over the Burmese combat zones.

The history of the North Burma campaign has confirmed the positive contribution air supply made to the successes of the American, Chinese and British forces. The hazardous practice of airdropping equipment, however, increased the rate of damage ordinarily expected from a combat zone. Consequently the 181ST did a very brisk business in repairing communication gear that fell victim to the airdropping routine.

Here, again, the 181ST found that their services could lead them into the combat zone. This was dramatically demonstrated when, sometime after the airfield was secured at Myitkyina, but before the final fall of the city itself, Carlyle Biggs was ordered to fly there, acting as nursemaid to a mysterious wooden crate. He was told that the nine cubic foot box contained secret communication equipment and had to be delivered personally to its addressee. In typical 181ST fashion he set out from Chabua. As the plane neared the Myitkyina strip and began its final landing approach, it suddenly veered away, to avoid ground fire, which was coming from a stubborn Japanese contingent dug in near the end of the airfield. The landing was finally made from the opposite direction and in due time Biggs delivered his mysterious box.

He then proceeded to search for a place to spend the night before returning to Dikom. In the process he was surprised upon discovering a half dozen members of the Fifth Team in several tents nearby. The date was probably June '44 and with the monsoon generating unbearable heat and humidity, his newly found hosts suggested that they all strip down to their under shorts and take a dip in the nearby Irrawaddy. What they failed to tell him, however, was that jungle streams can be extremely frigid, due to the dense canopy through which they flowed and the absence of much sun during the rainy season. At any rate, Carlyle recalled that he was severely shocked when he hit the water and scrambled out as quickly as he could. His comrades, who had suckered him into the river, and were waiting for his reaction, took great joy from his antics.

Foremost among these was James "Red" Hale, who had revealed his teletype-repairing skills at Tagap in late 1943. "Red's" stay in Myitkyina eventually ended in his being wounded. While the details surrounding his misfortune are lost, Charlie Wilson recalled attending a ceremony in Chabua, during which a General formally presented the Purple Heart to Hale.

Carlyle's one night stay outside of Myitkyina was punctuated by erratic small arms fire and somewhat alarmed, he happily boarded the plane for his return trip to Chabua. As he related his experiences to his friends back in Dikom, they pretended to disbelieve that the contents of his mysterious container was signal equipment and chided him, contending that it probably contained whiskey. In researching the 181ST story, this writer came across an account in Colonel Charles Hunter's book entitled GALAHAD in which General Stilwell learned that the Marauders had not received any post exchange, (PX) supplies. In his book Colonel Hunter commented, "Some time later I was surprised to learn that there were two liquor rations and some cans of peanuts for GALAHAD at our supply tent on the airstrip." Who knows??? The Fifth back at Chabua, after all, was servicing the needs of GALAHAD'S rear echelon headquarters.

Although, upon reaching Dikom, the Fifth was caught up in servicing combat units, its primary responsibilities were to the many organizations assigned or attached to Advance Section #2. The Team's charter also included the repair of special service equipment (radios, phonographs and projectors) for all units including the Air Force organizations in the area. Spencer Odgen, from the Fifth, also operated the local camp projector, grooming Oscar "Ossie" Brandsdorfer as his understudy.

A call was received one day, requesting that the Fifth set up projectors, audio, and signal equipment at the American section of the rest camp in Shillong in the breathtaking foothills of the Himalayas. T/3 Chuck Cortwright, who had held a "Ham" radio license and had also gained considerable experience while maintaining his high school's projecting and sound gear, took a crew, which included Ogden and Ossie to Shillong. The sergeant in charge was a former member of the University of Tennessee championship football team, whose coach had been General Bob Neyland. Observing that the sergeant's limitations were to matters athletic, Cortwright wasted no time in convincing his southern neighbor that the Fifth would handle his signal and theatre problems and, as Ossie related, was soon running the whole show. The crew spent several, very pleasurable months on the assignment.

Some time later someone from Advance Section #2 Headquarters appeared at the shop asking whether the Fifth had anyone who could fix a movie projector. Lt. Robb suggested that Cortwright go along to see what he could do and after discovering that it was an Ampro projector, Chuck checked out a working one from Supply. His diagnosis was that the AC power at the HQ tent theatre was overloaded and that the defective Ampro had a weak exciter lamp. Taking care of both of these problems and satisfied that the projector would work, he then set about building a pair of base reflex speakers from some high grade pine he discovered in a couple of packing crates and placed them on each side of the movie screen. He then designed a high-frequency driver out of the units from two metal horn sound systems and awaited the results. The whole project had taken about three days and when the next show went well, he returned to the shop, relieved that his efforts had been justified.

He was back in camp only two days when a staff sergeant drove up in General Cranston's jeep. When he said that he was looking for the repairman who had revamped the HQ theatre equipment, Lt. Robb suggested that this time Chuck swap his fatigues for suntans and go along with the sergeant. With more than a little apprehension Chuck reported to a lieutenant, the general's aide, who told Chuck that the general wanted to talk to him. After asking where Chuck was from and other personal questions, General Cranston explained that he also had a recalcitrant projector at his quarters . . . . and would Chuck take a look at it . . . . and stop back when he was finished. Since the general was a legitimate customer, Chuck agreed and accompanied the staff sergeant to a bungalow on one of the British tea plantations. The projector, this time an RCA, with which Chuck had more experience, was suffering from a shorted capacitor and, again, the power unit was overloaded. After looking to these problems, he replaced both the exciter and projection lamps, rejoined the sergeant and returned to the general's office.

Once the sergeant had confirmed that the projector was working fine, the general turned to Chuck and asked, "If you're not doing anything tonight why don't you come on over and run the projector?" Of course Chuck acquiesced, replacing the staff sergeant, who had had the duty until then.

As the reader has no doubt concluded by now, Chuck's future in the CBI was assured from that point on and he was soon attached officially to Advance Section #2 Headquarters.

The next request from the general came several weeks before Merrill's Marauders were finally relieved from duty in Burma. This time Chuck was asked to take two or three platoons of assorted individuals drawn from the Supply, Quartermasters and several other organizations to the rest camp and prepare things for the Marauder's arrival. The site that had been designated was an old British barracks about two or three miles from the town. After sizing up the condition of Galahad's future home, Chuck proceeded to order out a steam cleaner, several barrels of lime, some chlorine and other necessary items and put his charges to work disinfecting the entire premises, ridding them of an army of those insidious insects for which India was so infamous. Dozens of the patented Indian rope cots were installed and the job was completed in time for the arrival of the exhausted, semi-starved and disease-ridden Marauders.

Needless to say, Chuck's fortunes continued to improve and he was soon meeting the Hollywood stars from the USO troupes as they arrived at the Chabua airfield and escorting them to Shillong. Here they recuperated from the long flight to India and some of the native surprises such as Delhi Belly and other assorted humiliating ailments, which greeted them.

The Pat O'Brien-Jinx Falkenberg group which he escorted throughout Assam for two weeks were so impressed with their treatment through his efforts that they all signed a personal note to him, thanking him, wishing him good luck for the remainder of his CBI tour and inviting him to visit them when he returned to the "States". Many years later, Pat O'Brien, learning that Chuck, his wife Fran and some friends were in Los Angeles, stopped en-route home from New York to have a drink with them at their hotel.

U.S.O. TROUPE NO. 374, TOURING C.B.I.

APO 629
3 December 1944

T/3 CHARLES R. CARTRIGHT,
223rd Signal Company,
APO 629.

Dear Charlie:

Before leaving "C.B.I." we wish to thank you for the
things you have done for us while staying in Assam.

"Thank you", Charlie, is so little to say, yet all that
we can add is that it comes from the bottom of the hearts of
every one of us to you, who in the past two weeks have become
our friend.

God bless you and grant you a safe and early return to
the United States, and each of us invite you to visit us at
our homes so that we can have our families and our friends
meet our favorite "G.I.".

Sincerely yours,

*[signatures]*

Chuck was eventually promoted to Warrant Officer, attached
to India-Burma Theater SOS Headquarters and via Hastings Mills,
Calcutta and wound up in an Air Service Unit in Karachi.

. . . .

By the time that Myitkyina had fallen to the Allies, on August
3, 1944, almost all of the repair shop's efforts were being directed

toward fulfilling their original charter of servicing the surrounding army units and processing signal gear destined for China. As the number and variety of army units involved in supporting the Road in the race to meet HUMP tonnage projections grew, so too did the Fifth's business. The shop worked closely with the Signal Supply Section, inspecting, setting up, putting into operation, testing under load and, when necessary, repairing all equipment for shipment over the HUMP. After the testing process was completed, the Fifth also provided technical supervision for the repacking of the equipment for shipment.

In the course of achieving this goal most of their effort was directed toward healing the ailments of complete signal equipment units. Oftentimes, however, the most valuable repair challenges came when it was found that it was necessary to virtually remanufacture damaged components, for which there were no replacements. One example of this was brought on by the extremely damp climate which played particular havoc with the radios, causing a buildup of mildew fungus in the power transformers, resulting in shorts and the burning up of the coil windings. This occurred so often that a machine for rewinding them was devised from junk parts. Using tar, obtained from a nearby gasoline refinery, as insulation within the casings, Charlie Wilson spent many hours repairing and returning these critical components to service.

The assignment of this task to Charlie, whose army job was a telephone equipment repairman and a member of the Fifth's wire repair squad, under Sergeant Joe Cheeseman, was typical of the odd jobs usually directed to them. As a member of the wire squad with Lt. Bernie Silverman's First Team, this writer found that any job not classified as purely a radio repair task was usually steered to the telephone repairmen.

A classic example of this was the acquisition of telephone poles. While certainly related to the telephone industry, their procurement could hardly have been described as a repair activity. Nevertheless, Cheeseman kept a crew of three or four men permanently occupied with supervising the cutting and delivery of these vitally needed commodities. The task required that Cheeseman and his crew live about a day's ride from the Dikom-Chabua area, in the jungle where the poles were cut. Matt Fassio recalled that, on various occasions, he was with Cheeseman, along with Ben Tillman, Charlie Wilson and several others on a rotating basis. They often spent four or five months at the task and were housed on a British tea plantation. Matt remembered that the plantation featured massive wire fences to ward off elephant herds that roamed the area. The British tea growers, who were no doubt paid by the U. S. Government for housing our compatriots, were reported to be most hospitable.

Another job that fell to the telephone and Teletype repairmen was the manual cranking of hand generators, which supplied power for many field radios while they were being adjusted or repaired by the radio squads.

. . . .

Of course our comrades of the Fifth Team soon came to realize that within their magical powers of electronic repair lay the potential for improving the physical conditions in which they were living.

It wasn't long before they discovered that the surrounding army and air force units were the potential sources of foodstuffs not served in the local mess hall. The quartermaster and hospital units, particularly, had access to such tidbits as canned, boned chicken and tuna fish. These same military units abounded with personally owned radios, many in dire need of repair. It has been anonymously reported that Ray Altenbach, from Milwaukee, functioned very effectively as the repair agent within this plethora of commercial opportunity, engineering a steady flow of personal business for our busy repairmen. No one knows quite how he was able to accomplish it, but in due time, he was to be seen wheeling around in his own jeep.

As the heat and humidity began to reach unbearable proportions, Tech Sergeant Elbert Escherich, who occupied the same tent as Sergeant Carl Clampett, Oscar Brandsdorfer and Leo

Tridico, discovered a way to convert scrap dynamotors into small AC motors. He then fashioned several fan blades, which when attached to the AC motor, became an electrical fan. As the supply of dynamotors increased, Brandsdorfer and Tridico were assigned to mass-produce fan blades and a new industry was launched. Clampett assumed the role of distributor, with sensational results. It wasn't long before every Fifth-Team tent had several fans and a brisk business was being conducted with their army neighbors.

The food situation improved so much for the occupants of the Clampett tent that they began to receive an increasing number of evening visitors. One night Chuck Cortwright dropped in, accompanied by movie star Melvin Douglas and several others from Special Services who enjoyed a late night snack. Douglas was in the army (possibly a major) and operating from New Delhi, where, Bernie Silverman recalled, he " . . . was just another one of the boys."

## WE LOSE THE FIFTH

As discussed in the previous chapter, August of 1944 was the period during which the realignment of organizations due to the impending split up of the CBI into two separate theaters was occurring. Since the 181ST was, by then, operating in India, Burma and China, some decision had to be made as to its future deployment. One immediate result was the transfer of the Fifth Team out of the 181ST fold, on August 30th, 1944, to become the cadre for the newly activated 223RD Signal Depot Company.

It might be appropriate to mention at this point that the Fifth had been without an officer from June 14th until September 4th. During this ten-week period, Lt. Robb was hospitalized and the responsibility for the direction of the entire team and its transfer into the 223RD fell to Sergeant Cheeseman. The efficient performance of the Team during this period was so successfully maintained that Cheeseman received official praise for this very difficult achievement from the Inspector General and the Commanding General of the Section.

The organizational move to the 223RD also entailed a physical relocation to an area one half mile east of Chabua, under the jurisdiction of Intermediate General Depot No. 2. There they reported to a Major J. D. Carton (from New York Tel.) and began immediately setting up new shop facilities. Cheeseman, (now a master sergeant), Charlie Wilson and Matt Fassio from the old Fifth Team and Sgts. Meadows and Lumet directed most of the work.

The extent to which business had picked up since their arrival in Dikom was dramatically seen in the increase in floor space they were now occupying. From one building of 1200 square feet in Dikom they had grown to four buildings with a combined area of 14,400 square feet. Three of these, each covering 2400 square feet, housed the combined telephone-teletype-instruments shop, the classification and reclamation shop, and the carpenter shop. The fourth, as large as the other three together . . . was the home of the machine shop.

It comes as no surprise with the growth of the Fifth to much more than a purely signal repair organization, that it received the new designation of a depot company. Among the new services it offered to its military clients was the repair of a variety of sensitive test instruments. The motivating force in the organization and direction of the new shop was Technical Sergeant Truman Brock from Laurinburg, North Carolina. By the fall of 1945 Brock's shop had garnered a host of plaudits from Air and Ground Force Units whose chestnuts they had managed to pull out of the fire.

One of these was the 234TH General Hospital, whose various departments had been Brock's regular customers. On October 12, 1945, Major Henry G. Schaffeld, Chief of Laboratory Service for the hospital penned the following commendation to Major Carton of the 223RD, in appreciation of Truman's services:

> It is the desire of the undersigned to make this
> simple statement of commendation and appreciation for
> the service repeatedly rendered to this laboratory by

Tech. Sgt. Truman N. Brock of your organization. On many occasions he adjusted sensitive instruments and built others such as thermostats, necessary for our proper function. On one occasion he accomplished the repair of the gold wire on a string galvanometer in our spectrophotometer, an exceedingly difficult and tedious task, which I am sure could have been accomplished otherwise only in the Zone of Interior.

The undersigned has frequently been made aware of how valuable and resourceful this man has proven himself.

This commendation was passed upward to Headquarters, Intermediate Section, India-Burma Theater, where it received the concurrence and signature of the Commanding General, Brigadier General Joseph A. Cranston. For his assistance to the Air Force Units, Truman also received a Certificate of Appreciation, normally reserved for former Air Force personnel, from "Hap" Arnold, commanding general of the entire Army Air Force.

Brock also operated a photographic dark room. In the evenings it was a favorite haunt of Brandsdorfer, who gradually managed to comprehend some of the magic of "hypo" and "fixers". After winning first prize in a company contest, Ossie was awarded a supply of photo printing paper. Not owning a camera, he agreed to swap some of the paper with Truman in exchange for the use of his 35-millimeter. Ossie made good use of the barter and later accompanied Captain Robb on a trip to New Delhi, where he not only got in some busy photo-taking . . . but also learned, first hand, that his C. O. was a very quiet, shy but extremely learned individual.

A brief summary of some of the services rendered by the 223RD to their clients in the Chabua area is best found in the following excerpt from a HISTORY OF THE REPAIR SHOP published in 1945, much of it written by then Capt. Robb:

Although this history is necessarily a compressed and sketchy one, it would be incomplete if mention were not made of the many (extra) services provided by shop

personnel, such as work done for the Armed Forces Radio
station, electric wiring and installation of sound systems
for clubs and depot headquarters, such jobs as wiring of
the whole signal supply area, installation of local battery
telephone systems in various supply areas, camera repair
work, photo lab service, special assistance to the chemical
and medical laboratories, rewiring of hundreds of electric
fans badly needed by hospitals and other installations
in the section, the establishment, at the special request
of the Commanding General, of a typewriter repair shop
serving the whole section and dozens of similar services
that contributed not only to the more efficient operation
of the various units in Intermediate Section but also to
the comfort of the army personnel in a section where
conveniences had to be largely self-provided.

In watching the evolution of the role of this team, which had
been envisioned by its creators in far-off Washington, D.C. as that of
a relatively straightforward repair-oriented unit, into one that
eventually performed an endless array of technical tasks, one can
see an excellent example of the marked difference between our
singularly American way of doing things and that of the rest of the
world. The amazing list of services rendered by this band of thirty-
one individuals and those who joined them in forming the 223RD is
mute testimony to what can be accomplished with a strong purpose
backed by dedicated leadership and Yankee ingenuity and talent.
Their accomplishments are enhanced even more when one learns
of the political and military disagreements between the Allies, of the
bitter infighting among the military personalities who seemed to put
their selfish interests ahead of defeating the Japanese and of the
frustrations inherent in being lowest man on the Combined Chiefs'
strategic totem pole.

A measure of the level of sophistication to which the Fifth
had risen was that they achieved all of the above in spite of
miserable weather and living conditions. In overcoming the latter,
they demonstrated their ability to adapt to the survival game being

played by those military units, such as the air corps and quartermasters who controlled the movement and storage of those commodities, which made life a little more livable. To their credit, the Fifth did much more than what was originally expected of them, while, at the same time exacting their pound of flesh from those of their compatriots who were enjoying bigger pieces of the survival pie.

. . . .

When the powers in Washington finally got around to dropping the ultimate bomb on our ambitious friends in Japan, most of the men of the Fifth had weathered almost two years in India, starting with Ledo and eventually finishing in Chabua. During that period, which they started as tourists in Bombay, they gradually became familiar with and in a kind of sync with the customs, climate and non-military realities of India, particularly Assam. Thus it was only natural, when the pressures of work, boredom and the always-present frustrations of their living conditions needed forgetting, that they set forth to probe the region for whatever diversions it offered.

Ben Tillman related how, occasionally, a group would go off hunting at night in a weapons carrier they had rigged with a spotlight. The area they hunted was about three miles from a jungle village, which was approximately a days' ride from Chabua. Their routine was to pick up a village headman, who they had cultivated with a regular supply of canned food and other gifts. Arriving near midnight, they would stop at his bungalow and be immediately treated to tea and cookies, served by other natives in the village who were routed out of their beds by their higher-caste leader.

As Ben recalled, the "head-knocker" and his wife would then guide them to the edge of the jungle where they would ride up and down the trails in search of game, usually deer. When successful they gave the results of their night's work to the grateful, native Indians. One of their largest gifts was an 800-900 pound animal.

Shortly after unloading their rifles and dropping their hosts at their bungalow, one morning, three of our "great white hunters" found the road blocked by a good—sized tiger. Startled by the sudden appearance of the weapons carrier and the noise from its occupants as they hurriedly reloaded, the beast quickly disappeared into the tall elephant grass. Once reloaded, our heroes aimed their spotlight at the place where the tiger had entered the grass and began firing. After the huge cat had made good his escape, Ben suddenly recalled the danger the tiger, if wounded, could have posed and "thanked the Lord" that neither he nor his two companions had hit the animal. He also recalled several stories that had been circulating at the time, telling of several people, working on remote oil lines being killed by tigers.

On another occasion Ben had the unique experience of occupying the rear seat of a "howdah" on the back of a local maharajah's elephant, which had been borrowed or rented by an air force pilot. With four or five such elephants lined up, the local natives would form a long line and drive any game in their paths past the waiting gunners. Ben described this activity as "not much of a sport . . . like shooting fish in a barrel".

There were others, of course, who took their turns riding the elephants, Ray Bumgardner being one of them. Another was Ray Altenbach, super salesman, who parlayed the repair of an English civilian's radio into several tiger hunts.

. . . .

The two-year stint in Assam was broken up occasionally for the men of the Fifth by furloughs to the rest camp at Shillong or to Calcutta. During their two weeks at the girl's college in Dum Dum, outside of Calcutta, in late 1944, Joe Cheeseman and Reece Bailey joined Luke Strass from John Banks' third Team squad, which had just completed its tour in Burma. Carlyle Biggs received the news about the fall of the Germans in Europe while he was taking his turn at enjoying the delightful climate and scenery at Shillong in the foothills of the Himalayas.

Following the climactic A-Bombing of Hiroshima and Nagasacki, the men of the 223RD began to leave for home and when the unit was finally relieved of its role in Assam, it was replaced by the 191ST Signal Repair Company.

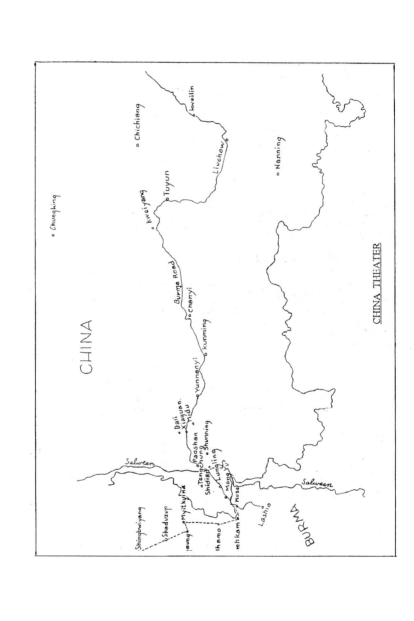

CHINA THEATER

# CHAPTER VI

# China (Y Force and SOS)

## CHINA—WAITING FOR THE RELUCTANT DRAGON

To continue with our story we must return to late November 1943 and our arrival at Ledo. By that time General Stilwell had had his fill of Chinese duplicity and corruption on the one hand and British arrogance and deceit on the other, plus repeated attempts by General Chennault to undermine his authority. In his letters to his wife, Stilwell expressed his terrible frustration in coping with the political environment he was forced to operate in by referring to it as the "manure pile".

To the 181ST, particularly those who were hustled into China shortly after arriving in Ledo, the resulting schedule disruptions produced repeated, nerve-wracking periods of "hurry up & wait". The burden of eternal waiting was magnified considerably for these men who lived for the better part of a year or more on a fare in which rice and water buffalo were the central ingredients. Fortunately for the 181st, however, most of the political jockeying through which Stilwell had been maneuvering since January of 1942, had already occurred by the time we arrived in India.

As the Sino-Japanese conflict spread, the United States demonstrated as it has done so often since, its well intentioned but pathetically naive brand of foreign policy. In October of 1940 Washington moved to keep China from making a separate peace with Japan by opening the door for a Lend-Lease arrangement similar to that then in place with the British. Immediately thereafter the Chinese sprung a request for 500 combat airplanes for implementing a plan devised by (then) Capt. Claire L. Chennault (USA-Ret) who, as a technical adviser, held the rank of Colonel in the Chinese Air Force. His plan, which was supposed to bring about the defeat of the Japanese with only a small air force, was to be a major source of fermentation in the "manure pile" until the scheme's failure late in 1944 . . . . an event, by the way, which caused no small concern to several of us who were in China at the time.

Another ingredient, which perpetuated the "steaming mass", also manifesting itself in the form of materiel requirements, was the Chinese plan to reorganize and rearm thirty divisions considered Chiang's own. As early as November, 1941 Chiang had promised to divert his personal thirty divisions from the 300 plus, which made up his four-million-man army. These thirty, (YOKE Force) were to be fed and trained by the American liaison teams and deployed across the Salween River in Yunnan Province to assist in reopening the Burma Road. Their objective was to drive the Japanese from Southwestern Yunnan and to link up with the Chinese divisions of the 1 ST Army (X Force) who were clearing the Japanese from northern Burma.

It took Chiang one whole year (until November of 1942) to designate the YOKE Force divisions but the unrelenting quagmire that was the Chinese political system prevented him from delivering them to Stilwell.

In December he sent Madame Chiang's brother, T.V. Soong to negotiate an agreement with Yunnan's very independent governor, Lung Yun (Dragon Cloud), which would permit the occupation of his province by this large contingent of Nationalist troops. With this last obstacle out of the way, the

Americans proceeded to wait through the first five months of 1943 for the Chinese to move on their commitment . . . . but in vain. About this time Chennault came up with his fantastic boast that he could beat the Japanese with air power alone. This was too much for Chiang to pass up as an excuse for his inactivity and he promptly hopped aboard Chennault's bandwagon.

At the Quebec Conference in August . . . and as the 181ST prepared to ship out . . . the Allies finally faced the realities of their opportunities in the C.B.I. and the Chennault plan disappeared. It was replaced by the one that was finally executed . . . code-named RAINBOW.

This plan called for YOKE Force to attack from Yunnan in September, as we boarded ship. Having had no real intentions of allowing that to happen, Chiang, once more pulled the string on the Salween attack. Here he fell back on one of his oft-stated reasons for reneging on his YOKE agreement, which was his insistence that the British also mount simultaneous land and sea thrusts into Southern Burma. Thus, as we went about the business of settling into our new quarters at Ledo, the Chinese YOKE Force in Yunnan had once again failed to keep its earlier agreement to launch its Salween offensive.

Everyone, including FDR, Churchill . . . and even Chiang . . . knew that landing craft and air transports could not be found for the British part of the plan. Nevertheless, as only politicians can do, both the Americans and British, at the SEXTANT Conference at Cairo during the last week of November, managed to get yet another promise from Chiang to cross the Salween . . . although he reversed himself four times before finally giving in to the Allies' demands. Then in typical Chiang-Kai-shek fashion, as he boarded the plane to return to China, he again reversed himself, without the knowledge of FDR or Churchill, stating once again that the British must do what everyone knew was logistically impossible.

Stilwell, who had been advised of Chiang's latest change of

heart, broke the news to Mountbatten. The latter, knowing that, with the Generalissimo, he was to jointly review the Chinese New First Army at Ramgarh, announced that he thought that he could sell the reluctant dragon the idea once more. Somehow he was successful and Chiang, on November 30th, confirmed the fact in a speech to the Chinese troops, placing them under the command of Stilwell and Mountbatten. This time the Salween fireworks were supposed to start in the spring of 1944.

· · · ·

The role that the 181ST was to play in the Yoke Force effort generally and more specifically in the Salween Campaign had been planned, no doubt, long before we left the States. With the new concessions wrung from Chiang on November 30th, both the Mc Veigh 2ND Team and Swanson's 4TH packed up their personal gear and, by December 7, 1943, had left Ledo, separately, for Chabua and China.

# KUNMING

Their destination was Kunming, the capital of ancient Yunnan Province. Located on a 6200-foot plateau in a valley of lakes and high-terraced rice-paddy fields, the city is bordered on the west by twenty-mile long Lake Tien. The two are linked together by a network of canals, which provide access for hundreds of junks and sampans to the very heart of the city.

Once the busy terminus of the now blockaded Burma Road, in late 1943 it was undergoing dramatic changes. For centuries it had been considered wild and uncultured, the haunt of barbaric Lolo and Miau tribesmen and surrounding warlords and bandits. It was also the place to which political losers and criminals were banished by each successive Chinese dynasty.

With most of China's major centers for trade and commerce under the yoke of Japanese occupation, Chungking and Kunming were catapulted into prominent roles in the war. The sudden intrusion of the conflict, American style, and the amazing behavior of the strange foreigners that it brought with it showed in the faces of the peasants, whose fore-bearers had survived for centuries in the rice paddies and hamlets that surrounded Kunming. They were also faced with the totally unfamiliar and devastating effects of the new economics that arrived with the hundreds of refugee bankers, tradesmen, prostitutes, industrialists, soldiers-of-fortune and scholars from occupied China.

Growing to what eventually became a population of 150,000, without the benefit of a well-ordered political game plan, Kunming had become a wide open city. Awash in every conceivable form of venereal and other diseases, ninety percent of it was labeled "Off Limits" by the U. S. military authorities.

One of four gates into the city

Sampans on the shore of Lake Tien

The airfield, located several miles south of the city proper, was large enough to accommodate both the busy fighters and bombers of the 14TH Air Force as well as the constant stream of C47's, C46's and C87's of the Air Transport Command (ATC). The field, also used by the civilian Chinese National Airways Company (CNAC), was eventually to be reported to be one of the busiest in the world.

At this point in time, it was also the frequent target of the Japanese Air Force, which was still a potent threat to the American installations in the country. The damages they inflicted on the runways were constantly being repaired by masses of coolies straining on a dozen or so long ropes attached to gigantic concrete rollers. As it labored to accomplish its incredible task, this vocal mass of humanity swayed in a sort of slow-motion cadence, accompanied by a rhythmic chant that was somewhere between an eerie wail and a long, low moan.

The Mc Veigh 2ND Team arrived first, on December 12th. After the eventful flight, described in Chapter 4, the ground felt reassuring ... and ... as the apprehensions which had peaked during their short but dangerous ordeal began to subside, our half-frozen travelers turned their attention to the setting for the next adventure in their strange Odyssey. One of the first things they observed, which reinforced their suspicions that they had indeed survived a truly dangerous trip was a significant coating of ice on the wings of the plane. During a long, miserably cold wait for ground transportation that followed, they were left to contemplate the dreary expanses of the airfield and the mournful spectacle of the coolies toiling with their gigantic roller over one of the runways. Their noses were assailed by an indescribable odor, which permeated the air everywhere . . . testimony to the native custom of fertilizing their fields with human manure called "night soil" . . . denoting the time of day during which it was collected.

. . . .

Eventually the men of the Second were whisked by truck to several nearby camps. These, called "hostels", were assigned numbers . . . the closest, "Hostel 5", being located just north of one of the runways. It was one of a chain of sixty provided by the Chinese National Military Council through its War Area Service Corps (WASC) branch.

National WASC headquarters was located in Kunming, which was also one of four WASC districts in China. Officially the WASC role was that of providing, not only room, board and even barbers for its Allied guests, but its impressive list of responsibilities also included "Recommending of Chinese Personnels, Training of Chinese Interpreters" and the organization of language classes, liaison with officials, social and cultural events and the "Rendering of Religious and Medical Services".

After so many years, most of the men from the 2ND Team are not too clear about where they were quartered while in Kunming. Several did recall, however, that they stayed in Hostel 5 during what was to be a period of only a matter of weeks. There they were housed in tiled-roofed, mud-brick barracks just north of and overlooking one of the runways.

The rest of the Mc Veigh team was taken north, along a dirt road toward the city. They passed through a countryside blanketed with a patchwork of rice paddies and seemingly endless expanses of semi-circular grass-covered mounds, marking the resting places of Yunnan's most venerable ancestors. Occasionally the view was interrupted by clay and mud-brick hamlets and a variety of military installations along the way.

About halfway to the city, three or four miles, they turned east onto another dirt road, which they were to learn was actually the continuation of the famed Burma Road. A few minutes later they made a right into a rather abbreviated version of an army camp. This facility, known officially as Hostel #4 was located on the edge of a vast sea of graves, which extended the three or four miles back to the airfield. The camp was still being expanded by coolies employed in what was for them the spiritually disturbing task of relocating the graves at what was no doubt considerable expense for our government. In this camp and Hostel #5 our fellows were to start what was to be a long association with members of other American Y-Force units.

Because of the small number of Americans in China in late 1943, hostel food, which included fresh eggs, cooked to order . . . . was a big improvement over the "corned willy" and luncheon meat (Spam) being served back in Ledo. Housing consisted of the classic double-roofed English tents, with charcoal-burning stoves attended to by Chinese houseboys. Toilets were outdoors and, although newly constructed for the U.S. troops, were still of the old "backhouse" vintage. Washrooms were provided along with a firm warning that the water was for bathing only and definitely not for drinking.

The boys soon learned that the latter was called "lin KA-EE shway EE" or "cooled, boiled water" and if they wanted more bread at mealtime it answered to the name "M YAN! BA-OO", which sounded like "me an bow". Cigarettes sounded something like "cheyenne" and matches "yong foo". It is some source of wonder to me that most of us who spent more than a year in China did not jump at the opportunity to take advantage of this unique and certainly inexpensive chance to learn the language. There were only a few who did . . . two who became fluent in spoken Chinese were Hugh "Hoot" Gibson from Asheville, N.C. and Millard "Jesse" Owens from Burlington, N.J.

Work for most of the team was conducted in a signal repair shop at a compound several miles from Hostel 4. On their first morning in this strange, remote country, the Mc Veigh team piled into their trucks and headed east for about two miles and then proceeded north at a "T" in the road for several hundred yards to a cluster of three compounds. These straddled the road . . . a Quartermaster facility on the left and Ordnance and Signal functions assigned to two on the right. Here again our compatriots found that they would be neighbors with their new associates from Hostel 4 and 5, from the Ordnance and Quartermaster units, who operated the first two compounds.

For radio repairman Weeks Andrews, Tarboro, N.C., his arrival at the signal compound was a reunion of sorts. Here he found many friends he had made from one of the "800" battalions, while taking a special course at Camp Crowder. Weeks was one of several who stayed behind when the rest of the company went to California to play "Lawrence of Arabia" in the Mojave Desert.

This twice-a-day round trip to and from the compounds was an eye-opening ritual. It took the newcomers past the mud brick hovels of the rice farmers, affording the men a bird's eye view of the early morning life of the peasants. On several occasions, huge flocks of ducks, geese and turkeys, and herds of hogs and cattle being driven toward Kunming delayed the trucks. These small seas of livestock sometimes extended for a good-sized city block . . . . and as we were all to learn, eventually, the Chinese driving them demonstrated, often in a most frustrating way their total disdain for time.

As the Mc Veigh gang took stock of their new workplace and prepared to assume their signal repair roles, a C87 (converted B24 Bomber) bearing their compatriots from the Swanson Fourth Team was in its final approach to the airfield. In a matter of minutes it had landed and deposited our stalwarts safe and sound on the tarmac. They did not get much farther, however, when they received a very dramatic demonstration of how life was going to be for the next five months. Somewhere between the airfield and Hostel 4 they were informed that a three-ball air raid alert was in effect and they were soon witnessing the spine-tingling spectacle of an actual Japanese raid on the airfield. Their introduction to the unimaginable uniqueness of China had begun.

With the scarcity of communications in the interior of the country, a simple but effective system for informing the populace of the air activities of their unwelcome visitors from Japan had been devised. Using a mysterious, cross-country signaling technique, when word was passed that Japanese planes had taken off from any of their fields and were headed inland for, what was assumed to be a raid, those villages and military outposts in their path immediately hoisted a large red ball, similar to a Chinese lantern to the top of a centrally-located pole. When it was determined further that the intruders were within about ten minutes of any of these locations, a second ball was hoisted, signifying that a two-ball condition existed. When the warning pole displayed a third red ball, good sense dictated that one had better be en-route to or already securely settled in some form of shelter, if one could be found.

This native-operated system was as mysterious . . . even spooky . . . as it was effective and the boys soon found out that the Chinese always knew of impending trouble before it was officially reported. When the Chinese started running our people knew it was time to do likewise.

While the aforementioned bombing raid was surprising the Swanson group en-route from the airfield to Hostel 4, Mc Veigh's gang at the signal compound were hurrying to nearby slit trenches. Some of their number, however, who were still at Hostel 5, and uncomfortably close to the airfield, did not know where to go. They sought what little shelter they could amongst the grave mounds that bordered the hostel. Willis Dengler and Milton Mac Donald, from Waterloo, IA and Chattanooga, TN, respectively, were less fortunate than those who fled to the graveyard. When the Japanese bombing and strafing attack descended on them, their closest refuge was a handy rice paddy, into which they unceremoniously dove. "Any port in a storm", may have a popular romantic literary ring to it, generally. The paddy proved to be anything but that, as it had been recently coated with a generous serving of human manure, which our heroes were obliged to burrow in for the duration of the Japanese air show. Understandably, their popularity rating with their peers, between each other and with themselves plunged to zero when the deadly festivities finally came to and end.

I must remind the reader that the foregoing was the first air raid experience for the 181ST in China. It turned out to be the first of many, often occurring at noontime. Although several individuals were never able to take them in stride, usually taking off for parts unknown at the announcement of a one-ball, anything short of a three-ball eventually became routine for most of the men.

Unfortunately, all of the alerts were not just exercises in the hoisting of red balls to the tops of poles. On December 18th, less than a week after the 181ST made its arrival in China . . . and again on the 22nd, the Japanese hit the airfield and its environs with devastating results. Several bombs landed in the vicinity of Hostel 4, killing a number of Chinese and leaving large craters amongst the surrounding graves, exposing the remains of generations past. Since many of the raids occurred during the daytime, most of the 181ST were at work, away from the hostels. This, however, did not always include truck drivers, who spent much of their time picking up supplies at the field. My guess is that they became quite familiar with where most of the trenches were in their travels between the field and the various Yoke Force storage points.

To the consternation of several of the men from the Mc Veigh Team who lived at Hostel 4, Lt. Swanson insisted on formations for morning muster and again at noontime after lunch. Most of them grudgingly humored him, however, with the marked exception of Jim Hoff, who religiously refused to fall out. With the frequency of the noontime raids by the Japanese, it was inevitable that one would eventually occur during one of the hated formations. This particular raid came uncomfortably close to the hostel and as the men in the formation broke for cover, a shell fragment tore through and shredded the outer layer of Hoff's tent. He was not only observed exiting in an unceremonious manner, and scrambling for cover while chomping down on a Sherlock Holmes-type pipe that he had become identified with, but from then on he was also seen as a regular participant in the lieutenant's formations.

For the newcomers, the raids were understandably quite traumatic, putting the fear of God into more than one of them. Charlie Boyd told of the Japanese planes coming in from East Mountain and swinging over the field and Battle Brown, Raleigh, N.C. remembered that sometime, after passing over the field, they came directly over the compound.

During one raid Millard Sturgell, from Portage, Ind. and the Mc Veigh Team, who was down at Hostel 5 and just off the end of the runway the Japanese were aiming at, managed to find an underground bunker. He described the 14TH Air Force as having exacted a grim toll from the foolhardy Japanese during one of the raids. Like any full-blooded radio repairman, however, he also managed to get a look at a radio from one of the downed bombers.

Ray Fichter, also from the Swanson Team, who had been pressed into the job of operating a switchboard for a Communication Unit within walking distance of Hostel 4, sat out the raids in a nearby slit trench. An officer maintained contact, there, with the telephone network via a field set patched into the switchboard over a length of wire strung to the trench.

The December 22nd raid was particularly punishing for the Japanese, however, who lost so many planes that day that, as Weeks Andrews, from the Mc Veigh contingent and Tarboro, N.C. declared, "They didn't bother to come back again." He had waited out that raid at the slit trench near the signal compound.

Having finally received the green light from Mountbatten, Yoke Force Commander Brigadier General Frank Dorn's operation staff at Hostel 1, north of Kunming, started to position its resources for the upcoming 1944 spring offensive. Communications between the forward bases at Yunnanyi and Paoshan had to be improved. Also a game plan for providing radio contact with and between the American liaison teams assigned to front line Chinese units had to be implemented. Charlie Boyd, from Detroit, recalled that some of the team, including Horace "Pappy" Gooding, (Williamston, N.C.), Stanley Greggo (Steubenville, Ohio), Clyde Oie (Ironwood, Mich.), Frank Downing, (Kansas City, Mo.)_ and Ray Fichter, (Palmyra, N.J.) were busy equipping Y-Force officers' jeeps with BC 610 radios. To accomplish this our fellows had to develop a way to modify the radio power units to work with the jeep batteries.

Having only a few vehicles of their own, some of the teams' drivers, among them Henry "Shot" Howell, (Gatesville, N.C.) and Duncan "Hamp" Mc Bride, (Asheboro, N.C.) were assigned to a Y Force motor pool, which had the responsibility for directing the transfer, by coolies, of signal supplies from the arriving ATC planes to trucks for delivery to warehouses before trans-shipment to the forward bases. Howell also won the job of driving a 6X6 truck, which had been converted to carry men on passes to and from Kunming.

But since the entire Yoke Force American contingent in all of China numbered only several hundred, everyone in it learned to pitch in on tasks not even remotely related to the parent unit's job description. A classic and most sacrilegious example of this occurred when Lt. Swanson magnanimously "volunteered" his and some of the Mc Veigh Team to oversee the transfer of hundreds of cases of Chinese rifle ammunition from the airfield to the signal compound on Christmas Day. Maybe he failed to inform them that, because of the level of Japanese air activity, a decision had been made that it was imperative that the airfield be cleared of this volatile cargo.

This decision by the lieutenant along with others, such as his insistence on twice-daily formations did nothing to salvage a rapidly disappearing level of affection held for him by the men. None of the other Yoke organizations operating at the compounds were being subjected to similar treatment and many of the men felt they were inappropriate in what was considered to be a combat area.

All was not air raids and grunt work, however, and our heroes were soon infiltrating all of the mysterious conclaves of Kunming, with the exception, of course, of "Dragon Cloud's" inner city fortress. They found out where to change American money called "gold" into Chinese yuan at the black market rate of 180 to 1 instead of the official rate of 30 to 1. They sampled the fare of every restaurant and attended the local movie house, where the American films were in Chinese with English subtitles. Some of the indomitable ones, of course, explored and sampled the attractions in the "off limits" district, returning with tales of experiences that outdid those of "Terry and the Pirates".

About a week after arriving, Bob Gunning and Sam Corritore decided to try some Chinese food. Picking up the menu, however, they found that western-style food was also served . . . and . . . opted for an order of spaghetti and meatballs. When it was discovered that these came with chopsticks instead of knives and forks, the boys took a chopstick in each hand and proceeded to wind the noodles on each one, guiding the food to their mouths by bringing the two points together. Suddenly they heard a shout and instantly had an audience of Chinese who were greatly amused by the unorthodox eating habits of the strange foreigners. The activity in the restaurant soon reached the street people who promptly streamed in to join in the observance of the interesting phenomenon.

Another group, which included Alton Croom, Ray Fichter, Roy W. Murphy, (Clymer, N.Y.) and John Nicholl, (Atlantic City, N.J.) made a short trip to see the nearby, lakeside home of General Stilwell. The outing was, for Murphy, one of the few times he managed to enjoy his time in Kunming. Most of it, unfortunately, was taken up by repeated stays at the hospital located east of the Kunming airfield, fighting off an extremely tenacious case of ameobic dysentery.

The abject living conditions of the Chinese masses, whether in the rice paddies or in Kunming itself, were not lost on these newcomers from the outside. They were struck by the meager diet of steamed rice and any little tidbit that could be found to give it flavor, even if it came from dogs or cats, which, it was discovered, were considered special delicacies. Our friends found the custom of splitting the rear seams of Chinese toddlers' britches as an alternative to the custom back home of employing diapers, to be quite novel and rather humorous. All in all, they discovered each day that their long odyssey, which started in Camp Crowder had finally brought them to the other end of the world.

An alternative to diapers

This region in China was almost devoid of trees and appeared to have been so for centuries. With lumber and other modern building materials being at a premium, the Chinese had learned to do with what was on hand. In constructing the compounds they had utilized bricks made of clay and straw. Each compound had warehouse-like buildings at the corners with additional buildings in between, all serving to form a large portion of the exterior walls. While this was expeditious as far as construction was concerned, it added a disturbing dimension to providing security at night. Although the clay brick walls, which were protected on top with picturesque curved waterproof tiles, appeared to have been able to withstand the ravages of weather for generations, a popular estimate among the Americans who guarded them was that a hard-working sneak thief could dig through a wall in eight minutes. On several occasions, it was discovered that one of the buildings had been entered by this method without the man on guard even suspecting that it was occurring.

In addition to the QM, Signal and Ordnance Compounds, "Y" Force operated at least one other, plus an ammunition dump several miles farther along the Burma Road. Guard duty, therefore, dictated that those in the "Y" Force contingent could be assigned to guard any one of these facilities rather than just the one in which they conducted business.

Lt. Swanson in the YOKE FORCE
Signal Compound

Drawing guard duty one night, our colorful associate, Fred Linton, now famous or infamous for his antics in the "States", was assigned to the standard two tours of "two hours on and four hours off at the Quartermaster Compound. This facility was the repository for a wide variety of supply items not specifically designated for signal or ordnance use. Among these were several dozen fifty-gallon drums containing gasoline and other fluids. Although the winters at the 6000 foot altitude of the plateau upon which Kunming was located did not reach severe below-freezing temperatures very often, there was still enough of a change between day an night to cause the drums to heat up during the day and expand, causing the tops to bulge outward with a resounding bang. Of course the process was reversed during the night as the temperature dropped, causing the same tops to contract . . . also with a loud bang.

Linton was dropped off at the compound by the "Corporal of the Guard's" vehicle and left to his own devices to patrol the inside of his post. It is not known whether it was during the first or second of his tours that the temperature finally dropped sufficiently to do its thing with the drums, but when it did, the results were spectacular. In this strange land only a week or so and after having been warned of the possibility of a visit from either saboteurs or black-marketer sneak-thieves, our hero was, no doubt, on edge and certainly apprehensive of what to anticipate on this first guard duty overseas with live ammunition. As the reader has, by now, deduced, the sound of the first drum expanding released all of his pent-up anxiety. Certain that someone had leaped from the compound wall onto one of the drums, Linton wheeled about and, as he did triggered the Thompson sub-machinegun he carried, spraying the area from which the loud bang had come. There is no report, now, of what damage, if any he wrought to the compound wall or to other materiel in his line of fire. We do know that, fortunately, he did not hit any of the gasoline drums or mortar shells purportedly stored in the compound.

Approximately six months later I was to share the same

assignment and under identical conditions. Linton's story could just as easily have been my own, except that when I wheeled about to face my imaginary adversary, I managed to marshal up just enough self-control to hold my fire.

For his lethal outburst Linton was scheduled to be court-martialed and was immediately confined to quarters. There is no record available of his eventual punishment, if any. An interesting sequel to his story; however, was told by Alton Croom from the 4TH Team and Robersonville, N.C., who, while guarding Fred and his weapon, made an error in judgment by allowing a sergeant, and no doubt one of Fred's drinking buddies, access to the sub-machinegun. It was later discovered that the firing mechanism had been filed down to make it appear that the outburst at the compound had been accidental. Fortunately for Croom, no charges were made against him and Linton soon disappeared down the road to Yunnanyi.

Shortly after their arrival in Kunming, the teams were invited to receive a personal welcome from the Generalissimo and Madame Chiang Kai Shek, who also translated her husband's words. Those men who were able to attend were given 1944 diaries as gifts, consistent with the Christmas season, which was upon them. I do not have the literal translation of what Chiang had to say . . . . but according to Charlie Boyd, a tech sergeant who headed up one of the radio repair squads, a Chinese standing nearby gave his own version of the talk, indicating that Chiang had spoken of his dislike for the British and of how he was using the Americans to obtain his own goals. This, of course, is what Charlie recalled of the incident and also that he was quite irritated by what he heard. Two known copies of these valuable diaries have survived and have been essential to the unraveling of the 181ST Salween story.

On Christmas some of the fellows attended a dinner party hosted by General Dorn at Y-Force Operating Staff (YFOS) Headquarters in Hostel 1. A very pleasant change of pace between the experiences of arriving in the CBI and those that were about to occur, the event enjoys a favorable place in the memories of those who attended. In contrast New Year's celebrations were a far cry from those normally held back in the USA. While some toasted 1944 with a bottle of wine at dinner in Kunming, others welcomed it in back at camp. One of these was Forrest Brown, from Independence, Mo. who described it as being, "The quietest spent in many a year."

Before 1943 passed into history, however, the forces that seemed bent on the dispersal of the 181 ST struck the newcomers. With the limited number of American ground troops in China at that time, those with particular skills were fair game for anyone in need of those talents. Soon after their arrival, our heroes, all of whom were now attached to YOKE Force, lined up to be photographed. The officer in charge of the process, being quite shorthanded, discovered that two of our stalwarts Pierson Roe (Phillipsburg, NJ) and Vincent William Wilkerson (Magnolia, NJ) had photo experience and soon had them working for him. What started as a temporary assignment with an ad hoc detail eventually became permanent when a photo company was activated and the two men were transferred out of the 181 ST.

## YOKE FORCE

By New Years day, the Second Team's time in Kunming had just about run out. The need for the upgrading and, in some cases the installation of communications from Kunming to the west were crying for attention. The 181ST had bought the assignment of helping to meet these needs . . . thus . . . the wild, rugged expanses of southwestern Yunnan, boasting only a slim semblance of a passable roadway system were beckoning to our apprehensive heroes.

One of the first to heed the call was T/3 Forrest Brown. He and two others, radio repairmen Jim Hoff (Palmyra, N.J.) and Bob Gallagher (Revere, Mass.) were informed that they would be assigned to a Y Force liaison team, which would assist the Chinese

53RD Army. What proved to be the start of a major escalation of the dispersal of the 181ST began with Brown leaving, alone for the west.

On January 3rd, he was ordered to Yunnanyi, 327 kilometers west of Kunming and the other side of Tienatze Miao Po, elevation 9200 feet, the highest point on the Burma Road. Host to a fighter unit of the 14TH Air Force Flying Tigers, Yunnanyi had been designated as a supply point for the Salween campaign. As such it was undergoing a substantial facelift, with which its communications capabilities had to keep pace.

Forrest was one of the physically toughest members of the company . . . so much so that he was often called "Bad Boy Brown". Although most of the company knew him by this nickname, only his closest friends dared to use it when addressing him face to face. I mention this brief characterization of him so that the reader will appreciate the amount of understatement he employed in some of the entries in the diary, which he had received from Madame Chiang. A classic example is his fourth entry, dated January 4, 1944 in which he described his trip down the Burma Road in an old truck and through some of the most spectacular mountain terrain in the world. His terse comments, "Was very glad to get here. Had a swell trip though (it) was a little cold . . ." tell much about a man who was short on words but very long on action.

The trip took the better part of two days and after getting situated and receiving his first mail while in China (18 letters and a Christmas package), he reported to the Y Force Signal office and was assigned work in, what was designated the "A" Area near Yunnanyi. By January 8th, he was climbing poles, a feat passed over very quickly in the telephone repair course back in Camp Crowder. Here again he recorded in his diary that he had fallen from the poles several times, " . . . but didn't hurt myself". His departure from the finite job description he had garnered back in telephone school and the adjustment to the Y Force concept that . . . if you do not do it yourself, it will probably not get done . . . had begun. Some of this had started back in

Kunming but it was to become standard operating procedure for everyone who followed Brown down the Road.

With the 4TH Team taking over the operation of the repair shop in Kunming, the 2ND was being rapidly assigned jobs by Y Force, either individually or in small groups. Whether repairmen or truck drivers, they, like Forrest Brown were quickly pressed into service by YOKE, with some becoming involved in stringing wire on the Road west of Kunming. This assignment was short-lived, when; on January 2, 1944 all of the members of the 2ND Team remaining in Kunming were ordered to relocate to Hostel 1. There they were the recipients of a morale-boosting snack party, hosted by the Yoke Force Operations Staff (YFOS) Headquarters contingent.

During the following week they devoted all of their time to preparing themselves and their trucks for the repair role they were about to embark on and the two days it would take their convoy to reach their next "home-away-from-home" . . . . Yunnanyi. On January 13th the entire team left Hostel 1 and after the better part of two days, during which they negotiated the same treacherous mountain road that Brown had traveled eleven days earlier, joined him at a tent camp near the old "Flying Tigers" barracks at the 14TH Air Force Base. Weeks Andrews recalled that during the trip he shared the back of a truck with Kermit Clark from Asheboro, N.C. and four other fellows and that it was a cold, uncomfortable ride.

This camp at Yunnanyi turned out to be an interim stop on their way to their permanent quarters and repair shop. During the several weeks that they spent near the airstrip, however, they managed to find use for their many talents. These were offered to the Air Force, who had some test equipment that was in need of doctoring. MIllard Sturgell recalled that they also breathed new life into a large battery-charger at the base maintenance shop.

In the meantime Brown, who had been holding down the fort learned that Clint Harwood, from Grand Rapids, Mich. was in the army hospital in Yunnanyi. A trip to deliver Clint's mail gave him a chance to see a familiar face, while rendering him a good turn.

But Brown was closer to the war than the new arrivals and as they were settling into their tent quarters, he was already making his contribution to the upgrading of Yunnanyi, while at the same time preparing for his role with the Chinese. During the weeks that followed he split his time between attending briefings on the British Bren machinegun, a standard weapon of the Chinese armies and the familiar Thompson sub-machinegun . . . . getting his truck in good running order and equipped for his up-coming assignment . . . . and . . . . continuing his bouts with the pole lines around Yunnanyi. On January 19th he attended a YFOS meeting and received a visit from General Dorn.

Two days later his partners-to-be in the pending adventures with the Chinese 53RD Army, Jim Hoff and Bob Gallagher arrived from Kunming. A brief insight into the stark primitiveness of the lifestyle he was preparing for is evident in that he considered the following as worth entering in his diary, "Rec. pkg. of candles from Major Ray (YFOS) for work done while a(t) Yunnanyi." That same day the three-man team packed for a trip they were to make the following day to Mitu (Midu) about 50 km southwest of Yunnanyi, where the 53RD Army was in the process of staging for the impending Salween offensive.

The trip to Mitu, while uneventful as far as creature comforts and vehicle performance was concerned was, nevertheless, another breathtaking experience with the rugged, lofty vastness of the forbidding world they were entering . . . . a world which, they had been told was the stomping grounds for fast-hitting, merciless Chinese bandits. They arrived without incident, however, and after reporting to the headquarters of the YFOS liaison mission and meeting their interpreter, Joe Lynn and a Captain Sweet, were informed that they had arrived just in time to pull guard duty that evening.

For the remainder of January and through February our trio made several jaunts to outlying Chinese units over what passed as roads, often transformed into quagmires. On one of the first of these they spent a very apprehensive night on the road in the rain when their truck nestled unflinchingly into a ditch. Coolies were dispatched to relieve them of their cargo and the following day they managed to find their way back to Mitu. The episode cost them the services of Hoff, who became so ill he had to be hospitalized for several weeks.

During February they also attended regular Chinese language classes, learned to eat with chopsticks, repaired signal equipment as required and became convinced that they and the other enlisted men with YOKE were never going to defeat the officers at volleyball. Mitu was a very remote location, with little to offer in the way of recreation. During one of their visits to town, Gallagher discovered a vender selling boxes of wooden matches that sold back home for a penny each but which he considered a real find at 300 CN (yuan) for ten boxes.

February was also the month during which Mc Veigh and his team, under the command of Tech Sergeant Gil Carlson (Falconer, N.Y.) finally moved about a mile into permanent quarters located in a large compound with several other Y Force units. In addition to quarters, the compound, which was a good hike from the town, was also home to their repair shop and mess hall.

Since Y Force did not have the luxury of receiving its rations from a central supply point, the unit had to fend for it self, purchasing food locally. Each individual had to use his own money and was eventually reimbursed by the army. Each was allowed $3 per day (per diem), which hopefully covered what he had already paid out of his own pocket. The scheme used by the Mc Veigh contingent was to pool all of their per diem and designate one of their own as mess sergeant and master shopper. This task fell to Morris Malinkowitz from Brooklyn, N.Y. In recalling their days in Yunnanyi, several of the 2ND Team made it a point to mention that "Morrie", who was not averse to trying his hand at the various games of chance the boys entertained themselves with, won more than the average . . . . often by dint of the fact that he had the biggest bankroll to support himself.

· · · ·

The team soon discovered that they were thoroughly involved in the YFOS task of converting what had been primarily a 14TH AF fighter base into a major supply terminus. Handling supplies was a big part of that task, much of which fell to truck drivers like Fred Linton, "Hamp" Mc Bride, Henry "Shot" Howell and Deward "D.B." Russell from Dallas Texas. Anyone who has seen photos of or actually traveled the stretches of the Burma Road between Yunnayi, Paoshan, Mitu, Shiakwan and the other towns, which were strung like beads along its snakelike path, can appreciate the skill and nerves required to negotiate its deadly curves and grades on a daily basis and in dry or wet weather.

In addition to taking their turns at driving, "Hamp" Mc Bride and "Shot" Howell shared living quarters in a small shack from which they maintained power generators that supplied 110 AC voltage to the area. When called on, they also repaired similar units for other organizations in the Yunnanyi vicinity.

. . . .

Since the team's primary assignment was signal repair, it plunged quickly into the business of servicing the local army units around Yunnanyi, testing newly-arriving equipment and readying it for use in the field. As had been discovered by their counterparts who were now scattered throughout the CBI, Mc Veigh's repairmen found that the variety of jobs they received required that they become general electronic practitioners. They also found out that much of their work was at their clients' locations, necessitating that they make some pretty remote and extended house calls.

. . . .

Millard Sturgell, who had received electronic training at the University of Kentucky prior to enlisting in the army and then attended radio classes at Camp Crowder, was called out on many such missions . . . oftentimes without getting time to catch up on some much-needed sleep. One such summons took him for a period of two or three weeks to repair and calibrate transmitter/receivers for an artillery battery, which was in position to fire across the Salween. He managed very little sleep during the roundtrip between Yunnanyi and YFOS Headquarters, over 250 miles, and the assignment took its toll on Millard's slight 135-pound frame. What he needed desperately and which, on his return, he did not waste any time in taking advantage of was a chance to finally put in some serious sack time.

But it wasn't to be . . . he had just closed his eyes when he was awakened by a captain from YFOS who apologized for breaking into Millard's much-needed slumber. The officer explained that his counterparts at a Chinese army headquarters in the town of Yungchang, west of Yunnanyi, had reported that a transmitter had just quit on them and had to be replaced as soon as possible. The countdown to the kickoff of the Salween offensive had started and the liaison team had lost all means of radio contact with Kunming.

Our hero gathered up his tools and joined a supply sergeant who had drawn a replacement unit. Although the trip was not a long one, the mission turned out to be one of Sturgell's most difficult ones. When he arrived, a corporal from the liaison team, probably the operator, was trying desperately to get the set working but without any luck. As our repairmen had all come to expect, the replacement unit was not identical to the original. Struggling with his terrible need for sleep, Sturgell was ready to throw in the towel after discovering that the cable to the power unit was not long enough. Scavenging frantically to find enough wire with which to meet their needs, he and his companion finally got the new transmitter/receiver fired up and calibrated. They then made their connection to the antenna, tried to transmit and failed completely. At this point the American colonel in charge of the liaison team went into a minor fit of exasperation mixed with anger. Sturgell, now totally exhausted, hurriedly explained that he was confident that there was nothing seriously wrong but that unless he got some kind of rest, he doubted whether he would be able to find their trouble. Somehow logic prevailed and the good colonel backed off. The sudden lifting of the murderous pressure both he and the corporal had been under immediately caused a light to go on in both of their minds and they blurted out, almost simultaneously, that they must have reversed the polarity to the antenna. The change was quickly made and Yungchang was back on the air. To the colonel's credit . . . he apologized to Millard for his behavior under fire, whereupon our diminutive hero quickly assured him that, having spent most of his recent career putting out similar fires throughout the Salween area, he understood, as much as the colonel did, the importance of maintaining radio contact.

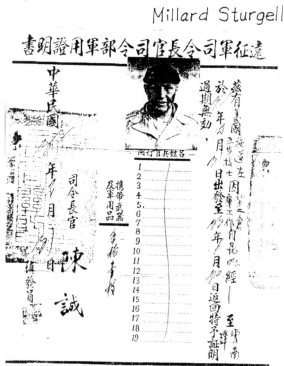

CHINESE GOVERNMENT PASSPORT – IDENTIFIES THE BEARER AND INCLUDES REWARD FOR AIDING HIM – ALSO A PERMIT TO CARRY A WEAPON

Sturgell's Chinese Passport

The demand for repair service continued relentlessly, with word being received that the transmitter at the air base weather station was ailing and again Sturgell won the job. Accompanying Lt. Mc Veigh, he once again demonstrated his talent, getting the weather station back on the air.

There was no let up in the variety of tasks required of the 2ND. Among these was the responsibility for instructing Chinese in repairing radios. Six or seven kits were assembled, calibrated under the leadership of Morris Stern (Neptune, N.J.) who held an amateur operator's license in the "States" and distributed as needed.

Fascination with Army Air Force electronic scrap apparently was universal with the 181ST. The 2ND was no exception, making a trip to a downed plane and salvaging such a treasure of wire, relays and insulating material that they could not carry all of it back to the repair shop. Like all of the other Teams, they also devised a machine for rewinding power transformers.

Although these were busy times for the 2ND, they were certainly in touch with what was happening around them. While Yunnanyi was no Kunming, it offered enough diversion to interrupt the Team's preoccupation with the upcoming Salween fireworks. Like everyone in China the team put up a volleyball net and before the campaign got going took its turn on the firing range.

There was a bit of excitement shortly after the 2nd Team settled into their permanent home at the compound when a B29, which had lost an engine, made an emergency landing at the 14AF Base. It remained for many months until the runway was lengthened and a replacement motor found its niche on the viciously fought-over Hump tonnage priority list.

· · · ·

As the 2ND assumed their multi-faceted role in Yunnanyi, bringing the repair shop on line and receiving their Chinese Army assignments, the 4TH was doing their thing back in

Kunming. The double duty of repair and supply responsibilities of the Team, along with the endless transportation chores for which its drivers were volunteered guaranteed them a full measure of job security.

Like their contemporaries in India and Burma, they learned all too quickly the deplorable supply conditions accruing to the C.B.I. as a result of its lowly position on the War Department's priority list. It is ironic that the many otherwise unnecessary tasks that were presented to the Team by the shabbiness of the supply effort for China were described by some of the members as "routine" . . . another testimony to the "can do" attitude of the American G.I. One such "routine" task, assigned to Bob Gunning, a radio repairman from Wendel, Idaho, was the winding of plate coils for Collins radio transmitters, which were shipped minus same. Bob recalled that, "This job took much experimenting with the correct number of turns and spacing them, from No. 8 copper wire, intended for telephone lines." This laborious improvisation was finally abandoned when it was discovered that with some adjustments and modifications with plexi glass and the use of banana plugs, the spare-parts plate coils for the V-100 radio transmitters, made for the Chinese Army by Pilot Radio Corporation of N.Y. could be made to work with the Collins unit.

. . . .

Of course the Japanese air force had not forgotten that Kunming was becoming a real challenge to their imperial appetites and continued their bombing runs aimed at the airfield. Signal repair activity was interrupted frequently with two-ball alerts, forcing our heroes to take cover in the slit trenches on a nearby hillside. Gunning recalled that about the middle of February a large V formation of bombers, accompanied by a "swarm" of zeroes appeared from the southeast. Bob remembered that the concussions from the exploding bombs "knocked us against the sides of the slit-trenches." The attack wreaked havoc in the vicinity of Hostel 4, leaving gaping craters in the countryside and taking a grim toll of the native population. Bob also recalled that the shrapnel-ridden bodies of the coolies remained for a long time before being finally picked up and laid to rest with their surrounding ancestors.

This air raid brought with it more than the usual degree of apprehension experienced during earlier events, since it followed on the heels of a paratrooper alert, which was prolonged from February 10th through the 15th. News of an anticipated visit by Japanese paratroopers triggered a feverish reaction by the Team. Hurrying out to the repair compound, where radios were still being installed in jeeps, our heroes were issued live ammunition and given hasty instructions on how to emulate the actions of the gallant defenders of the Alamo in the event that the alert turned out to be the real thing.

Alton Croom recorded in the diary he had received from Madame Chiang, " . . . . Everyone had (their) gun(s) loaded and waiting. I was a walking arsenal with so much ammunition and guns." Needless to say confusion reigned supreme and reached its zenith when Dan Russo from New York City, in loading his rifle, managed to blow a hole in the repair shop roof. The ensuing air raid was so devastating, however, that it kept the Team's attention diverted from any thoughts and apprehensions that had been generated by the paratrooper alert.

. . . .

March of 1944 was one of those pivotal months during which the fortunes of the 181ST changed direction, reflecting the historical events that were occurring. In India Generals Slim and Stilwell met to develop a game plan for thwarting the Japanese invasion of Southern Assam . . . . a threat that brought Robb's 5TH Team face-to-face with the realities of the war. John Banks' squad from Wilson's 3RD Team was poised in Shingbwiyang, within earshot of the big guns that were pounding the Japanese at Maingkwan. The remaining members of the 3RD, under the direction of Lt. G. Holmes Wilson and Tech Sgt. Willis Nichols were whipping their repair shop, back in Ledo, into a facility which they knew would have to respond to the signal and electronic servicing needs of everyone in that area and along the Road to Shingbwiyang. As we just discussed, Mc Veigh's 2ND Team was settling into their role in Yunnanyi and . . . in Kunming . . . Swanson's 4TH, while operating a brisk Y-Force supply and repair business, was readying itself for its upcoming role in the Salween campaign.

The already unpopular lieutenant, on March 9th, added yet another provocation, although an obviously necessary one, to the Team's list of real or imagined grievances against him, by calling for a surprise shakedown inspection. The rationale for the lieutenant's order became coldly evident when, on March 24th, as recorded by Alton Croom in his diary, the word was out that the Team was about to leave Kunming.

On March 13th the folks at C.B.I. Headquarters, gambling on the Chinese crossing the Salween, ordered Silverman's 1ST Team (this writer included) to China to take over the 4th Team's YFOS responsibility. By the 23rd we were in Chabua waiting our turn at clearing the "Hump".

. . . .

President Roosevelt, however, was not convinced that Chiang would indeed turn the YOKE FORCE loose as promised. After Chiang's performance in Cairo in November 1943, FDR had finally become more realistic in estimating Chinese military effectiveness. The August 1943 Quebec Conference had revealed also that Chennault's boast that he could beat the Japanese by air power alone was not possible, particularly with the limitations of supplying it via the "Hump". The only practical course of action, still limited by the logistical needs in Europe and the Pacific, was to complete the Ledo Road to China.

This was Stilwell's baby and he was "off and running" against the Japanese 18th Division in Northern Burma. Its successful completion, however, depended on the start of the Salween offensive. Here too FDR made an about face, finally supporting Stilwell's oft-repeated contention that Chiang needed a push. Thus in a heretofore unprecedented move, FDR on April 3rd sent a message to the Generalissimo informing him that, inasmuch as the British were taking on a most formidable Japanese force which was threatening the Assam supply line . . . . and with the initial successes of the Chinese and Americans in Northern Burma, it was inconceivable that Chiang was reluctant to commit two entire group armies (12 divisions) against the watered-down Japanese 56TH Division that was holding a thin line, blocking the Burma Road west of the Salween.

FDR's radio message also informed Chiang that if YOKE, which was American-supported was not to be deployed, it was illogical, then, to continue to supply it with critical Hump tonnage. The April 3rd message, unfortunately, was delivered to Madame Chiang, who elected not to let her husband see it. When the Americans heard this, General Marshall directed General Hearn, acting for Stilwell, to propose transferring YOKE's April Hump allocation to the 14th Air Force. When word of Hearn's plan reached Chungking, General Ho Ling-chin, the Chinese National War Minister and number one contributor to Stilwell's "manure pile", after a hasty conference with Chiang, formally approved the go-ahead for the Salween crossing. An interesting aside for the reader . . . in issuing his proclamation on April 14th, the slippery Ho also announced that the Chinese government was not responding to pressure but was making the decision entirely on its own.

. . . .

One point should be raised, however, in defense of the Chinese reluctance. As Stilwell had predicted in the spring of 1943, the Japanese had decided to send their response to Chennault's escalation of his air attacks on their shipping and communication facilities in eastern China. On April 17th, as we stood poised to cross the Salween, the Japanese crossed the Yellow River in Honan Province. Two days later two of their divisions started a drive southward along the Peiping-Hankow railroad . . . . their ultimate goal . . . . Chennault's East-China air bases. Posing a real threat to Chiang's armies positioned along the railroad corridor, the Japanese drive was of grave concern to him, and, I believe, gave him the first valid reason for not wanting to open a second front in southwestern Yunnan at that time. FDR's message and the threat to divert Hump tonnage, nevertheless, convinced him that he could not afford to delay the Salween campaign any longer. Although much valuable time had been lost due to his foot-dragging . . . . and even with the start of the spring monsoon too close for comfort . . . the stage was finally set for the much-delayed Salween Offensive.

On April 29th, only two weeks before the Salween D-Day, Brigadier General Frank (Pinky) Dorn established field headquarters for his American Y-Force Operations Staff (YFOS) at Paoshan. Quite logically it was near the headquarters of the Chinese Expeditionary Force (CEF) commanded by General Wei Li-huang. In outlining the American liaison role, Wei made it clear that we had no command power over the Chinese. YFOS was to (1) assist in training, (2) assist in supply, (3) perform its own administration, (4) exchange intelligence with the Chinese, (5) furnish air-ground liaison and (6) report to the CEF the conditions and needs of the frontline Chinese troops. The Americans would also operate portable-surgical field hospitals, man anti-aircraft batteries at bridges and airfields, provide aerial photo-maps and train and rehearse the Chinese troops in rubber-boat ferrying on the Mekong River.

The American liaison teams, some of which were already with their Chinese units, were to vary in size from six to twenty men. They would include infantry, artillery, engineering, ordnance, signal, quartermaster and veterinary personnel. Since the 181ST would be supplying many of the signal people on these teams and would be necessarily scattered throughout the Salween offensive area, the liaison structure was automatically a blueprint for the further breakup of our repair family.

In the process of taking inventory of the units, which would be supporting the Salween offensive, Dorn elected to visit the 181ST's 2ND Team repair shop in Yunnanyi. Millard Sturgell recalled with much pride that the general was visibly surprised at the wealth of talent and repair potential he found among the men of the 2ND and was obviously satisfied at the answers he received to all of his questions.

. . . .

While Washington was putting the heat on Chungking and General Ho was preparing his boss for the inevitability of releasing the Salween Armies, Lt. Bernard Silverman's 1ST Team flew the "Hump" to Kunming. Before dawn on Easter Monday, April 10th, we packed our gear . . . and . . . after what seemed like hours, received the word to "move out". A short trip by truck and we were deposited next to a runway. But things were not to change for us . . . as we were then informed that the C46, which was to take us to China, had a flat tire. In due time we did finally clamber aboard, after being fitted for parachutes and after receiving a short briefing on how to exit the plane should the need arise. The ensuing three-hour flight, while bitterly cold, was uneventful and we soon smelled the potent aroma of China and watched the same coolies pulling the same gigantic rollers over the repairs being made to Chennault's airstrips.

Like the two teams that preceded us, our destination was Hostel 4. By this time, however, barracks had been built to supplement the English tents and I (still a lowly T5) was soon tossing my bedroll onto an upper bunk over one claimed by T4 Charles A. "Willie" Wingler from Champaign-Urbana, Illinois.

Our role, for the moment at least, was to replace Lt. Swanson's 4TH Team at the YFOS Signal Compound. This we proceeded to do, experiencing all of the reactions to China and Kunming that have already been described. The air attacks had abated, however, although we were occasionally treated to a one or two-ball. As our predecessors had done before us, we made the four-a-day truck trips between the compound and the hostel for meals.

During these we were able to view the damage caused by the March air raid described by Bob Gunning. Many of the craters were still unfilled. One of these, which bordered on the road to the compound, held a strange, morbid fascination for some of us. It contained the body of a small pre-school boy. He was crouched with his knees bent under him and his rear end pointed skyward, constituting the highest point of his anatomy. After several days of passing this sobering spectacle, we suspected that he would probably never be accorded the basic decency of a regular burial. Our suspicions were soon confirmed when the pre-monsoon rains began and the crater began to fill with water. Just before the body was completely covered, the only thing still visible was his little bare buttock. If the reader is asking why we did not do what would certainly have been done at home, I can only comment that the enormity of the suffering, death and squalor of the region precluded any such action by the few American troops assigned there. It simply was not our role as guests in the country and largely for religious or political reasons we were advised that it was "none of our business".

During the month of April, some of us had a chance to renew acquaintances with the fellows from the 4TH whom we had not seen for five months. April, however, was also their countdown month prior to their departure for Paoshan. On the 18th Croom was told that he, Aaron "Artie" Dorf (New York City) and Charlie Boyd would be assigned to work with the Chinese 2nd Army. On the 23rd T/3 John Chase, Roy W. Murphy and Willam Floyd Mercer (Whitesburg, Ky) flew to Yunnanyi, continuing by truck to Paoshan. About the same time Tech Sergeant Varner Shippy, the Team's platoon leader, accompanied by Clyde Oie (Ironwood, Michigan), Dan Russo (New York City), Bob Gunning (Wendell, Idaho), Dave Thorn (New York City) and Ray Fichter (Palmyra, N.J.) took the same route to Paoshan, where the 4TH was to assist General Dorn in establishing YFOS Headquarters. Shippy and his charges bedded down overnight in Yunnanyi before continuing by truck to Paoshan.

By May 1st all of the 4th had begun their trek to Paoshan, leaving only John Nicholl from Atlantic City, N.J. behind. John had the unique reputation of being the champion complainer in the 181ST and was often referred to as "The Bitcher". His persistent attempts to gain a transfer out of the 181ST had finally worn Lt. Swanson down and John parted company with the 4TH. Oddly enough, and to the great relief of many on the Team, the lieutenant also failed to join the general exodus, choosing to follow at a later date.

Although we remained organizationally as a complete repair company for four more months, the departure of the 4TH Team completed the final physical dismemberment of the 181ST. From that day on, although we occasionally encountered each other during our individual Odysseys, we were never again assembled as a company entity.

· · · ·

The 4th Team's assignment in Paoshan varied somewhat from that of the 2nd's in Yunnanyi. While the latter location was essentially a supply point for the YOKE Force operations, Paoshan was the nerve center for developing and directing the Chinese and YFOS battle plans. Both Generals Dorn and Wei directed their people from Paoshan.

As a communication hub it was a natural spot for the 4th Team to show off its talents. While one half of the Team received assignments with the Chinese Armies and Divisions, the other half were quickly caught up in the myriad variety of signal activities. The town of Paoshan was surrounded by dozens of compounds, from which the many Chinese and American organizations functioned. These were tied together by a switchboard located away from town in a hut, in which a Chinese-owned British H1 Carrier terminal station was housed. Thorn, Oie, and Bill Mercer (Whitesberg, Ky.) were assigned to operate the switchboard. Gunning bought the job of maintaining the carrier, which was superimposed on a pair of open wires that ran between Paoshan and Hsungyin, near Yunnanyi and from there to Kunming.

· · · ·

Weeks before the 4TH Team left Kunming for Paoshan, down on the Burma Road the momentum had begun to build toward what was now seen as the final start of the oft-discussed Salween Campaign. During the first two weeks of March Forrest Brown left Mitu and rejoined the 2ND at Yunnanyi in their permanent quarters. He joined the Team on the firing range and tried his hand again at pole climbing. After attempting to breathe some life into several Japanese, Chinese and German telephones, but without much success due to lack of replacement parts, he prepared to return to Mitu.

By mid-March he was back in Mitu, where he again jumped in to try to improve, not only the telephone network but also the lifestyle in camp. In addition to assisting the engineers in building a bridge, he spent about a week with them constructing a bamboo pipeline from a spring from which coolies had been carrying water to the mess hall. An example of the high value that was placed on space on the Hump flights appeared in an article in the theater newspaper "China Command Post", which stated that " . . . the "little inch" kept from calling on the "home front" for 600 feet of metal pipe and saved 678 lbs. of cargo space, enough for 7500 rounds of .30 caliber ammunition."

On March 17th, St. Patrick's Day, Brown made his March and April contribution to the American 53RD Army's YFOS ration fund. The following day Lt. Mc Veigh and several of the men from Yunnanyi paid a visit, during which they all took a shot at eating with chopsticks. On the 19th Brown finally received his per diem for the money he had laid out for January and February.

Continuing to exercise his Yankee ingenuity and to demonstrate the YFOS policy which required one to perform tasks well outside of his limited army training, Brown worked on the commanding American colonel's radio and antenna . . . repaired a phonograph used for code classes . . . and helped erect a mess tent and building which was to house the HQ kitchen.

During April he also took his turn in HQ as the CQ (Charge of Quarters) . . . managed to get a much-needed haircut in town . . . viewed a film on malaria control and visited a Chinese carnival at Shiakwan.

On April 24th Jim Hoff, who had become ill when the trio spent the night on a rain-soaked road, returned to Mitu from the hospital. Three days later the trio, Brown, Hoff and Gallagher received their per diem for March and April and settled their mess hall bills. Time for their departure with the 53RD for the Salween had finally arrived.

The last entry in the Brown diary notes that he had visited Battle Brown (Raleigh, N.C.), Frank Mc Craw (Hendersonville, N.C.) and Eddie Vossler (Closter, N.J.) from Lt. Swanson's 4TH Team, who had just arrived from Kunming and had taken over telephone line maintenance between Yunnanyi and Mitu.

In explaining why his diary had stopped at this point, Brown informed me that he had left it behind when the 53RD received their marching orders, since if he had continued to make entries in it, it might have become useful information to the Japanese, were he taken prisoner.

By now several others in the 2ND team had been designated for duty with the Chinese. While some of the survivors remember serving with them, at this late date most of them can no longer recall with which army units they traveled.

One of the groups, however, which would follow the fortunes of the Chinese XI Group Army Headquarters and its 71ST Army, included radio repairmen Weeks Andrews and Harry Gramavot (New York City) and telephone repairmen Tech Sgt. Arley (regular army) Palmer and James Henry Hopper (Somerset, Ky.), who had been my companion on guard during the frigid rail trip from Missouri to California.

In late February Andrews left Yunnanyi for Paoshan, staying in an ordnance compound about ten miles out of town and commanded by a Colonel Svensguarrd. Here Andrews, a radio repairman by army definition demonstrated the depth of his homegrown mechanical ability and his readiness to serve the YOKE cause. The only real artillery possessed by the Chinese was an American 75MM Mountain (pack) Howitzer. It could be disassembled and carried by mules and/or coolies. The desired charge was customized by the operator by his selection of the appropriate number of powder bags. During their training, the Chinese soldiers had developed the habit of using too many powder bags at a single firing, with the resulting explosion invariably shearing off two small bolts in the main housing of the gun, rendering it useless and irreparable in the mountain scenario of Southwestern Yunnan.

When Andrews discovered the Colonel's quandary, he produced a small drill from his "radio" repair box and devised a way of drilling the sheared studs from the gun housing. He then went through the very tedious process of filing the heads from two ordinary stove bolts as replacements for the sheared-off originals. A single test firing of the 75MM confirmed that it was again available for use. Also sharing the compound with Svenguarrd's ordnance unit was a group of engineers who would eventually be formally organized as the Burma Road Engineers.

During the two and a half months he spent in Paoshan Andrews managed to visit Lt. Mc Veigh, leaving right after Lt. Swanson's 4TH Team arrived during the first week of May.

From Paoshan the Andrews contingent made several (almost weekly) repair missions to the town of Shih-tien, home of the Chinese 200th Division, which was held in reserve for supporting either of the Group Armies. Shih-tien also became a major marshalling point from which the XI Group Armies launched their part of the Salween offensive. From there our fellows occasionally traveled down the Road to a point from which they could view the steeply descending, winding grades leading to both sides of the site of the Road's Huei-tung Bridge. Andrews vividly recalled the long lines of burned-out vehicles clogging the Road for almost ten miles on each side . . . useless souvenirs of the retreating Chinese as they destroyed the span in 1942.

Shih-tien, located in the rugged mountains bordering the Salween Gorge, was the terminus for several trails. While servicing their customer allies, the Andrews Team bivouacked in pup tents alongside one of these paths, just as it cleared the crest of a hill. From there they sallied forth in every direction to ply their trade. On one occasion, the day after Tech Sergeant Arley Palmer had returned from a distant telephone repair house call, a small column of bedraggled-looking GI's struggled to the top of the trail, sweating and panting. When they reached a low wall, at a bend in the pathway, they did not waste any time in seizing the opportunity to get off of their feet. Palmer, never known to be short on words looked up and addressing one of the heavy-breathing group, none of whom displayed any rank, queried, "Rough out there, ain't it soldier?" The reply "It sure is sergeant!" came back quickly with much emphasis. Andrews, who was witnessing the conversation suddenly straightened up, when he realized that Palmer was making small talk with the YFOS commander, General Frank "Pinky" Dorn.

By May 1st Swanson's 4TH Team had also received their Yoke Force assignments. For Alton Croom, his separation from the Team and the 181ST started when he reached Yunnanyi. While his companions in the flight from Kunming boarded trucks in the morning for Paoshan, Croom remained behind and by afternoon was in one headed for Mitu instead, arriving just before dusk. There he also met Mc Craw, Battle Brown and Eddie Vossler but Forrest Brown, Hoff and Gallagher had left to join the Chinese 53RD Army en-route to the Salween River. The following morning, May 3rd, Croom boarded a truck, this time for Ch'ang-ning (Shun-ning), across the Mekong River, forty air miles southeast of Paoshan and twenty air miles east of Shih-tien. His diary reported that he arrived after midnight having had dinner about 9:40 PM at a Hostel 22. Alton recalled that Shun-ning was located in a beautiful but lonely setting. Since this was to be his jumping-off place for the Salween, he remained several weeks, long enough for his mail to catch up with him.

Here he also discovered that Aaron (Artie) Dorf from New York City and Charlie Boyd from Detroit (and the motorcycle incident on the Ledo Road) were to join him in his upcoming adventures with the Chinese 2ND Army. On May 20th the trio, along with ten other Americans, had dinner, capped off by a Gombei (bottoms up) drinking party with a half dozen officers from the Chinese 2ND Army Headquarters.

Boyd (MI), Croom (NC), Dorf (NYC)
2nd            3rd          5th
from the left (standing) join Chinese clients and other members
of the American liaison team in drinking a Gombei
(bottoms up) toast to the upcoming campaign

CHART #1

CHINESE EXPEDITIONARY FORCE

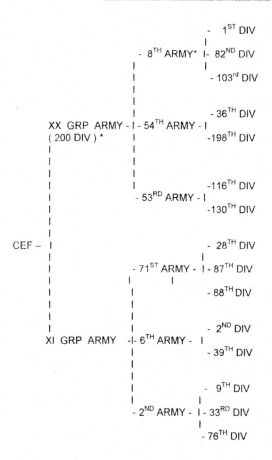

- 1ST DIV
- 8TH ARMY* - 82ND DIV
- 103rd DIV

- 36TH DIV
XX GRP ARMY - - 54TH ARMY - -198TH DIV
( 200 DIV ) *

-116TH DIV
- 53RD ARMY -
-130TH DIV

CEF –

- 28TH DIV
- 71ST ARMY - - 87TH DIV
- 88TH DIV

- 2ND DIV
XI GRP ARMY - - 6TH ARMY - - 39TH DIV

- 9TH DIV
- 2ND ARMY - - 33RD DIV
- 76TH DIV

* = Reserve

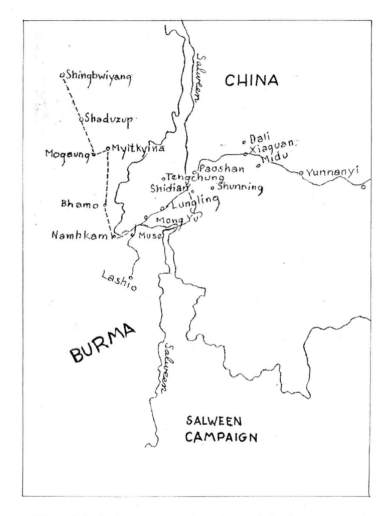

Nine o'clock the next morning Croom left Shun-ning with a
pack mule supply column for the town of Yoa-pin-gi. This was
his first try at walking with the Chinese on what turned out to be
a three-day return trip. His apprehension, which was subsequently
painfully justified, became a matter of recorded history when he
told his diary " . . . well to-day we part company for awhile. Please
wish me luck!" By the afternoon of May 24th he was back in
Shun-ning, suffering miserably from a case of severely blistered
lips and sore and aching feet and "no Dr. in miles."

# WE CROSS THE SALWEEN

When the Salween campaign began, the Japanese thinly-spread 56TH Division had the responsibility for defending the entire area west of the river as far south as the Burma border. The Chinese plan to dislodge them, code-named RAINBOW had two major objectives.

One was the walled town of Tengchung, due west of Paoshan, beyond both the Salween and Shweli Rivers, tucked high up in the rugged Kaoli-kung Mountains and accessible only by pack trails once traveled by Marco Polo. Tengchung was also connected by trail to Mytkyina in Burma. The capture of both towns would give the Chinese their first land connection to the west since the fall of Burma in 1942.

The other objective was the key town of Lungling, located on the Burma Road 78 kilometers south of where the Road crossed the Salween. A major obstacle to the Chinese drive toward Lungling was heavily fortified Sung Shan (Pine) Mountain, fourteen miles south of the river and virtually overlooking the site of the Hwei-tung bridge which had been destroyed by the retreating Chinese in May of 1942.

The "RAINBOW" plan assigned all activity north of the Burma Road to the 20TH Group Army, with everything south of the Road the responsibility of the 11TH. It called for the 20TH to cross the Salween at two points well north of the Road, with the 39TH Division, from the 2ND Army in the southernmost crossing to work its way twenty miles south to the main Burma Road Hwei-tung bridge site. The 53RD and 54TH Armies would cross at the two northern locations, negotiate the mountains through two lofty (9000 and 10,000 ft.) passes into the Shweli River Valley and eventually converge on and lay siege to Tengchung.

South of the Hwei-tung bridge site and the Road, the 11TH Group Army's 71ST and 2ND Armies would bypass the Sung Shan Mountain fortress, engage and neutralize a Jap force in the village of Pingka and sweep westward to the Burma Road, cutting off supplies moving north to the Salween. After reaching the Road behind Sung Shan, the 71ST Army would proceed southwest to attack Lungling.

In reviewing the structure of the Chinese Expeditionary Force (Chart #1) which, although 40 per cent under strength, was available to dislodge the anemic Japanese 56TH Division, one can readily understand President Roosevelt's impatience with Chiang's reluctance to move. The long wait for the Chinese to do so, however, was over. Ho Ling-chin's proclamation of April 14th turned out to be genuine and on the night of May 11th the Chinese Expeditionary Force (CEF), commanded by General Wei Li-huang launched "RAINBOW", crossing the Salween at five points. Negotiating the river at the northernmost point, opposite Mamien Pass, was the 198TH Division of the 54TH Army. Under the supervision of American YFOS GI's, this was accomplished on rubber boats and bamboo and oil-drum rafts.

During May 11th and 12th elements of the 54TH Army's 36TH Division and the 53RD Army's 116TH Division similarly crossed to the south at Meng-ka Ferry, opposite Ta-tang-tzu Pass.

The third crossing, by units from 11TH Group's 6TH Army's 39TH Division occurred about five miles north of the Huei-jen Bridge, opposite Hung-mu-shu Pass. South of the Burma Road, the 88TH Division of the 71ST Army, moving out of Shih-tien, avoided the Sung Shan Mountain fortress by crossing south of it. The 88TH landed about seven miles north of the road to Pingka, while the 76TH Division of the 2ND Army was taking up positions eleven miles south of town.

. . . .

At this point in our story, in the interest of continuity we shall follow the experiences of each group of repairmen as they traveled with their Chinese clients through and over the monsoon-drenched trails of the lofty and precipitous Kaoli-kungs. To appreciate their truly heroic accomplishments the reader is asked to keep in mind that the incessant rainfall in near-freezing temperatures often transformed the trails and roads, which were often engulfed in sleet and fog into slippery death traps. It should also be understood that these men were not hardened combat-trained soldiers, ready for the long uphill hikes alongside of obstinate pack animals, but only technicians who were trying to do the best that they could for the allied effort. What they did possess, however, was the philosophical and physical determination to see the war through to its end so that they could return to whatever they were doing when they were faced with the need to answer the call.

Because of the terrain in which the Salween Campaign was waged, YFOS conceded right from the start that supplying the almost 100,000 troops which were scattered over a 100 mile front, was going to be extremely difficult. With few roads available that could support motorized vehicular traffic and with little on hand in the thinly populated region through which the troops would be traveling that would enable them to live off of the land, supply had to be via coolie porters or by air. History reports that the Air Corps 27TH Troop Carrier Squadron, which joined the 14TH Air Force in late May 1944 at Stilwell's request, complained about having to support the entire Chinese effort with only thirteen C-47's.

Some of our fellows discovered that it was indeed impossible and were forced to survive on starvation rations on several occasions until breaks would occur in the monsoon-soaked clouds.

. . . .

While the maneuvers of the 71ST Army were underway to reach and cut the Burma Road south of Sung Shan, the Chinese 200TH Division from the 11TH Group Army, crossing on rubber boats took up positions confronting the defenders of the stronghold. With them was the jeep team of Weeks Andrews, Harry Gramavot, James Henry Hopper and Arley Palmer, along with a contingent of Burma Road Engineers (BRE). The latter's objective was to build a bypass road around the south side of the mountain fortress. Here they discovered that the Japanese had extended their defensive positions onto the lower slopes, well out in front of the tunneled bastion, which had been hollowed out of the several peaks comprising the mountain.

As the BRE attempts to cut a road began, they immediately came under heavy fire from the Japanese guns, losing several of their precious heavy-duty machines. This action was observed by the Andrews team from behind a hill out of view of the enemy. Another hill provided cover for the Chinese 200th Division, which was getting its first taste of battle conditions. Following the aborted attempts by the BRE to get past the entrenched Japs, the Andrews quartet, along with their fahn-yee!-gwahn (interpreter) decided to run the guantlet and also came under the guns of the defenders, fortunately without being hit. A Colonel Woods, also attached to the Chinese Army Headquarters, gave orders for his jeep to be dismantled, after which it was literally carried by the Chinese around the mountain obstacle.

Surviving several very punishing counterattacks, the 53rd and 54th Army units, in the north, hammering at the passes that guarded the way to Tenchung gradually began to get their acts together. In an attempt to slow the advancing Chinese and to re-enforce the garrison at that remote Jade center, the Japanese were forced to withdraw some of the units from the 56th Division in the south. Exploiting the opportunity this move presented to the Chinese in the south, General Wei Li Huang opted to release the reserve divisions from the 71st Army. These, the 28th and 87 th, put another 20,000 men across the river seven miles south of the site of the main Burma Road Hwei-tung Bridge.

The 28th attacked the enemy outposts that had fired on the BRE and the Andrews repair team, driving the Japanese back into the mountain fortress. At the same time the 87th Division swung around Sung Shan and headed south down the Burma Road toward Lungling. With their army headquarters was the Andrews team.

. . . .

By now it was early June, 1944 and after their violent introduction to the Salween campaign, our heroes were destined to spend more than four months, sharing the endless frustrations of working with the Chinese. The following instructions they received on how to perform their repair duties reveal the personality and stubbornness of their curious allies. The typed pages which were distributed were filled with admonitions, designed specifically to allay any suspicions among their clients that the Americans were not trying hard enough or that they were altering the identity of any equipment for which their olive-skinned allies would literally give their lives, were it lost.

## GUIDE TO REPAIRMEN IN THE FIELD

The Chinese soldier looks toward the American who works with him with great confidence. The reason for this is, the American has taught him all he knows about modern tactics and American equipment. To insure his confidence one must work with the greatest self confidence possible.

Nearly always the Chinese soldier who operates the equipment you are working on will be by you, and watching you work, and he will be very much interested in what you are doing.

Although whatever he brings to you may seem O.K. to you when you first check it, always do something to it if it is not more than burnishing some contact points or cleaning it up bit. This will insure in the Chinese mind that you are helping him and he will have more confidence in you and his equipment.

When you pull into an area for the first time with the average Chinese outfit, and set up your trailer for work, the Chinese will be rather skeptical about the work you will do. They will probably bring a set or two and watch you very closely, and after they see you repair equipment they will bring everything that they can no matter how minor the trouble. The best policy is to always do what you can if it is only replacing a few screws.

One thing to remember is never mix equipment. Never take a part off of one piece of equipment and use it to repair another.

Although it may seem to you that you are doing a favor the Chinese cannot see it that way.

When a Chinese soldier is given a piece of equipment such as a radio or telephone, it is his responsibility to take care of it and probably his life if he loses it. So you cannot blame him for trying to keep it intact.

Always control your temper although sometimes it takes a great deal of self-control.

The Chinese will crowd around you while you work, make them stand back, if necessary, place a Chinese guard nearby, this is easy to do if you have an interpreter with you. Nearly always you will have. Never curse Chinese or threaten them because when you do you simply lose face. The Chinese officials will take care of any serious misunderstanding so always go the long way around to stay out of trouble.

## DO'S AND DONT'S

Don't leave equipment torn down. Try to repair it, if you see that it is impossible, at least put it together.

Don't leave your own equipment unlocked or unguarded. Trust no one, your equipment is valuable and there are men in the field who know it.

Avoid professional jealousy. There are good repairmen in the field and probably the lack of spare parts is the reason for the trouble.

The eccentricities of the Chinese military were not limited to their policies regarding signal equipment. American advisors discovered all too readily that much of the combat tactics that they thought they were imparting in training were quickly ignored when the Chinese finally engaged the Japanese. Our allies made it clear that, to a large degree, they had been humoring us in keeping with their own brand of oriental politeness, when in fact they had no intention of letting any foreigner instruct them in how to fight. Their reluctance to commit entire units in their attacks against the well-defended Japanese positions and the terrible waste of valuable ammunition were of particular aggravation to our combat advisors. They were forced to watch in disbelief as one small detachment after another was literally annihilated during their futile charges at the enemy. The net result, of course, was the unnecessary lengthening of the campaign.

In the case of Lungling, which the Japs held for months after the initial assaults, the terrible losses suffered by an overwhelming Chinese force caused the Reluctant Dragon to threaten to call off the campaign unless Stilwell mounted a totally impossible and premature attack against Bhamo in Burma when Myitkyina had not yet been taken.

Following the bypassing of Sung Shan by the other 71ST Army units encircling Pingka to the south, the Chinese swept aside minor resistance in several fortified villages and proceeded south to attack Lungling. The latter, which sat astride the Burma Road, was also the southern terminus of the only good supply road to Tengchung to the northwest. For these reasons, the Japanese re-enforced it, determined to hold it at all costs.

Since it is not the purpose of this narrative to cover the details of the Salween offensive, we will only report that the 71ST was stopped in its tracks for many weeks. During this time army headquarters occupied the town of Hwangtsoapa to the north.

By September the Salween campaign had been finally reduced to the sieges at Tengchung and Sung Shan and the continuing assault on Lungling. During the summer of 1944 the Andrews Team, now officially part of an American Technical Instruction Group (TIG), moved along with the successes and failures of the 71ST, spending time at Hwangtsoapa and other locations needing their repair expertise.

Their odyssey, usually by weapons carrier but too often on foot through the roads and trails that marked the adventures of the 71ST and the 11TH Group Army, lasted throughout the summer of 1944. On September 7th word came that Sung Shan Mountain had finally fallen to the Chinese. When it reached Andrews and his companions, they were occupying a former Japanese Headquarters somewhere between Sung Shan and Lungling to the south. Although well received, the news came with grave implications for our little band. Fortune, it seemed, had conspired to place them squarely in the path of any retreating survivors from the mountain stronghold. Armed with British Bren machine guns, they deployed one on each of the four corners of a porch, which encircled their building, anticipating the worst. The night, which followed was probably the longest ever experienced by our heroes. Their concerns, however, proved to be unfounded when it was finally evident that the enemy stragglers had apparently taken another route south.

The battle for Lungling, however, was still raging and as the number of Chinese Army units that joined the fray increased, so too did the number of calls for repair service. This had the Weeks Andrews Team scrambling from unit to unit. En-route to making a house call on the 200TH Division, Weeks and his interpreter, Chou Chi Yu, were fired on by Japanese artillery twice, first while going across a rice paddy and again while returning. Business remained very brisk up until late, October 1944 when the Japanese finally decided that they had had enough and began to withdraw. By November 3rd their rear guard had been dealt with and the Chinese occupied the town.

For the next month Andrews and his traveling companions also moved into town and took up residence in a tent. They remained long enough for mail and packages to overtake them, Andrews finally receiving a pair of eyeglasses to replace those broken weeks earlier. Also included in this treasure from the other side of the world were two bottles of Coca Cola, a commodity absolutely unheard of among the ground troops in the Salween. Deciding that sharing this with anyone else was too much above the call of duty, Weeks slipped stealthily behind the tent and privately relished this nectar from home.

Some extensive shopping in town produced a small canned "Yunnan Ham". Encased in brine and of an unknown age, this rocklike find resisted our heroes' initial efforts to pry an edible particle from it. After a lengthy soaking, however, it was magically transformed into an unexpected delicacy.

Once the team had had a chance to breathe some strength back into their tired, aching bodies, they moved again back to Hwangtsoapa and the 11TH Group Army, which was poised for the final push south into Burma. They were not too far from the long-awaited junction with there much better fed and clothed countrymen from Stilwell's "X-ray Force". The Chinese 1ST Army and The Mars Task Force (the successors to Merrill's Marauders) were at that moment driving toward a linkup with the original Burma Road in Burma.

By this time Tengchung had also fallen to the Chinese, releasing their 53RD Army for use in a flanking maneuver parallel to the Road in China, a tactic that prevented the Japanese from stopping long enough to put up road blocks. When 11TH Army Group Headquarters decided to follow the crowd en-route to Burma, our little band of repair stalwarts went with them. Somewhere near the border, either in China or Burma, they discovered Bob Gallagher from the Forrest Brown, Jim Hoff trio who had been with the 53RD Army through the siege of Tenchung. Bob was resting comfortably in a scenic bamboo grove setting, which the Japanese had obligingly prepared for them. Andrews, although not able to name the location, did recall that it featured a swanky Greek-style resort with hot spring baths accessed via a grand stone staircase. He also remembered seeing vast fields of opium poppies growing on the nearby hills.

Team's modified weapons carrier repair shop

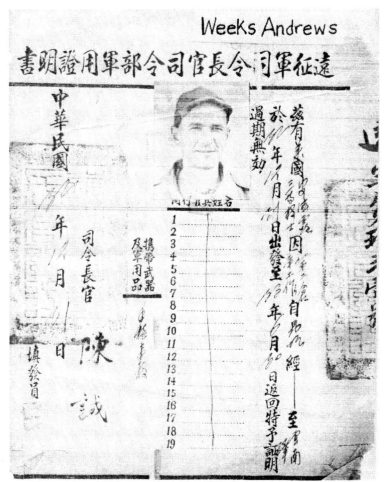

CHINESE GOVERNMENT PASSPORT – IDENTIFIES THE
BEARER AND INCLUDES REWARD FOR AIDING HIM –
ALSO A PERMIT TO CARRY A WEAPON

Andrews passport with the Chinese Army

Andrews Team

Palmer (standing with Japanese rifle)
Hopper (KY), Gramavot (NYC), Andrews (NC)

With the cessation of hostilities, the Andrews party found their way back to Paoshan, crossing the Salween this time over a pontoon bridge at the site where a new permanent structure was being built for the Road. One of Andrews' last memories of the Salween campaign was of the general from the Chinese 88TH Division attempting to hitch a ride, with all of his furniture, on a truck which was leaving Paoshan for Kunming . . . and Kermit Clark forcing him off of the running board while brandishing a .45 automatic.

Harry Gramavot added a short sequel to this segment of our story. Sometime during the campaign he was informed that Lt. Mc Veigh, back in Yunnanyi, had for no reason that Harry could ascertain reduced him in rank. Knowing that Mc Veigh was less than a model of what a commanding officer should be, Harry could only guess that the lieutenant had someone else upon whom he wanted to bestow Harry's T4 rating. At one point in his tortuous wanderings, Harry met General Dorn and asked him if he could find out what Mc Veigh's motivation was. Sometime later, Harry was contacted by Brooks Atkinson the well-known war correspondent and was told that the general had kept his promise and, upon receiving Harry's approval, would take the necessary steps to correct the apparent injustice. Questioning the wisdom of proceeding any farther, and being at heart a civilian anyway, Harry told Atkinson to call off the general.

Harry did not get his T/4 stripes back but the general had decided to right the wrong in his own way . . . . since, after returning to civilian life, Harry was summoned to Governors Island, in New York harbor and awarded the bronze star medal for his services to the Chinese Army. While he was obviously pleased, he knew that another injustice had been done to his three companions, who were equally deserving of the same honor.

. . . .

Although much of the history of the Salween Campaign is occupied with describing the singular nature of the battles fought, significant space has also been devoted to the almost-impossible task of supplying the Chinese Armies with food and ammunition. While reporting the obstacles to supply that were presented by the brutal terrain; monsoon-ravished weather and the bulldog-minded enemy, the historians also pointed out additional and certainly unnecessary delays caused by the ever-enduring politics within the Chinese command structure.

Following its successful crossing of the Salween south of Pingka at the beginning of the campaign . . . . and after throwing a blockade around that key Japanese-held town, the Chinese 2ND Army dispatched elements of its 9TH Division south and west in a sweeping move. This maneuver achieved the establishment of a key block across the Burma Road south of Mangshih, which cut off the supply route to the Japanese, who were at that time defending Lungling from the 71ST Army.

The initial elation by their American YFOS associates over this brilliant accomplishment was quickly dispelled, however, when the Chinese, who had been complaining bitterly about not being supplied by their headquarters, decided arbitrarily to remove the block, and return to their previous positions. Investigation by the disappointed and frustrated Americans soon revealed that there were indeed bad feelings between 11TH Group Army Headquarters and their 2ND Army counterparts.

The difficulty of supplying the 2ND Army was indeed real and as chance would have it, was the scenario for another segment of our 181ST adventure.

Earlier in this chapter, we left Altoon Croom, a radio repairman from Robersonville, N.C. with a severe case of blistered lips and sore feet at Shun-nng . . . . where he was assigned to the YFOS contingent, traveling with the Chinese 2ND Army Headquarters. Recalling his arrival there from Mitu the morning of May 4th, 1944, he described it as a beautiful but lonely place. During the ensuing seventeen days, which were disturbingly lacking in activity, he found himself with too much time to think . . . . of home and what he knew lay ahead. For diversion he buried himself in a novel he had appropriated during his travels and waited impatiently for his mail to overtake him. Occasionally, and as a release from the monotony, he took his meals in town.

On the eleventh of May, for want of something to occupy his time, he started to build a British 48 (portable) radio but for reasons his diary did not divulge gave up in disgust after two days. His battle with boredom and apprehension continued until he left on his ill fated try at packtraining, which we have already described and from which he returned on May 24th, nursing his blistered lips and sore feet.

Fortunately he was mercifully granted several days to recover but by May 29th the word was out that a large contingent of the 2ND Army, along with another pack train would depart for the Salween the following day. The old game of "hurry up and wait" began again, with the primitive assemblage of non-descript animals and their equally non-descript contracted handlers and coolies finally leaving Shun-ning on June 2nd.

As before, their route was over the same rugged rain-swept mountain trails that led to Young-pin-gi and beyond. Responsibility for keeping the ragtag caravan moving in any semblance of order fell to an American veterinary Captain. From the very start, however, and for the two days it took to reach this remote village, things did not go well. What Croom's diary referred to with the single word, "trouble", was his futile attempt to describe the constant haggling of the Chinese muleskinners over their fees, which were negotiated, apparently, on a daily basis . . . . the confusion and frustration of reforming the picturesque column each morning, after discovering that during the night animals, their precious cargoes and their shifty owners had disappeared . . . or the overloading of protesting animals with supplies taken from the backs of beasts that were injured or too ill to continue. Add to these the countless other mishaps that were inevitable to an endeavor whose success depended on mercenary natives who were being paid to travel reluctantly through one of the wildest, dangerous and most remote regions of the world.

On June 5th the column pulled out of Young-pin-gi, swinging west and south toward the Salween, still ten days march away. By this time Croom had also acquired his own set of personal concerns. These became more than just the sinking realization that his feet were beginning to ache again . . . but took on a disturbing psychological bent when the lieutenant, who had assigned him the exclusive task of sticking close to a packhorse laboring under the weight of two wooden boxes, stunned him with the revelation that they contained more than a million dollars in Chinese currency. Much of the success of the supply train was dependent on their contents since they were used to pay the muleskinners and coolies at the end of each day.

The farther the pack train got from civilization and closer to the Salween, the more difficult and heated the daily negotiations for the day's fees became. The rate of animal and muleskinner desertions also increased exponentially and on several occasions the Captain failed to appear for the evening meal, triggering all sorts of conjecture as to his fate. To Croom's relief, after each occurrence, however, he did eventually catch up with his charges.

On June 10th, eight days out of Shun-ning, a sizeable number of horses got away, necessitating a halt at a town called Mong-pong, until replacement animals were acquired. Four days later the train started again for the Salween, arriving at 6:30 PM the evening of the 15th, thirteen days after leaving Shun-ning.

It is appropriate, here, to mention that to his credit, Alton Croom, a youngster like myself and not very large in stature, had neither the physique nor had he come from a rough and ready lifestyle, which would have prepared him for the rigors of this experience. Instead, he was a product of a typical genteel southern upbringing, which our brief training in the "States" had done little to enhance. Nevertheless, like almost all of the civilian-soldiers of the 181ST, he faced his adversity, this time alone, with a determination to see it through to the end.

This determination was sorely put to the test the next day when he crossed the rain-swollen, turbulent Salween on a raft. By this time only about a dozen of the one hundred or so animals that had started the journey remained . . . and most of the million inflated Chinese dollars had been doled out to the handlers and coolies.

Once the remnants of the pack train had been collected, the Captain's now abbreviated retinue headed west from the river to the town of Tempo (spelling uncertain). Somewhere between the river crossing and Tempo, Croom lost the service of his packhorse. This, then, became his new "home-away-from-home" until July 6th while he waited for another animal, which turned out to be a cow. This time in Tempo was memorable to Alton since he remembered that he celebrated July 4th, (Independence Day) with a dinner of "C" rations, corn mush and rice.

Two days later he was off again, in search of 2ND Army Headquarters. This time it was three days of slogging through the mud and wrath of the monsoon. His stay at headquarters was short-lived, however, and about 3:00 PM of the eleventh he reported to a seven-man YFOS team attached to the nearby Chinese 76TH Division. The team included a veterinary captain and his sergeant, a medical major (who shortly became ill and left the team), a radio operator, code man/operator and an interpreter.

From this point, and for two and a half months, Croom battled the mountains, still on foot, with the 76TH, functioning as a sole one-man radio repair team, sometimes without the luxury of an interpreter. His most disturbing memory is of becoming lost on the trails, while carrying radio codes to one of the Division's remote locations. Accompanied by the interpreter, two Chinese "bings" and two pack cows, and upon reaching the crest of a trail overlooking a deep valley, his little party detected activity on the far slope. Gambling that it indicated the presence of a unit from the 76TH, his little band descended into the valley. When they reached the bottom an artillery duel suddenly broke out overhead between the occupants of the opposing ridges. With little choice left but to continue on, they reached the far slope, finding, to their enormous relief, several Chinese artillery batteries and their American advisors.

The assignments of the 181ST repairmen to the various Chinese units, spread over the entire southwestern map of Yunnan Province, were painfully lonely . . . made more so by the reluctance of the Chinese government to fight an aggressive war. So it was no small event when our fellows' paths crossed. This happened only once for Alton Croom, when after trudging for hours, often over vertical trails, his little band turned a bend and came face-to-face with the Andrews contingent and their 200TH Division clients catching their breaths.

By October 1st, (1944) Croom's assignment to the 2ND Chinese Army had run its course and he received his orders to return to Kunming and a stint at a rest camp. Traveling by truck this time, he headed north on the Burma Road and by the 5th rolled into Yunnanyi. Expecting to retrieve the rest of his clothing and other belongings, he could find no trace of them . . . . and continued on to Kunming. Feeling like the forgotten man, but elated to be back in civilization and among his many friends, he discovered that his luck had not yet completely changed, however, when he learned that there was also no room for him at the rest camp.

You will recall that, before jumping off on his adventures with the Chinese 2ND Army, Croom was joined by Artie Dorf and Charlie Boyd at a gombei party and dinner. While Artie was unable to provide us with any specifics, such as which units he was with, he did recall that he also traveled with a Chinese Army pack train and repaired an occasional radio or two, while enduring the same privations as the others. Boyd's memory, on the other hand, was not as lacking, but while abundantly full of colorful details, it unfortunately, did not contain an identification of the Chinese units with which he served.

The reader must remember that, aside from those facts, which have been borrowed from recorded history and several individuals' diaries and notes, much of my story has been extracted from the memories of the participants. As they tried to relive those so distant days, it was inevitable that facts of time and place would not always be accurate. In piecing their many stories together, I feel, however, that I have been reasonably successful in correcting most of these inaccuracies. What I have not done and possessed no license to do was to modify the versions of their experiences as told to me. Consequently, I feel that although their stories are essentially factual, depending on the personality of the individual teller, each contains some degree of imagination and embellishment.

In listening to Charlie Boyd's account of his adventures, I suspected that he was indeed adding some degree of hyperbole as he described his period with the Chinese. In researching this story, however, I have heard several true accounts of Chinese behavior that were even less believable than those related by Charlie. Thus I have no way of determining how much enrichment is contained in Charlie's story and have, therefore, recorded it as told to me.

Having enlisted early, he had more time in the army than most of us and had held the rank of tech sergeant for a long time. He was also an excellent radio technician, sporting an amateur license. By army standards Charlie was small in stature (about five feet seven), weighing no more than one hundred and forty pounds. He more than made up for his size with an energetic, quizzical, challenging but warm personality, qualities which worked so well for him with his compatriots and which were also not wasted on his Chinese clients with whom he made many friends. He was convinced that his assignment to the Chinese Army was a direct result of a run-in he had with Lt. Swanson in Kunming. In view of the role the 4TH Team subsequently played in the Salween Campaign, the more likely scenario was that the difference of viewpoints between the two men only made the lieutenant's selection of a candidate a mite simpler.

Following the dinner and gombei party with the officers of the Chinese 2ND Army at Shunning, he somehow found his way to Paoshan. It was from there that he departed with a pack train, headed for the river. Unlike his contemporaries, who crossed via boat, footbridge or raft, he insisted that he forded the Salween with the aid of ropes. From subsequent events I have deduced that, if he stayed with the 2ND Army, he was probably with either the 33RD or 9TH Division, since Croom, who was at one time with the 76TH had not met him. Like several of his contemporaries, however, he also was the only representative of the 181ST with his YFOS group.

At some point in his meanderings, he must have been pretty far forward because he received a thigh wound and was left behind by the Chinese column for three or four days at a remote compound. Eventually two coolies were dispatched with a stretcher to retrieve him. Suspended between the shoulder carrying poles of his two benefactors, Charlie recalled that the ensuing trip was, "kind of thrilling going up and down the mountains." Throughout the journey, which took several days, however, he had a knawing fear of being accidentally or intentionally tossed off the trail over one of the numerous cliffs that it skirted.

Not bashful by any measure, Charlie became very friendly with the liaison group's interpreter and several of the Chinese officers, including one of the generals. On several occasions the latter invited him to dinner at his private quarters. The general was partial to a type of meatball, which Charlie conceded was very tasty. He recalled that he had tried unsuccessfully to find its counterpart when he returned home but commented that, possibly the principal ingredient used in preparing it was one of those singular Chinese "delicacies" and that, as an afterthought, maybe he really did not want to find out what it was.

He spent several months with his Chinese customers, most of them in the company of, what he called, the Fu-gwahn, who Charlie described as the adjutant to the commanding general of the division he was servicing. In one of the compounds at which the unit was stationed, while conversing with an American blacksmith Charlie described as a "red-headed dude", Charlie and the Fu-gwahn were interrupted by one of the many illiterate Chinese "Bings" who wanted to borrow a hammer from the farrier. The soldier had come from a group huddled at the far side of the compound and when his request was honored by the horse-shoer he returned to his friends. Several minutes later, Charlie, looking across the compound at the group of Chinese saw the fellow who had borrowed the hammer suddenly raise it over his head and to Charlie's horror, was taking aim at the nose of an 81mm mortar shell which he had stood up on its tail fins. His objective, apparently, was the removal of the multi-colored rings by which the projectile's firing range was set. Instinctively, Charlie shoved the blacksmith aside and the Fu-gwahn, in broken English blurted out, "There goes your hammer." The resulting explosion, in addition to killing the unfortunate Chinese soldier and some of his friends, also destroyed a building and much of the compound wall.

Those of us, who had the opportunity to observe the ordinary, often illiterate Chinese private, do not find this type of story to be as outlandish as it may seem. Another of Charlie's tales was of the unit taking over a compound that had been recently evacuated by the Japanese. Among the many "don'ts" that were ordered by the Fu-gwahn, as the Chinese occupied the compound was the use of the Americans' latrine, which had been booby-trapped and which had a sign to that effect tacked over the door. The inevitable occurred, of course, and Charlie described a scene of one of the "Bings" dashing into the structure and being demolished with it as it exploded. At this point Charlie received his horrifying indoctrination into the Chinese' disregard for life when the Fu-gwahn returned from the gory scene laughing at the bizarre sight of "arms and legs everywhere."

The incredulous behavior of these unfortunate men was demonstrated again to Charlie when, after witnessing a dry-run demonstration to two rows of Chinese troops, standing back to back, on how to operate flamethrowers, he stared in horror as they turned to face each other and fired the strange weapons for the first time with terrifying results.

Evidences of the total ignorance by the "Bings" of the nature of the instruments of war that were entrusted to them, such as the mortar round mentioned earlier, too often ended in tragedy. As the Japanese gave ground and moved southeast to protect the

Road, which supplied the defenders of Lungling, the Chinese often occupied the evacuated areas and set up their command posts. On one such occasion, as Charlie and a YFOS compatriot began to set up a radio station, they were shaken by a tremendous explosion from an area up ahead. Their first fears were that the retreating Japanese had bracketed the occupied area for artillery purposes. When the Fu-gwahn returned from the direction of the explosion, he explained that a group of "Bings" had constructed a crude fireplace from several captured 75mm shell clusters and had set off a chain reaction with other nearby shells. Again he shocked Charlie with his laughing description of "arms and legs everywhere."

As the campaign progressed, Charlie and his Chinese compatriots left the mountains behind. Approaching the border of Burma, apparently near or in the Salween River Valley, they were now in a jungle setting. In one of the airdrops, by which they were routinely supplied, they received some American hand grenades. Up to this point the Chinese had been accustomed to the old German potato-masher type. As Charlie related, the Pings (Bings), whose uniforms were not designed so that they could carry many equipment items, elected to string the pineapple-shaped grenades by their fuse pins, like so many beads. They then set off into the jungles and as one could have predicted, the sounds of the explosions as the pins worked themselves loose as the men marched along, marked the routes they had taken.

Charlie was appalled at the atrocities inflicted on the few Japanese prisoners that were taken. He insisted that none of them survived the hangings and torture at the hands of the Chinese, who marched them to the rear, for transport back to Kunming. Charlie not only witnessed these executions but also took photographs of the unfortunate victims. Like so many others from the 181ST, the records and momentos of his tour in the C.B.I. were subsequently lost . . . his, in a garage fire . . . . another penalty we have received for waiting so long to tell our story.

I was unable to pin him down to any of the towns that he encountered during his long tour with the Chinese, although he recalled hearing of Lungling but was certain he had not been there. My guess is that he was with the 2ND Army's 9TH Division which entered Mangshih, on the Burma Road on the heels of the retreating Japanese and later, on January 19th, 1945, demonstrated that they were learning to fight the American way when, in a superbly coordinated battle, they drove the enemy from Wanting on the Burma border.

My theory about Charlie's affiliation with the 9TH gains some foundation in that he was with the Chinese when they made contact with the American successors to the Marauders, the Mars Task Force and the Chinese 1ST Army from Stilwell's XRAY force near the Burma border.

He was still with his Chinese clients near the Burma border when the first convoy from India passed on its way to Kunming, also in January of 1945.

I believe that Charlie Boyd's tour with the Chinese was one of the longest experienced by anyone from the 181ST. Having crossed the Salween early in the campaign, probably in May or June of 1944 and leaving on an L5 plane for Kunming shortly after viewing the convoy passing in January of 1945, he spent about nine months with the Chinese.

Charlie joined the army long before the draftees from Forts Dix and Bragg, thereby amassing a very large point-score near the war's end. In the summer of 1945 he left Kunming for Calcutta and Karachi, India on a converted C54, continuing to and touching down at Abadan, Iran and the Azores en-route to Bangor, Maine. Heading for his home in Detroit, he boarded another plane for Chicago. Upon arrival he learned that the Atomic Bomb had been dropped while he was en-route. He also celebrated VJ Day while still in the "windy city."

. . . .

With all of the ground that was wrested from the Japanese during the Salween Campaign, when the initial smoke had cleared, they still held the three major objectives . . . Lungling, Sung Shan and Teng-chung. While the Japanese at the latter two locations were aided by topographical and singular physical features enhancing their defenses, Lungling did not. Although the Chinese had started their attack on the town on May 28, 1944, by July 15th the 10,000 troops that they had employed were not only repulsed, but were severely punished by only 1500 Japanese defenders. In fact the latter, counterattacking new Chinese positions around Hwangtsoapa, three miles north of the town, were only stopped by the arrival of reinforcements, a heavy B-25 raid on Lungling and harsh orders from an infuriated Chiang-Kai-shek. It wasn't until November 3rd, after the fall of both Sung Shan and Teng-chung, and with the forces in Burma threatening the Burma Road south of them, that the Japanese defending Lungling finally decided to give up the ghost . . . leaving only a small rear guard to slow up the Chinese occupation.

With only the link-up with the X Forces working their way east from Bhamo left to accomplish, all of the remaining troops from the Salween Y Force were concentrated on pushing the Japanese south along the road and out of China. In late September another group of seven repairmen from the 181ST was dispatched from Yunnanyi to service one of these reconstituted Chinese units. Among them were Bernard Metz (from Chicago) and Henry "Shot" Howell from Gatesville, N.C.

Shot's assignment was to drive and nursemaid their vehicles and to keep the team's auxiliary power unit running. He recalled that the team and its vehicles, a jeep and weapons carrier were ferried across the Salween in, what he described as a kind of boat or raft. He remembered that the Chinese had to paddle a good distance up stream before they turned into the current and paddled furiously toward the opposite shore, hoping to land across from where they had originally started. At some point in their wanderings the repairmen had to relinquish their vehicles, and like their earlier counterparts, continued their travels on foot and over mountain trails. He also recalled watching the Chinese battle to dislodge their stubborn adversaries from hilly machinegun positions. He and the team were out about three months and stayed with their Chinese clients all the way into Burma, witnessing their eventual union with the Mars Task Force and Stilwell's Burma Chinese.

. . . .

The campaign to take Tengchung differed from the Lungling operation in which Andrews, Palmer, Gramavot, Hopper, Dorf, Boyd, Croom, Howell, Metz and others had participated. The terrain, though similar to that south of the Burma Road and the Hui-tung bridge site, was much more formidable. The 53rd and 54th Armies that crossed the Salween at the three locations north of the bridge site had to negotiate the lofty, snow-capped, icy, monsoon-drenched Kaoli-kung mountain passes and the swift-flowing Shweli River before they could lay siege to the massive walls of Teng-chung itself.

During the night of May 11th the northern-most crossing of the Salween, opposite Mamien Pass was started in rubber rafts by the 198th Division of the 54th Army. Man-for-man, the inexperienced and poorly led Chinese were no match for the professionalism of the Japanese units that defended the strategically fortified mountain pass. Only Japanese patrols were left at the river, offering no resistance to the landings. The first real contact occurred at the entrance to the pass, ending with an initial success for the Chinese but negated by a fierce counterattack by the Japanese. With the weight of superior numbers in their favor, however, and displaying unbelievable bravery, as they charged the enemy positions, the Chinese did eventually overrun them. Japanese resistance at the entrance to Mamien Pass ended on May 13 and on May 29th a footbridge was operating across the Salween. Once the 54th was through the pass and into the Shweli River Valley beyond, it fought its way south towards Tengchung.

The 54th had prepared for its role, in the impending offensive in the vicinity of Yunnanyi. During its staging period American liaison teams were assigned to it, one of which included four or five men from Mc Veigh's Second Team. Bill Friedman (New York

City) recalled that he and Milton W. Mc Donald (Chattanooga, Tenn.) were on this team. One of the team's first tasks was to instruct the Chinese in the operation of SCR284 transmitter/receivers, which would provide contact between the 54th Army Headquarters and its divisions during the upcoming offensive. Like their counterparts assigned to other YFOS liaison teams, Friedman and his companions also were called upon to repair a variety of non-signal equipment types. One of these that Bill remembered as being kind of unique was a mine detector.

On May 8th, 1944, Friedman, Mc Donald and several others left Yunnanyi by truck for Paoshan. From there, they continued to the Salween, crossed the river on sampans and joined a Chinese pack train column. Bill was assigned to a mule, which carried the precious SCR284. Unlike some of the 181ST teams assigned to different Chinese units, he was not present at any of the battles. Like most of the others, however, he witnessed another example of the disregard for human life and the untold bravery of the Chinese. In order to advance in some sectors, the 54th found it necessary to clear mine fields. On more than one occasion, when none of the detectors that he had repaired were available, Bill watched in numb horror and disbelief as a line of Chinese, walked, holding hands, across the suspected area with devastating results, each time they stepped on a mine.

Friedman's tour with the 54th covered between two and three months, after which he returned to Yunnanyi via Paoshan, crossing the Salween on the footbridge. During his time in the field, when the monsoon would permit it, supplies were often airdropped to the troops that he, Mc Donald and the others were with. Upon his return to Yunnanyi, he discovered that several of his comrades from the 2nd Team had volunteered for the airdropping operation . . . another diversion from signal repair.

When Bill arrived at Yunnanyi, Lt. Mc Veigh had been sent home on a medical disability. Bill went back to work at the repair shop until November when Lt. George Holmes Wilson came over from Myitkyina to take over the team. The lieutenant soon learned that Bill could type and promptly installed him as his secretary and shop clerk. To this writer, at least, it came as an unbelievable fact when I learned, during the researching of this part of the 181ST story, that Lt. Mc Veigh failed to promote Bill Friedman, who had completed radio school and was qualified as a repairman, to at least the rank of T5 before sending him into a combat zone. Bill remained a Private until an edict was promulgated by FDR that anyone who had been a private for at least one year should be raised to at least PFC rank.

. . . .

The next crossing, also on May 11th, occurred about twenty miles to the south, opposite Tatangtzu Pass. The responsibility for this operation fell to the 116th and 130th Divisions of the 53rd Army.

That same day Ray Fichter (Palmyra, N.J.) left Yunnani, his objective, Paoshan, and then by pack mule train, to join the 53rd Army. His first overnight stop was at Hsia-kuan (Shagwan) and the second at Kilometer 641, 27 kilos short of Paoshan. Sometime during May 13th, after reaching Paoshan and accompanied by a Lt. Murphy (a ground liaison officer for the 27TH Troop Carrier Squadron); a radio operating team; a mule skinner and another Signal Corps lieutenant, he joined a pack train, which was starting for the Salween. The next leg of his journey involved a two-night stopover at the town of Wa-fung-Gi. The fourth and last overnight was finally endured at Dalang, another one of those drab, dusty, mud-brick villages that were so typical of the Yunnan countryside. The following morning, May 16th, the column set out for and eventually came upon the headquarters of the 130th Division. Here they were treated to a five-day respite, which gave them a much-needed opportunity to take a breather and to prepare them physically and psychologically, for what was to come. On May 21st they headed back to Dalang and the staging area for the 130th Division itself. After a final detour to the airfield for supplies, the long column of animals and humans headed for the Salween.

Pack mule column leaving Paoshan

Their mission, as it turned out, was to furnish coordinates for the 27TH Carrier Squadron, which was supporting the Chinese ground troops that were trying to dislodge the enemy from Tatangtzu Pass. The pack train, including the mules, crossed the Salween over a footbridge. From there they took on the precipitous trails that traversed the lofty mountain pass. By this time Ray and his weary companions began to encounter Chinese litter bearers bringing casualties back from the battle raging ahead of them. Ray recalled that whenever one of their wretched burdens had the fortune, good or bad, to expire, his corpse was unceremoniously tossed over the edge into the valleys and gullies below. Ray also reported that the smell of decaying bodies was stifling.

Their food supply, which was airdropped to the team, fluctuated from feast to famine, subject to the whims of the monsoon. On one occasion they managed to purchase a pig, which they shot. Their only shelter at night was to have been provided by jungle hammocks. With few trees to hang them on they found themselves forced to lay the hammocks flat in rice paddies, which offered the only flat ground available. The monsoon refused to cooperate, however, and during more than one night Ray recalled being awakened, as he was inundated by the rising water.

Fichter's (NJ) jungle hammock
With the 53 rd Army's 130 th Div.

On June 10th they reached the battle scene where a regiment from the 130th was attacking a Japanese mountaintop position. Here, the Chinese were employing tactics that had their American combat advisors totally frustrated. Instead of bypassing the enemy positions and placing blocks on their supply routes or committing large forces to overrun the Japanese emplacements, the Chinese, instead, persisted in sending units of squad or platoon size into the lethal fire of the well-trained enemy guns, with sickening results. The Japanese were also rolling hand grenades down at the hesitant Chinese. Their predicament was made even worse by a near-freezing, weeklong deluge by the raging monsoon. During this period, Ray's only refuge was the same, inadequate jungle hammock. When breaks came in the storm, Ray cranked the hand generator for the radio, as the operator relayed coordinates to the drop planes and watched the fighters from the 14th Air Force as they tried in vain to dislodge the stubborn Japanese from their tunnel defenses in the mountain.

Ray learned that Lt. Swanson was coming in by L5 to visit the team and went to meet him, taking along some mules to pick up supplies. At the field he was treated to the dubious experience of witnessing a Japanese mortar attack. Swanson arrived in time but became ill and had to make his stay a short one.

Eventually the breaks in the weather stopped altogether and for more than a week, each team member survived on one quarter of a can of "C" rations per day. When the weather finally opened up again and the belabored troops waited for an air drop of life-saving food, they discovered to their dismay and frustration that the first bundles contained only raincoats for the freezing Chinese. Failing to defeat the Japanese by military means, the Chinese were finally able to eliminate them by setting the entire mountain on fire.

According to the official history, the efforts by the Chinese to clear the Japanese from Ta-tang-tzu Pass occurred during the period from May 12 through most of June. These coincide with dates, which were taken from per diem vouchers found in a scrapbook, covering his army life, which was kept by his wife. His relatively short stay with the Chinese may have been caused by a deterioration in his physical condition as a result of the short rations he had been forced to contend with. Back in Kunming we were told that he had reported to the medics in Paoshan and been diagnosed as being in the first stage of starvation. I was not able, however, to get his confirmation of this story when personally interviewing him. Taking into consideration his quiet, overly modest personality, I am not yet convinced that there was not some truth in the report. Of course another bit of logic could be that the large number of casualties that this unit of the 130th had suffered made it temporarily useless in the drive to clear the pass and, therefore no longer in need of American liaison support.

Whatever, the reason, by June 15, 1944, Ray's assignment with the 130th was over and by the 18th he was back in Paoshan, where he discovered that the entire 4TH Team had arrived and set up shop. Still recovering from his ordeal with the 130TH Division, he began taking his turn with the rest of the telephone and wire squad on the YFOS switchboard.

. . . .

Another team that spent time with the 53RD Army featured Bill Roby from Reynold Station, Kentucky and John Mc Dermott from Long Island City, New York, both radio repairmen.

After several months at the Mc Veigh Team's repair shop in Yunnanyi, where they gave lectures to the Chinese on the proper use and care of telephones and radios, they received orders attaching them to the 53RD. Like their compatriots, they also joined their Chinese clients and their pack mule trains in Paoshan. Roby recalled the long walk to the Salween and crossing it over a rickety suspension bridge. He also remembered that it required a trek over the precipitous trails of eighty grueling miles before they reached the combat area. Their path took them past the Headquarters of the American Brigadier General and his contingent which was acting as liaison to the Chinese 53RD Army Headquarters.

Once they entered the combat zone all of their movements, from twice to six times a day, were done either at night or in early morning. They camped just off the trail, taking turns at standing guard. Roby remembered these times as being very nerve-wracking because they were never quite sure where they were. Because all of the traffic on the nearby trail was oriental and since none of the Americans in his group understood either Chinese or Japanese, there was a considerable degree of apprehension as to the nationality of their nocturnal contemporaries.

Like most of the Americans who accompanied the Chinese into the battles of the Salween Campaign, Roby and Mc Dermott bore witness to the attempts, some suicidally heroic and others pathetically hesitant, by the Chinese to dislodge the efficient Japanese from their well-fortified positions. Roby also recalled that he watched as the frustrated Chinese lined up coolies in front of them as shields as they advanced against the lethal Japanese fire.

While Roby was watching a spectacular attack by Chinese artillery and American planes against the enemy, a nearby American lieutenant, who was also fascinated by what was occurring, suddenly shouted that he had been hit in the helmet. Upon closer inspection, however, it was discovered that he had been hit by an expended ammunition clip, from one of the planes.

In addition to their repair assignments, Roby related that they also instructed the Chinese on how to display the ground panels that guided the vital airdropping planes in their lifesaving supply sorties. His experience regarding food was much like Fichter's and all of the others who had to rely completely on air supply for sustenance. Roby's consisted of two socks (such as one would wear on his feet) of rice each morning. This was always cooked in their helmets.

Their attempts to flavor the bland taste of the rice proved to be Roby's undoing, however, when someone, possibly their interpreter, produced a little meat for the purpose. To Bill's misfortune, it turned out to be rancid, leaving him with a severe case of ptomaine poisoning. The resulting gas pains and diarrhea were so excruciating and disabling that he was ordered to return to Paoshan. The meat, it turns out, was cut from the hanging carcass of a horse that was swarming with flies and maggots, even as the Chinese were still cutting slices from it.

Bill tried to get treatment at a Portable Surgical Hospital near the battle zone, where he saw the body of an American doctor on a stretcher. But still suffering the worst symptoms of the food poisoning and still unable to hold anything on his stomach . . . with no way, other than by foot, to retrace the eighty miles, plus another fifteen or so . . . . Bill was forced to set out, with two Chinese soldiers to guide him. The several days it took to make the long torturous walk were utter agony for him and he recalled that several times he really did not think he would survive it.

· · · ·

The role of the 130th and its parent 53rd Army in the effort to reach and lay siege to Tengchung had just begun, however, which augured more involvement for the repairmen of the 181ST. As the 53rd battled its way west thru the Ta tang tzu Pass, the 54th was paralleling their efforts in the Mamien Pass to the north. Clearing of both would open routes from the Salween to the Shweli River, leaving the way south open to Tengchung. Desperately outnumbered, the Japanese shuttled troops between the two passes in attempts to slow the Chinese advances. After several fiercely fought battles at key towns in the Shweli Valley, the Japanese withdrew towards Tengchung, leaving large quantities of materiel and ammunition. By the end of June 1944 elements of the 53rd and 54th Armies from the 20th Army Group stood before their quarry, Tengchung, with orders from Chiang-Kai shek to take it.

Tengchung, with a population of 20,000, was completely surrounded by an earth wall, forty feet high and up to sixty feet in width . . . . its face also protected by great slabs of stone. In spite of its remote location (on the original Marco Polo route), it was considered a major jade center. An outer ring of pillboxes and 6000-foot Lai-feng Shan Mountain, "The Place Where The Birds Come" with 600 men and all of the Japanese artillery defended the town. Two thousand men were garrisoned within the wall, which formed a great square with a gate on each side at which the Japanese had set up command posts. Rifles and machine gun emplacements protected the entire perimeter of the wall. It was to prove to be a hard nut to crack.

The Chinese infantry began their attack on July 2 nd, taking seven of the outlying pillboxes on a height four and a half miles northwest of the city. By the end of the first week the city was completely surrounded by five Chinese divisions. A break in the monsoon in mid-July permitted the capture of a much needed airstrip southwest of the city and the battle for this key to the success of the Salween Offensive was fully joined.

· · · ·

From the end of April 1944 the Signal Repair team of Forrest Brown, Bob Gallagher and Jim Hoff, whose activities in the Mitu area we have already described, accompanied 53rd Army Headquarters along its torturous route to Tengchung. Starting from Mitu (Midu) their odyssey found them sometimes bouncing along in an old Chinese truck but more often experiencing the same litany of aggravation, agony, adversity and apprehension that so many of their counterparts were sharing as they followed the pack mule trains of their Chinese clients. Beyond the Salween, which they crossed over on what Hoff described as a "rickety" bridge, they were confronted with the unbelievably difficult challenge of traversing the treacherous, ice and mud covered trails of the ten thousand foot pass through the Kaoli-kung Mountains. It has been reported that during the brutal trek to Tengchung, more than 150 coolie carriers fell to their deaths from the monsoon-swept trails.

As the 53rd confronted each pocket of fierce Japanese resistance, Brown, Hoff and Gallagher and their American associates on the YFOS liaison team did what they could to assist the Chinese. Too often this involved them not only in occupations not related to their army "MOS" numbers, but sometimes thrust them into the center of the actual hostilities themselves. Brown related an incident in which the liaison personnel came under a severe and unexpected mortar attack. All sought cover except a major, three enlisted men and their interpreter. In a vain attempt to reach a safer haven they bolted into the open, only to fall victim to deadly sniper fire, with no survivors.

From early May until the middle of July the Brown Team continued to play nursemaid to the Chinese signal equipment, eventually reaching Tengchung in mid July, about the time that the air field was secured.

· · · ·

Like many of the cities and larger towns in China, the area just outside the walls was carpeted by a spread of mud huts and other buildings, each of which the Japanese had fortified. Several of the Chinese divisions, with their American advisors, were intensely engaged in reducing these, one at a time. During this period Brown took on the task of delivering the mail to his American compatriots. This he was successful in doing even while under artillery fire. After making his delivery, he and several others paused to watch the progress of the battle. As he did so, an American captain, who was also a spectator to the events before him, was shot in the head.

With the airfield secured, the Chinese turned their attention to the area between it and the city itself . . . They discovered immediately that the Japanese artillery, which had serenaded Brown during his mail delivery assignment, would have to be dealt with first. In reconnoitering the Japanese artillery positions on Lai-feng Shan Mountain, Chinese patrols reported that the Japanese had only fortified the slopes facing Tengchung. Responding, finally to the criticism of their American friends, and after the 14th Air Force P-40's and B-25's blasted the northern wall of the city and the artillery positions on the mountain, the Chinese attacked the mountain en-masse. This time they abandoned their usual practices of stopping to loot and rest but continued the attack until they stood at the top.

Sometime, during which the attempts to clear the Japanese from their footholds outside the walls of the city were taking place, while carrying ammunition near the airfield, Jim Hoff and another American were suddenly confronted by a Japanese soldier, whom they pursued and killed.

Brown recalled that the repair team spent much of its time in the vicinity of the airfield. He remembered a P51, which had lost the use of its landing gear, making a belly landing. As the pilot staggered out of the cockpit, he crossed in front of the plane. Brown and others ran out to assist him and just got themselves and him clear of the plane before the wing guns electrical system shorted out and the guns started firing wildly.

Many of their supplies were ferried to the airfield by L5 liaison planes, and as a result there were often several parked there at one time. During the early period when the Japanese could still provide some air activity, one of their fighters suddenly appeared and managed to destroy seven or eight of the little workhorses. Sometime later, one of the mechanics who apparently was a relative newcomer, while inspecting the damage to the planes, was heard to mention that he was sorry he had missed the attack and that he would really like to see one of the Japanese planes. Within minutes, another Japanese plane decided to take a run at the airfield with the hapless mechanic catching one the strafing plane's bullets right between his eyes.

Although the airfield was essential to the success of the Chinese attempts to take the city, it did not make it possible for Brown and his team to receive rations, thus they were again on a per diem basis and therefore had to find their own food supply. He reported that food was very scarce, as were anything resembling PX supplies. They did manage to get cigarettes, however, and Brown, who did not smoke, recalled that the rate of exchange was one pack of butts for a dozen eggs, when one could find any.

. . . .

Near the end of August 1944 the Air Corps, with an innovative skip-bombing demonstration, were finally able to poke a hole in the wall, large enough for the Chinese to get a foothold in the city and by September 15th, over stubborn and costly Japanese resistance, the Generalissimo's order to take Tengchung had been fulfilled. Several Burmese women, who had been forced to accompany the Japanese were discovered in the city and were liberated. Evidence of the city's prominence as a jade center was everywhere, with the precious stones lying around for the taking. By the time that the team was ready to leave Tengchung, however, the Chinese craftsmen were hard at their trade again, processing the jade into objects of art and jewelry.

The work for Brown, Hoff and Gallagher was not yet finished, however. What was left of the 20TH Group Army and the 53RD now headed south down the Schweli Valley to assist in the final phase of the Salween Campaign and the linking up with Stilwell's X-Ray Force, which had finally reached the old Burma Road. The Japanese now withdrawing from Southwestern China, but still astride some sections of the Road, made the advancing Yoke Force Chinese pay dearly for every mile they gained.

Without any details of the activities of the members of the Brown Team during this period, it is not known to what extent each contributed to the Chinese battles. From photographs, we do know that they remained together with the Chinese until the latter finally affected the link up with their countrymen, who made up the Chinese 1ST Army component of the X-RAY Force. This occurred at Muse, just over the Burma border.

The event signaled the end of the role of the 53RD in the Salween Campaign and it and all of the other units of the 11TH and 20TH Group Armies were ordered back into China. This, of course also ended the Brown Team's assignment to the 53rd and they prepared to fly back to Paoshan.

CHINESE GOVERNMENT PASSPORT – IDENTIFIES THE BEARER AND INCLUDES REWARD FOR AIDING HIM – ALSO A PERMIT TO CARRY A WEAPON

Brown's Chinese Passport

Gallagher (MA), Brown (MO),
Hoff (NJ) try their hand at chopsticks

Brown (MO) with one of the losers after the Battle of Tengchung

Brown and Gallagher get a souvenir

Brown and Hoff leaving for Paoshan

For his service to the 53RD Brown was awarded two Bronze Star Medals. The order and citation for one of them reads as follows:

HEADQUARTERS
CHINESE COMBAT COMMAND
UNITED STATES FORCES
CHINA THEATER

200.6                                                        APO 286
                                                            27 Oct 45

SUBJECT: Award of the Bronze Star Medal.

TO : T/4 FOREST M BROWN, 4919 Parrism, Kansas
     City, Kansas

3.    Forwarded herewith is General Order No.63, this
      Headquarters, dated 15 Oct 45, awarding you the
      Bronze Star Medal.
2.    Medals and ribbons may be requisitioned from your
      local Military District.
3.    The Commanding General regrets that presentation
      could not be made prior to your departure from this
      theater.

FOR THE COMMANDING GENERAL:

WILLIAM T. HAYNER
2nd Lt. AGD
Asst. Adj. Gen.

*CITATION*

Technician Third Grade FORREST M. BROWN, 37 148 491, Signal Corps, Army of the United States, is awarded the Bronze Star Medal for meritorious service during the period from 1 September 1944 to 14 September 1944. During this period Technician Third

Grade BROWN, continually went from sector to sector of the TENGCHUNG battle field adjusting and repairing the telephones at each unit Command Post and observation Post so that a continuous flow of accurate information could be relayed to Headquarters. This arduous work was done under constant artillery fire as well as mortar and small arms fire, sniper fire killed many of the personnel around him. His heroic devotion to duty reflects great credit upon himself and the Armed Forces of the United States.

The second BSM was awarded for his contribution to the 53RD during its efforts to accelerate the Japanese withdrawal from China down the Burma Road and covered the period between December 1944 and January, 1945. While he did not receive the official notification of this award until he was back in the civilian ranks, before he left Muse Lieutenant Sweet sent the following note to him:

*53rd Army*

Muse, Burma Dec. 20 to Dec. 30
Ta Ching Shin Hill, Burma Dec. 23 to Jan. 1
Mongyu, Burma Jan. 1-Jan. 30

Brownie, The one you got was signed by you and approved by Capt. (_____) J. Major F.A., Asst. G1, Awards and Decorations Off. Will try and get a copy to you to-morrow from Bw. I give you this info because you may be processed before I get there.

Sweet

Bronze Star Medals were also awarded to Jim Hoff and Bob Gallagher. At this writing we do not have a copy of either the order that conveyed the award to Gallagher or the citation, which accompanied it.

The order and citation for Jim Hoff's award reads in part as follows:

HEADQUARTERS
CHINESE COMBAT COMMAND (PROV)
UNITED STATES FORCES
CHINA THEATER

APO 286

24 August 1945

GENERAL ORDERS)

NUMBER 30)
AWARD OF THE BRONZE STAR MEDAL . . . . I

## 1. AWARD OF THE BRONZE STAR MEDAL:

Pursuant to authority contained in Letter AG File No. 200.6, subject, "Decorations and Awards", Rear Echelon Headquarters, United States Forces, China Theater, dated 26 February 1945, and under authority contained in Paragraph 8, AR 600-45, a BRONZE STAR MEDAL is awarded to the following named Officers and Enlisted Men:

TECHNICIAN FOURTH GRADE JAMES G. HOFF, 32 483 154, Signal Corps, United States Army. For meritorious service from 27 July 1944 to 27 September 1944.

BY COMMAND OF MAJOR GENERAL McCLURE:

Brig Gen., USA
Chief of Staff.

OFFICIAL:

(signed)
JAMES E LIGON,
Lt. Col., AGD,
Adjutant General

CITATION

TECHNICIAN FOURTH GRADE JAMES G.
HOFF,32 483 154 Signal Corps, United States Army
for heroism during the period of 27 July 1944 to 27
September 1944, at the siege and capture of
TENGCHUNG, Western Yunnan Province, China.
Technician Fourth Grade Hoff, a radio repairman,
repeatedly visited the siege city under heavy Japanese
fire to repair Chinese and American liaison radio
equipment at the forward Command Post. With
another American soldier, Technician Fourth Grade
Hoff pursued and killed, by small-arms fire, an armed
Japanese soldier near TENGCHUNG Airfield.
Technician Fourth Grade Hoff's outstanding heroism
and technical work under enemy fire and his alertness
reflect great credit upon himself and the Armed Forces
of the United States.

. . . .

The team of Forrest Brown, James Hoff and Robert Gallagher
arrived at Paoshan in time to join a truck convoy that was
preparing to leave for Kunming. As chance would have it, the
truck that they were in broke down shortly after leaving Paoshan
and to prevent its being ravaged by Chinese passersby, they
volunteered to stay with it until a wrecker could come out for it.
They were hesitant to do so, until they were offered a deal that
included air travel to Kunming instead of having to endure the
discomforts of the torturous, thirteen-day convoy road trip. The
following day the truck was retrieved by someone from Paoshan
and Brown & Co. were relieved and returned to town. As promised,
they were given seats on a plane, only to discover that the offer
included a detour all the way back to India before heading back
to Kunming. While they were able to avoid the agonizing trip up

the Burma Road that their compatriots were then enduring, they had to cross the Hump twice. By his own estimate, after leaving Ledo in December of 1943, Brown was away from the company for about nineteen months.

## MINDING THE STORE

With the start of the Salween Campaign in early May, and the imminent departure of almost two thirds of the 2ND and 4TH to join their Chinese clients, their compatriots, at both Paoshan and Yunnanyi, were left to take on the supporting roles that had been assigned to the teams. By Mothers Day, 1944 the YFOS liaison teams were all gone and those who remained turned to face the yet undefined mission that was now expected of them under the game plan for the offensive that had just begun.

Now familiar with the unwritten rule, which applied to any American unit attached to Yoke Force, they knew that their tasks would not end with the mere maintenance of signal equipment. During the first weeks of the offensive, those who remained were hard pressed to fulfill their new roles and soon found that doing so required that they leave the secure environment of their repair shops to venture far and wide into the remote vastness of that area of Southwestern Yunnan that lay between Yunannyi and the Salween River.

### *YUNNANYI*

During the many months that were required to dislodge the Japanese from the Salween and Schweli River Valleys, the demands for the services of the 2ND were many-fold. Occurring in no particular order, they generally included the shuttling of new materiel and equipment to the repair shop or local warehouses from the incoming planes arriving from India over the

"Hump" . . . the repair or alignment of signal equipment for use in the campaign . . . forwarding it to either the airfield for trans-shipment within China or transporting it by truck down the Burma Road to Paoshan and other locations which served as bases for the Chinese and American forces . . . and of course . . . . the servicing of the signal and electronic needs of all of the surrounding organizations in the Unmanly area.

All of these activities were performed by the 2ND Team at the direction of 1st. Lt. James F. McVeigh and platoon sergeant, Tech. Sgt. Gilbert L. Carlson (Falconer, N.Y.). As mentioned earlier, Morris S. (Morrie) Malinkowitz (New York City) was pinch-hitting as mess sergeant and one of the radio repair squads was under the wing of Tech. Sgt. Roy Hendricks (Bridgeport, Indiana). In no special order, the rest of the group included Millard Sturgell (Kentucky) . . . . Henry (Shot) Howell, Duncan (Hamp) Mc Bride, Richard H. Ferguson, Kermit H. Clark (North Carolina) . . . . Bernard Metz, Ed Rozmerski (Chicago) . . . . James Beck (Little Rock, Arkansas) . . . . Salvatore Corritore (Nebraska) . . . . Morris Stern (Neptune,N.J.) . . . . Bill Singer (New York City) . . . . Fred Linton (Memphis, Tennessee) . . . . Percy Olsen (Commerce, Oklahoma) . . . . Manuel P. Perez (New Mexico) . . . . Deward B. (DB) Russell, William H. Little (Texas) . . . . Willis Dengler (Iowa) . . . . and . . . . Clinton E. Harwood (Illinois)

. . . .

Calls for the services of Millard Sturgell, described earlier continued after the campaign had started. Receiving an assignment to YFOS Headquarters automatically guaranteed that he would see considerable time in the field. One of these took him all the way to the Salween for two or three weeks to repair and calibrate radio receiver/transmitters for a Chinese artillery battery that was firing across the river valley.

The tasks the men were given covered the entire gamut of

YFOS activities with the Chinese. The reader might recall that one of the military occupations the Americans were permitted to engage in during the Salween offensive was the manning of anti-aircraft batteries at the bridges over key river crossings. One of these units, which had been guarding the bridge over the Mekong River, where it intersected with the Burma Road was eventually recalled when Japanese air activity was no longer a threat.

In leaving, however, they left behind an amount of materiel and equipment in a compound that they had occupied. To prevent its confiscation by the Chinese or anyone else passing though the area, Bill Roby, who had recovered partially from his ordeal with the 53RD Army in Ta-tang-tzu Pass and Willis (Willie) Dengler were sent to watch over the compound and its contents until arrangements could be made for its removal. Anticipating that a change from Yunnanyi might not be "all bad", our two stalwarts accepted the assignment, expecting it to be non-eventful if not down right peaceful. Their expectations were indeed realized with one startling exception. What they could not have known was that the AA Battery contingent, as part of their battle with what must have been a mostly boring assignment, had taken to feeding a pack of apparently wild dogs, which frequented the vicinity. When the unit left their compound, there was a period during which the dogs went hungry.

One morning, shortly after his arrival Dengler, upon opening the compound gate, was confronted by one of the largest of the savage, hungry brutes. The situation required swift decisive action, which Roby provided by dispatching the unfortunate animal with his rifle.

Sometime after the fall of Myitkyina, while delivering several vehicles to Paoshan, 205 grueling miles west of Yunnanyi, Mc Bride, Linton and Russell, after turning a sharp curve, were stopped and accosted by a group of Americans. These folks were apparently newcomers to China and the Road and had some words to say regarding the speed at which our heroes had been traveling. When these became overheated, one of the newcomers lost his "cool" and began shouting to one of the officers, "Give me that gun captain . . . give me that gun!" . . . . to which Mc Bride retorted icily, as he flipped the retaining flap from the 45 automatic at his belt, "Go ahead captain . . . give him the gun!". Of course nothing could or did come of the incident but it does illustrate the rugged, wildness of life along the Burma Road.

This extraordinary episode also had a bizarre conclusion when, after delivering their vehicles and now without road transportation back to Yunnanyi, the trio accepted a plane ride to Myitkyina in Burma. After a night in which they were treated to American beer, not attainable by ground force enlisted men in China, they returned, also by air, to Yunnanyi.

. . . .

Defeating the Japanese was still the reason for the American presence in Yunnan, of course, a fact that the enemy had not lost sight of. Testimony to this, particularly during the early weeks of the campaign, came in the form of air strikes at the airfield. Hamp Mc Bride, who shared a small hut, about a half-mile from the airfield, from which he sallied forth to repair gasoline-powered electric generators, recalled a night when the Japanese hit a gasoline storage revetment. He said, "You never saw such a fire in your life."

. . . .

The forays into the area surrounding Yunnanyi and down the Burma Road, though sometimes dangerous and difficult, did help, however, to break up the long wait for the Salween Campaign to end. With no American food included in the priority list of items that made up "Hump" tonnage, the menus in all ground force mess halls had rice as the central ingredient. Water buffalo meat was another prominent leader in the list of native offerings. About the only familiar fare that was available as conditions dictated were chicken eggs, cooked in any style requested.

For most of the 2ND Team their Salween adventure lasted from February 1944 until January 1945 or later, long enough for the most iron-willed soul to succumb to occasional moments of frustration and even bitterness. The usual string of diversions, from poker to volleyball, the latter a standard with the 181ST wherever it went, were sometimes effective in consuming some of the seemingly endless days and weeks.

At one point, the ever-present, infamous but lovable Fred Linton also made his contribution toward the war on boredom when he appeared in the repair shop with a large empty artillery shell casing with its firing cap still intact. He promptly clamped it into a vise and set the cap off blowing a large hole in the gravel floor. Always looking for some form of mischief to get into, with money he borrowed from Hamp Mc Bride, he upstaged some of the "Special Service" folks by meeting a group of entertainers at the airfield and taking them to dinner.

Where there was still room for promotions, they were awarded, Sturgell finally getting a well-deserved raise to T-4 (technician fourth grade) which paid the same as a three-stripe buck sergeant . . . . and Kermit Clark was elevated to tech sergeant.

When the novelty of Yunnanyi finally wore off, the tourist juices in our heroes' veins rose to the surface, prodding them to look beyond for new worlds to conquer. One such objective was the town of Tali (Dali), a major source of marble and another stop on Marco Polo's long itinerary. A weapons carrier was checked out for what turned out to be a two-hour jaunt. The time spent in probing the secrets of the ancient settlement revealed yet another example of the many wonders of this mysterious land. As Bill Friedman of New York recalled, however, these were soon forgotten during the trip home. What should have been a routine exercise of adjusting to the geological eccentricities of the road suddenly became a deadly race to upset the designs of bandits. In telling his story, Bill related that, at first, he did not connect the small popping sounds with any impending danger and was unpleasantly surprised when their truly ominous nature was revealed. Not having factored such an eventuality into their travel plans our friends soon discovered that they were woefully short of firepower. Several, including Bill, however, were carrying small-caliber pistols purchased from the street venders in town. Fortunately there was no opportunity to discover their dubious usefulness, as the weapons carrier was gunned through the gauntlet of fire coming from the unfriendly darkness, leaving the memories of the Tali adventure to remain much different than what the men had at first anticipated.

Of the sixty men who had entered the army via Fort Dix in New Jersey en-route to joining the 181ST at Camp Crowder, a dozen or more, from New York City, were Jewish. A handful of these had found their way to Yunnanyi and with others from neighboring units were in need of a chaplain. Despite the enormity of China itself and because a small minority of the GI's in the country answered to the Jewish faith, the army had designated only one rabbi, Alvin Fine from Rhode Island, as chaplain for the entire country. The men from the 181ST, in responding to the situation, promptly accepted Bill Friedman as their unofficial acting chaplain. Bill conducted weekly services for the men for a while until the theater rabbi was finally able to get down the Road to attend to their spiritual wants. When he discovered what Bill had been doing, with Bill's concurrence, he started the paperwork to have him transferred and to become the official chaplain's assistant. The move fell through when Lieutenant Mc Veigh refused to let Bill go.

In view of the fact that almost all of us who had completed radio or telephone school in Camp Crowder and who had been with the company through the entire desert maneuver had been promoted to Technicians, Fifth Grade (T5) the lieutenant's motives were certainly suspect. This became even more apparent when he allowed Bill, who was a qualified radio repairman, to venture across the Salween into a combat zone with the Chinese 54TH Army . . . . still a buck private.

. . . .

During the summer of 1944 several changes occurred in the personnel in Yunnanyi. One saw five or six men from Lt. George H. Wilson's 3RD Team, stationed at Ledo, fly from India to Kunming and then on to Yunnanyi. In this group were Paul Mrogenski (Brookfield, MO.), Sabatino Gentile (NJ) and Evan Evans (Brainard, MN).

Near the end of the summer or early in the fall Lt. Mc Veigh reported to the medics complaining of asthma, a surprise to most of us, since he was a dedicated cigar smoker. With the blessing of the medics, which allegedly included a friend of his, he packed his bags and ordered Hamp Mc Bride to drive him to the airfield. When Hamp asked him where he was going, he stunned him with the simple statement, "I'm going home."

As in every war there are those who decide that they are no longer going to participate in what they perceive to be a meaningless exercise. Like the deserter in California who made his decision and move while we were still in California, the 181ST had three others who apparently came to the same decision but each acted upon it in a different way. Two of these were with the 2ND Team.

One, a very able telephone repairman announced one day that he had "had enough" of the way the war was being conducted in China and that he was going to get drunk and stay that way for the duration. For the majority of his stay in Yunnanyi he was true to his word, causing some of his comrades considerable concern and effort. Since he was a very large man, they developed a procedure during air raids in which they dropped his huge frame into a garbage pit, which was the nearest thing to the barracks that passed as a slit trench. When the "all clear" was sounded they then had the most unpleasant task of cleaning him up. Their treatment of him during the many months was an extraordinary act of loyalty and compassion for one, who when sober, was himself an extremely friendly, likable and outgoing person. Unfortunately, he accomplished more than just avoiding the war. One year later, in August, after the Atomic Bomb had been dropped and we were back in Kunming waiting for transportation home, he was still in the same condition and possibly on the road to alcoholism.

The other person in the 2ND who decided to quit the war, at least the one in China appears to have been one of the lieutenants. Always a cocky, self-assured operator, he was accepted as such by most of the men with whom he often played poker. His decision apparently was made about September, when the Theater was going through tumultuous changes that included the split into the India-Burma and China Theaters and the recall of General Stilwell. It has been alleged that, before boarding the plane in Yunnanyi he had collected an unknown number of per diem vouchers from men out in the field with an offer to cash them in the next time that he was in Yunnanyi or Kunming. It has also been reported that he was intercepted at Karachi in India in possession of a large amount of cash.

. . . .

His departure left a void that was subsequently filled when Lt. Wilson, accompanied by Luke Strass arrived in Yunnanyi via Kunming in November, as described in Chapter 4. A much more businesslike individual, one of the first things the new C.O. did was to recognize Bill Friedman's abilities including the fact that he could type and immediately assigned Bill as repair shop clerk and Wilson's secretary. He also saw that Bill received a PFC stripe, small enough compensation for the treatment he had previously received.

With Tengchung, Lungling and Sungshan Mountain all now in Chinese hands, the Salween Campaign was now entering its final phase. The Japanese characteristically had not yet given up the fight and to the surprise of many an enemy plane following on the tail of a landing American transport dropped anti-personnel bombs aimed at the Yunnanyi airfield. They fell, instead, in the vicinity of the barracks with no casualties. Although someone had been in the process of ordering a formation, most all had the good sense to get under cover instead. When Wilson learned about the attempted formation, he became irate and took the guilty officer to task.

. . . .

As it did all over the world, the war took its toll in many ways. In the 2ND it struck down Salvitore Corritore. At this writing it is not known whether he had been out with any of the Chinese armies. A rumor had found its way back to Kunming that he had and having a slight disability in one of his legs, had found it impossible to keep up with the rest of the column. The rumor went on to explain that he had been found wandering along one of the trails and was returned to Yunnanyi. We will never know the real story but several of his compatriots have attested to the fact that he became suddenly violent in the repair shop at Yunnanyi and had to be disarmed. The last report was that he had been hospitalized and subsequently flown out of China. All attempts to locate him since the beginning of this narrative have been unsuccessful.

. . . .

While this is not the end of the 2ND Team's story, most of it, like all of the personal experiences of the men involved, has been lost for eternity. When the Ledo and Burma Roads were finally joined and a land link was completed to Kunming, some of the 2ND remained until the end of the war while others returned to Kunming for reassignment in the campaign to reach and establish a port on the China Sea.

Malinkowitz (NYC)

Old water detail

New water detail

(L to R) Mrogenski (MO), Stull (NY)
Beck (AR), Russo (CT), . . . with some
Friends

# PAOSHAN

The role of the American YOKE FORCE OPERATIONS STAFF (YFOS) in Paoshan was quite different than its counterparts' in Yunnanyi. With the latter playing essentially one of supply, the folks in Paoshan, and the command center for the Chinese Expeditionary Force (CEF), performed a function parallel to that of their Chinese Allies. Although the U.S. had no command power over the Chinese armies and divisions, it was their responsibility to oversee all of the activities of the American liaison and support units. It followed, then that American and Chinese units were scattered all over the Paoshan area.

Servicing their communication and signal repair needs became the burden put upon Lt. Kermit Swanson's 4TH Team. The platoon leader was Tech Sergeant Varner Shippy (Holden, MO), who enjoyed the backing of another excellent group of men. After the team had been diminished by the departure of about half of its personnel to the Chinese Armies, those left behind to mind the store included Battle Brown (Raleigh, NC), Horace Gooding (Williamston, NC), Lawrence Hundley (Thomasville, NC), William Floyd Mercer (Whitesburg, KY), Clyde Oie (Ironwood, MI), Millard (Jesse) Owens (Burlington, NJ), Ed Vossler (Closter, NJ), Harry Prince (Yonkers, NY), Roy W. Murphy (Clymer, NY), Ken Merritt (Lake Hopatcong, NJ), Dave Thorn (New Orleans, LA), Frank Mc Graw (Hendersonville, NC), Dan Russo (New York City) and Franklin Trivette (Boone, NC). These men, and several others whose names can no longer be recalled, participated, not only in the maintenance of the YFOS switchboard, which tied together all of the allied military units in the Paoshan area, but continued also to be directly involved in its operation.

Of course, servicing the circuits, many terminating in a Chinese carrier station, another one of those non-repair shop job activities was picked up by the Swanson Team. Here Bob Gunning, who had demonstrated his considerable talents in Kunming, was again called on to exercise his Yankee ingenuity. He recalled that . . .

This carrier consisted of modulator and demodulator circuits, the east direction operated at 1650 cycles and the west direction at 1350 cycles, with a ring-down circuit at 1000 cycles. The db gain was controlled with H type pads and T type pads of 4 db intervals, from 4db to 16 db. The gain had to be changed every morning, due to moisture leakage on the long lines and then reduced again when they dried out. This changing required soldering and unsoldering of bridging wires on the pad terminals. To eliminate this inconvenience, I constructed a small panel from scrap sheet metal, from a crashed airplane, and mounted two rotary switches and two octal tube sockets, wired to the T-pads and H-pads respectively. Then I used the bases from worn- out tubes to plug into the H-pads, by properly bridging the required pins for the necessary db gain. These were labeled for each gain needed, from 4 db to 16 db, requiring four bases for each H-pad. The panel was permanently mounted to the equipment demodulator cover, with stand-off brackets."

Thus, as the lines dried out during the day, maintaining the proper gain became a simple matter of exchanging plugs. Gunning found that, "This modification served the purpose well."

Connections soldered throughout the carrier system by Chinese technicians who were using irons heated in charcoal fires were discovered to be unreliable and the cause of most of the troubles they cleared. Re-soldering them whenever they were encountered became a second career for Gunning and his American companions.

By June, one month after arriving in Paoshan, Gunning was back in Yunnanyi, making the same modifications on the Hsungyun-Paoshan and Hsungyun-Kunming circuits. This accomplished, he was ordered to Hsungyun where he helped operate a BD 72 field switchboard. One of its circuits was a line to an American Motor Pool and repair facility in Hsia-kuan

(Shagwan), forty miles west of Hsungyun on the Burma Road. One side of the circuit utilized a ground-return, which endowed it with a metallic sounding hum that, at times rendered the circuit useless. To Gunning this was not only a communication problem, but was also a professional challenge. After several attempts to locate and eliminate the mysterious electronic culprit, which often kept the signal drops on the switchboard in the operated position, Bob finally deduced that the interference was caused by occasional electronic eccentricities generated by the earth's magnetic field over which even the 181ST had no control.

Gunning was subsequently joined in Hsungyun by Battle Brown, Ed Vossler and Frank Mc Craw, the same trio that had been encountered near Mitu by Forrest Brown and later Alton Croom. At the time they had been participating in the construction of telephone line circuits between Yunnanyi and Mitu. Upon arriving in Yunnanyi, they had been pressed into a YFOS pole line construction gang, thrown together and guided by a Captain White from Kentucky. In Hsungyun they, along with Gunning were given room and board and medical and dental care by the American Field Hospital, which was also one of Gunning's switchboard customers.

The other circuits on the board were trunk lines to Paoshan, Yunnanyi and Kunming. Maintenance of these also became the order of the day for our quartet, with Brown buying the additional task of installing Teletype service to the Hsia-kuan Motor Pool. While Mc Craw, an accomplished pole-climber, was earning his keep nursemaiding the open-line circuits, Vossler, a portly fugitive from a New Jersey power company, was assigned the job of maintaining the health of the team's jeep and, under orders from Brown, who out-ranked him, sallied forth whenever there was an outage on the Teletype line. Since the latter used a phantom circuit superimposed on the erratic ground-return configuration mentioned above, Vossler was kept very busy. As chance would have it, most trouble seemed to occur just at mealtime, which was especially annoying to Ed, who was very fond of the food served by their hosts at the hospital. The result was an increasingly long and continuous verbal exchange between Vossler and Brown, who was under strict orders to keep the critically needed line to the motor pool in working order. Ed ultimately developed a healthy dislike for Teletype, which he referred to as "tomato cans." Gunning recalled that the argument continued for several months, until he was finally promoted and recalled back to Kunming, after the Salween fireworks were over.

From the accounts that have been given by the members of the Mc Veigh 2ND Team and Swanson's 4TH, one can deduce that there was some overlap in geographical responsibility, particularly in the Yunnanyi-Hsungyun-Mitu-Hsia-kuan areas. On one occasion Millard Sturgell (from the 2ND) found himself working with Bob Gunning (from the 4TH) servicing a repeater station at Pin-ch uan, north of Hsia-kuan.

Back in Paoshan, Roy W. Murphy, a radio repairman from Clymer, New York, accompanied a string of pack mules, carrying equipment to a remote village and spent a long, lonely vigil guarding it until someone finally arrived to claim it.

Horace Gooding remembered that he was often called away from Paoshan. "Up in those hills!" as he described the locales where the Chinese units were based. Typical of the variety of jobs that came his way was one request that came in for the rewiring of a PE-95 110 volt power unit to 220 volts so that a Chinese general's son could be x-rayed.

Ray Fichter, after returning from his adventures with the Chinese 53rd Army across the Salween, took his place at the Paoshan switchboard. It was from his memorabilia that the actual traffic diagram, taken from the Paoshan switchboard, was unearthed. A devout Catholic, Ray also volunteered to assist the chaplain by serving mass on Sundays and holy days.

As the nerve center for the Salween Offensive, Paoshan was naturally the target of the Japanese air force. For a time they appeared nightly. When the three-ball alert was up, standard procedure was to take off into the nearby hills. Varner Shippy, who was the platoon leader and a fellow telephone repairman, recalled that Fichter, with whom he was very close, usually ran the farthest and, during a particular night raid, did not return until morning . . . having apparently gone to sleep while waiting for the all clear to sound. Shippy told another story of him and several others taking refuge during one of the night raids. They had taken off as usual and, in the dark, selected a large structure as a good place under which to stay. When it became lighter, they discovered, to their dismay that the protection they had sought was under a gigantic gasoline tank. Several members of the 4TH recalled an incident, which occurred as a flight of American B-25s, returning from a mission beyond the Salween passed over the town of Paoshan during the night. As they watched the flight approach, a single plane opened its bomb-bay doors and, apparently mistaking the town as a target of opportunity let go with its entire string. The effects on the town and its inhabitants were devastating. I noticed, during my reading of the official history of the CBI conflict that no mention was made of this incident.

Like the 2ND at Yunnanyi, the 4TH also had a dissenter, who had apparently lost patience with the progress of the CBI war. Sometime while the conflict dragged its feet, due in part to the eccentricities of the Chinese leadership and the numbing effects of the tenacious monsoon in the Salween and Shweli River Valleys, one of our New Yorkers somehow wangled himself a seat on a plane heading west over the "Hump". He was not apprehended until he, during a possible change of heart, reportedly checked into a medical station in New Delhi.

. . . .

Once Tengchung, Lungling and Sungshan were taken in the early fall of 1944, and the battles were over for the Chinese Expeditionary Forces in Yunnan, some, including Shippy, Fichter, Gunning and Stanley Greggo (from Ohio) were summoned eastward to start all over again in the 1945 campaign to open a seaport on the Chinese coast. Weeks Andrews and Jim Hoff also headed for Kweiyang in Kweichow Province, from which the now beefed up American Chinese Training and Combat Command of which YFOS had become a part, was preparing to assist the Chinese in opening a port at Ft. Bayard. Others from the 181st, both in Yunnanyi and Paoshan, were still serving the needs of their areas when the first truck convoy passed through on its way to Kunming from Ledo in late January 1945.

# CHAPTER VII

## Between The East

## And The West

### THE FIRST FINALLY FINDS ITS NICHE

The phrase "Hurry up and wait!" very aptly describes the two major conditions under which the average GI had to function during World War 2. It is also a pretty accurate description of the context within which the military went about its business of generating edicts that contributed to the mental frustrations of those of us who were not privy to the army's game plans. The eventual revelation of these plans and the orders that emanated from them either put these same frustrations to rest or generated a whole new set of anxieties. Thus it was with very mixed feelings the fellows from Lt. Bernie Silverman's 1ST Team, of which I was a member, responded when on March 13, 1944 Special Order Number 73 was received in Ledo, India, stating in the army's very own private pig Latin:

"15. Following named O and EM, 181st Signal
Repair Co, are placed on DS with "Y" Forces at APO
627."

This part of Order Number 73 was followed by four more lines of
military shorthand which outlined the mode of travel to be utilized
and under what circumstances the O and EM would be entitled to
the grand sum of six dollars per day (per diem) for food etc. If written
in English the order would have said simply that we were to catch a
plane in India and fly to Kunming and if we couldn't find mess halls
along the way, we would each get six bucks per day for food.

The order then went on to list all of the members of the team.
At the risk of boring the reader, I have included that list . . . .
first because I am proud to have been associated with them and
secondly because it is the only team that I have a complete roster
of. This stellar group included the following:

1st Lt. Bernard Silverman

Radio Repair                    Radio Repair

T/Sgt Alvin P. Wagler       T/Sgt William W. Wraspir
T/3rd Robert W. Callinan   T/3rd Colden D. Chesser
T/3rd Raymond E. Hardee  T/4th George A. Simon
T/4th Lloyd G. Teske        T/4th Isadore Kishner
T/5th Arthur L. Follett       T/5th Phillip E. Thompson
T/5th George E. Raabe       T/5th Richard A. Williams
T/5th Donald P. Sanders     T/5th Rene J. Sandoz
Pfc. William C. Evans        T/5th Earl Troy
Pvt. James M. Spalding      Pvt. Lois L. Orman

Telephone Repair

T/Sgt William A. Hasse
T/3rd Alvin F. Kljun
T/4th Jeffrey A. Bennett

T/4th Alfred C. Stursberg
T/4th Charles A. Wingler
T/4th Alfred C. Stursberg
T/5th Sam Firman
T/5th John H. Omer
T/5th Joseph W. Harding
Pvt. Lorin H. Bolin
Pvt. Ben Marcus

(back row) Thompson (PA) Wingler (IL) Sanders (NC) the
writer . . . . (middle row) Kishner (CA) Troy (NJ)
Callinan, (NJ) Simon (MD) Stursberg (NJ) . . . (seated)
Wagler (IA) Marcus (NYC) Williams (MN)
Silverman (VA) Hasse (OR) Wraspir (ID) Bennett (NJ) . . .
(missing from photo) Hardee (NC) Teske (ND) Follett (KS)
Raabe (WI) Spalding (KY) Chesser (NC) Sandoz (NJ)
Orman (NC) Firman (IL) Omer (IA) Bolin (NM)

My first association with Lt. Silverman did not really occur
until the team had reached China, since Al Kljun and I were
still playing nursemaid to our six-circuit switchboard up in

the jungles outside of Hellgate when he arrived at Ledo to take Lt. Petri's place. Bernie was a young (one month my junior), idealistic Electrical Engineering Graduate of Virginia Polytechnic Institute and had been raised in a normal, patriotic family in the Richmond area. He, like so many others, took advantage of the ROTC program at the school and thus entered the army as a second lieutenant. He believed that at the time that he joined the army, it was singling out college students in its ranks for assignment to headquarters organizations and that his post in New Delhi was a direct result of that policy. At Delhi he had anticipated a much more active role in the war than the one he was given, however, and on January 28th, 1944 he jumped at the chance to escape from the office intrigues that it engendered.

Once he had managed to shed himself of the newness inherent in assuming the command that he received upon reaching Ledo, he settled down to become a credible officer and handled his assignment with the 1ST Team in an even-handed manner.

In addition to his position as leader of the telephone and Teletype repair squad, T/Sgt William A. Hasse . . . a tall, rawboned, sharp-witted westerner from the Oregon horse country . . . was also the platoon sergeant. It is my opinion that, in assessing their chances for victory in the Pacific, the Japanese woefully underestimated the degree to which Hasse and so many others like him, whose stories we are already familiar with, would react to the events at Pearl Harbor. The enemy also failed to recognize that the plethora of skills that these men brought to the army spelled certain doom for their imperialistic adventures.

I could spend many more positive words on each of the gentlemen listed above but will only summarize by acknowledging that each made his own individual contribution to the Team's activities.

· · · ·

Our subsequent travels from Ledo to Kunming, covered in more detail in Chapter 5, brought us to Hostel 4, north of the airfield on

April 10, 1944. There several of the team were assigned to tents while others, including the writer, were fortunate in finding empty bunks, albeit some of them uppers, in a newly-constructed wooden barracks. This hostel was provided and managed by the Chinese War Area Service Corps (WASC). The kitchen was also run by WASC and to our astonishment served eggs for breakfast, a pleasant change from the corned beef and luncheon meat menus in Ledo. Whereas we had been forced to improvise methods for washing our own clothes in India, we now found that being in a country of Chinese laundrymen, WASC also relieved us of that chore.

The contrast between life in the jungles of Assam and our new station on the outskirts of Kunming was enormous. In India with its imposing foliage, we had experienced the urgencies of initiating a newly formed ground offensive without being told what our contribution toward it would eventually be. Our roles as pinch-hitters for the soon-to-be-arriving 96TH Signal Battalion and other miscellaneous jobs that fell to us, however, could have been likened to those of second stringers at an athletic event. Prior to receiving word that our real assignment was to be in China, some of us wondered exactly what roles awaited us. The Ledo area, which was building up for the Herculean task of driving the Japanese out of Northern Burma and the construction of a road across the entire country, was bustling with activity. Yet we, in the 1ST Team, were not plugged in as an integral unit.

Conversely, in the drab, vast expanses of rice paddies and distant treeless mountains of China, which seemed to swallow up the scattered American installations, we had finally found our ultimate niche in the historic event called World War 2. For the 1ST Team, at least, it had also changed its tempo. In place of the accelerating pace of the Allied units in and around Ledo, and with the pitiful shortages of materiel and the utter disregard by the Chinese for time, we soon discovered that our war had suddenly slowed to a snail's pace. The low-flying transports, bombers and fighters of the Air Corps that buzzed continuously over our little military installation dramatically demonstrated the only apparent activity.

As reported earlier, we were assigned to the Yoke Force signal compound, which housed the repair shop just vacated by our comrades from the 4TH Team, who had departed down the Burma Road to Paoshan. With an apparently minimum amount of Y Force equipment left in the Kunming area, there was, at first, very little repair activity. Some of the men, following in the footsteps of their comrades from the 2ND and 4TH Teams, soon discovered that, in Y Force, army military occupation labels (mos numbers) were irrelevant to the tasks to be performed. Consequently, several repairmen, as well as the vehicle drivers spent most of their time meeting transport planes at the airfield and distributing their cargoes within the Kunming vicinity, essentially performing signal supply functions. Those of us who reported to the repair shop soon fell into a daily pattern of travel between the Y Force signal compound and Hostel 4 several times a day for meals.

Troy (NJ) and Omer (IA) waiting for the truck to take them to work at the signal compound

Sam Firman (Chicago) and friends killing time
while waiting for the truck

This routine proved to be short-lived, however. The army had either changed its mind or had discovered that they had made a mistake. On May 7, 1944, just short of a month after our arrival, they rewrote those same orders reassigning the 1ST Team to Advance General Depot #1 SOS (Services of Supply). By a stroke of the typewriter, we were transferred from the Army Ground Forces to the Army Service Forces . . . or as some of the more earthy members of the fighting forces would put it . . . we were now "Blue Star Commandos", a derisive title prompted by the ASF shoulder patch, which featured a blue star in a red circle. We had also become *"garritroopers"*, another derisive term which described the holders of such a title as being in a combat zone, thus not considered *"garrison troops"* but also located too far from actual combat to be labeled *"combat troops"*.

The immediate effect of our new assignment to SOS was that we could no longer be served at the Hostel 4 kitchen. Living quarters, which, later, were to be at Hostel 5, a much larger facility and nearer to the airfield, however, were not yet available. Thus began several long weeks of traversing the pathways across an expansive Chinese cemetery for our morning and evening meals. It was also while negotiating our way over the toe path that wound its way between the graves that we made the somber discovery of the resting place of several dozen American military casualties, mostly fallen airmen. The Chinese section of this cemetery near Hostel 4 had received more than its share of Japanese aerial bombardment with many graves being disturbed. Some had been totally destroyed while others had been sliced cleanly in half with one end of their caskets open, exposing their contents to the curiosity of any passerby. At first the trek between the hostels and the viewing of the grisly contents of the open coffins competed with one's bodily demand for nourishment. But when it became depressingly evident that the fare at the mess hall at Hostel 5 revolved too often around entrees of water buffalo and unbleached rice, the apparitions, which emanated from the resting places of the honorable ancestors lost their impacts on our appetites.

. . . .

During our first days at the signal compound there was precious little repair or other activity to occupy idle hands. Consequently some of the men used the time to visit with the last group from Swanson's 4TH Team who were still readying their gear for their assignment down the Burma Road. Several others from the 1ST Team discovered that the 4TH's repair bus-body was standing idle in the middle of the compound . . . immediately commandeered it . . . and soon had a brisk "crap" game going. In due time it was inevitable that they would be discovered and when this occurred Lt. Silverman wisely decided to convert the work shop into a classroom. Having been caught as an observer in the bus-body, I can still recall much of the detailed functioning of the superhetrodyne radio receiver that was subsequently taught to us by Sergeant Paul Wagler (Iowa).

. . . .

Our first experiences with overseas guard duty started with Y Force, putting us at night within the walls of the same compounds that our predecessors from the 2ND and 4TH Teams had watched over as described in Chapter 6. The fascination by blackmarketeers from town over the possibilities of the materiel housed within the walls of the warehouses in the compound was evidenced by their persistent attempts to gain entrance. Constructed of clay and straw bricks, these same walls were easily dug through. When level places were bulldozed upon which to erect these walls, a continuous embankment of ten-foot piles of earth had been left, encircling the compound on three sides. Access could then be made by simply placing a plank of proper length between the top of one of these earth piles and the top of the wall itself. In the Signal Compound, which housed a large store of Chinese rifle ammunition, access was even easier by continuing the plank bridge to the top of the pile of cases, which had been conveniently placed only a few feet from the wall.

At first the guards were only responsible for the area within the walls and warehouses, the latter being locked at night. My first guard assignment was the same Quartermaster Compound that our compatriot, Fred Linton, had peppered with his Thompson submachinegun . . . . and I was introduced to the same spine-tingling sensation of "popping" fifty-gallon drums that had triggered his unfortunate action. Also, during the same tour, I was viciously admonished by the corporal-of-the-guard for not having been aware of the fact that someone had dug a nice neat hole into the outer wall of one of four corner warehouses of the very compound that I was supposed to be safeguarding. Fortunately for the allied war effort and me my nocturnal visitor had been denied entry by a long stack of coal shovels, which blocked the hole. Thereafter all of the guards were given keys to the compound gates and were responsible for both sides of the walls.

. . . .

As members of the Y Force population charged with guarding their military real estate received assignments that took them away from the area, the supply of bodies available for guarding the compounds dwindled considerably. A decision was then made that only two individuals would be assigned to each of the guard posts and that they could divide their night's work between them as they so chose. This edict subsequently resulted in an evening in which I and a fellow New Jerseyite, Rene "Sandy" Sandoz, inherited the responsibility for safeguarding the Signal Compound. This, of course, was the one in which the Chinese ammunition was stacked so conveniently close to the wall, a fact that the daytime coolies had no doubt relayed to some of their contemporaries. In due time it had been noticed that cases of the rifle ammunition were indeed being taken and one morning it was discovered that the thieves had even left their plank-bridge still in place after conducting their evening's work. This was too much for Sandy and me to disregard so we decided that we were going to be the ones to catch these nocturnal culprits in the act. We removed the planks that had been left behind and took two of the ammunition boxes and stood them on end, hoping that they would act as bait for the sneak thieves.

We decided that we would each split the fourteen-hour shift in half, with each of us standing seven straight hours. Sandy, however, had been partying the previous night, probably a Saturday, and had had very little sleep. Consequently he asked that I take the first shift from 6pm until 1am the following morning, so that he could catch up on the lost shuteye. This I agreed to and after unsuccessfully employing all of my trick maneuvers . . . doubling back, suddenly climbing over the gate to circle the outside of the compound, and other gyrations that must have appeared puzzling to anyone laying in wait in the rice paddies behind it . . . . I woke Sandy. I also had to report my failure at not having even seen anyone and then retired to the far corner of an empty warehouse and a folding cot. Sometime later, about

3am or 4am, I sat upright when the door of the warehouse swung inward and a very excited Sandy shouted that one of the ammunition cases was missing. He could not explain how it had happened, swearing that he had not been sleeping, although we all rested occasionally in a chair that was propped against the outer wall of a warehouse facing the main gate across the expanse of the compound. He said that it had just happened and that the perpetrator could not have gotten very far.

He took a position on top of the ammunition pile and I swung over the gate and headed for the back of the compound. It was one of those nights when the air activity was pretty brisk and the clouds were intermittently covering the moon. Timing my movements to coincide with a darkened sky and the noise of a plane on its incoming glide path, I began to work my way from paddy to paddy, hoping to catch up with the culprit, who I assumed would be heading for a small hamlet about a half mile behind the compound. This consumed several minutes and as these became longer and longer for Sandy . . . and just when I thought that I might be gaining on my imaginary quarry, he could take the waiting no longer and shouted, "Are you O.K. Joe?" This, of course was the end of my little escapade . . . and . . . we did not report the missing ammo case when our tour was over.

That ammo pile was to the Chinese, like a streetlight was to a moth. Donald Sanders while putting in his guard stint, decided to spend a couple of minutes in our favorite chair one night. He did not remember just how long he was in that position, when a Chinese suddenly leapt from the pile and bolted for the locked gate. Although he was shocked momentarily Don did manage to get off a couple of shots but the fleeing Chinese was over the gate and gone. Thirty-five years later I asked him if he recalled the event and if he could give me any of the particulars. His only response was that he had tried to hit the man but for many years worried that he might have been successful.

. . . .

With the blackmarketeers apparently developing maybe a little too much moxie, the brain trusts decided that it was time to mount spotlights on the outside walls of the compounds. The telephone men from our team won the job. At various times Jeff Bennett (an AT&T Long Lines splicer who could climb poles better than most monkeys) . . . . Charles "Willie" Wingler (a former eighteen-wheeler truck driver) . . . . Al Kljun (a former steel worker from Ohio) . . . . and "yours truly", who had climbed about five steps up a pole back at school in Camp Crowder . . . . could be seen hauling ladders, pulling wires and climbing the half dozen poles near the compounds. All of the latter was done with standard climbing spikes that were strapped onto one's legs. Late one afternoon, after spending a half hour with my knees locked in position atop a twenty-five foot pole, I discovered that they were not working very well and had difficulty initiating the necessary rhythmic motion to start down the pole. Bennett, who I was assisting, went into a sort of frenzy trying to get me started down. I was finally able to convince him to sit down and enjoy a smoke and after assessing the probable damage I would incur if I jumped and after several abortive attempts, I suddenly got the hang of it and descended without mishap. The new lights, which we had installed at diagonally opposite corners of the compounds, proved to be the necessary deterrent to our unwanted nocturnal contemporaries and the guard business became mostly a battle with sleeplessness, the corporal-of-the-guard and the monsoon.

Bennett (NJ) and Kljun (OH) adding #8 copper
between three YOKE compounds for lighting to discourage
Chinese nocturnal thieves

. . . .

Among the other members of the Y Force detachment were a handful of infantrymen, two of who were American Indians. One, named Jim Hawks was dubbed "Big Chief" by his irreverent white comrades. The other, whose name I did not know, was conversely called "Little Chief". No one will ever know the complete story . . . but . . . one night during his turn at guard duty, "Big Chief", while either asleep our just resting and while seated with his back to the wall, blew a hole clean though a young Chinese who had the misfortune of picking that precise time to crawl between two earth piles that bordered on the compound wall. His body was placed next to the road in front of the compound. Feelings by the men varied from stunned disbelief at their sudden meeting with the realities of our new environment . . . . to more callous opinions that the interloper had received his just desserts. The following day I was on duty as gate guard, when the poor devil's young, pretty wife came to claim the body . . . and was the target of her fury and grief. Fortunately or maybe otherwise, the language gulf between us made it impossible for me to convey my own feelings regarding her loss.

The most memorable event that attaches to "Little Chief" occurred during the day while we were all at work in the Signal Compound. After a time the Y Force contingent was housed in barracks . . . and each given a wall locker. I learned, after the smoke had cleared that, for some reason, "Little Chief" had been sitting on my bunk, which was now at floor level . . . cleaning his rifle. There is also some conjecture that he may have been under the influence. Regardless . . . in the process of restoring the bolt of his Springfield '03 and pulling the trigger, he managed to blow a good-sized hole in my wall locker. Shortly after the above happenings, our two Native Americans disappeared from the Kunming scene.

There always seemed to be something happening out at the YOKE FORCE compound where we had relieved our friends from the 4TH Team. A really mundane task that fell to some of us lowly ones was taking a turn at gate guard. This consisted of making sure that any Chinese that requested permission to enter had legitimate business inside. It was usually a very boring task, with most of the time spent sitting in a four-foot square sentry shelter that was barely tall enough to stand up in. It was very reminiscent of one that was featured in a popular Sunday comic strip entitled THE LITTLE SENTRY . . . but lacking its brilliant red, white and blue decor. A very distasteful part of the job was frisking the coolies coming and going through the gate. We soon learned that it could be accomplished with less chance of sharing their populations of lice or worse by conducting our searches with the muzzles of our weapons. This included a gentle stab in the vicinity of the individual's crotch, since it had been discovered that several had concealed their stolen objects in that area.

Getting the assignment several times, I finally decided to bring a camera along one day. Although the subject matter was limited to who our whatever passed my guard post, I did get several that I think were unique. One that impressed me, still adjusting to the newness of China and its culture, was of a little old Chinese wife, clad in standard blue denims . . . and carrying a load of lumber over her shoulder and trying desperately to keep up with her unencumbered husband-carpenter who was building work benches in our shop. I could not bring myself to subject her to the routine search described above, although her hotshot husband was not so lucky.

The carpenter's wife

Sandoz (NJ) . . . gate guard

There was, of course a variety of vehicular and human traffic that struggled through the dust or mud of the nearby road. Another example of the little value placed on life in this vast and strange country occurred when a lowly Chinese private collapsed and died as the column of troops he was with trudged by. His comrades never even lost a step, continuing on and leaving his pitiful corpse right where he had fallen. He laid there for almost a week and when the smell became more than we could stand, some of the men took up a collection and after convincing several coolies to ignore his evil spirits, paid them to bury him, which they did right where he had fallen. The following morning, several prayer sticks were discovered burning on his grave. We never discovered who put them there.

Another example of Chinese values, that of how little was placed on female children was brought home in a startling manner one hot afternoon when a middle-aged man approached several of us on the road in front of the compound with an offer to sell his teenage daughter, who was with him, for fifty American dollars . . . . no there were no takers! Not having yet become cognizant of the extent of the poverty of the area, we were surprised to learn that cats and dogs were considered to be culinary specialties . . . watching one morning as a man very meticulously skinned what looked something like a collie dog that he had hung up by its tail.

. . . .

Our short stay at Hostel 4 was a very interesting period for all of us. It was during our stay there that we first marveled at the uniqueness of China generally and our place in it. The first venture into the ancient, walled city of Kunming with its narrow, cobblestone streets started just down the road from the hostel, where the road intersected with the one that connected the airfield with the city. This corner was a favorite waiting place for several rickshaw entrepreneurs . . . who . . . in the timeless mood of China itself waited patiently for the Americans who they knew would be heading for the city eventually.

It is difficult to describe my feelings as I gingerly boarded this legendary conveyance. It is even more difficult to describe a sense of . . . guilt . . . almost, that nagged me at the thought of exploiting an apparently miserable human by utilizing him as a beast of burden. This feeling took much of the excitement out of the extraordinary experience, because it was re-enforced by the sight of his slight torso as he loped along on the two-mile trip to the city gate.

This was my first trip into Kunming and it was like a living page out of National Geographic. When a companion, Jeff Bennett, who was following in another rickshaw, arrived, we plunged into the crowd, working our way farther into the city. Several blocks and we were before a movie theatre, in front of which was one of our enterprising comrades from the 181ST. He reminded us that we had only American money and that he would lead us to the place where it could be exchanged at the black market rate of 200 Chinese yuan to 1 U.S. dollar (the official rate at a bank was 40-1 at that time). Another block or so . . . around the back of a wooden two story building . . . up an outside rickety stairway . . . a knock on a door and we were talking to an apparently well-educated young fellow, who confirmed the going rate of that day. It only took as long as reaching into ones pocket and making the exchange . . . . and the deed was done. A short "How are you doing?" conversation then ensued during which I managed to expose my stark naiveté of the conditions of the population by asking our English-speaking broker, why the Chinese, who were supposed to be our friends, were giving us so much trouble out at the compounds. He did not answer me . . . . but the look of incredulity that came over his face said all that was necessary to convey to this ignorant newcomer what the rules of survival were and to what extent the Chinese people would go to cope with the incredible suffering and sorrow that was there lot. As we were to eventually discover, we would be in the Kunming vicinity for a little over a year . . . ample time in which to witness the details of the message in his look.

After exploring as much of the city as time and our stamina

would permit . . . and after sampling Chinese cooking and an imprudent quantity of mulberry wine, at a photo studio we obtained pictorial mementos of our first trip to a truly intriguing city. It is curiously interesting that the return trip by rickshaw to the spot where we had started our day did not trigger any of my earlier philosophical musings over the lot of the human machine that returned me to my military lifestyle.

During the war, Kunming was home, not only to the native Chinese population and those who invaded it from other sections of the country, but also to a plethora of non-Chinese entities. These ranged from the obvious visible American military units and those not so visible, e.g. the Organization of Strategic Services (OSS), the Sino American Cooperative Organization (SACO . . . a naval espionage unit also known as the "Rice Paddy Navy", which worked with the Chinese secret police) . . . to the Communist cells of Ho Chi Minh. The fact that we in the army were not the only representatives of the USA was brought home to Callinan and his very close buddy and roommate, Joe Shirley (Randleman, N.C.) who, while in a Kunming nightclub, encountered six or eight American sailors. After teasing them by asking where their ship was berthed in Kunming . . . and after several rounds at the bar, our friends learned that their drinking companions were en-route to the Gobi Desert to gather weather data.

Not all of the fellows in the 181ST limited their excursions into Kunming to expand their "cultural horizons". Two whose motives were directed at assisting religious missionaries, of which most nationalities and denominations were represented, were Al Stursberg a Lutheran (Bergenfield, N.J.) and Arthur Follett (Sylvia, KS.) a devout Seventh Day Adventist.

. . . .

Shortly after our arrival in China, two radio repairmen, Don Sanders, (Lumberton, N.C.) and Phil Thompson, (Sharon, PA.) were called out on a house call to the Chinese 53rd Army, which was preparing for its bout with the Salween. The assignment, which lasted about two weeks turned out to be very boring, due mostly to the fact that they were the only Americans present and, having just arrived in China, had absolutely no knowledge of the native tongue, thus no way of communicating with their strange new clients.

From the little that Don could recall of their task there, it seems that the Chinese were experiencing an abnormal number of radio components burning out in the sets that they were charged with. Our heroes finally traced the trouble to the hand-operated generators that were cranked by an assistant when the radios were in use. The Chinese had been mistakenly assuming that a small adjusting screw, which regulated the voltage output of the generator, was loose, because they could turn it. They had apparently "tightened" it, inadvertently increasing the voltage in the transmitter\receivers and burning out the components.

Reporting their findings, however, was another problem for Don and Phil. They had observed the extreme interest and even concern that was evidenced by the Chinese who were responsible for the precious equipment and soon realized that if the negligence of the operators was reported as such, the consequences for their new allies could be very grave. Don could not recall how this problem was overcome but he and Phil did manage to leave without incriminating anyone.

## HOSTEL 5

The anticipated move, which was dictated by the change in our orders, finally came about and we packed our gear and took up new residence in the vicinity of Hostel 5. We inherited a building that was north of the 14TH Army Air Force main airfield and on the east side of the road that ran from it to one of the several picturesque gateways into Kunming. It was not unlike a motel, but of the Chinese variety, with quaint, curved roof tiles, a long cement portico, with about ten rooms facing along its length.

The northern end held a bathroom with sinks and a shower room. On the wall over the row of sinks was a sign strongly admonishing anyone from drinking the water, which was provided only for bathing, shaving etc. The rooms, which faced the road, were a vast improvement over anything we had so far experienced since debarking from the Mariposa. Each room accommodated up to four men who shared double-decker bunks. At this date I can only remember that I occupied an upper bunk over one assigned to Technical Sergeant Bill Wraspir, one of the finest men I have ever had the good fortune to be associated with. This singularly unique structure was our home until about March 1945, when the hostilities in Burma and the Salween were over and the first convoy had made its tortuous way from Ledo to Kunming.

Our oriental motel—Thompson, Teske, Raabe

Our trips to the Y Force compounds ceased several weeks after our arrival in China when we moved into a brand new repair shop about three hundred yards behind our picturesque, Hostel 5 dwelling. The daily trek from our Oriental motel to our workstation was through an area that was home to a company of MP's and past an army stockade holding the poor unfortunates who had the misfortune or bad judgment of running afoul of army regulations.

This workshop occupied most of the southern wall of a compound, which, unlike its Y Force counterparts, was constructed of real bricks and was not going to be dug through by anything less than a carboloy drill. Completing that side was an army movie film library, run by a half dozen men from a 3371ST Signal Service Detachment. The remaining three walls of the compound consisted of warehouses, which were under the control of the folks from a 3344TH Signal Service Detachment who were operating a rather lethargic signal supply enterprise. The main gate was located on the west side, facing the army stockade. Just inside and to the right was a small building in which Charles (Willie) Wingler (Champaign-Urbana, IL.) and Arthur Follett (Sylvia, KS.) repaired and maintained gasoline driven electric generators. Inside the repair shop and just to the left of its entrance was an open section, which functioned as an office. Also to the left and behind the wall of the office section were two rooms. They served as home to George Simon, (Baltimore) in one and to Bob Callinan (Rumson, N.J.), Dick Williams (Hibbing, Minn.), Joe Shirley, (Randleman, N.C.) and Luke Orman (High Point, N.C.) in the other.

The occupants of these rooms were the envy of the rest of us in the platoon . . . first because of their privacy and the fact that they did not have to participate in the early morning trek, up hill and often through the mud and downpour of the monsoon, from our "army motel" to the work shop. The rooms had one drawback, however . . . . they were infested with mice. To cope with this annoyance our enterprising compatriots devised a very effective, if not brutal, apparatus for the extermination of their unwelcome roommates. As described by Callinan,

> "It consisted of a metal strip about two inches wide,
> running across the center of the floor. About three inches
> above that we had a wire suspended above the length of

> the strip. Then we fed 30 to 50 thousand volts to each so
> when a mouse transgressed between the strip and the
> wire, said mouse would be zapped. It worked like a charm
> with one flaw. One of us would have to get up and pull
> the plug and extract the mouse. Cooking mice don't smell
> so good."

In their private accommodations Bob Callinan and his roomies soon developed a lifestyle, which differed in various ways from that enjoyed by the "motel" dwellers. Among their pursuits, with which they battled the boredom that was to descend on us like a psychological blanket, Bob and his buddies installed a darkroom for developing photo film. From my own teenage recollections of dabbling in this same activity, the process consisted of essentially two steps. After the first of these, during which the film was immersed in a developing solution, the former was then placed in another bath containing an agent called a "hypo" which stopped the chemical action of the developer and "fixed" the film. While experimenting with the process, our friends in the back room discovered, to their surprise, that the composition of the undrinkable Chinese water was such that it could be used in place of the "hypo".

· · · ·

Shortly after our arrival in China, because of his mechanical skills and the added fact that he was a qualified radio repairman, Follett was selected by Lt. Silverman to act as driver for several engineering officers who were assigned the task of surveying a suitable route for the future construction of a pipeline between Kunming and Kweiyang. Knowing Follett's religious affiliation with the Adventists and their teaching regarding the taking of human life, even in wartime . . . . and not wanting to place him in a situation that could possibly require him to defend himself, the lieutenant explained the nature of the assignment. It was not until Follett assured him that he could, if necessary, fire his weapon in self-defense, that Silverman recommended him to the officers.

After working all night to install a radio in a jeep, the party, which included the three officers, Follett and an interpreter headed east over the continuation of the Burma Road. Approximately one year later, I was to travel the same route in a convoy that took three brutal days ... over the most terrifying mountain roads I had ever encountered. It was a seemingly endless series of flat valleys, followed by severe grades, superimposed onto breathtaking switchbacks. As one approached Annan, about a day's ride from Kweiyang, it was necessary to negotiate a section of road that consisted of twenty-one switchbacks before reaching the summit. Many manuscripts have featured this piece of roadway, several of them incorrectly identifying it as a section of either the Burma or Stilwell Roads west of Kunming.

Their task eventually took them beyond Kweiyang and well into the combat zone. They became aware of this fact when, after traveling three hours over a section of road, another convoy was shot up pretty badly after following them over the same road. Art recalled that their camp was camouflaged and that many wounded Chinese soldiers were brought back to the area he was in.

After the team completed its work and disbanded, Art was ordered by a colonel to remain in Kweiyang. His original orders, however, were finally honored when a radio message was received from a Captain Barnes instructing him to return to Kunming. He had been assigned a jeep during the surveying job and, with it, headed back toward Kunming, managing to catch a convoy that was just leaving.

. . . .

My comrades in the 181ST were possessed of an apparently bottomless bag of talents. There were two, for instance who were very accomplished in playing the harmonica. They were my partner, Al Kljun, from the remote jungle message center in Hellgate, back in India, and Donald Sanders, one of the younger draftees from Lumberton, N.C. Al had often brought his instrument along when we were hiking in the states and serenaded us with strains of "Elmer's Tune" during a mile long trek after we debarked from the train that took us from the docks of Calcutta to the British camp at Deolali. Don was a little more intensive student of the mouth organ and related a story that started while we were in Chabua, waiting our turn to challenge the "Hump". Threading his way through a tent area, en-route to the latrine, he was entertaining himself by playing his harmonica, when, he was suddenly accosted by an individual who sprang from one of the tents. He asked Don if he could examine his harmonica and then introduced himself as Forrest Scott, a former member of the world-famous Borrah Minevitch's "Harmonica Rascals", well known prior to the war. He too, was waiting for transportation to China and eventually he and Don found each other in the Hostel 5 area. Don recalled that Scott taught him much about the chromatic harmonica and "most of what I still remember about chord construction". They eventually formed a trio and spent some very pleasurable hours entertaining folks in the Kunming area. Don's most memorable "gig" was a command performance for General Chennault during the intermission between boxing matches at the Air Corps recreation hangar. Don told us that his friendship with Scott continued after the war, until the latter's death in 1988.

. . . .

To the ordinary G.I., whose seemingly endless days were mostly consumed by his battle with boredom, frustration with the pace of the war and the Spartan living conditions, the real events that were occurring in Kunming were invisible. There were those amongst us, like Follett, Stursberg and others who made the necessary contacts that ultimately revealed what was happening behind the many walls that partitioned the city. I do not know who to give the credit to, but someone arranged for the entire team to visit a secret Chinese war plant in the nearby hills. This visit brought out in dramatic fashion the true nature of the Chinese effort to survive the tragic destruction of their means of survival by the relentless Japanese occupation.

Our tour of the facility was very properly conducted by a middle-aged gentleman, who could have served as a model for our own public relations experts. Without a source of metal ore, a major product, wire, was being made from coins. We were shown the process from beginning to end, starting with the sight of literally barrels of coins in a small warehouse. Our tour, which covered the melting and forming processes was interrupted by a delightful and tasteful lunch. It was served at round tables with the main ingredients, chicken, sweet and sour pork, rice and round golf-ball-sized bread balls available only via the use of chopsticks. It is too bad that the hand-held camcorder was not yet invented as the scene of more than a dozen Americans struggling to feed themselves with the basic eating implement of the far east would have surely won a prize on one of the current television shows. A finished product of the plant was telephone-switchboards, surprisingly similar to those, which, at home, were made by the Western Electric Corporation in the nearby town of Kearny, N.J. Being a short-time employee of this company prior to my induction, I was fascinated by the sight of a one-position switchboard used in commercial PBX installations in the U.S. that not only was made of the same beautifully finished hardwood, but also used the Bell System color code, (blue, orange, green, brown, slate) in the wiring of the front equipment answering and trunk jacks. It was obvious that some Chinese had brought more than souvenirs back from a visit to our country.

In front of the Chinese war plant

We are invited to a Chinese-style dinner
at the Chinese war plant

Our arrival at Hostel 5 in May of 1944 also held a whole new set of experiences for Lt. Bernie Silverman. As a newly arrived officer at the hostel, he was immediately invited to a welcoming "gombei" party by his contemporaries. What he was not told was that it had been arranged beforehand that their Chinese hosts were to take turns, individually, in toasting their recently arrived ally. The word "gombei" literally translated means "bottoms up" and when one is being toasted by another, he is required to consume the entire contents of his glass. The result of this grueling exercise was, of course, that in due time our leader was very much "under the influence".

On August 4th he received orders to return to India to secure the Team's allotment of trucks and to bring them to China via the Hump. To make this feat possible, the truck bodies had to be actually cut in half with acetylene torches in order that they could fit into the cargo planes. Of course the opposite had to occur when they reached Kunming. Even though the vehicles were ours . . . according to the army Table of Equipment (TOE) . . . in typical CBI style, which we had learned to anticipate, all but one of them were commandeered by the SOS depot.

. . . .

As Hump tonnage increased and the American contingent in the Kunming area grew, signal repair and supply activity did also. The equipment items that graced our repair benches mirrored those that our contemporaries were mending, both in Ledo and Chabua. For some reason, motion picture amplifiers, Ampro and Bell and Howell, were very popular candidates for repair. The technique employed by Sergeant Paul Wagler (Burlington, IA) and his crew, in testing these, consisted, during their operation, of using actual 16mm sound movies. Only one or two of these, however, were used by his industrious cohorts and after several weeks everyone in the shop knew the dialogues and music on them by heart. One, whose lyrics I can still remember almost 100%, was a version of the song "Making Whoopee" sung by Tony Pastor. At the time the words would not have been considered to be in good taste, although today they would not even evoke any comment.

Occasional requests for the demonstration of our talents were also received from our Chinese hosts. One of these, which was responded to by Bob Callinan and one of his associates took them into Kunming to repair a transceiver. The unit was located in the quarters of the Chinese operators, which was crawling with bedbugs. As our heroes hastened to complete their mission they were serenaded by a continuing series of volleys coming from the adjoining courtyard. When inquiring about the purpose of the shots they were informed that the firing squad was taking care of the morning's business.

As the men of the First Team's tour in Kunming grew, so too did their rapport with the population and others whose fortunes, military or otherwise, had brought them to this forgotten outpost of the war. One of our many colorful characters, Sam Firman, a charter member of the Omer/Koch entrepreneurial association, made friends with a man named Y.Y. Chi, a former member of the Chinese 1936 Olympic Basketball Team. When he learned that his new acquaintance had a dysfunctional radio, Sam wisely enlisted the aid of Bob Callinan. The trouble was quickly located and a 117L7 vacuum tube was identified as the guilty component. To my comrades' amazement, Mr. Chi promptly produced one, a virtually irreplaceable item in a country where material goods were so much in short supply, it was rumored that a handful of nails, removed from a packing crate could bring the price of a dinner in town. Chi was so pleased with the response by these new allies to his predicament that he invited them to an impressive dinner at his western-style home. It was learned that Chi had been forced to abandon a lucrative jewelry business in Shanghai when the Japanese invaded, but that he and his wife had been able to carry a considerable quantity of their stock with them to Kunming. Callinan also recalled that Sam and he subsequently became so close to the Chi's that they had to decline an invitation to attend an opium party to be held by one of their friends.

. . . .

The talents of the team were tested many times. When what were supposed to be ten pilot radio receivers turned out to be ten kits, a production line was improvised. Estimates are that about 1500 jobs were logged into the repair shop and about the same number not logged.

Radio repairmen Sanders, Wagler and Thompson

. . . .

As usual the wire repair squad, including this telephone repairman, would have starved had we been operating a commercial enterprise. The fate that befell my counterparts in India, the operation of a Rube Goldberg transformer coil-winding machine, became my baby. This one was rigged using a small motor found in Chennault's Air Corps junkyard. It had been used to deploy and retrieve a radio antenna on some aircraft. Our initial experiments with the coil winder, however, left much to be desired. The first stumbling block occurred when we found that we could not get the original can covers back on our finished product. This, we discovered was caused by the use of the wrong size wire. The wire, which had been procured from the same Chinese plant that we had visited outside of town, had been measured using an American Wire Gauge table. Lt. Silverman subsequently theorized that most of the rest of the world were on working terms with the Standard Wiring Gauge instead, which called for a smaller wire size and that we had just ordered the wrong size from our previous hosts. With this obstacle overcome, the next was the unavailability of a reliable insulating material, which when melted was poured into the completed transformer. Since I was only the coil winder, I do not remember how this was finally remedied. The last memory I have of this event was of Sergeant Bill Hasse melting down ordinary roof tar and trying it unsuccessfully as a substitute.

Marcus (NY) Silverman (VA) Stursberg (NJ) Hasse (OR)

Inside view of SOS signal compound, warehouse
and loading docks

A typical example of the lengths to which our repairmen had to go to service the needs of those organizations within our jurisdiction was the successful repair of 2 circuit breakers for the 14th Air Force. These units would have been routinely scrapped and replaced, but because of the supply situation in the CBI this was impossible. After several organizations in the Air Corps proclaimed that the items in question were unrepairable, they were referred to us at the 181st. With replacement not an option our fellows simply rebuilt them, which triggered the following commendation from the Air Corps:

RESTRICTED
HEADQUARTERS
CO "C" 559 SIGNAL AW BATTALION
APO 627, C/O POSTMASTER
NEW YORK-EW YORK

GLH/feo
11 April, 1945

Subject: Commendation

To   Commanding Officer, 181st Signal Repair Co., SOS, APO 627, Theater, THRU: Commanding General, 14th Air Force, APO 627, Attn,: Communication Officer.

2.   This headquarters has been notified by Lt. Henry P. Bartolf, commanding Officer Reporting Platoon #7, of the excellent work done by Lt. Silverman and the 181st Signal Repair Co. in restoring two (2) defective circuit breakers to working condition for this organization.

3.   Subject items of equipment had previously been submitted to other maintenance organizations in this area and returned as unserviceable. Replacement parts are not available.

4.   The attitude displayed by 181st Signal Repair Co. in attempting numerous approaches to the problem is greatly appreciated and it is felt that it should be commended.

FOR THE COMMANDING OFFICER:

(signed)

George L. Hogeman

1st Lt., Sig. C.

This commendation was processed upward until it reached the desk of our commanding general. Major General G. X. Cheves, who added his own commendation, which was returned to Lt. Silverman.

. . . .

The fall of 1944 was another of those critical turning points in the fortunes of the CBI generally and the 181ST particularly. The animosity between Chiang-Kai shek and General Stilwell reached the bursting point and President Roosevelt was forced to relieve the latter and replace him with General Wedemeyer. At the same time the CBI was split into the India-Burma and China Theaters of War. We had lost the Fifth Team and were about to lose half of the Third as plans were being made for the HQ Team in Ledo to be part of a convoy that was to leave for Kunming when the road was completed.

General Stilwell's prediction that the air corps' boast to defeat the Japanese by air alone would cost them all of their airfields in eastern China was, unfortunately, coming true. The Japanese had reacted violently, executing a plan labeled ICHIGO. In it they continued their earlier drive down the East China railroad from Hunan Province, with the goal of capturing all of the American air bases from which the 14TH AF was severely punishing them. As the enemy moved relentlessly southward, taking Hengyang and Changsha and threatening Kweilin, Stilwell's earlier insistence that the Chinese Army should have been trained and supplied in order to be prepared to stop the Japanese was also ringing true.

With the end of the Salween campaign now predictable and with a new American theater commander in place, primary attention was directed to the events taking place in the east. The degree of importance that was given to the improvement of the supply situation from Kunming eastward was manifested by the appointment of a new commander of the Services of Supply (SOS) in China, Major General Gilbert X. Cheves. Arriving in early November 1944, he immediately began to set up his base of operations in a large compound adjacent to Hostel 5. In addition to his own office, the compound was home to a host of lieutenant colonels who reported to him and had various roles in the conduct of SOS business. General Cheves had made his reputation in Calcutta where he had eliminated a serious bottleneck at the docks. In a similar manner he set about the task of injecting a large dose of efficiency into the supply procedures in Kunming that, up to that time, had pretty much been dictated by whatever came over the HUMP.

One of the steps he ordered was that a buzzer system be installed between his office and those of his lieutenant colonels. This job was assigned to Jeff Bennett, a fellow Jerseyite and me. For me it turned out to be one of the most memorable experiences of my military tour. In the "States" this would have been a simple, routine task and would have been in China, also, had we had quality materials with which to work. Instead, two of the items required to accomplish the job, wire and buzzers, were really inadequate. The wire we were given was nothing more than the two-wire cable used for demolition purposes. The buzzers which were apparently made locally, had more operating eccentricities than a pinball machine and defied all of our efforts to adjust them to the various loop lengths between the individual offices and a key control panel on the general's desk. To our credit and that of the 181ST we persevered until we had matched the personality of each buzzer to a circuit it agreed to work over.

After the wires were in place at the outlying offices, I assumed a position on the floor at the right side of the general's chair and with a head-set worked the keys as Jeff moved from office to office trying each recalcitrant buzzer until he found one that worked over that particular circuit. This was not a speedy process, taking several days to complete. It was delayed one morning when a "two ball" air raid alert sounded and Jeff, en-route to the job, had to take shelter in a slit trench. At first he was the only occupant, when suddenly it was full of Chinese girl employees from the SOS compound, some of whom had had bad experiences with Japanese air attacks in the past. In his own words, Jeff related, "They were draped all over me looking for protection".

When I reached the compound a little later and as I approached the General's office, I saw a half dozen American GI's, all dressed in plain woolen olive drab uniforms without any identification on them. I thought it strange that they should be loitering on the general's front porch and as I brushed past them into the building, I noticed that there was something different about them. They were obviously not from any of the units that normally did business at the compound. As was our custom, we started work at least an hour before the general started, if he was in town . . . so I assumed my position on the floor behind the desk, waiting for Jeff to contact me. Because of the air alert, we had started later than usual and in a very short time the general arrived and joined me at his desk. Then a most extraordinary scene began. In walked the strange GI's who had been waiting outside. Four of them came forward and were directed to chairs facing the general. He then offered them cigars, which they took, and when urged to relax, two of them put there feet up on his desk. I was stunned at the total absence of military courtesy but was soon a witness to one of the most heart-rending examples of suffering and heroism of the war.

These men were survivors of the Bataan Death March. They were also some of the few survivors of a Japanese ship that was sunk by Allied action while it was transporting prisoners from the Philippines to Japan. They had been picked up by the Chinese, who delivered them to the Americans, where, for two weeks, they were cared for, until they were able, physically, to be transported to Kunming. One reason that they appeared, when I first saw them, to be just another group of GI'S, was that they did not show any outward signs of their ordeals. For at least an hour, they poured out their individual stories to the general, who demonstrated a human side that I am sure very few of his men suspected he was capable of. After so many years, I do not recall any of the details except one. One of the men did not speak and was obviously suffering from some form of emotional shock. When the general could not get a response from him, one of the others told this story:

> The man had been kept in a prisoner-of-war camp along with Filipinos who had fought on the side of the Americans. During his time there he had become very close to one of them. The fellow who was relating these events made note of the fact that the Japanese guards had a particular hateful attitude towards the Filipinos for having fought beside the Americans. He recalled that the Japanese guards took great delight in beating and torturing these men. On one occasion, knowing of the relationship between his comrade and his Filipino friend, their captors marched the two of them to a field outside of the camp, forced them to dig a grave, shot the Filipino and forced his American friend to bury him.
>
> He had been in his current mental state ever since and was kept alive only by the efforts of his fellow prisoners.

I wondered then and since, why the general allowed me to remain while these unfortunate men poured out their tragic stories. Needless to say, I had a most difficult time concentrating on what I was doing. I also felt pretty foolish and embarrassed at how these men must view a mere draftee spending his war at nothing more useful than installing a general's buzzer. It took some explaining to Jeff, later, as to why I was not as responsive to his calls via the headset as he thought I should have been. The entire experience gave me pause for several weeks, particularly whenever I was prompted to complain about what had suddenly become trivial discomforts and inconveniences of my military lifestyle.

. . . .

Whether related to General Cheves appointment as the new SOS commander or not, on November 5, 1944 Lt. Silverman and Tech Sergeant Bill Wraspir were ordered to Yunnani on signal depot business. With them were a Captain Frederick Fogarty and Staff Sergeant Harold O'Dell from the 3344TH Signal Service Detachment.

. . . .

With the arrival of the new SOS commander and the continuing increases in HUMP tonnage made possible after the capture of Myitkyina, the tempo in the 1ST Team repair shop and the 3344TH warehouses picked up considerably. Supplies needed by the repairmen, however, were not keeping pace with the demand. Coincidentally, word was received from the 3344TH's Captain Fogarty, who had flown to Calcutta to reconnoiter the signal supply situation at dockside, that the answer to our needs was languishing in a warehouse that he had somehow gained access to. Our astute management responded with alacrity to this news and, taking a page from the air corps book, immediately dispatched Bob Callinan and Joe Shirley to Calcutta.

They caught a B-25 that was heading that way. Bob was invited to ride in the co-pilot's seat, affording him an excellent view of their route, which was not over the highest peaks but in between them. He recalled being disturbed by the large number of blackened, burned out patches of jungle, each of which was the scene of a tragic airplane crash. At Calcutta they were given " . . . carte blanche to go through the depot and help ourselves" by the ubiquitous Fogarty. Cal recalled that the depot was two storied with each " . . . the size of a football field". For several days they busied themselves with the almost giddy task of filling a wooden crate, 3' x 3' x 6', with, ". . . all kinds of items we were hankering for in China". In between the days, they studied several motion picture projectors and amplifiers and also took advantage of the opportunity to visit Calcutta several times. Following is a portion of a letter, dated April 26, 1989 I received from Bob just 15 days before his death:

> In the evening Joe & I had a pretty good time. Went to Firpo's Lim. restaurant a couple times. One thing I remember was all the dead bodies lying in the streets and carts going around picking them up to be placed on pyres. Then there (were) soup lines, blocks long, hours before they served, some people in line were asleep, some lying under their sheets making love and some just lying there dead.
>
> On one trip to Firpo's Joe & I had to walk around and over dead bodies to reach the front entrance. Once inside it was like another world, buff walls with gold accents and tables, red table cloths and napkins. The food was excellent—but one wonders how they can be so callused as to actually enjoy anything. Seems we mortals adap(t) to anything.
>
> That soup line outside showed the limits. Some guys sleeping, some guys making love, some guys dying and some who did die.

Having been on the receiving end of the most anemic supply artery in the world, Cal rightfully anticipated that getting their booty back over the Hump would require an innovative game plan. Assuming that declaring their precious crate as cargo would only ensure its delay, if not demise, he decided to declare it as personal baggage. Their path homeward to Kunming entailed an intermittent stop at Chabua in Assam and when they boarded for that first leg of their return journey, Bob recalled:

> . . . lo & behold there was our crate (and another) tied down in the middle of the plane. It looked *so* out of place, on the sides it was flanked by two plush rows of seats. In these seats were seated a bunch of VIPs. Joe & I just walked around the crate(s) and took

our seats. We just made believe we never saw the crate(s) before.

In Chabua Bob was summoned to a major's office and received " . . . the (worst) reaming of my army life." He tried to explain how desperate we were for the repair parts but was told that in the future to use cargo planes when shipping cargo. Once he had finished venting his wrath, the major's tone softened and he promised that we would have the crate in Kunming in two days, which is exactly how long it took.

Our heroes' troubles were not yet over, however. While waiting to board the plane for China, Bob nosing about discovered one of the kingpins on a landing gear had worked its way out with only about 1/4" keeping the gear from collapsing. He sought out the crew chief, who paled when he saw the kingpin and got his very tired "bushed, bearded, dirty" crew to fix it. By nightfall they were en-route finally to Kunming and had cleared the Hump when the left engine of the plane caught fire. The pilot found an available airstrip, possibly Cheng-tu, and even though the field was experiencing an air alert they turned on their lights for the crippled aircraft. The trouble, a leaking fuel line was remedied and a short time later Bob and Joe were back in Kunming.

The mystery of the second crate, which was marked in orange as containing signal equipment, was subsequently disclosed when we were all awarded our first beer ration since leaving India . . . . no doubt the work of the good Captain. This revelation coincided with a Christmas party that was held at the compound, attended by no less than the general and a bevy of Chinese girls and their chaperones.

. . . .

Part of the Japanese ICHIGO plan was the dissemination of propaganda that their objective was not to inflict casualties on the Chinese, but only the capture of the American airfields. Whether this ploy by the Japanese was a factor or not, on

November 10th, Kweilin and Liuchow were evacuated by the Chinese. Two weeks later, Nanning, the last major link in the Shanghai-Hanoi Railroad also fell.

The actions of the Japanese, as they raced to implement ICHIGO, promised to make life interesting for those of us on the First Team in Kunming. Air raid alerts increased and rumors that it had become an objective of the Japanese advance began to surface. To allay the fears of the more fainthearted, the local command announced that Kunming was not threatened, but should that eventuality materialize, everyone would be safely evacuated.

To counter the Japanese successes, on November 21, 1944 General Wedemeyer presented a plan for the defense of Kunming, called ALPHA, to Chiang-Kai shek. It called for the redeployment to eastern China of some of the Chinese forces fighting in Burma and those, which were part of the Salween Yoke Force. ALPHA also included plans to retake the lost airfields and to open a seaport at Ft. Bayard on the China coast.

An entry in his excellent book, DRAGON BY THE TAIL, in which he relates his experiences in China during the war, John Paton Davies, Jr. included the following comment and a quote from a message General Wedemeyer sent on December 16, 1944 to the American Chief of Staff in Washington:

> "in the midst of prevailing alarm that the Japanese would advance on Kunming and Chungking, Wedemeyer unburdened himself:
>
> ""In early conferences with the Generalisimo, I pointed out that we should . . . insure the defense of the Kunming area.
>
> I presented a plan for this purpose and he approved that plan . . . Now I find that he is vacillating—in fact, he has ordered movements of divisions from the Kunming area without my knowledge . . .
>
> If he [Chiang] goes to the Kunming area, the governor of Yunnan may kidnap him or at least place him under protective custody . . ."

Had the contents of Wedemeyer's message been known at the time, some credence would have been given to the concerns of some in Kunming. The tension reached its height when, just before midnight on Christmas Eve, one or more Japanese aircraft managed to make a run on the airfield, dropping a string of bombs, some of which hit slit trenches that, fortunately, had not yet been occupied by the folks in the area. This writer was jolted out of his upper bunk by the reverberations. Preparing to attend midnight mass, I was fully clothed with the exception of my shoes. The dash up the hill to the compound was made in record time. An interesting aspect of these moments was that, as we passed through the area inhabited by the MP's, we discovered that they were all in their slit trenches but had not yet activated their air raid siren. It turned out to be a long, cold night. With several inches of water in our slit trenches and when some of us elected to sit on the edges, rather than stand in the water, Lt. Silverman had to order us down. In the morning Lloyd Teske, North Dakota, was feverish, eventually developing pneumonia.

Slit trench and Chinese graves behind compound

Evidence of the presence of saboteurs and others sympathetic to the Japanese were reported . . . . the most dramatic example occurring when rockets were observed rising from the corners of the airfield just prior to the start of the bombing attack. The night before, Bob Callinan while acting as "sergeant of the guard" at an ammunition dump outside of Kunming, was fired at. He described how at least two rounds were aimed at him, the second passing through his hair. He insisted that one was so close to his scalp that it stung him. He also said that his hair has never grown normally on the spot since. His tour ended just about the time that the attack on the airfield started the next night, leaving him with no sleep for over twenty-four hours.

Although the hostilities along the railroad corridor in the east continued to heat up, after this single air raid, no significant enemy activity occurred in the Kunming area.

One quasi-enemy event that loomed as being of much more immediate concern to Ray Hardee, myself and several others in the Hostel 5 area was an upcoming touch-tackle football game against a similar group of gentlemen from Yoke Force Operations Headquarters who plied their trade at Hostel 1. The game played on New Years Day and facetiously called "The Rice Bowl", was really a grudge affair between the "Grunts" from the YFOS field units and their "college-boy" counterparts from HQ. Played without any equipment and with "no tackling" as the only variation from the real game, it exacted a grim physical price from all of the participants. Although my memory has surrendered the final score to time, I do believe that we won by a small margin. Our quarterback was a lad named Ben Chapman from St. Bonaventure's College, who did not see too well. He more than compensated for this infirmity, however, by locking his eyes onto his prospective receiver and enjoying deadly accuracy. This writer caught two of his passes. Located north of Kunming City, Hostel 1 was host to the carnage. Our victory lost much of its gloss when, back at Hostel 5, we were ordered to strip to our under-shorts by the medics, who almost gleefully painted our bruised and scratched torsos with burning medical alcohol.

# CHAPTER VII

# Our Final Breakup

## THE ROAD IS FINALLY OPENED

The opening of the year 1945 carried with it much hope and promise that there would soon be some resolution to the war and an end to our ordeal in the CBI. These hopes bore their first fruit when we learned that on January 10th patrols from the Chinese 1ST Army's Burma X Forces had met with their Y Force counterparts at Meng Mao in northeastern Burma. The Allies' confidence that the Japanese would soon be cleared from the Road's path was dramatically demonstrated by the departure, two days later, of the first Kunming-bound convoy from Ledo. The good news continued, also, when Bob Finkel's commission finally was approved January 17th, although the gold bar was awarded on the condition that he agreed to spend an additional year in the CBI.

On the 23rd the lead vehicle of the Ledo-to Kunming convoy reached Myitkyina . . . . a day before the official end of the Salween Campaign. The 25th saw the Chinese 38TH Division open the Burma Road and on the 27th their main body linked up with their comrades in Y Force. A day later the convoy crossed the China-Burma border at Muse, where elaborate ceremonies were held. On February 2nd Paul Mrogenski (Brookfleld, Missouri), George Henze (Iowa) and Evan Evans (Brainard, Wisconsin) watched it as it passed through Yunnanyi and two days later, on February 4, 1945 it made its grand entrance through the gates of Kunming. I and several other tenants of the Hostel 5 "Oriental Motel", that served as home to the 181ST First Team, waved and shouted our welcome to the lead vehicle as it passed on the road and seemed to be headed for the SOS compound. With almost one voice we shouted, "Where is the beer?". The answer, "We drank it all", told us that the new supply line was not going to contribute very much to our personal wants.

. . . .

With the end of hostilities west of Kunming, a convoy of about twenty six-by-six trucks, under the capable guidance of Sergeant Bill Hasse, was sent down the Burma Road to Yunnanyi. Driving two of the trucks were Luke Orman (Thomasville, NC) and my companion at Hellgate, Al Kljun (N. Royalton, OH). Presumably their mission was to secure signal and other supplies and bring them back to Kunming, a distance of about 250 kilometers, round trip. Again the latent talent that identified with the men of the 181ST revealed itself during the journey. With gasoline, which had to be flown in from India being so scarce in China, the truck carburetors had all been adjusted to burn a mixture of 25% alcohol and 75% gasoline. All of the vehicles carried only enough extra fuel in auxiliary tanks to get them to Yunnanyi, having been assured that there would be enough at their destination to handle the return trip.

Upon arriving at Yunnanyi they discovered that the only fuel available was undiluted gasoline. When they were ready to start back to Kunming and started their motors, great clouds of black smoke billowed from their exhausts. Hasse deduced that the problem was in the carburetors and immediately sought out his resident compatriots at their still-functioning signal repair shop to borrow some tools. From a carburetor taken from one of the trucks, he removed its jet and filled it with solder. Then starting with a small drill bit, he opened a hole through the jet. He reinstalled the carburetor and instructed the driver to start the motor, which ran very roughly, indicating that the mixture was too lean. He then repeated the process several times, progressively using larger drills until he had the truck running normally. He then instructed all of the drivers to remove the jets from their carburetors and bring them to him for modification. The trip back to Kunming was trouble-free and in his words, "We brought back what we went down to get."

. . . .

Once the excitement over the arrival of the Ledo convoy had subsided . . . and . . . . with the Salween Campaign starting its journey into history, the brass turned to the business of planning and implementing the difficult task of regaining the lost airfields in the east and the opening of a seaport on the China Sea. The prospect of our probable role in these undertakings portended that there was still plenty of war left for us to contend with . . . . and we soon got about the business of initiating what turned out to be the last chapter of our overseas adventures.

For Jeff Bennett and I, however, there remained one more assignment that resulted from the completion of the long-awaited land link to China. Within weeks of its completion, knowing that we were Catholic, Lt. Silverman designated us to be part of an honor guard that was to participate in a solemn high requiem mass, which was to be held at one of the Catholic missionary churches in Kunming. It was being celebrated to commemorate the men and women from all of the allied military ranks who had been killed while serving with their units during the building of the Ledo (now Stilwell) Road.

We were dropped by jeep at the gate of the mission, rang a bell to seek admission and were greeted in stony silence by a middle-aged, bearded Caucasian monk in the brown robes of the Franciscan Order. We informed him of our reason for being there and asked for directions to the proper entry to the church. He nodded his head, removed one of his hands from his sleeve and pointed to a distant doorway . . . but never uttered a word. We reported to a sergeant inside, who upon questioning informed us that our silent guide belonged to a Capuchin order that was sworn to silence.

The mass was a very unique experience for both of us. While the physical aspects of the church were familiar, the clergy that participated in the ceremony represented all of the nationalities that had contributed to the defeat of the Japanese in Northern Burma and the actual building of the road itself. It was the first time that I had ever seen Chinese nuns, a Chinese bishop, an English monsignor and a half dozen priests and brothers of several nationalities. High masses are usually very long but this one seemed to never end. A Chinese bishop, an English monsignor and an American monsignor each delivered lengthy sermons. At the front of the center aisle was a symbolic bier, holding an empty coffin and pall, representing those for whom the service was being held. Two Chinese soldiers stood at attention at each of the two front corners of the bier, while Jeff and I, carrying our carbines at the slung position, did the same at the two rear corners. After the first hour, it became a contest to see whether the Chinese could hold their position of attention longer than Jeff and I. As foolish as it may seem now, we were quite proud that eventually we prevailed over our oriental comrades, who finally started to twitch and shift position.

. . . .

With our move to Hostel 5 in May 1944 and our association with SOS, most of us were able to find gainful employment of one kind or another. This did not hold for everyone, however. There were several, not classified as repairmen, upon whom the war in China had not yet made any particular demands. One of these was a young, dark-haired, dashing individual named Loren Bolin from Roswell NM. In the unit's organizational makeup he was listed as a private and truck driver. He was about my age but a truly free spirit, totally bored and frustrated with his role in the 181ST. Many years later Bernie Silverman recalled Bolin coming to him and requesting permission to volunteer to serve with the folks, called "rice-kickers" who rose each morning, long before sunup, to board the C-47s that were air-dropping supplies to the troops engaged in the Salween. Bernie also confessed that, "One of my shortcomings was not finding a way to utilize fellows like Bolin who did not have a repair skill." On February 9, 1945, General Cheves awarded Distinguished Flying Crosses to thirteen members of the Burma Road Engineers, "For air dropping missions over mountainous terrain and enemy occupied territory." One of these men was Loren H. Bolin. After the war, Bolin rose to the rank of supervisor in a power company in New Mexico.

．．．．

After almost a year in China we were suddenly informed that the air force had allocated us ten beds per week at their rest camp that was located several hours ride south of Kunming, astride the Kunming-Hanoi Railroad. Reports had it that it was still running between these cities and that Yunnan Province warlord and governor, Lung Yun's, nephews were operating a brisk black market trade over it. The camp, named Camp Schiel, overlooked a large, beautiful lake, surrounded by mountains.

The information was correct and . . . with thirty enlisted men in the First Team we began to send groups of ten men each to this Shangri-la. To those of us, who had been acquiring most of our protein from entrees that, too often, featured water buffalo, the camp was very much just that. Of the ten men in the group I was with, I can recall only my close friend, Jeff Bennett, Al Kljun, Charles "Willie" Wingler and Earl Troy; the fellow Hardee had dubbed "Jungle". Not only the food was something we had been deprived of in Kunming, but also the entire atmosphere of the place was truly restful. Besides the freedom to hike in the surrounding hills, one of which held a small, secluded temple, we had free run of several sailboats and a pier with a diving board. We immediately proved that we were not sailors, however, usually managing to sail across the lake, but having serious trouble in learning the mysterious technique of "tacking" back. We also discovered, the hard way, that the pilots of fighter planes returning from missions in Indo-China to the south, knowing that some of their associates were at the camp, would buzz the lake to see if they could capsize the sailboats

We had our weapons with us and, in the hills behind the camp, tried our hand at firing them. Here I met and became friendly with a member of the China detachment of the Office of Strategic Services (OSS). He fired my carbine and I his '45 automatic . . . while he explained the nature of the OSS and gave a very sketchy description of its function, after which I exclaimed, "You're a spy?" which he confirmed with only a slight nod and a mysterious smile. Photos were taken of both of us, and some others from our team and several weeks later, I delivered copies of the prints to the OSS office right in the center of the city of Kunming. Knowing who these fellows were, but following my friend's instructions, I simply handed them to one of the men and stated that they were for him, whose name I can no longer remember. At the mention of his name, everyone in the room turned to observe whom it was that was making a delivery to him. From the several looks I received, I imagined that I was being assessed as anything from a chance acquaintance to an enemy counteragent. The only comment that was offered was a very curt, "Thanks, we'll see that he gets them."

This "Shangri-la" we were guests at did have several drawbacks. It was home to a goodly number of rats. They usually made their presence known as soon as lights were out in the barracks. The bunks, with their mosquito-netting enclosures were arranged in two rows, with a long center aisle in between. As soon as lights were out, our rodent friends would begin their version of drag racing, scampering up and down the middle aisle. Occasionally one would get carried away and dive onto someone's mosquito netting, evoking loud and profane outbursts from the occupant.

The other drawback to the camp was that some of the aircrews that were sharing their facility with us were in dire need of the quiet it offered. Too often their nightmares, wherein they relived the tensions and excitement of their recent air battles would surface and individuals would suddenly start shouting and screaming as they again battled their recent adversaries.

In spite of these minor faults the rest camp served its purpose for us and upon returning to Kunming and Hostel 5, we were indeed refreshed and eager to know what we could expect, now that the war had finally taken a positive turn towards completion.

. . . .

Back at Hostel 5, however, conditions were not improving. Though only a lieutenant, Bernie Silverman, as a platoon officer, commanded one of the units assigned to Advance General Depot #1, SOS. As such it was his duty to attend weekly meetings that were called by the Area commander, a Colonel Owenby. At these functions the Colonel urged the unit leaders, who attended, to feel free to air their ideas or any grievances that were coming from their men. The most longstanding of the latter revolved around conditions at the Hostel 5 enlisted men's mess hall. These started with the outside and the fact that the long lines of men, which paralleled the dirt road on which the building fronted, were subjected to clouds of choking dust whenever a vehicle rumbled by. The grievances continued to address conditions inside, the least of which was the dismal shortcomings of the fare, which too often featured water buffalo meat. This rare delicacy was so tough that half of one's serving could not be chewed to a consistency that would permit it to be swallowed.

Determined to make these facts known to the meeting, Bernie loyally presented them, with several suggestions as to how they could be dealt with. Now Colonel Owenby was an elderly National

Guard veteran with a typically well-traveled, colorful army itinerary behind him. Having formerly held a post in Calcutta, he was reputed to have initiated a program in which U.S. Army medics routinely inspected the local prostitute population as a strategy for reducing venereal diseases among his American charges. In typical army fashion he immediately appointed Bernie assistant mess officer so that, "Young man . . . . you can put all of these things into effect." Reluctantly Bernie took on the job. Diesel fuel was spread on the road and the dust disappeared, a practice today's environmentalists would certainly not have condoned. Our lone truck was lent to the mess sergeant, who used it to do a better job of food shopping, especially for fresh vegetables. The story does not end there, however. In due time, when the Colonel was conveniently out of town, Captain Gebhardt, the adjutant, mercifully relieved Bernie of the job and assigned it to the local army dentist, whose practice was not moving too swiftly. He was a close friend of the mess sergeant, with whom he operated a photography darkroom. The Captain added his own touches, including paper flowers on the tables as well as allegedly improving the menu. As the fortunes of war go, months later the eatery was eventually host to the new area commander, General Cheves, who after partaking of the dentist's improved food and dining room ambiance, awarded him the Bronze Star Medal.

The logic of this episode completely escapes this writer, who for almost a year had to endure the horrendous offerings of this grotesquely overrated establishment and to this day cannot remember ever having been served a reasonably decent meal there. The abysmal quality level of the offerings in the Hostel 5 SOS mess hall was dramatically revealed to me and several other fellows one Sunday after Catholic services. The custom in those days was to refrain from breakfast when receiving Communion at Mass and usually our own mess hall would open when services were over. For some reason, on one morning, SOS Mess was closed and the chaplain had made arrangements for us to have breakfast at an Army Air Corps Service (AACS) organization's facility, which was directly across the road from our own. We were stunned when the cooks rolled out American style bacon and eggs and the works. The lesson we learned, of course, was that the air corps, which had actual, if not official control over what came over the Hump to Kunming, was, as should have been expected, taking care of its own. Still very young and naive, however, I was not mature enough to forgive the U.S. Government for allowing such a heartless inequity to exist.

## THE CURTAIN COMES DOWN ON THE 181ST

Shortly after his escape from the mess hall assignment . . . . and . . . . having had some time to contemplate on the naiveté of having tried to do something about his men's complaints, Lt. Silverman received orders for what turned out to be a very interesting assignment. It was to be his last as a member of the 181st. The orders did not designate any particular reporting destination but only directed him to, " . . . . proceed from this station (Kunming) on or about 15 March, 1945 . . . . to such points as necessary in (the) China theater on temporary duty in connection with Signal activities . . . ."

The job, he discovered, was the installation of a clandestine radio for an organization called the Air Ground Aid Service (AGAS). Its main function was to assist downed airmen by arranging for their medical and physical needs and by providing a means for their return to their parent organizations. Too often these services had to be rendered in Japanese occupied territory.

Like every other country concerned with internal security, the Nationalist Chinese did everything possible to discourage espionage, even by their allies. In China, however, because of the internal corruption, which even included business dealings with the enemy, their vigilance had a twofold purpose. All secret service activity in China was controlled and directed by one of Chiang's generals, named Tai Li, who was known for his extreme cruelty. The only American espionage that he condoned was that, which was conducted by a U.S. Naval unit within an organization called the Sino American Cooperative Organization (SACO). Ti, of course, was on good terms also with General Chennault, who was a close friend of Chiang's. All attempts by the OSS, which was a signatory to SACO, to participate in the gathering of vital intelligence were opposed by Ti and the U.S. Naval Unit in SACO, even though they pretended to be cooperating.

Although authorized to carry on the covert activities required for it to be successful in its rescue role, AGAS had no Table of Organization (TO) nor did it receive any visible source of funding. Because of the nature of its business, however, it was in position to pick up much needed information for those excluded from Tai Li's inner circles. So AGAS was performing two distinct functions. While it had no routine funding source, it did receive equipment from various players in China, including, on occasion, Major Bergman, the commander of the 3344TH Signal Service Detachment, our neighbor organization in the signal compound. The radio, which Bernie was to install and which was mounted in a large suitcase, was one such case. AGAS responded in turn with expressions of their appreciation . . . . one example . . . . a new 38 caliber automatic and shoulder holster that Bernie had been given.

The lieutenant headed east with a jeep, a trailer and a Chinese radio operator. The trip took two plus days and was uneventful until they experienced a blowout on the jeep. With the spare on, Bernie sent his Chinese companion back along the road to an American Ordnance station to get the tire repaired while he, Bernie, spent the night in the trailer. With the new spare aboard, they continued on, now going north, until they reached their destination, a small village, which was home to a Catholic mission. When he arrived, one of the priests told him that they had known of his coming for two days, another example of the mysterious communication systems of this very mysterious country. While installing the radio posed no special problem, when it was ready to use, they discovered that the Chinese operator did not speak or understand the local dialect and a replacement had to be sent for. Having to spend more time than he had originally anticipated, Bernie became quite friendly with the missionaries, who he thinks were from my home state, New Jersey. They were pleased to be visited by a fellow American, apparently not a very frequent event. Bernie recalled that he marveled that these folks, who must have had a subscription to Time magazine, had a copy of every one that had ever been issued.

Also in the village was a large Swedish national, so large that he had lost all of the buttons on his suntan shirt. Being a typical efficient ROTC graduate, Bernie, just happened to have a sewing kit in his musette bag and surprised his new acquaintance by making him a gift of it. His Swedish friend had been employed by the American Government to buy rice, grown in the area, and transport it by river barge to the Yoke Forces fighting in the Salween Valley. In attempting to guess where the village was located, taking into consideration that it took more than two days travel to reach . . . the directions they had taken . . . and based on the fact that there was a large enough river to support barge traffic, it is probable that the village was located on the bank of the Yangtze where it dips south to form the northern boundary of Yunnan Province. Once the replacement operator had arrived, the radio was fired up on a nearby hilltop and contact was made.

. . . .

As was noted earlier, this was the lieutenant's last mission as a member of the 181ST Signal Repair Company for, upon his return to Kunming, he learned that the company had been deactivated. The final curtain had indeed come down on our military family and our last scattering was about to occur. On March 20, 1945 General Order # 40 was issued. It read in Part:

S-E-C-R-E-T
REAR ECHELON
HEADQUARTERS U. S. FORCES
CHINA THEATER

APO 627
20 March 1945

GENERAL ORDERS)

E-X-T-R-A-C-T

NUMBER . . . . 40)

4.  *ACTIVATION, DISBANDMENT AND
REORGANIZATION OF UNITS.*

1.  Pursuant to authority contained in paragraph
19c WD Circular 256, dated 16 Oct 43 and radiogram
from the War Department, the Adjutant General, dated 5
March 1945, the 4011th Signal Service Battalion is
activated effective 15 March 1945 at APO 627 . . . .

It also stated that the new unit would include both Battalion
and Company Head- quarters . . . . and . . . Mess, Storage and
Issue, and . . . Auto Mechanic Teams. The repair section would
have ten radio repair teams of nine men each and three
officers . . . . and . . . . five wire equipment repair teams of ten
men each with two officers. The order directed that the 4011TH
was assigned to the Service of Supplies, China Theater at APO
627 (Kunming). Total authorized strength of the new battalion
was 15 officers and 259 enlisted men.

The order then went on to declare that, effective March 15,
1945, both the 3344TH Signal Service Detachment and the
181ST Signal Repair Company were deactivated and all
personnel were transferred to the 4011TH, including those men on

detached service, who would continue in their current assignments.

The final blow was that General Order # 40 was cut at the command of Major General Chennault.

So there it was . . . . the history of our military family was finished . . . . not so the exploits of the men, however, who had cast their lots with the 181ST back in 1942. The war in the east beckoned and some of us were destined to be part of it.

Ironically, on March 20th, the same date that the order came out that deactivated the 181ST, another was issued awarding the "Good Conduct Medal" to seventeen members of our 1ST Team, identifying them as members of the 181ST.

. . . .

Back in India the news of the reorganization found the men of the Third Team, now commanded by Bob Finkel, scattered wide and far . . . . operating repair shops both in Ledo and in Myitkyina. Several were leading the good life on rest and rehabilitation (R&R) furloughs in places like New Delhi, Agra (home of the Taj Mahal) and Calcutta.

Although we have been unable to establish the precise time frames during which they occurred, several accounts, received from the men from Lt. Wilson's Third Team, include references to working and living with people from the 191st Signal Repair Company. On November 1st, one week after the splitting of the CBI Theater (October 24, 1944), Sergeant Nichols, with the assistance of Bottary's motor pool gang, took a squad to Myitkyina to establish a permanent repair shop. Besides Nichols and Bottary, in the group were Warren Diesel, George Loftus, Ernie Gioia, Jack Hale, Harold Webb, Hugh Gibson, Sam Monteleone and a John Clark, who was not a member of the 181st when it first reached Ledo in late 1943. It is very likely that he was probably part of the 191st. Nichols recalled the excellent job that Clark did in wiring the shop.

The squad took their meals with the 96th Signal Battalion, sharing KP and guard responsibilities. In January of 1945 a radio message, ordering some of them to return to Ledo was relayed through the 96th. Bottary recalled that when they finally reached Ledo, they found the entire Ledo contingent prepared to join a convoy, which was about to make the long trip to Kunming. In addition to the entire HQ unit, the group preparing to leave included one half of the men from Finkel's Third Team. Quentin Brandt (Danbury, WI) recalled that those working in the Ledo repair shop, who were transferred to the 4011TH, were chosen by the simple exercise of drawing straws.

In the meantime, several from the Third Team, who were away on R&R were blissfully unaware of the demise of the 181ST. Henry (Hank) Frank, New York City . . . Herman Berger, Houston, TX and Eddie Blake, Burbank, CA were living it up in the romantic Kashmir. When they returned to Ledo they were confronted with the stunning fact that they were no longer in the 181ST. They received another shock when they discovered that half of their repair team, along with the 181ST headquarters contingent, motor pool and all, had disappeared over the Road en-route to China. Some of their bashas were now occupied by a host of new faces. They soon learned, also, that they and what remained of the 181ST Third Repair Team were now part of the 191ST Signal Repair Company. Up in Myitkyina, the gang that had flown up with Sergeant Nichols in November of 1944 was also inducted into the 191ST.

Robert (Robby) Robertson, Riverton, NJ and Bill Snider, Greensboro, NC, who had been working with a signal supply unit since shortly after our arrival in Ledo, were now officially in the 3199TH Signal Service Battalion. Snider was offered and accepted a commission as a 2nd Lieutenant, with the same provision as that which Bob Finkel had agreed to . . . . that he spend an additional year in the CBI. As events subsequently dictated, they were both spared that fate when the Japanese ill-conceived plan to rule Asia was dealt a deathblow by the A-Bomb.

. . . .

The official dissolution of our military 181ST family was now complete.

On March 16, 1945, the day following the activation of General Order #40, a gallant band, composed of the entire HQ platoon and the remnants of the 3RD Repair Team formed their convoy, under the command of Bob Finkel, who by the way assigned Warrant Officer Joe Hardwick to the last vehicle. Their trek across Burma into Yunnan Province took more than a week. Finkel recalled that he celebrated his birthday, March 25th, while still in convoy. Following the route that the first official convoy had taken only a few weeks earlier, they made their tortuous way over the Patkai's and through the rain forests of the Hukawng and Mogaung Valleys. At Myitkyina they spent the night saying their final good-byes to their friends from the 3RD Team, now members of the 191ST. In Burma they marveled at the drastic changes in temperature from the steaming heat of the valleys to the near-freezing cold of the high mountain passes. On this once-in-a-life-time journey they stopped to get their photos taken at the remote spot in Northeastern Burma where the Ledo and Old Burma Roads intersected . . . . then into the vastness of Southeastern China and Yunnan Province, where they had another opportunity to visit ever-so-briefly with some of their compatriots at Paoshan and Yunnanyi. Hamp Mc Bride recalled that at the latter, Felix Orsini, the HQ's mail man and heretofore right-hand for 1ST Sergeant Hess, even spent the night in Henry "Shot" Howell's bunk, "Shot" off somewhere on a maintenance "house call". Eventually our travelers reached Kunming and were assigned quarters in the tent camp adjacent to the Signal Compound.

181 ST (now 4011 TH) leaves for China

Somewhere in Burma

Mongyu—Joining of the Burma and Ledo Roads

Salween River "Huitung Bridge"

# THE 4011TH

We could have ended our manuscript here and still been true to the thesis, which started out as the telling of the story of the 181ST Signal Repair Company. To do so, however, would have left a significant number of its members adrift in the remote reaches of the CBI and we would have also lost an opportunity to record their experiences which occurred while working for their new masters. Thus our story continues . . . .

As it had in 1943 when we were preparing for our bout with the Mojave Desert . . . and . . . again in 1944 as we joined the campaign to open a land route to China . . . April in 1945 also turned out to be a pivotal month for our struggling signal repairmen. Not only had their military identities been altered by their transfers to their new organizations . . . but also the environment in which they were now to function had also changed. In China all eyes were now directed to the East where the Japanese were reconsidering the wisdom of their recent advances along the north-south railroad corridor. The ending of an era in American and world history also occurred with the death of President Roosevelt on April 12th.

. . . .

The process that followed, the integration of six officers and about one hundred and twenty enlisted men from the 181ST into the new battalion, was a typical, cold, army exercise. No recognition of the fact that these men had already served more than a year and a half in the theater, starting when living conditions and supplies were worse than Spartan . . . and . . . that many of them had been close enough to the war to have earned citations . . . was forthcoming from our new management. Having spent their tour in the CBI in the country club environment of the SEAC headquarters in Kandy, Ceylon, they had no conception of the obstacles that China presented to quality repair and supply performance. The commander, a Lt. Colonel Webster F. Soules, did not waste any time in finding fault with our repair operation in the signal compound. When Lt. Silverman gave him the twenty-cent tour, his criticisms flowed freely. Bernie recalled that during our many months in the Kunming compound, when tools were at a premium, we had somehow become the owners of a second hand power saw, a veritable prize. The good colonel, however, managed to comment that the saw, which had a slightly off-centered shaft was leaving a burn mark on the boards that it was cutting for packing boxes.

Bernie also recalled that the colonel brought with him his own stable of subordinate officers, who were quite unhappy with the loss of the vacation-like amenities they had enjoyed at their last assignment and that they were not very friendly. Added to the officers from the 181ST, together with those from the 3344TH Signal Service Detachment, who had shared the compound with us, the colonel's contingent created a surplus of officers in the battalion. On April 5th, therefore, he penned a request to General Cheves, Commander SOS China Theater, whose buzzer system Jeff Bennett and I had installed, that Lt. Silverman, who was overdue to be sent back to the "States", be relieved of his assignment with the 4011TH, pending his rotation back home. The answer came back that SOS HQ had already reported the lieutenant eligible for rotation back on March 6th, that he would be placed on the next War Department Requisition and that until that was received, he was "not eligible to return stateside".

One of the colonel's next moves was to assign all of the officers to their various jobs in the battalion. On April 9th per his "Special Order #2" Lt. John Petri, our former 181ST company commander's main duty became Assistant Executive Officer. Lt. Robert S. Finkel and his long-time adversary Warrant Officer Joseph O. Hardwick became Supply Officers, while Lts. Silverman and George Holmes Wilson, who had replaced Lt. Mc Veigh at Yunnanyi, were assigned to Radio Repair. Lt. Kermit Swanson, who had been in charge of our repair team at Paoshan became a wire officer. Lts. Petri and Finkel were also given additional responsibilities.

. . . .

Ironically, on April 11th, two days later, Bernie Silverman's 181ST First Team received a commendation from the 14TH Air Force's 559TH Air Warning Battalion for having restored "two (2) defective circuit breakers to working condition". This was followed on April 19TH by General Cheves' personal commendation. It read in part, "1. This file is forwarded with my personal commendation and appreciation. It is the desire of this headquarters that all units through ingenuity, initiative and whole-hearted attitude of cooperation that you have shown, endeavor to do not only their regular job but help our sister Agencies whenever possible." We have no record, however, of whether Colonel Soules saw either of these communications and if he did, what his reaction might have been.

. . . .

Our world had indeed changed . . . even our living quarters. We discovered that while we had been enjoying the amenities, such as they were, at the rest camp, some one had had us evicted from our Oriental Motel and we found that we had been moved to a barn-like barracks. The reason that filtered down to us was that the powers-that-be had decided to "improve our living standards". It was indeed closer to the mess hall and the center of activities at Hostel Five, but it was shared by us with a "Grave Registration Detail". Their grisly job was to visit the scene of some poor devil's demise, scrape him into a body bag and arrange for his burial. In the Kunming vicinity the fatalities were usually suffered by the Air Corps. So that even finding the bodies in the plane wreckage was difficult and indeed gut wrenching. When the word came, often in the dead of night, the detail would be awakened and regardless of the weather, monsoon or not, would hasten to perform their gory duty. For several reasons, these fellows occupied the cots nearest to the back entrance to the barracks. As had become the custom with these unfortunate GI's, upon returning from their gruesome ministrations, they were often known to settle their nerves with a generous libation of alcohol. The inevitable finally happened in the dead of one night . . . . when one of the men, after having surrendered his senses to the alcohol, managed to drop the bottle, which broke when it hit the floor. In his inebriated condition, rather than turn on the lights and suffer the rage of his sleeping comrades, chose instead to light a match. The result was spectacular and when the scream of "FIRE" penetrated the dreams of the fifty or so inhabitants of the barracks, the scene became one of panic mixed with anger. Fortunately my bunk was a good fifty feet from the fire, which was quickly extinguished.

. . . .

While the month of April continued its relentless campaign to remake what, for more than a year, had been the long-suffering role of the men from the former 181ST, the war in the east continued to heat up. Having succeeded in wresting from the Chinese all of Chennault's airfields that were located in the major cities sewn together by the Hunan-Kwangsi Railroad, on April 8th the Japanese turned westward with an eye to taking Chihchiang (Chick-ee-yang') in western Hunan Province. Its fall would leave the way clear to our major base at Kweiyang (Gway-yang) in Kweichow (Gway-chow) Province . . . . and the road to Kunming.

With the Salween Offensive only recently completed . . . and with the Chinese and American efforts to move troops and materiel eastward just getting under way . . . . the timing of the attack caught our leaders not quite ready to mount a fully coordinated defense of the area. American liaison teams, who were in the middle of their programs for acquainting the Chinese armies with their new American weapons and maneuvers, had to cut their classes short and join their charges as they were deployed to meet the Japanese advances.

Material support for the defending forces was also in a state of flux. When the major base at Kweilin fell in late 1944, its American garrison had withdrawn to Chihchiang only to face the possibility of a repeat performance of their earlier retreat. As they struggled to service the Chinese armies that were arriving and those already in the field, some supplies became hard to get, if not impossible. This was made dramatically clear to us in the repair shop at Hostel 5 one day when a jeep roared into the compound and its passenger charged up to our service counter carrying what was left of a small power transformer. He explained his haste by blurting out that no replacement was available in Chihchiang and that the radio that it had come out of was critical to the defenders air-warning capability.

By now I had become well schooled in the intricacies of coil winding, having learned all about "primary and secondary windings" . . . . "number of turns per volt" etc.

Our frantic customer's transformer was, therefore, entrusted to my care . . . and . . . as he watched over my shoulder, I rewound it to his specifications and as soon as it was reassembled and tested, he shot out of the compound just as hurriedly as he had entered.

. . . .

While the month of April prepared to spring its next surprise on our heroes, the fight to deny the Japanese Chihchiang was reaching its climax. In the rush to re-enforce the Chinese and their American advisors, Kweiyang was rapidly being made into a major point for the support of Chihchiang and the buildup for the campaign to retake the 14TH Air Force airfields and open a port on the China coast. The 4011TH had been delegated to be part of both objectives and on April 24th, only six weeks after its activation, was ordered to Kweiyang. This did not excuse it from its repair and supply responsibilities in Kunming, however, and four days later, on the 28th, Special Order #2 was cut by battalion headquarters creating a Detachment #1 which was to continue the repair and supply role in Kunming. Technically it called for a unit, which included two officers and forty-seven enlisted men. Someone must have discovered that when the list of folks who were to head east to Kweiyang was deducted from the total battalion roster, there remained a surplus, which exceeded the number called for in the order. This might explain Special Order #6, issued on the very same day, that not only listed the names of the individuals assigned to the detachment but also increased the number of officers to five (two from the 181ST) and enlisted men to sixty-five (nineteen from the 181ST). The list also included seven men who were reassigned from the 3371ST Signal Service Company, which was operating a film library next to our repair shop in the signal compound.

. . . .

Shortly after the release of the two orders, the battalion, less the men who were assigned to Detachment #1, formed a convoy and headed by Lt. Petri, began its trek eastward toward Kweiyang. After thirteen months in Kunming I, and a dozen of my comrades from the First Team were finally going to get a different view of China.

. . . .

Less than a week after we arrived in Kweiyang, the electrifying news that the Germans had accepted reality and given up the ghost in Europe was announced.

. . . .

Back in Kunming, both of the men who had led the 181ST First Team for over a year and through its most difficult times in China . . . . left the 4011TH. Platoon Sergeant Bill Hasse, whom I had been associated with since way back in San Bernardino in the late spring of 1943, was relieved of his assignment with the battalion on May 14th and began preparations for his return to the United States. By the 14th he was in India, awaiting embarkation and eventually arrived at Ft. Totten, Long Island, NY on June 25th.

Remembering all too clearly the earlier action taken by Colonel Soules to hustle him out of the 4011[TH], and deciding to save the good colonel and himself any more aggravation, Platoon Officer Bernie Silverman contacted a former contemporary at the old YFOS HQ at Hostel 1, who informed him that they were looking for instructors at the Chinese Training Center. On May 24th orders were issued affecting his transfer. The assignment there was cut short, however, by a June 7th order for his return to the United States that came from China Theater Headquarters. The next day he also flew from Kunming to Calcutta where, after several days he took "a slow boat" to the US. Having been overseas since January 1943 (two years and six months), he was discharged, after a thirty-day leave from Ft. Meade, MD. During his leave at home in Richmond, VA the first A Bomb was dropped in Japan.

# WE MEET SOME STRANGERS
# IN KUNMING

For the rest of the 181ST men still in Kunming, especially those who had returned from more than a year in the remoteness of Southwestern Yunnan Province, following the end of the Salween Offensive, life became a little more livable. Located right at the main terminus of both the Burma Road and the Hump Route, they no longer had to play games with per diem vouchers, but instead could enjoy the stability of the Hostel five mess, such as it was. Some of the men who had been repairmen were assigned to the warehouse, Col Soules deciding that his own first team was going to include as few of the 181ST personnel as possible. Having never fully relinquished their civilian status to their draft boards, and knowing that the war was beginning to wind down, I do not imagine that these men cared very much what the good colonel did. They were seeing signs that their days of endless waiting in this forgotten, God-forsaken theater might finally be coming to and end.

Besides the encouraging news from the Pacific and the knowledge that, with Europe now in Allied hands, it was reasonable to expect that Washington would have no alternative but to give more of its time and material support to what once was the CBI. Another fact, that we should have considered, but did not, was that when Germany fell, so did their puppet government in Vichy . . . . leaving the Japanese in Indochina without an ally.

. . . .

As mentioned earlier, most of the incidents that involved my wartime companions, came from years of conversation and questioning. Deciding which parts of the resulting mass of material was worthy of repeating, was of course, a real challenge. Thus it became necessary to sort through the many stories told, to try to identify those that contained the most truth and the least amount of exaggeration. In making these judgments, one does not always bat one thousand. Two of these stories, which I was to hear several years apart and from two very dependable individuals still left me with serious doubt as to their veracity. Time and the seemingly endless research of the history of the CBI war eventually convinced me that they were indeed true.

The first was related to me by Bob Callinan. Early in my research, he claimed that he had met none other than Ho Chih Minh at the repair shop in Hostel 5. At the time I could see no logic in his story and filed it deep in the back of my memory. About four years later, Weeks Andrews repeated the same claim, and though I did not doubt his word, I had found nothing, historically, to corroborate the story. Callinan had insisted that a thin, gaunt, strange, civilian had been brought into the signal repair shop in the Kunming compound. He was not told whom or what nationality his visitor was . . . only that he was to be taught how to operate and maintain several transceiver equipments. It was not until thirty years after the war, when an article appeared in ARGOSY MAGAZINE, that he concluded who his mysterious client had been. Only recently was I able to learn, in a history of the OSS and a television program, that following the chance rescue by the Viet Minh of an American airman, who had made a forced landing in northern Indochina, Ho agreed with both the OSS and Chennault to gather intelligence information for the Americans. This agreement was made in Kunming and when Ho explained his ignorance of the workings of the radio equipment he was to use, he was taken to an American location and instructed accordingly.

The other story, which also started with Callinan, and which I originally could find no confirmation of was of the French Foreign Legion marching through the streets of Kunming. This one, mentioned several years later by Millard Owens, Burlington, NJ, was also discovered in the OSS history to be a direct result of the end of the Vichy government in France. While they were still allied with the Japanese, the French in Indochina were tolerated and accepted. With the fall of their homeland to the Allies, history has recorded that their behavior became suspect by the Japanese and when attempts were made to jail them the French Army fled north into China.

. . . .

As the summer of 1945 approached, other strangers, in American uniforms and wearing paratrooper boots began to appear on the streets of Kunming. They were, of course, the vanguard of the forces that were to be relocated from Europe and who would play some role in the opening of a port on the China Sea. The stories that began to circulate about them were not of a military nature, however, but instead revolved around some of their exploits in evading the military police in the red light sections of Kunming.

# CHAPTER IX

## Eastern China

### HERE WE GO AGAIN

The opening of the Ledo and Burma Roads and the end of hostilities in the Salween Valley in January of 1945 signaled the downsizing of the American presence at Paoshan, Yunnanyi and the other garden spots in Southwestern Yunnan Province. With the focus now being turned to the task in the east, the American liaison personnel, formerly with the X, Y and Z Forces were quickly reorganized into the Chinese Combat Command headed by Major General Robert B. Mc Clure. Those men from the 181ST who were in the field with their Chinese clients packed their gear and headed east, some stopping at Paoshan and Yunnanyi to collect their belongings. Leaving some of their comrades, still "minding the store", they continued on to Kunming.

Weeks prior to that, in October 1944, a small contingent, led by Platoon Sergeant Varner Shippy from Swanson's 4TH Team and including Ray Fichter and Stanley Treggo had already left Paoshan. Taking a repair bus body and a weapons carrier with them they stopped briefly at Kunming and continued eastward. Their destination turned out to be Chihchiang, located up against the western border of Hunan Province, where they arrived just in time to become directly involved in the fall of Kweilin to the Japanese. They were immediately dispatched with the weapons carrier and trailer to the doomed town. Fichter recalled that they loaded up with gasoline drums and "left in a hurry." Both going and returning they had to cross the Yuan Chaing River at An-Chaing in Hunan Province on an improvised ferry. During their escapades with their new clients they traveled with the New 6TH Army, which included many of the Chinese troops who had been with Stilwell in Burma. They were still in Chihchiang when the Japanese flew in to formally surrender as the war finally came to an end in August 1945.

. . . .

There were others like Bob Gunning who arrived in Kunming in December 1944, from Yunnanyi, joining Otis Bannon (Portland, OR) . . . Alton Croom, Lawrence Hundley and Franklin Trivette all from North Carolina . . . . Frank Downing (Kansas City) and William Floyd Mercer (Whitesburg, KY) who were occupying a rapidly growing tent camp that had sprung up next to the Signal Compound. After New Years, with Downing driving a weapons carrier, he, Gunning and Bannon joined a convoy heading east for Kweiyang. Gunning recalled that on the second day it got so cold that, "we had to break out the winter underwear from our barracks bags."

Their destination was a former college, which was located on a hill in the central part of the city. Here they reported to the Signal Officer, a Colonel Boye and his aide, both of whom, curiously, were wearing cavalry breeches and boots. Living in a dormitory with varnished floors, and with the use of a gym and showers, a day room and cafeteria and best of all the service of Chinese boys and cooks, they discovered that they had fallen into the best assignment they had enjoyed since they first arrived in the CBI. Utilizing a former classroom, Downing and his comrades were engaged in the repair of V-100 radios from the Chinese armies and some manufactured by the British. They also set up and maintained public address amplifiers and speakers.

They found that many of the Americans at the school were recent evacuees from Kweilin and Liuchow. On March 1st they were joined by Nisei troops from Merrill's Marauders, whose job was the questioning of Japanese prisoners.

. . . .

On February 1, 1945 Millard Sturgell, at Paoshan, received similar orders to return to Kunming. He flew back in time to be part of the welcoming party for the first convoy when it entered the city. Checking out a jeep he sought out some of the folks from the 2ND Team, who had returned from Yunnanyi and who had also checked into the tent camp adjacent to the signal compound. As our long lost comrades filtered in, they joined the others in the camp or were immediately pointed east for places like Chanyi and Kweiyang.

. . . .

At the same time, some of us at the Signal Compound were getting the same messages. One group that got the official word, also on February 1st, included our Lt. Silverman and Lt. Henry P. Tomczak, Staff Sgt. Harold J. O'Dell and Pfc Harry Fox, the latter three formerly with the 3344TH Signal Service Detachment, fellow tenants in the signal compound. They were ordered to Chanyi also, " . . . in connection with activities of this Depot . . ." Chanyi was rapidly becoming a key to supporting the activities in the east.

. . . .

Also, several days later Sergeant Roy Hendricks (Indianapolis) from Carlson's Yunnanyi Team headed east bound for Chanyi. Included in the truck he was driving were Sturgell,

Joe Little (not from the 181ST), Orace Bowman (Oklahoma) and a captain. Sturgell described the ride as "frightening and dusty" with the occupants in the back prepared to bail out . . ."especially when the truck had to back up on the sharp curves". One night was spent in a camp and another by the side of the road . . . ." . . . near an irrigation ditch where we washed some of the road dust off".

Chanyi turned out to be somewhat less than hospitable. After first settling in a tent in a large encampment, but then learning that there was a possibility of enemy attempts to sabotage the base's transmitters, they moved near to one outside of camp. Here they were also about fifty yards from a large ammunition dump. Their fears were realized when Hendricks found an American hand grenade, with the pin pulled, outside one of the transmitters. He tossed it away, expecting it to explode, but when it did not, he notified the MP's who buried it.

The next act of sabotage, suspected to be coming from Chinese sympathetic to the Japanese, surfaced with the discovery of arsenic in the food at the mess hall. It was promptly closed and another opened, but not until after several men had become ill. While the problem was being taken care of, Sturgell and Little, on the way to get hair cuts, were stopped by an officer with a large truck and ordered to drive him to the airport . . . . his driver was one of those who had fallen victim to the tainted food. Neither of our heroes had ever driven a truck before but, with Sturgell at the wheel, did manage to deliver their passenger to his destination. They then abandoned the truck at the airport and walked the five miles back to camp.

The would-be saboteurs were persistent, however, and had wired the base commander's door in such a way that opening it would have blown the ammunition dump. Fortunately he discovered the wired door. When a report also circulated that Japanese suicide troops had been dropped in the area, a contingent of ex-Mars Task Force troops arrived and set up camp near the transmitter.

In addition to their main responsibility, which was the maintenance of the transmitters and receiver, the latter located on the other side of the camp our little team also maintained the Mars mobile radio equipment. While servicing one of the base transmitters, Sturgell accidentally came in contact with its output current and was knocked, "clear across the tent. My hands and arms were burned to the elbow. I think the shock was the worse I ever had."

Sturgell recalled that one day " . . . . a Chinese Army Major came and asked us if I could go and check his radio. Upon arriving (I) was amazed at what a crow's nest. By luck Joe Little and I straightened his equipment into operating condition." The entire group was rewarded with a dinner invitation and when Sturgell turned down the offer of a drink, the major said that he was surprised that someone from a whisky-producing state like Kentucky did not drink.

Wherever one went in wartime China, he or she was sure to witness the squalor and misery of the population. In Chanyi our small repair team discovered an eight-year old boy, who was almost deaf. Hendricks promptly adopted him and the men fitted him with a pair of earphones connected to a source of music. Sturgell remembered that he would not remove them, wandering around most of the day, fascinated by them.

This group of men remained in Chanyi until V-J Day, after which they left for Kweiyang to join the main body of the 4011TH. Sturgell finally returned to Kunming on September 15th. While waiting his turn to go home, he regularly visited a Lutheran school for the blind in the city, fascinated when hearing the children sing in both Chinese and English. On October 1, 1945 he was on board the first flight to Calcutta.

. . . .

During April of 1945, while those of us back in Kunming were going through the trauma of our transfer to the 4011TH, Paul Mrogenski (Brookfield, MO) and four or five others flew in from Yunnanyi. They rejoined their former platoon sergeant, Gil Carlson, (Falconer, NY) and within days loaded a repair bus body and headed east to Kweiyang. From there they turned south . . . . their destination Nanning . . . . at the southern end of the string of airfields lost in 1944 to the Japanese. To reach Nanning they had to pass through Liuchow . . . . arriving just as the Chinese 29TH and 46TH Armies were in the latter stages of its occupation in June 1945. As the Japanese evacuated Liuchow they burned 60% of the city and left the airfield runways riddled with large craters. When Carlson's little group reached Liuchow they were struck with the spectacle and the extent of the recent destruction. Wrecked Japanese vehicles and corpses . . . animal and human . . . were everywhere. Chinese cleanup squads were still wandering about, prodding bayonets into strings of Japanese prisoners roped together. From Liuchow Carlson's little group continued south to Nanning. They remained there until the war ended but, unfortunately were, not able to remember very much about the time they spent there. The only event that stood out in Mrogenski's memory was of being kidded about the Chinese 1ST Army's Missouri mules, he being a Missouri native.

. . . .

All of the foregoing incidents occurred to the east of Kunming, reflecting the impending buildup for the campaign to recapture our airfields and to open a port on the China Sea. In consort with this effort, the allied plan called for pressure to be exerted on the southern border of China, where it met Indo-China. It followed, then, that some of the 181ST repairmen soon found themselves in or near towns with names like Wenshan, Mengtzu or facing the Japanese across the Red River, which marks a section of the Indo-China border.

While their stories are not as numerous or detailed, we know that, before he left the 4011TH, Lt. Bernie Silverman, accompanied by Technical Sergeant Bill Wraspir, my roommate the night of the Christmas Eve air raid, and several others from the former 3344TH, also spent several days in the Mengtzu area. Others who were sent to southern China were Leon Olson

(Gloucester Heights, NJ) . . . Millard Owens (Burlington, NJ) . . . Hamp Mc Bride, Battle Brown and Franklin Trivette . . . from Asheboro, Raleigh and Boone, NC respectively. Trivette was another of those singularly talented civilian/soldiers, holding down the position of radio repairman. Battle Brown reported that, in his spare time and to streamline his personal laundry chores, Trivette fashioned himself an electric washing machine . . . which he brought back to Kunming after V-J Day.

Owens recalled that Chinese bandits stole the Christmas mail in Wenshan and when the Japanese threatened to advance on Kunming, some of the fellows were seen removing the chevrons from their sleeves.

. . . .

Besides these men there were some who opted to volunteer to return to India and drive vehicles over the now-opened Stillwell Road . . . anticipating that the food and PX situation was better there than where they were. Two who jumped at the chance to get out of China, if only temporarily were Hugh "Hoot" Gibson (Asheville, NC), and Roy W. Murphy (Clymer, NY) who had spent a considerable part of his time in China in the base hospital in Kunming, battling amoebic dysentery and several other Chinese maladies. Jeff Bennett (Long Valley, NJ), my closest friend, who had served as honor guard with me at the memorial mass in Kunming and Sam Firman (Chicago) also decided to take a shot at the Road. They, with several others from the 181ST, drove jeeps towing trailers.

Back in India, Jimmy "Red" Jones (Kingsville, MO) from the 5TH Team, (subsequently the 223RD) and George Loftus (San Antonio) who had followed Stillwell's Northern Combat Area Command through Burma to Myitkyina, also signed on to one of the convoys that was forming. Under the control of a company of black GI's, with a white C.O., the convoy started from Digboi, near Chabua. The trip took eleven days and covered 1100 miles. Jones made it all the way to Kunming but Loftus, due to a strange series of events, was ordered back to Ledo by the convoy commander. Prior to starting, the order was given that there was to be no passing and that anyone who was caught doing so would have to return to India. Somewhere well into Burma, Loftus was told to stop and pick up some Chinese members of a tank unit . . . . which he did. The convoy, however, started up and left him before he had everyone aboard. In relating the story, Jones explained that he and others had been told that when the trucks reached China, they would change color to a light green. Naturally he doubted the credibility of such a statement, only to discover that when they did reach China, due to the reflection of the rice patties or some other natural phenomenon, the vehicles did indeed look lighter in color. This eventually turned out to be Loftus' downfall . . . because as he tried to catch up and resume his former position, he did not do so until the convoy crossed into China. Deceived by the apparent change in color of the trucks, and assuming that they were from another convoy, and still trying to find his own, he unfortunately passed the convoy commander's jeep. Jones tried to intercede for him, relating what had happened . . . but in vain. The commander's sergeant explained to Jimmy that "rules are rules and they would'nt be of much use if folks were allowed to break them". Jimmy was in Kunming about three days, but never had an opportunity to meet with any of the men from the 181ST, by then the 4011TH. He flew back over the HUMP to Chabua, rejoining the 223RD.

Roy W. Murphy drove a 6x6 truck loaded with thirty drums of gasoline in one of the first convoys over the newly opened Ledo Road, starting at Calcutta. Much later, he volunteered to drive in another, which was going to Chungking. Again he carried a load of gasoline and after delivering it, remained there as a radio repairman until the war was over.

. . . .

During the last week of April 1945, the 4011TH Signal Service Battalion, less Detachment #1, left Kunming for Kweiyang. Those of us, who were not driving were assigned to trucks as passengers. With me were several new faces from the Ceylon contingent and two of our own, Phil Thompson (Sharon, PA) and George "The Gonk" Raabe (Milwaukee, WI), two very capable radio repairmen and very good friends of mine. A hint of what was ahead of us surfaced when we were all issued kidney belts. After having spent fifteen stressful months in China, at first some of us scoffed at our need for them. But as is so often the case, wiser heads prevailed and it was not too long before our skepticism turned to acknowledgement of their value.

Commanded by Lt. John Petri, the convoy started eastward on what was actually the continuation of the famed Burma Road. In the truck that I was assigned to, there were just enough spaces in the two fold-down benches to afford everyone a seat. Up to this point most of my travel in 6X6's had been on paved or sandy desert roads in the U.S. or in relatively short hops in India. This time I was faced with 300-plus kilometers of very rough road over lofty mountain passes and literally scores of spine-chilling switchbacks. The downward version of the latter were made extremely difficult to adjust to (a polite word for fear) due to the need for the drivers to distribute the wear and tear alternately between the brakes, clutches and transmissions. They did this by shifting into a relatively high (third) gear as they began to descend, in order to spare the clutch and transmission. Depending on the length of the decline, they would consequently be traveling at a good clip when they reached the bottom, at which time they would then apply the brakes and spin the wheel to confront the next decline. Inasmuch as too many of these "bottoms" could easily have doubled as what are referred to in the North American mountains as "scenic overlooks", a failure of the brakes would most certainly have left us airborne and plunging to the valley or the next switchback below us. For a city boy from New Jersey, three days of this action was indeed "trying" if not downright terrifying.

The first day out was uneventful except that one of the trucks carrying passengers had mechanical trouble and had to leave the convoy. We were soon well into the remoteness of the mountain ranges that lay between us and Kweiyang and beginning to experience some of the apprehension that Sturgell had encountered five months earlier. Lunch break, which was enjoyed along a lofty stretch of a most remote section of the road, consisted of cold "C" rations. While enjoying the rare servings of meat and vegetable hash we became aware that we had become the objects of several of the curious, sun-browned natives who tended the nearby terraced rice paddies. The most striking of their swarthy features, were the almost universal profusion of very large goiters, understandable in light of the very limited variety of edibles available in the lofty remoteness in which they and their forbearers had apparently survived.

By days end we approached a small hamlet and as we rolled though its only street, we caught a brief glimpse of a bottle of Five Star Rum, a native concoction that we had sampled without dire results back in Kunming, which was perched on the top shelf of a small, dingy roadside stand. The convoy came to a halt about a mile the other side of town next to an airstrip, which was bustling with activity as C-46's were taking on planeloads of Chinese soldiers for transport to the east. My guess is that we were somewhere near either Chanyi or Kutsing. Gathering everyone around him, the lieutenant's first comment was that the town was off limits. After deciding that the mud behind the truck that had been carrying us was suitable for supporting our bedrolls we started for town . . . the goal, of course, was to retrieve the bottle of rum that we had spotted. About half way there, we met the lieutenant and another officer coming out. After learning that we were not drivers, listening to our very limited objective, carrying the permanent rank of master sergeant in the regular army prior to the war . . . and . . . a bit of a rounder himself, he allowed us to pass.

The next day, however, we had to contend with the results of our folly with one more bit of aggravation being added to the dust and heat of our journey. Added to this was the discovery that, although the stricken truck had finally caught up with us, it could

not continue. When we lined up before starting, we also
discovered that we were to take on its passengers . . . meaning
that half of us would have to take turns standing. As the
lieutenant strolled casually along the convoy, he stopped and
facetiously asked about our comfort. When he received a
loudly voiced negative response he smiled and replied "tough
s—". This was not a wise move under the circumstances, as a
fellow standing next to me voiced a similar epithet, coupled
with "has anyone got a gun?" The good lieutenant lucked out
that morning.

Our route on day "two" began over some of the same hair-
raising terrain of the previous day. For the greater part of the
morning we made our way gingerly down the face of a mountain
that fell off so steeply, we could not see the floor of the valley
below. At the bottom we threaded our way through this same
valley and for several hours followed it to where it broke out into
a series of lesser hills. By mid-afternoon we had put most of these
behind us only to find that we had arrived at the foot of one of the
most blood-tingling sights that I have ever seen. Before and
towering above us was a series of switchbacks (twenty three, we
counted them) that wormed their way up the shear face of a
mountain. This man-made wonder has been the subject of many
photo publications and, in some cases has been incorrectly
identified as being in Burma or elsewhere. It is actually in the
vicinity of, what was then called, Annan and a good days travel
west of Kweiyang. The apprehension experienced during the
ensuing climb rivaled anything that has since been generated in
Coney Island or Disneyland. As Sturgell had described, some of
the trucks could not make several of the turns in one try and had
to back up until their trailers were actually hanging over the
edge of the "scenic overlook" to complete the maneuver. Although
it was about two o'clock in the afternoon when we began our
ascent, it was dark when we reached the summit. Another hour
or so brought us to a transit camp just in time to miss dinner. The
following day we reached Kweiyang and although we still
encountered the inevitable grades and switchbacks, the day's

events were no more than anti-climactic compared to those of day number two.

Our first stop in Kweiyang, in the southeast outskirts, was next to a small tent encampment. While the lieutenant and his brain trusts sought out information as to our exact destination, some of us grasped the opportunity to dismount. We knew that some of our compatriots, who I have discussed earlier in this chapter, were about somewhere . . . . and . . . . poking my nose into one of the tents I found Frank Downing and Otis Bannon intently ministering to an alcohol-producing still. I do not know what ingredients they were using in their process but was informed by Downing that they judged their final product to be ready to drink when it burned with a blue flame.

. . . .

In due time the order was given to board the trucks. At this point, a very significant action occurred . . . . those trucks carrying the upper management of the battalion veered left into the town proper, headed for the college on the hill that Bob Gunning had described. About two-dozen of us, including Lt. Petri and Sergeant Hess turned right, instead, finally bedding down in a tent area on the southern outskirts of town.

. . . .

The headquarters of the 4011TH had reported to and become part of the SOS Area Command at Kweiyang. Several of our former 181ST officers were present in this detachment. On May 26th, one of these, Lt. Bob Finkel and a former supply sergeant, Maurice Lichty (Kansas) were assigned to Chihchiang on temporary duty. On June 1st the order was issued awarding the bronze service star, to be worn on the Asiatic/Pacific campaign ribbon, to all those in the former 181ST who had participated in the India-Burma Campaign. Upon returning from Chihchiang, Finkel, who had been assigned as a battalion supply officer in April, on June

23rd was given yet another job as Investigation Officer. Bob's recollections of that assignment included the issuing of a report on a Pvt. Ira J. Brewer, who had curiously elected to refuse to perform punishment that had been meted out as a result of having been drunk at work. To celebrate the memory of our country's independence, the battalion brass, on July 4th, also decided to appoint Bob Information and Education Officer for Base Section 3 (Kweiyang). They were not about to relieve him of his battalion supply duties, however, sticking him, on July 10th, with the title of Assistant Battalion Supply Officer.

That was not his final title . . . on the 16th he was assigned his principal duty, as Radio Officer. During this period he assumed the responsibility for the operation and maintenance of the army radio station XWRA, which broadcast from the American Red Cross building in Kweiyang. It had been started, originally, by a hard-working lady named Gladys Wavrek. To operate as an army station, however, the ground rules were that it had to be under the official control of the military. The initial effort to take over the excellent work she had accomplished, however, was handled callously by Bob's predecessor, without any recognition being given to her role in the station's beginnings. To his credit, when he and his crew assumed responsibility for its operation, Bob went the extra mile by extolling her very patriotic efforts and making sure that her superiors were aware of her contribution to the amiable transfer of responsibility.

. . . .

While several of today's 181ST survivors remember their time in Kweiyang as having been spent at the college site described by Gunning, some members did not. I and a score of others who had been assigned to the tent camp on the southern outskirts of town were leading anything but the country club life of those fortunate enough to be with battalion headquarters. Instead we were soon struggling in the mud and rain, to prepare trucks and bus bodies for deployment, with their repair personnel, to the

Chinese Units that were attempting to dislodge the Japanese from our eastern air bases. The weeks that I spent there were miserable. I had, unfortunately, contracted a severe case of diarrhea, while at the same time being assigned the task of repairing tires for the two-and-a-half ton trucks and other menial motor pool jobs.

Everyone's morale, including my own, needed a shot in the arm at this point. Instead, it took an additional nosedive when Lieutenant Petri gathered us together to impart two pieces of news. The first, the good news, was that the war was finally over in Europe. Before we had an opportunity to envision the wonderful implications that this announcement might have on our current situation, he continued on, dropping the second bit of news on us. It came in the form of a proclamation that the ground rules for rotation back to the "States" had just been revised. He read aloud that the regulation, that made those men overseas for eighteen months or more eligible for rotation, had been changed. While the eighteen months still held, it no longer applied to two "essential" organizations, namely finance and signal corps, who would not be eligible for rotation until after having completed twenty-four months overseas. At that moment in time everyone in the 181ST had accumulated twenty months.

. . . .

When the sulpha drugs from the medics failed to give me any relief, I discovered that my good friend, Jeff Bennett, had received a bottle of paregoric medicine from home. Through his generosity I began to improve. While on the road to recovery, I was told to assist a tech sergeant named Charles J. Cella, one of the newcomers to China, in equipping a bus body, which was destined to be used by a liaison team that was scheduled to work with the Chinese 71ST Army. Proving the old adage that "luck is not always bad", Cella revealed to me that he was very apprehensive about joining the 71ST Army, as he had virtually no signal repair experience. He was one of those fellows who had been transferred repeatedly, receiving promotions with each move.

He had finally reached his present rank without having had any
schooling in the task he was about to take on, which was to lead
a five-man repair team. Here was the opportunity I needed. I
assured him that he should stop worrying . . . . that his problem
was all but solved . . . and that I knew just the men he needed. I
explained that with my experience with Western Electric and the
army's schooling, I could fill his requirement for a telephone
repairman and that my good friends, Thompson and Raabe were
well qualified in radio. I never learned whether he had verified
my facts but on May 30th, SPECIAL ORDER #18 was indeed
cut directing the three of us, plus a stranger named Frank Bailey
and Cella to " . . . PROCEED . . . . ON OR ABOUT 1 JUNE
45 . . . . TO 71ST ARMY, CCC, ON TDY IN CONNECTION WITH
SIGNAL ACTIVITIES . . . . AND TO REPORT TO THE SENIOR
ARMY OFFICER . . . .

Although I still have a copy of the order, Thompson, the
only other surviving member of the team, still cannot recall
the incident. It did occur, however, and "on or about June 1,"
we did indeed, with another vehicle and the bus body set
forth on the road heading south in search of the American
Chinese Combat Command liaison team that was advising the
Chinese 71ST Army.

The same order directed Alvin Paul Wagler (Burlington, IA),
my benefactor Jeff Bennett (Long Valley, NJ), Bill Roby (S.Pekin,
IL) and two newcomers to the 4011TH to proceed to the Chinese
54TH Army. It also ordered another former 181ST supply
sergeant, Morris Hollander (NYC), Kermit Clark (Charlotte, NC),
Hugh Gibson (Asheville, NC) and Tom Stephenson (Selma, NC)
back to Kunming . . . over the same piece of Burma Road that
we had recently traveled.

We were to discover that others had also found their way to
the Chinese armies that were confronting the Japanese in Kwangsi.
Two of these, whom we were to meet later were Weeks Andrews
who was traveling with the Americans attached to the Chinese
29TH Army and Jim Hoff, both having earned bronze star medals
in the Salween Campaign.

# THE CHINESE 71ST ARMY

During the latter part of 1944, the Allies, to counter the Japanese offensive in the east, had executed a plan called ALPHA. Its main purpose was to prevent the enemy from reaching Kunming and Chungking via Kweiyang. The plan included the redeployment of those Chinese forces, which had been freed up as the Salween Campaign neared its conclusion. When the Stilwell Road was finally completed, those Chinese divisions that had been equipped and led by General Stilwell in Burma, plus the American battalions from the Mars Task Force were also transported to the east. Among the various Chinese units from the Salween, was the 71st Army, which Weeks Andrews and his crew had been with and the same one that had had its troubles at Sungshan Mountain and Lungling.

The threat to Kweiyang ran out of steam in early December of 1944, when the Japanese, who had driven north from Liuchow on the road to Kweiyang, got as far as Tushan (Dushan). Events in the Pacific and the impending threat to their home island; the overextension of their supply lines and several other factors caused them to stop at that point. From there they elected to begin the slow withdrawal of their troops from the cities along the railroad in southeastern China.

Once the Allies had observed this, they converted their ALPHA PLAN from a defensive to an offensive one, called BETA. The roles that were to be played by the armies were to be directed at reoccupying Chennault's airfields and eventually opening a port on the China seacoast.

## *TUYUN*

The trip from Kweiyang by the Cella Team to the 71ST took us all day, with the only delay occurring at a fast-moving river. Here we waited while several GI's, operating a flatbed ferry, powered by two huge outboard motors, worked feverishly to reduce a quarter mile lineup of vehicles that were waiting to cross. When the bus body's turn came, they insisted that it was too heavy for their gallant craft and, leaving Cella with it, three of us, with Bailey driving, continued on our way. At first we followed an easterly route that, had we stayed on it, would have taken us to Chihchiang. By late afternoon we reached and turned south on the road, which terminated far to the south in Liuchow in Kwangsi Province. It was well after dark had fallen that we finally pulled into the northern outskirts of the town of Tuyun (Duyun) where our new masters were doing business.

If first impressions mean anything, ours were not too encouraging. Looking for somewhere to spread our bedrolls, Bailey and I spotted a two-story barn and theorizing that it had to be more substantial than a small group of pyramidal tents that apparently housed our new compatriots, we took over the second floor, which was completely empty. We should have known that this was not a good sign . . . . and sure enough, somewhere in the dead of night, we were both awakened by the feeling of something crawling on us. By the light of a flashlight we discovered that we were covered from head to foot with bedbugs.

In the morning, after finding the mess hall, we reported to the signal officer, a Lieutenant Larson. An interesting insight into the workings of the army brain trusts is revealed by the logic they must have employed when, based on the fact that he was a tall-timber tree topper in Minnesota, they somehow reasoned that he belonged in the signal corps. Half Scandinavian and Canuck, he was an easy-going fellow and made it clear that he was happy to see us, after which he told us to find ourselves spaces in the tent area.

The American liaison group had set up shop in a raised park-like grove immediately behind a huge stage, which faced westward, overlooking a large parade ground. A dirt road continued on the far side of it, curving to the right and losing itself somewhere north of the encampment. As found in most Chinese cities, the stage displayed a large replica of the Chinese Nationalist Star, flanked by equally large portraits of Chiang Kai shek and Sun Yat-sen. A cart path to the right of the parade ground climbed a hill for about a hundred yards to a latrine and two tents, occupied by the liaison group's commander, a full colonel and his personal aide, an infantry sergeant . . . . both reported to have arrived directly from North Africa. Between the main tent area and the cart path was a small building that housed the American Headquarters and the mess hall. Across from this building was an assortment of old frame structures that included the infamous barn, a jury-rigged shower facility for the Americans' use and the quarters of the Chinese civilians employees and their families who saw to the Americans' needs.

The most visible of these folks was a man who had held the auspicious title of head chef on one of the large Pacific Ocean passenger vessels. An apparent refugee from the coast, he had had to settle for the demeaning role of cook with the Americans attached to 71st Army Headquarters. The surrounding area must have yielded fruit orchards because "Charlie", as he was affectionately called by his new employers, served some of the best peach cake I have ever tasted. Rumor had it that this very temperamental individual, who was convinced that his high-class culinary talents were not being sufficiently appreciated or rewarded, attempted to renegotiate his contract with the Americans at the end of every month.

Among the other civilians were a youngster about fourteen years old, who was called "Boy" by his new benefactors and his two twin five-year old brothers. The three of them had been orphaned by the war, staying alive by their wits and the goodness of the other civilians and the liaison folks. One of the twins was a mild mannered, well-behaved little fellow but the other was a holy terror. Where the 71st went, they went also.

If we had anticipated seeing any action against the Japanese, we were denied that, when it became apparent that the 71st and its American contingent, deployed about an hour north of Tushan on the Liuchow Road were assigned the role of reserves in the oncoming phases of BETA. The Americans with 71st Army Headquarters, numbered somewhere between twenty and thirty.

They represented most of the army's special forces ranging from a veterinary major to representatives from the infantry, chemical warfare, medics, signal corps and artillery organizations . . . . and even a lad from Georgia who filled the role of saddle-maker. When he wasn't occupied with his unique assignment, which included repairing our G.I. shoes, he entertained us, on the banjo, with "down home", foot-tapping, country music.

Within a day or two, Sergeant Cella arrived with the bus body and we set up shop right next to the parade-ground stage. Here again any expectations we might have had of making a significant contribution to the war were soon deflated. Someone brought in a radio, which was turned over to Thompson and, while he did his thing with it, I cranked away at the hand generator. It soon became apparent that not much repair business was going to come to us in Tuyun and that Thompson and Raabe could better serve the purposes of the Chinese Combat Command (CCC) elsewhere. They only remained with us for a matter of days before they were ordered away . . . Thompson to the Americans working with the Chinese 6th Army, which was east of Chichiang, working its way toward Kweilin . . . . and Raabe to the Indo-China border.

. . . .

Before they left, however, Lieutenant Larson had one more assignment for them and me. With the end of the war now just a matter of time, Chiang's forces were preparing for the impending civil war with the Communists. The Americans, who were still struggling to get supplies and equipment to the Chinese BETA forces, discovered that many of these units were, instead, squirreling away these same supplies for use against the Reds. The lieutenant assigned us a jeep, with instructions to proceed to a spot near the town of Ma-ch'ang-p'ing, about an hour's drive to the north and to inspect and repair the radio and telephone equipment of the Chinese unit there. He made a point, however, to impress upon us that the real reason for our mission was to make a count of all of their equipment.

Following a map that he had given us, and which I carried for weeks, hoping to keep it as a souvenir of the war, we pulled up in front of a typical Chinese walled-in compound. It was guarded by a single sentry, wearing a World War 1 German helmet, a small square pack, short pants, knee socks and straw sandals. He ushered us into a cobblestone courtyard where a company of Chinese soldiers (bings) stood at attention in extended order, each with a unit of signal equipment at his feet. We were greeted by their officer . . . . returning his salute. We then proceeded to inspect the equipment, actually making some minor adjustments to several of the radios. As usual, the telephone equipment needed no repair, although I spent time inspecting each unit to see that it was in operating condition, while making the count that the lieutenant wanted.

Then an incident occurred that I still remember vividly. With the shortages of replacement clothing in the forward areas and the general relaxing of army regulations regarding any dress code, most of the Americans wore fatigues and many without any chevrons, denoting rank. We were no exceptions, thus there was no way of knowing whether we were officers or enlisted men. As we prepared to leave, our host again ordered his men to the positions they were in when we arrived. Whether out of curiosity or whether to protect his "face", he turned to me, who for some reason he must have assumed was in command, and asked me what my rank was. If I had it to do all over again, I would have told him that I was at least a Colonel, which would have done much for his "face". Without taking the time to consider my answer and its impact, I informed him that I was a corporal. In the blink of an eye, I realized my mistake. First he glared at me and as the effects of my naive response began to sink in, the blood started creeping up his neck and into his face. My first impulse was to turn and run for the compound gate. Instead, I held it all together, walking as normally as I could manage behind my two companions, who had already started toward the gate and who had not seen my exchange with the Chinese commander. To this day, I do not know what I had expected his final reaction would be . . . maybe any thoughts he had of exacting some revenge for this obvious show of disrespect for his rank gave way to the realization of what the ultimate result of any violence would net him. This was the last episode with Thompson and Raabe, who left shortly after we returned to Tuyun. I do not recall what happened to Sergeant Cella but he, Bailey and the bus body were also ordered elsewhere, leaving me alone with the 71st.

. . . .

One event occurred just prior to their leaving, however, that revealed an atmosphere of apparent disregard for the traditional, uniform, military way of doing things that had evolved among my new American associates. It no doubt was the result of having just completed a very long, difficult and certainly unorthodox period with their Chinese clients in the malaria-infested Salween Valley . . . . a period during which they received very few of the amenities normally available to the average military organization.

A truck arrived carrying a load of much-used telephone field wire, which was dumped onto a small clearing in our park-like encampment. It had obviously seen more than its share of use and was to be destroyed, a job that was assigned to Bailey and me. The lieutenant suggested that the best way to accomplish this was to burn it. It seemed to me that the beautiful setting, into which the wire had been dumped, was hardly the place to start, what was sure to be a large conflagration. But orders were orders and we set about the task, I with some trepidation but Bailey diving head first into the job. At first we could not get the four-foot pile to burn but Bailey fetched a can of gasoline and soon had spread a goodly amount of it onto the target. Remembering the similar incident in Ledo when one of our unnamed non-coms had attempted to burn our garbage, I backed well away as Bailey, despite my protests, knelt to strike a match. The result was spectacular . . . . with a loud "poof" the gasoline vapors ignited sending flame in a large circle a good sixteen feet from the center of the pile. The edge of it engulfed Bailey for a split second. Fortunately he was not burned . . . . but when he rose and turned to face me, he was missing his eyebrows and was white as a sheet. Once the tar-like insulation started to burn, a column of fire and black smoke rose more than twenty-five feet into the air. To my amazement, instead of triggering the anticipated disciplinary action by anyone from the liaison team, nothing was said of the event, as though it was the accepted, routine way of disposing of just one more distasteful job.

In addition to the wire that we had just burned, the Chinese had returned what was left of an American EE8A portable telephone. Its leather case had been burned away and its innards were charred beyond use. Lieutenant Larson suggested that it be discarded also. But I decided that since, after two and one half years in the army . . . having done every chore except repair a telephone . . . . and . . . during most of that period, having carried a twenty pound tool case and all of the necessary parts . . . . I was going to repair my first telephone. It was the last job I did in the bus body, but I was pretty proud when I presented the brand new instrument to the lieutenant, who accepted it after giving me a strange look.

The next morning Cella, Bailey and the bus body left. It was the last time I saw either of them . . . . who, like so many of the men I was associated with during my three years in the service, just disappeared from my life.

. . . .

With my companions from the 4011th gone, I soon acquired new ones, two were radio operators and another a big Irish infantryman, named Curgan, from the south side of Chicago. He told of the efforts he and others had made to teach the Chinese bings from the 71st how to crawl across the battlefield, just prior to their abortive try at dislodging the Japanese from Sungshan Mountain . . . . and . . . . how he watched in disbelief as his students, instead, fashioned their version of a "banzai" charge into the waiting muzzles of the Japanese machineguns. Most of the Chinese phrases I managed to pick up, I learned from him also.

. . . .

My abbreviated career as an active military telephone repairman was also about to end. While in Tuyun, I made two house calls to Chinese units in the vicinity. The first was a visit to one of the 71st Army' division headquarters with the lieutenant. Its commander operated from an upstairs office in a building on a cobblestone street in the center of a very quaint walled town. The room resembled a small town law office, with carpeting and a spacious mahogany desk. The lieutenant spoke briefly with the officer behind the desk, probably the division's commander . . . and we were on our way. Our destination turned out to be a large dried mud compound, which was perched like a medieval fort, on a small island in the middle of a vast rice paddy. Just inside the massive gate was a large, high-ceilinged room where a Chinese soldier was waiting with a foreign version of our EE8A telephone. The lieutenant directed me to do what I could for him and then disappeared through a distant door. With no interpreter handy, but with the aid of the few phrases I had learned from Curgan, I soon realized that I was being asked to make the strange instrument well. Probably of German vintage, it resembled the American unit . . . but upon close inspection I discovered that, instead of two "D" battery dry cells, it actually received its transmission source from two small, rectangular, glass wet cells . . . . which were dead. Assuming that even if there was a battery charger in the compound and knowing that I would never be able to form the required question to my host . . . . I removed the wet cells and handed them to him. With the use of clips, I connected two "D" flashlight batteries into the circuit, crossed my fingers . . . . and held my breath until I heard side tone in the earpiece. Then, against my better judgment but with no other alternative, I hard soldered the two batteries in place, hoping that the lieutenant would conclude his business before they, too, went dead.

. . . .

Several days later one of my new telegraph operator friends invited me to accompany him to another Chinese unit, where one of his contemporaries, a sergeant, had a repair problem. It turned out to be a very frustrating and humbling experience for me. I quickly learned of the shortcomings of my own technical knowledge and of the shallow content of the schooling I had received at Camp Crowder when the sergeant produced an American unit that I had never seen. He called it a radiotelephone and asked if I could repair it. None of the telephone components were familiar to me and, of course, I had no real practical knowledge of how the radio side worked. Apparently I was not the first to be presented with the sergeant's problem and he tried to relieve my frustration, stating that he would keep working on it himself and maybe someone would come along that was familiar with the unit.

The location of this American group had another down side . . . . the climate was extremely hot and humid, the mosquitoes were as big as sparrows and I had forgotten to bring along my mosquito netting . . . . forced to spend two nights trying to sleep with my head under a woolen army blanket. Fortunately, however, there was an up side. I shared a tent with the sergeant, who was a rabid chess player and who was spending some of his war competing by mail with an army friend in Europe. He wasted no time in taking advantage of my company and before I left for Tuyun, I had mastered the basics of chess.

The food was very good, featuring eggs cooked to order at breakfast. I also picked up another Chinese phrase, interspersed with occasional American four letter adjectives, from a young, frustrated Italian GI from New York City who was struggling to acquaint his Chinese charges with the proper method of assembling and mounting a new pack unit onto some of Mrogenski's and Jimmy Jones' Missouri mules that had just arrived. In spite of my failure to help the sergeant with his problem, the two days I spent with him and his comrades, who, with their Chinese clients, were literally living off of the land . . . . were quite memorable. These men, who had been through the entire

Salween Campaign, had a quiet, confident and resigned air about them, which was not lost on me.

. . . .

In deploying the Americans with the Chinese, the CCC had assigned units from the Mars Task Force as security for the various liaison groups. Ours was a Company "G" from one of the battalions and had set up camp on the far bank of a small river that formed the southern border of Tuyun. As a veteran unit, which had seen its share of combat in Burma, they, understandably, did not mingle with the 71st Army Americans . . . . with one exception. He was a very young lad, named Byrd, who hailed from somewhere in Nebraska. In time, he and I, with too much time on our hands, became constant companions. The nerve-wracking Japanese "banzai" charges that he had helped fight off in Burma had matured him well beyond his nineteen years . . . . and I would bet . . . . are still with him if he is still alive. I became, not only his friend, but also the outlet for his need to tell someone about it.

He also became intrigued with the metal leg pole climbers that I had and was always after me to try them out. Eventually the opportunity arose. Word came from our switchboard that the line to Company "G" had just gone out. Byrd and I set out immediately in a jeep, trying to follow the wire, which appeared to use the poles in town, as it headed south. With much difficulty we managed to trace it to a pole in the center of town, where it became lost in a tangled mess of wires. I put on the climbers and with the EE8A over my shoulder, struggled up the pole . . . . which was about ten feet from a stone building. As I was in the process of tapping into the wire we had been following, a window was opened in the stone building and a very pretty young Chinese woman leaned out and, in perfect English, asked if I was having any trouble. At the same time our operator back at the 71st Army informed me that I was on the wrong circuit. This was continuing to be a very strange war for me. The woman informed me that the building was the civilian telephone office, which explained the number of wires on the pole. She also invited us to come in for a visit . . . . which we did.

The transition from the dusty, packed mud street, with its rows of outdoor venders shouting their wares and the pungent smells of Chinese cooking . . . . to the interior of the telephone office was like being able to step across 14,000 miles to the good old USA. Almost everything in the office was identical to those in the United States that I had seen as an installer for the Western Electric Company, down to the color code on the wiring of the cables connected to the switchboard jacks and lamps.

But we still had to find and repair the open wire to Company "G", so we drove back to our starting point just outside of the building, which housed the 71st Army switchboard. Exercising more care than we had started out with, we discovered that the line did not go through town, but instead followed a small dirt road that veered off to the left. Within minutes we found the break. It was in a section of the road that was bordered by one of China's many security walls. Someone had climbed the two poles and neatly cut the span between them. Up I went with a length of wire and began to splice onto the wire coming from the army's direction. As I settled onto the climbers and started to strip the wires I peered over the wall and there was our wire, which was then holding up the lady of the house's laundry. In about five minutes we had communication with Company "G" back in operation.

. . . .

Several days later, while I was observing one of the radio operators code and send off a message to an American liaison group that was working with one of the Chinese units, the parade ground began to fill up with people. As soon as the transmission was completed, we left his tent, which was directly behind the parade ground stage and positioned ourselves just to its left. An American correspondent, who I believe was Lowell Thomas, joined us and in minutes several hundred Chinese troops had formed. We then watched in amazement as our American veterinarian major inspected them. Before he had finished, the troops were joined by scores of civilians from town, their officials assuming their appropriate positions on the stage. When the major had completed his inspection, a Chinese officer addressed the crowd. Although we did not understand him literally, it was obvious from the animated way in which he delivered his speech that something important was occurring.

When he finished talking, two Chinese soldiers appeared almost dragging a half-dozen middle-aged civilians, including two women, who were roped together. As he began to speak again, the reason for the event became obvious as a pile of drug paraphernalia was dumped in front of the stage and ceremoniously set fire to. The speaker completed his final admonition directed at the pathetic individuals, who had apparently just been tried and found guilty of using drugs. He then directed that the prisoners be marched off on the road that went beyond the parade ground. Several minutes after they had disappeared, gun shots were heard . . . . a graphic example of Chinese justice in action. I learned of another way in which it was meted out, when someone told me that just prior to our arrival in Tuyun, there had been a pair of ears tacked up on a pole in the center of town. They did not know any specifics, however, of the crime that had been committed.

## THE TUYUN-LIUCHOW ROAD

The Japanese invasion of China, which had begun in the early 1930's, essentially reached its climax when their attempt to take Chichiang was stopped by the Chinese in May 1945. As the Japanese divisions in Southeastern China and along the Hankow-Nanning railroad corridor were being recalled to the north, the Chinese advanced and began to reoccupy the cities they had evacuated in late 1944. While few, if any major battles ensued, the process was not bloodless. As they withdrew their forces, the enemy left behind very formidable rear guard units, whose charge was to keep open the routes over which their troops to the west and south could be withdrawn. Most of these were funneling through Liuchow, the southern terminus of the road that led south from Tuyun.

The same road is the scene and subject of the novel THE MOUNTAIN ROAD by former Time correspondent and author Theodore H. White and was later made into a movie, starring James Stewart. Reading north to south from Tuyun, its major towns were Tushan, Hochih and Ishan. On June 10th the Chinese had worked their way down the road as far as Ishan, which they took from the Japanese . . . . only to lose it back. Three days later it again was theirs. Similar activity took place in and near Hochih and on June 22nd the Japanese set fire to Liuchow, destroying sixty percent of the city and making the airfield unusable. The city was finally occupied by elements of the Chinese 29th and 46th Armies on July 1st. From that point on, the allies' goal was to reach the coast and establish a port of entry at Fort Bayard on the tip of the Liuchow peninsula (no relation to the city).

. . . .

The fall of the city of Liuchow was the signal that spelled the end of the need for the 71st to remain in Tuyun and elements of our liaison group began to pack up and leave for the south. Within a week or so, we also received the word and prepared to follow them.

As the vehicles were lined up, the untold story of how this family of Americans had weathered their forgotten status during more than a year of being at the end of the longest supply line in the world . . . . became evident. During their travels they had acquired Chinese civilians, who worked for them and who they almost treated as family . . . . taking them wherever the war dictated. The occupants of the trucks reflected this relationship as "Boy" and his two brothers . . . . a character called "Burr Head" . . . . Charlie the cook and a dozen other men women and children, with all of their worldly goods clamored aboard. They looked more like a gypsy caravan than a military convoy. Given "C' and "K" rations for three days and a small Coleman stove,

Byrd and I were assigned to a jeep, with an empty trailer. Then in typical GI fashion Lieutenant Larson admonished all of the drivers not to speed and to stay together. Whereupon he started his jeep, into which he had stashed a large jug of Chinese wine and raced off . . . . not to be seen again until we had reached Liuchow.

Byrd insisted on driving. The first day was uneventful as he and I stopped only to refuel the jeep and eat our meals. Water was scooped from streams, boiled on the Coleman stove and treated to a couple of "halizone" tablets. As each vehicle had its own set of humans, who in turn, had different reasons for causing delay, the convoy gradually began to string out and we eventually discovered that we were quite alone on the road. While it did not rival the switchbacks at Annan, the road certainly had its share of them . . . . but navigating them in a jeep was a far cry from managing them in a two-and-a-half ton truck. By nightfall we reached what was probably the vicinity of Hochih and backed up to a loading platform in front of a warehouse. As some of the others in the convoy began to arrive, Byrd gathered up his bedroll and disappeared. The empty trailer, we had been pulling, had a canvas cover and unfolding an army cot that I had thrown into the back of the jeep, I fashioned myself a private bedroom.

Our progress during the morning of the second day mirrored that of the previous day and in a short while we, again, had the road to ourselves. About two o'clock we caught up with a long column of Chinese troops who were led by a single officer on horseback. At the time we were in a vast valley between two mountain ranges. As we passed the men they all gave us the universal "thumbs up" accompanied by shouts of "ding hao". When we neared the head of the column, however, Byrd suddenly turned to me and said, "Watch this". I had no idea what he had in mind but when we were opposite the officer, he floored the clutch and began gunning the motor, causing the horse to start bucking. He then engaged the clutch and, in a cloud of dust, left the column far behind. Our sins, however, have a way of sometimes catching up with us and after several miles, that same clutch decided that it had enough for one day . . . . and ceased to function. In due time the same Chinese column was in sight and was soon about to pass us. It was not one of my better moments. We lucked out, however, as the officer decided to ignore us, and the "bings" were full of grins as they filed by and eventually disappeared over a rise.

So we sat, helplessly stranded in the center of a vast, and what appeared to be, an uninhabited valley . . . . confident, however, that one of the vehicles from our spread-out convoy would eventually come by. In less than a half an hour a cloud of dust appeared, coming from the far end of the valley. It soon materialized into a six-by-six truck, driven by two of Byrd's red neck associates from Company "G". In minutes they attached a tow chain to the jeep and we were on our way again. The ride, however, then proceeded to take on an entirely different and menacing quality. Whether our benefactors feared that we were in Chinese guerrilla country, which we probably were or they also had a jug of wine in the cab of the truck . . . . they took off at top speed . . . dragging our disabled jeep, totally engulfed in a massive dust cloud . . . less than six feet behind. Byrd found out almost immediately that our brake or horn made absolutely no impression on his two infantry comrades. They barreled along as though they had a hot date waiting for them . . . . stopping only long enough to eat or to attend to our other human needs. By dusk we had left the valley and were climbing to challenge a formidable-looking range of mountains. Except when they battled the upgrades, our inhospitable Samaritans continued to push their vehicle at break-neck speed, with us literally bouncing over the crude bridges that spanned ravines, small streams and any other irregularity in the dirt roadbed. As night closed in, our friends stopped briefly for a pit stop and to switch drivers. With Byrd now quite exhausted, we elected to do the same. What followed was the most fearful and frustrating experience of my three-year stint in the army. Contending with the ochre dust and struggling to keep the jeep between the two taillights of the truck was a monumental physical challenge. But as the night wore on, I found the battle to keep my eyes open an even bigger task. In the passenger seat, Byrd had collapsed into a deep sleep, totally oblivious to my predicament. In desperation I reached into his pocket, pulled out his cigarettes and lit one. I vowed that I would not go to sleep and fully intended to burn myself if I thought it necessary. After an eternity the first hint of dawn mercifully made its appearance, the road began to descend and as daylight arrived, we pulled into the outskirts of Ishan.

With not so much as a "How are you? . . . . or . . ."Did you enjoy the ride?" the occupants of the tow truck unhooked the chain and were gone, leaving us alone again . . . albeit in civilization. At that early hour there was no activity on the road . . . Byrd was still out . . . . and I climbed up on the hood of the jeep and surrendered to the impulse that I had been fighting for the last half dozen hours.

. . . .

The battles that had been fought for Ishan were still pretty recent news and the Chinese had decided to remind everyone of their victory by displaying a very large assortment of arms that the Japanese had left behind. Byrd and I rummaged about among the piles of weapons, and equipment. I learned later that photos had been taken of the war booty by someone with our liaison group and subsequently acquired a copy, which I still possess.

With the jeep inoperable, I soon found a seat in the back of a truck. Byrd had disappeared again . . . . and had probably joined some of his associates from Company "G". As a matter of fact, I do not recall ever seeing him again. Most of the convoy had arrived in Ishan and in due time we were off again . . . this time for Liuchow itself.

## Liuchow

The first indication that we were nearing Liuchow was the appearance of the unique, sugar loaf-like mountains that seemed to pop out of the ground like huge chicken croquettes that were peculiar to that section of Kwangsi Province. Our first contact with the Liuchow area itself was when we came upon the airfield. It was still sporting the after-effects of the Japanese very thorough demolition effort . . . . with huge bomb craters scattered intermittently over the entire length of the runway. We crossed over near the north end of the airfield and picked up a road that led us to the city itself . . . . passing several abandoned Japanese planes . . . . which I assumed were probably booby-trapped.

. . . .

As we neared the city, itself, the road veered to the left, skirted the north side of town and ended in a steep drop to the bank of a very wide river that divided Liuchow from its eastern environs. Here we were carried across by another ferry, much larger than the one we had encountered en-route to Tuyun. As we proceeded, I saw for the first time the devastation that a war could bring to a pretty large urban area. Shopkeepers and other small entrepreneurs as well as residents were actually living in and going about their daily routines from the shells of partially demolished buildings.

In a matter of minutes we were clear of the devastated area and about a mile beyond the river we pulled up outside of what appeared at first to be another park like location. It featured a wide, beautiful, long rectangular walled-in garden split by a single walking path, which ran west to east and which extended the entire length of the compound. The path was interrupted about a third of the way by an impressive covered shrine and altar over which a solemn, statue of Buddha kept watch. Testimony to the reverence he enjoyed was evidenced by dozens of punks, which burned at his feet. On each side of the altar were single rooms, which I soon found were being utilized by American medical personnel from our liaison unit. Continuing down the center path, beyond the shrine, and about two thirds of the length of the park itself, was another shrine, also with rooms on each side of it. One of these, I soon learned, contained tables and chairs and functioned as a small mess hall. Outside the wall of the compound and nestled in a wooded area was a tent camp, which was accessed by a side gate in the southern wall. Here I shared a tent with two of the telegraph operators. Little did I suspect that this tent would turn out to be my last permanent home-away-from-home in World War 2.

The food continued to improve, with Charlie still turning out his fabulous peach cake. All of our meals were eaten in the little mess hall adjacent to the shrine. During some of these we were apprised by the S2 (intelligence) officer of the deployment of the various Japanese units to the south and east of us.

Again there was no telephone repair work. Instead I was assigned the task of stringing double field wire from a small PE 75 power generator to each of the tents to power a single light bulb. I was also responsible for the generator's maintenance. Summer in Liuchow was very hot and humid, making this assignment, which required some degree of climbing, most uncomfortable. Thus most of the time that I spent climbing trees during the wire-stringing chore, I was bared to the waist. This worked well until, while attempting to use my pole climbers to secure the wire to a tree, a large chunk of bark broke loose forcing me to hug the trunk. I was immediately covered with small fiercely biting ants, which refused to let go until I managed to dislodge them by diving headlong into a fifty gallon drum of water that Charlie kept outside of his kitchen.

Some of us occasionally piled into a vehicle and tried swimming in the river that divided the city. One of the men came up with an eye infection, however, which put a halt to this activity. The only real diversion in Liuchow at that time was an outdoor movie that was sometime shown, by an American unit, in a small amphitheater on the far side of the town, on the other side of the river.

With the new regulations regarding rotation back to the states and the knowledge, gained from the S2's daily briefing that the Japanese were deployed in large numbers and fighting doggedly to slow any forward progress of the Chinese, we became convinced that our tour in China was going to be a long one. The resignation to this apparent fact did nothing to boost morale. I, for one, found that I had become quite callous to the suffering and misfortune all around me. This was brought home very graphically, when after a severe rain, which caused the river to flood, I was sent to try to find a pole along its swollen banks. As I ran along the bank, hoping to find something that we could use, I came upon the body of a small Chinese child. The toddler's corpse was lying face up and had sunk into the mud so that it was level with it, impossible to be seen until one was right over it. Not even hesitating, I leapt over it and continued what turned out to be a vain search. But as I ran along, I was suddenly struck with the realization of the degree to which I had become hardened to the war and the plight of those affected by it.

## IS IT REALLY OVER?

As we entered the month of August, 1945, the mind set of the Americans attached to The Chinese 71$^{ST}$ Army Headquarters was justifiably influenced by the prospect of a long campaign still before it in China. Little did we know of the dramatic events that were about to occur? Maybe our first inkling should have been from an announcement by the S2 officer one morning at breakfast of the unexplained and sudden general movement of Japanese units to the north. Within days of this news, a Chinese interpreter poked his head into my tent and very excitably blurted out something about a super bomb having been dropped on Japan. At first I ignored him, and suggested that he take his tall tale elsewhere. My compatriots soon confirmed his message, however. We had not heard the term "atomic bomb" and assumed that it was an updated version of the severe firebombs that we knew the Japanese were currently being served.

Shortly afterward, word came of a second bomb having been dropped on Nagasaki and then the incredible, unbelievable news that the Japanese had surrendered. Each of us handled this totally unexpected turn of events in his own way. Word got around that the Lieutenant Colonel and medical officer for the liaison group had given his permission for the doling out of some of his precious medical alcohol. Whether that was true or not, I will never know. I do know that my large Irish friend, Curgan, produced a bottle of it into which we mixed some lemon extract left over from a "K" ration that we had been issued during our dash down the Tuyun-Liuchow Road. He then proposed that we take ourselves across the river to attend a movie that was scheduled for that evening.

This we did, with one of the group driving us down to the river, with instructions to pick us up again later that night. The crossing was negotiated without any difficulty and with the bottle in hand and carrying a colorful Chinese parasol that I had found very useful during the intermittent monsoon rains, we made our way up the steep streets of the west bank and eventually to the U.S. Army outdoor theater.

When it became dark enough, the show started and we settled back to enjoy it. Knowing that I was not much of a drinker, I sampled our new concoction very cautiously . . . not my large friend, however. With the recent news still taking its time to sink in and trying to believe that we might really be going home to the States, it was impossible to concentrate on the movie. Sometime after the projector operator had changed to the second reel, a strange, large, black, round cloud appeared in the southwest sky. It moved swiftly coming right for us and in minutes we were in one of the worst downpours I have ever witnessed. By the time that we had left the movie and started for the river the water was cascading down the city's steep cobblestone streets like turbulent mountain streams. Our concern, of course was getting back across the river. The water was almost up to our knees and my parasol was slowly being destroyed. At the river the scene was one of complete panic and confusion. A very large sampan was filling up with people who also wanted to reach the other side before it became too late. To my amazement and disbelief, Curgan waded right into the middle of them and when he could not convince any of them to leave the vessel, began to throw them bodily overboard. Before he had made any hole in the crowd, a very calm and articulate Chinese voice inquired, "What seems to be the problem here?" The voice came from a Chinese officer, who informed us that he was a member of the American-trained Chinese-American Composite Wing. Still dazed by Curgan's brazen performance, I expected that we were in trouble. When Curgan explained who we were and that we were trying to rejoin our unit, the officer turned to an ordinary Chinese soldier, who had been sitting in the cabin near the bow and gave him an order in Chinese. Within minutes the "bing" had cleared the sampan of everyone except himself, the CACW officer and us.

By this time the river was boiling and after an interminable time the polers had taken us a half-mile upstream and were preparing for the dash to the other bank. As they placed their poles on the bottom and shoved off for the opposite bank, we were immediately swept downstream at a fearful rate. I sat with my back facing upstream. About halfway across, Curgan shouted to me, "Look behind you!" Coming straight for the spot where I was sitting was a huge tree. It came root first, measuring about twelve feet across and was bucking like a rodeo horse. Having been raised in New Jersey and having learned to swim in the ocean surf there, I wondered whether I could swim in the turbulent water with the clothes I had on plus my army shoes. In seconds, however, before I could complete my thoughts, the folks pushing on the poles had managed, miraculously, to evade the galloping tree and, although we landed well below our target, we soon were on the opposite bank.

The impact of the deluge on the city itself was catastrophic . . . the ensuing flood swallowing up more than a city block on both banks. The weakened and semi-destroyed buildings were no matches for the downpour and several collapsed, sometimes on the occupants who were trying to avail themselves of the scant protection they afforded. The scene in the morning was tragic and within days cholera reared its ugly head, spreading throughout the city. Each morning the death toll was determined by simply counting those who were still lying on the ground.

. . . .

A week later I received orders to join several others from the 4011th as they too straggled in from their various Chinese army assignments. At this point, I tried to explain to some of the Chinese, especially the ones we called Boy and Burr Head, who was about twenty years old, that we were going to leave China and return across the ocean to America. Burr Head cried and asked to go with me. He was a simple, uneducated young man, only one step above being a coolie. There was nothing that I could tell him other than that we had come to China to defeat the Japanese and since that had been accomplished, we had to leave. It truly hurt to think of how he and the others would survive without us.

. . . .

Chichiang Airfield
The Japanese surrender delegation

Shortly after VJ-Day, the following leaflets were air-dropped throughout China.

**LEAFLET DROPPED IN CHINA BY THE ALLIES AFTER VJ-DAY**

八月十二日，日本又得接受波茨坦宣言的條件，向中美英蘇四國接受日皇要接受盟國最高統帥的命令，負責履行投降的條件。條件的要點是這樣：

（一）軍完全解除武裝。（二）日本主權止於本土以及小島（即本州、本土、九州、四國及……）……軍佔領直至和平正義的新秩序能在日本建立為止，想對一切軍閥化（日）成立……保證民主政治實施的政府。

中國朋友們，這樣子最後勝利已經到來了。你們自然高興，我們也替你們高興。但是，中國淪陷區還有許多日軍未完全解除武裝之前，雖保沒有混亂的情形，所有被迫附日的偽軍應該立即歸順，並負責維護人民，保持治安，真正和平快樂的日子才會更愉快的到來。

在華美軍 印

TRANSLATION IN HAWAII BY FATHER OF FORMER

CO-WORKER

Friends,

In July '45 Japan was offered terms of surrender by USA, China and Great Britain but refused. In August, Russia attacked Japan, and in August Japan accepted surrender terms proposed jointly by USA, China, Great Britain and Russia. These are the surrender terms:\

Japanese must:

1. Lay down all arms.
2. Move back to Japanese islands.
3. Remain confined to Japanese islands.
4. Assume full blame for war.
5. Set up a democratic government in Japan

There will be possible problems developing as the Japanese move out of China. There may be problems with Japanese sympathizers. It will be some time before stability returns.

(Co-worker comment) "Joe, now you know ... after thirty-five years..... Ping.

(Author's note) This one person's translation only .... still very interesting.

With the realization that the war was finally over for us, we prepared to leave the 71ST. Our clients had one other chore for us, however, and I was ordered to join some of the other Americans, who were assembling in the road just south of our camp area. To our amazement, we learned that we were to take part in a victory parade with our Chinese partners. It was not much of a parade, as parades go. I and another GI were placed at the very tail of the column, joining a "bing" who was leading a mule. With the very minimum role that the 71$^{ST}$ had played in the current campaign, and the fact that the turbulent river forced the Chinese to confine their demonstration to the unimportant east side of the city, the whole exercise seemed rather ludicrous and certainly irrelevant to us Americans.

Not until I began my research efforts to discover the 181$^{ST}$'s story, however, did I attach some significance to one event that occurred during our afternoon walk through Eastern Liuchow. As the column made its way past a group of very swarthy, rugged-looking men, I was impressed at how different they looked from any of the Chinese I had seen during my sixteen months in the country. I guessed, then, that they might possibly have been Chinese Communists. With the Civil War then only months away, that now appears as not very logical. It is more likely that they were some of Ho Chih Minh's Vietnamese guerrillas, who were operating out of Liuchow and other southern Chinese cities, at the time.

. . . .

After exchanging "Goodbyes" with the men of the liaison group and gathering up my gear, I climbed aboard a truck, which took me across the river and to several old friends from the original 181ST who were awaiting orders to continue back to Kunming. One of these was an old Jersey compatriot, Jim Hoff, who had distinguished himself in the Salween Campaign. I hadn't seen him for a year and a half and his first words were to congratulate me on being promoted to technician fourth grade [T/4], a fact that I had not been informed of. He had seen it on a bulletin board somewhere, about the time that the A-Bomb was dropped. Also there were Weeks Andrews (Tarboro, NC) and James Henry Hopper, (Somerset, KY) who had been together also in the Salween Campaign, but who had lately been with the Chinese 29th Army. Frank Downing, (Kansas City, MO), Otis Bannon, (Portland, OR) and Kermit Clark, (Asheboro, NC) were also waiting for orders to return to Kunming.

Liuchow—After VJ-Day
181 ST Members of the Chinese Combat Command
standing (left-right) The writer, Jim Hoff, Weeks
Andrews, Frank Downing
Crouching (left-right) Kermit Clark, James Hopper
(extreme right) Otis Bowman

Soon Joe Shirley, (Randleman, NC from my old 181ST platoon arrived toting a half gallon of Japanese whisky that had been liberated by the Chinese 13th Army from a dock somewhere along the river. George "The Gonk" Raabe, who had left me at Tuyun came up from the Indo-China border with a tale of having watched the Japanese each morning across the Red River but with orders not to fire on them. He also raved about the fact that the folks at the Indo-Chinese border had been eating ten-in-one rations, which featured dehydrated potatoes. Our mutual buddy, Phil Thompson, who had also left me in Tuyun, flew in by L5 from Kweilin after a stint with the Chinese 6th Army. He recounted that he was on a balcony in that town on VJ Day. He also relived his wanderings after leaving the 71st Army at Tuyun.

Shortly after Thompson's arrival he, Raabe and I received orders to return to Kunming on the following day. At that very point a classic example of the CBI mail delivery system was graphically demonstrated when we were inundated with dozens of previous-year Christmas packages that had been languishing in the warehouses in India. There were several for each of us and we tore into them with a vengeance, saving only those items that could be eaten that night. We gorged ourselves with a strange assortment of delicacies, which we washed down with some of Shirley's liberated whiskey.

After we had stuffed ourselves with as much of the newly received manna from home that we could, we crawled into our mosquito nettings, preparing to dream of home. In short order, however, all hell broke loose in the tent as Thompson suddenly was seized with a severe malaria attack. This was my first experience with the malady and I watched helplessly as he alternately shivered violently with chills and then sweated profusely as he burned with fever. It was a long night for all of us.

In the morning, with Thompson having recovered somewhat from the events of the previous evening, the three of us were met by a jeep and headed for the airfield. En-route, we decided that a stop at the medics was prudent, in view of Thompson's recent performance. With the jeep driver having been told to wait, the three of us entered a large tent facility and were met almost immediately by a tall imposing nurse. We explained the situation and as Raabe and I turned to leave she ordered us to "Sit." Disputing her order being out of the question, we sat until she returned. She gave each of us the "needle-pricking-on-the-end-of-the-finger" test and would not let Raabe and me leave until the results exonerated us.

Raabe and I then proceeded to the airfield, which boasted a small wooden shack as its terminal, in which an enlisted man, behind a simple wooden counter, reviewed our orders and directed us back to the airstrip. There we sat on a wooden bench, waiting further developments. In due time, our airline executive stuck his head around the corner of the terminal and informed us that he had one seat for Kunming coming in on the next airplane. He also reported that he had no knowledge of any other flights that were scheduled for Kunming. I do not remember how it was determined, but we agreed that this one would belong to Raabe and I would take my chances that something else would be available later.

By this time, I had developed, as most of us had, the necessary talent for coping with the "hurry up and wait" syndrome, which was so much a part of the army experience. Of course I was not the only poor soul hoping for transportation back to civilization. My companion, on my right, was not coping with the waiting very well and made no bones about it, voicing his complaints in the then standard army vernacular, which more often than not included the free use of four letter adjectives. As we made small talk and were sympathizing with each other's plight, the fellow in the shack shouted to me that he now had one coming in that, while it was not going to Kunming, was scheduled to land in Luliang, which was en-route and only a short distance from it by air. I opted for this and as I rose to board the anticipated arrival, I noticed only then that my agitated companion had a cross on his collar. A long stay in China could do that to you.

The arriving plane turned out to be an empty C47 cargo ship. I threw my gear toward the back of the plane and assumed a sitting position with my back up against the bulkhead that separated the cargo space from the pilot's cabin. Here I found two more companions, both Air Corps lieutenants, one a fighter pilot and the other an Air Transport Command (ATC) pilot. In addition to their flight bags, each of them had a personal parachute. When I inquired where mine was they suggested that I would probably find one in a pile of gear that was also in the rear of the plane. My first impulse was to register a complaint with the management, but not wanting to jeopardize my good fortune, I decided to put my faith in the pilot and the very reliable C47.

As expected, the flight was uneventful, taking about three hours, covering a distance that had taken me three days several weeks earlier. As we completed the taxi at Luliang, a young, thin, blonde youngster appeared in the door of the pilot's cabin.

He could not have been much more than twenty years old . . . but he was our pilot. As the war had progressed, the brass in Kunming decided that it was in the best interest of peace and order that the city be open to enlisted men and officers on alternate days. The youngster informed us that he was going to get a bite to eat, refuel and take advantage of what was left of officer's day in the city and that we were welcome to join him. Since military discipline was somewhat lax in the part of China that we had just come from, it was not unusual for officers and enlisted men not to wear their insignia. Thus it was no trick for me to pass as one of them. It was about three in the afternoon when we entered the mess hall. Here I got another example of the difference between air corps food and what had been passing for such with me for the last sixteen months when the mess sergeant apologized for the fact that all he could give us were roast beef sandwiches. I knew then the war was really over. As we waited to be served, I found a telephone, called the 4011th in Kunming and informed them when I would be arriving and requested transportation from the airfield. The rest was like a dream. It was difficult to believe that I was really on the way home until I was met by none other than my dear friend from North Carolina, Ray Hardee driving a weapons carrier.

The American facilities in Kunming had undergone significant changes during the three months that had elapsed since Lt. Petri had lead our convoy eastward to Kweiyang. Ray turned into the same road that had led to Hostel 4, but I do not recall seeing it. Instead we stopped at a brand new facility called Camp Easy. It was very large and although living quarters were pyramidal tents with wooden sides and floors, the camp also included a good-sized auditorium and stage, as well as a day room that boasted a bar. Softball was the main outdoor activity while the bar featured vodka eggnogs, utilizing the very popular "Joe's Russian Vodka" which, I believe was made in Japanese-occupied China, probably by the White-Russian population there. Two distinct memories of my short stay in the camp are the rendition of the then popular song, "Sentimental Journey", played by an army orchestra on stage. The other was a disastrous experience with several of the vodka eggnogs served up by bartenders Joe Shirley (NC) and Sam Firman (Chicago).

It was here that we all congregated, waiting our turns to go home and greeting long lost friends as they straggled in from the four corners of China. I had found an empty cot in a tent with Jim Hoff and Charlie Martenson (White Plains, NY). As the others arrived, we all swapped war stories. Little did I ever suspect at that time that a half-century later I would try to reconstruct the events that were occurring then?

During the next several days we turned over our weapons and any ammunition that we possessed to Sergeant Hess. I remember a certain sense of reluctance to part with my carbine, although I knew from having tested it while guarding an ammunition dump several months back that it was no longer very accurate. Its sights had endured too many critical adjustments as it had been dragged and bounced on and off numerous trucks since being placed in my custody back in California . . . . .two years earlier. After carrying and almost fondling it for so long, it was like giving up a part of myself.

At this time we were also given medical examinations to ensure that we were not about to bring home any unwanted souvenirs of the orient, such as leprosy or any other skin disease. Needless to say, the days at Camp Easy did not pass very fast, although our period of adjustment back to civilian life was actually begun there.

. . . .

VJ Day in the CBI was like a snapshot in time. While the end of the war came as a dream come true for us, it also signaled the start of the civil war in China. As the hostilities against the Japanese came to a halt, the men of our gallant band were scattered from rest areas in Kashmir and Shillong, in India, across a thousand miles that included Assam Province in Northeastern India, all of Burma, Yunnan Province in Southwestern China and Kweichow and Kwangsi Provinces in Eastern China. Some may have even accepted assignments in places like Chungking, Shanghai and Tientsin in Northern China.

Carlyle Biggs (Lumberton, NC) was languishing peacefully in a British rest camp in Shillong, enjoying some much-needed R & R when the "bomb" went off.

For others, the situations they found themselves in were anything but peaceful. In Yunnanyi, in Yunnan Province, Bill Friedman recalled that he and other Americans were mobilized to defend the airfield from a Communist takeover. He remembered that, "They gave us hand grenades. They even mounted a 50 caliber machinegun on one of the trucks and we went out to protect the field." In recalling the event, he believed that the Communist troops were formally the same Nationalist 54th Army that he had accompanied beyond the Salween River. He also remembers turning to someone and declaring that, " . . . if I get killed now I'll be pissed off."

Several hundred miles east of him in Chihchiang, Bob Finkel (California) and Maurice Lichty (Kansas), were given the incredible order by the Americans in the Chinese Combat Command to literally bury their Bus Body truck. After hearing his account of this extraordinary action verbally and not wanting to depend for its accuracy on my fast-fading memory I requested and he confirmed the story by e-mail. It said,

> . . . . My orders to return to Kweiyang included the burial of our Bus Body and all its equipment. There was fear that the Chinese were about to attack us and steal the equipment to sell to the remaining war lords. Lichty and I began shoveling, no easy task making a hole big enough to bury a Bus Body. We did and drove the truck into the hole with Thousands of Dollars of equipment. When I was about to be sent home, there were a lot of questions as to what I did with the Bus Body. I did not have the orders in my possession and I guess they thought I was somehow going to take it home. Finally I was given clearance, though I got a lot of stares. I guess I was the Bus Body Bandit."

# CHAPTER X

## Trip Home And Separation

### THE LONG ROAD HOME

When we were drafted, we had been told that we would be the government's guests for the duration of the war. With the latter milestone having finally been reached, the only question remaining then was when and how we were to return to whatever we had been doing when we were so rudely interrupted by the war.

Fortunately for us, the War Department had already devised a method for returning us to our loved ones. It was a system, which awarded points for time spent in the service, plus various activities that were deemed to have been significant contributions to the successful conclusion of the conflict. While all of the details of the system have now become dim, I recall that points were awarded for each month in the service, with double credit given for those spent overseas. Additional points were also awarded for married men; heroic medals earned; purple hearts and campaign or service stars. For example: on September 28, 1945 an order issued in Kunming authorized twenty-nine men of the 4011<sup>TH</sup> to wear a Bronze Service Star on the Asiatic-Pacific Theater Ribbon for having participated in the China Offensive Campaign. The list included seventeen of us from the original 181ST Signal Repair Company. This unique contribution to the war gained us each five points towards separation from the army. On September 29TH, however, no points were garnered when the Chinese government awarded the China War Memorial Badge to all American personnel who served in China during the period from December 8, 1941 to September 2, 1945.

. . . .

Everyone from the 181ST knew that they had achieved a point score that would surely qualify them for the trip home. So the waiting started all over again. This time, however, the end goal was known and eagerly anticipated. But it was still a time that had to be passed somehow and to the army's credit, it did its best to supply as much diversion as it could under the unique limitations it still enjoyed in the former China, Burma, India, Theater of Operations.

The arrival at Camp Easy was a homecoming of sorts. I found many old friends from the original 181ST. In addition to Jim Hoff from Palmyra, N.J. and big Charlie Martenson from White Plains, N.Y. I was particularly pleased to find that several of the men from Lt. Bernie Silverman's First Team, who I had spent over a year with in the repair shop near Hostel 5, had not yet started for home. We sensed that this was, indeed, the last time that many of us would ever see each other, a sobering thought that somewhat dampened the excitement of knowing we would soon be back in the United States.

In preparation for leaving, we were ordered to surrender some of our clothing and informed that, since we would be flying to Calcutta, we would be limited to a certain amount of weight.

The ground behind the building at Camp Easy had been leveled and developed into a softball diamond. Early in the life of the 181ST a few of us had prided ourselves on our skill in this sport and, to kill some of the waiting time that we knew was ahead of us, took advantage of the opportunity to hone up these skills. During the war, General Chennault's 14$^{TH}$ Air Force had boasted of the proficiency of its softball team on which the general, himself, was known to have played. As we occupied ourselves on the softball field, someone scheduled a game for us with the then current version of this Air Force aggregation. One of our fellows, Willis "Willie" Dengler had had a very impressive career as a pitcher in an Iowan industrial league before entering the service and, when we engaged the 14$^{TH}$ at their field, he demonstrated the fact that he had not lost much of his talent. The last fond memory I have of my eighteen months in China is of savoring our subsequent victory over this much-touted team.

On August 23, 1945, while awaiting the orders, which would send them homeward, the members of the 4011$^{TH}$ were informed that it had been awarded the Meritorious Unit Service Plaque. The catch that came with the award, however, was that it rated the members of the battalion no points toward separation from the service and could only be worn by an individual while he was still an active member of the battalion. In light of these restrictions, our heroes who could not wait until they were no longer members of that astute organization were not too excited about the event. Made in the form of a laurel wreath and in view of its questionable value, our "soon-to-be-civilians-again" promptly dubbed the award with the disrespectful title "The Toilet Bowl".

So now our most immediate concern was when and how we would be transported home. Our experiences with the poor service this remote theater had been subject to forewarned us that we still had one very big test ahead of us before we could once again sport civilian attire. We were still on the other side of the world from the good old U.S.A. While this fact was cause for concern, the military's stellar success in keeping the existence of the Atomic Bomb from everyone except those immediately involved in its development and deployment added yet another impediment to our coming logistical undertaking. The sudden end to the war with Japan caused untold confusion in the transportation organizations—disrupting their global game plans on the books—and even worse, those in the act of being implemented. Troopships that would be required for bringing home those who were still overseas were, instead, still carrying personnel and material to the Pacific Theater. The net effect on us in the C.B.I. was additional delays, while the logistical transportation rats nest was being unraveled and ships could be freed up for our use.

. . . .

Eventually the going home process began in earnest and also the final breakup of the remaining members of the once 181st Signal Repair Company. There were essentially three routes to the U.S.A.—by ship from Calcutta; by ship from Karachi and by air. The most common route from Kunming was by C-54 non-stop to Calcutta, and after a staging period in a tent camp in nearby Kanchrapara, by ship to the U.S.A. The men in Burma and India were most often shipped home from the port of Karachi on the Indian Ocean. Getting there, however, if not by air, was a long, hot, dusty train ride across the widest part of India, including the Sind Desert.

. . . .

But we did finally take on this last test of our fast-fading patience and the parade of ships out of Calcutta and Karachi began. Unfortunately, the sudden dispersal of the 181ST veterans from what was once the C.B.I. via these known routes and probably others has prevented us from compiling any meaningful record of their long treks for home. This information is irrevocably lost. What we have managed to discover, however, and what fits a logical scenario, is that the men from the original cadre, who first formed the company in early 1942, and consequently had racked up the largest point scores, were the first men released from their sentences in Asia and ordered home. Some received this welcome news even before VE Day in Europe, but most of these orders were cut soon after that world-moving event.

The first of these, that we have knowledge of, was given to our own beloved First Team platoon sergeant, William Hasse. Bill was from a horse ranch near the town of La Grange, in Eastern Oregon, where his father was in dire need of help. Based on the number of points that he had accumulated and the emergency nature of the situation at home, on May 14, 1945 he received an order that relieved him of his assignment with the 4011th. A subsequent one, dated May 22[ND] directed him to fly to Calcutta to board a ship, which took him, to New York and Ft. Totten on June 25[TH]. From there he traveled by air to Colorado, where he was discharged from Ft. Logan.

. . . .

On June 7,1945 Lt. Bernard Silverman, the C.O. of our First Team received a similar order, which also relieved him of his 4011[TH] assignment and directed him to Calcutta, via Myitkyina in Burma, from whence he eventually boarded a, "slow boat" to New York. There he obtained a 30-day leave and was home in Richmond, VA when the Atomic Bomb was dropped. He received his discharge from Ft. Meade, MD.

. . . .

Next on our list to leave was Robert Gunning, whose home was in Wendell, ID. His turned out to be one very long airplane ride. It started in Kweiyang in Kweichow Province when, in mid-June 1945, he reported to a Green Project Officer at the airport, from where he then flew to Kunming. Bob had garnered a total point score of 86, which made him eligible for the final trip home. At Kunming he turned in all of his belongings except his musette bag, two changes of clothing, suntans and his personal equipment. After two days at the Kunming airport hotel and a visit with Battle Brown from Raleigh, NC and one other former 181$^{ST}$ repairman, he left on a C54 for Dum Dum just north of Calcutta. One night at Dum Dum and he was off, again by air, for Karachi, via New Delhi. His wait at Camp Malir in Karachi lasted several weeks, during which, because of the intense heat he, "took several baths a day to keep comfortable" and described an American rodeo on July 4$^{TH}$ in which his contemporaries, "could not bulldog the Brahma bulls." On July 23$^{RD}$ he left on a C46, which was loaded with mail for the USA, arrived at Abadan, Iran at 2AM. One hour later he and several other GI's were aboard a C54 headed for Cairo, Egypt . . . . was over Jeruslem by 6AM and arrived at their destination at 8AM. There they were confined to the airport overnight, partaking lunch at 11AM the next morning. His comments regarding the meal were that they were, "served by young, pretty French girls." The menu was in "French and English (but he) had to point to (the) desired items." One hour later he was en-route to Casablanca, where he arrived in the evening.

At Casablanca troops from the European Theater were also being processed. Among these, Bob reported, were several very young veterans of that theater. He was impressed by the fact that they were extremely nervous, jumping at the least sound. They were very interested that he had come all of the way from China and engaged in some brisk swapping of francs, lire and marks for Chinese money. Noon of the 24$^{TH}$ of July he left on another C54 for the Azores, arriving that evening. After two more nights of good food, movies, ping pong, magazines, the Stars and Stripes and reprocessing, he was assigned to a new, but smaller group and a C54 equipped with additional gasoline tanks mounted behind the pilots cabin. The last leg of this amazing journey was over the Atlantic at about 1000ft, often on autopilot while the " . . . crew played cards with the cabin door open." Accommodations included a chemical toilet in the rear of the plane, a relief tube outside of the compartment, cot-like seats, under which he placed his musette bag and web belt, which held his canteen. After eighteen hours, that Bob described as a, "long boring flight, some sleep" they touched down in Presque, ME (July 31$^{ST}$). August 1st found him on a train to Boston and Camp Miles Standish for more processing and meals served by German prisoners. I suspect that the next leg of his journey was also by train as he arrived at Ft. Douglas, Salt Lake City in the evening of August 8$^{th}$, the day before the first A-Bomb was dropped. He was discharged and the next morning was at his parents' home in Twin Falls, ID. He reported that they had aged but were very happy that he had survived the war. Bob had spent 5 years, 1 month and 13 days in the army.

. . . .

Since we have no complete record of how and when the original cadre started their individual treks back to the "States", we cannot share them with the reader. There is no question that many of them, but not all, were gone before the draftees from Forts Bragg and Dix received their traveling orders. One of the original members of the 181$^{ST}$ who we do know about was Percy Olson, from Commerce, OK. He wasted no time cashing in on his point score and was on his way from Ledo shortly after VE Day . . . Another was Charlie Boyd, from Detroit, MI, whose exploits we learned about in an earlier chapter. As we reported then, he had amassed a very large point score, followed the same air route as Bob Gunning and was in Chicago when the A-Bomb was dropped on Hiroshima . . . . Two others from the cadre, also from Chicago, were Henry Cieszykoski, who had been the 181$^{ST}$ mess sergeant from the time that we left California in 1943, and a T/4 Bernard Metz, who had been with Lt. Mc Veigh's Second Team in Yunnanyi on the Burma Road. Both had apparently flown to Karachi . . . from whence they made their trip home on the USS General Bliss. They were discharged from nearby Ft. Sheridan.

# CAMP IN DESERT OF INDIA STARTS GIs ON WAY HOME

## Reach Karachi from Long Trail to China

### BY ALFRED WAGG
[Chicago Tribune Press Service]

KARACHI REPLACEMENT DEPOT NO. 1, MALIR, India, Oct. 8— Nineteen miles inland from Karachi, on the sun scorched Sind desert, is the most unusual mushrooming city of adobe huts and rock barracks. There

Replacement Depot [arrow].

the majority of the homeward bound American personnel of the China-Burma-India theater are being processed before boarding ship.

### Like Wild West Roundup

Spread over the countryside of sand dunes and desert scrub the camp's perimeter is nearly 40 miles around. Its rock walls were crumbling and dusty only a few weeks ago. It now teems with nearly 20,000 men. The men arrive in groups of about 1,000 daily. One day 2,700 men came in a rush.

Under command of Lt. Col. Franklin Pruyn, air corps replacement depot No. 1 will handle upwards of 30,000 Americans monthly until this theater is cleared. Already Pruyn's men have loaded three ships, and dispatched thousands of men by air.

Capt. Bates Fertig, a New Yorker, does the initial processing. He has a couple of barns of lumber and tin. Fertig's corral looks like a wild west round up.

Unauthorized equipment, for instance guns, are taken away from them. Their orders are taken up and they are assigned to groups, according to where they will go.

### Chicagoland Contingent

The Bliss, bound for New York, on Oct. 2, and expected to arrive there Oct. 24 or 25 carried these Chicagoland men for the separation center group at Fort Sheridan:

Capt. Edward Stempel, 4720 N. Spaulding av.; Corp. Edward Was, 1634 N. Hermitage av.; Lt. Marian Klaus, 2846 N. Spaulding av., Chicago; Capt. Robert Vasek, Cicero, and Lt. Richard Vogt, 239 N. Spring st., Elgin.

Other Chicago men:

Tech. Sgt. Jesse Seaman, Staff Sgt. Joseph Strzdovski, Sgt. Stanley Becker, Sgt. Blanchard D. Menzemer, Roy Staubin, Albert Parth, Master Sgt. Louie L. Ogens, Sgt. Harold Mortenson, Sgt. Leo A. Raines, Tech. Sgt. Albert E. McFall, Tech. Sgt. F. C. McNicholas, Staff Sgt. Howard Flowaty, Tech. 4th Grade Chester Lada, Corp. Arnold E. Greer, Corp. Felix Kissel, Corp. Cliff Young, Tech. 5th Grade Anthony Nesmerak, Tech. 5th Grade Arthur Payton, Tech. 5th Grade William Thomas, Pvt. 1st Class Jacob Dorner, Pvt. 1st Class Robert Houston, Tech. Sgt. Frank Kaplan, Tech. Sgt. Clarence A. Montgomery, Staff Sgt. Henry Cieszykoski, Staff Sgt. E. Szura, Sgt. Albert Cara, Sgt. John Nokotis, Sgt. Edward Sporleln, Tech. 4th Grade Bernard A. Metz, Tech. 4th Grade Harry Reynertson, Tech. 4th Grade Bodo von Meding, Tech. 5th Grade John Fry, Tech. 5th Grade William Harris, Tech. 5th Grade Peter Kozik, Tech. 5th Grade Elmer Kriske, Tech. 5th Grade Joseph Viscvaty, Pvt. 1st Class Utilano, Pvt. 1st Class Fred Horvath, Pvt. 1st Class Alfonso Leon.

The following men are for the Fort Sheridan reception station group:

Lt. Frank Irland, 1347 Granville av.; 2d Lt. Walter Suberg, 4038 Southport av.; Lt. Melvin Rippe, Euclid av.; Capt. John Patt. Lt. Dae Thrapp, Tech. 4th Grade Albert Swirshy, Chicago; Lt. Robert Neely Jr., Urbana, and Pvt. 1st Class Kenneth Alsman, Peoria.

Processing and transportation facilities picked up considerably in September. On the 11$^{TH}$ of that month, another of the original cadre, one of the leaders of the First Team, and one of the finest men I have ever known, Technical Sergeant William Wraspir, from Aberdeen, ID started a twenty-eight day Odyssey to that western state. Bill, who was the leader of a radio-repair squad, left Kunming, China by air for Calcutta. His stay there lasted five days, which afforded him a rare opportunity to dine at Firpos famous restaurant in Calcutta, probably the first decent meal he had had in two years. By September 16$^{TH}$ he was on his way again, this time to New Delhi, another layover of five days and another opportunity . . . . a visit to the Taj Mahal at nearby Agra. A night flight on the 21$^{ST}$ brought him to Karachi on the 22$^{ND}$. Here he experienced another seven-day delay as his transportation, the USS General "Snorton" Norton underwent repairs and refueling. He was finally on his way on the 29$^{TH}$ and with two days, each, spent crossing the Arabian Sea, the Indian Ocean and the Red Sea headed into the Suez Canal. Passage through this waterway took another three days, delayed somewhat when, as he described it, ". . . the locks were on the fritz." Three days in the Mediterranean and a three-day layover in Algiers and he was off again. The last leg of his journey, crossing the Atlantic, took another eight days, culminating in the final docking in New York on October 22, 1945. On the 24$^{TH}$ he left by train, arriving at Ft. Douglas, UT on the 27$^{TH}$ and two days later received his discharge.

. . . .

One of the most uncomfortable and exasperating routes was the one by train from Ledo to Karachi. The passage, which took six days or more, was anything but comfortable in what passed as passenger cars. More than half the route was across the blazing heat of the Sind Desert in what is now Pakistan. Leo Tridico (Louisiana) who reached the rank of Tech Sergeant in Lt. Robb's Fifth Team and was transferred into a quartermaster unit for transportation purposes remembered this trip. Leaving Chabua in November of 1945, he described not only the physical discomfort, but also watching the Indians, who like hitch-hikers, were hanging all over the outside of the cars. Assigned to Camp Malir, in the desert, he endured the scorching heat, and also experienced an earthquake that literally threw him out of his bed. On November 25th Tridico left Karachi on the USS General Norton, the same one that Bill Wraspir had boarded two and a half months earlier. He recalled that it made port at Malta and passed through the straits that separated it from Sicily. A memorable event of the voyage was the sighting of a mine and its detonation by the ship's crew. The docking at New York and the sight of the Statue of Liberty still stand in his mind. He was discharged from Camp Shelby on Christmas Eve, 1945, talked and drank all night with his brother and hasn't drunk any alcohol since.

Another group of men, who made this journey in late September 1945, were also from Lt. (by then Capt.) James Robb's Fifth Team that had been absorbed into the 223[RD] Depot Company, and had spent most of the war in Chabua, India. They included Charles Matthews (Bethany, CT), W. C. Wasco (Toronto, OH), James Jones (Kingsville, MO) and Oscar Brandsdorfer (New York City). For Matthews, events conspired to delay his homecoming by an additional thirty days. Upon arrival in Karachi, all of the men were also consigned to Camp Malir, which at one point housed 30,000 Americans awaiting passage homeward. Matthews was separated from the others into a group that was destined for New England and which was to be transported on the USS General R. E. Callan. Unfortunately the good ship was in need of repairs and Charlie had to "cool" his heals for a month in the heat of the camp.

Such are the fortunes of war. Events were kinder to Quentin Brandt from Wisconsin, who was spared the infamous train ride and, instead, flew to Karachi. He did, however, join Matthews on the USS General R. E. Callan and was subsequently discharged from Camp Mc Koy in Wisconsin . . . . Matthews from Ft. Devens, MA.

Right behind the General Callan contingent was the remainder of the 223[RD]. Among them were Benjamin Tillman, and Raymond Bumgardner. Since the Army practice was to transfer the lucky candidates into organizations that had been tagged for transportation, the folks from the 223^RD found new temporary homes with either the 853^RD or 308^TH Aviation Engineering Battalions. Leaving several days apart, their companies boarded the same Karachi Express that Matthews had endured. This aggregation was assigned passage on the USS General Harry Taylor. Tillman reported the following itinerary of the trip after boarding the ship on 12/10/1945:

    12/12—upped anchor at 12:00 noon
    12/15—passed Aden entered Red Sea
    12/20—Port Said, Egypt for refueling
    12/25—passed the Rock of Gibraltar
    1/03/1946—sighted USA at 9:00 AM

Docking was at Pier 88 in New York City and reception at Camp Kılmer, NJ. For the men from the 181^ST, this was to be their last moments together and their final scattering then began. Tillman and Bumgardner were sent to Fort Bragg, NC from which they were discharged.

. . . .

A week after the Callan had reached New York, our best telephone repairman, Harry Koch from New York City, a charter member of the "Omer, Firman, Koch 181^ST Entrepreneurial Association", also found his way to Karachi. A most colorful and popular member of the 181^ST, but sometimes short in memory, Harry related how he had spent time in Camp Malir on the Sind Desert, and in his inimitable fashion, managed to scare up a chicken dinner, just outside of the camp. He claimed that he traveled on a ship from a French Line that lost its "propeller" but also docked at Pier 88 in New York arriving January 3, 1946.

. . . .

The last known of our Karachi—bound travelers was Robert "Robbie" Robertson (Riverton, NJ). Shortly after our arrival in Ledo, Assam on November 10, 1943, he and William Snider (Winston-Salem, NC) had been assigned to duty with the 3199$^{TH}$ Signal Service Battalion and eventually transferred into that unit. Sometime in November 1945, Robertson also flew to Karachi and traveled home on the USS General Richardson.

. . . .

Snider, who had accepted a field commission as Second Lieutenant in March of 1945, still with the 3199$^{TH}$, came home much later. He recalled getting a ship out of Calcutta to Seattle, via Hawaii. He was still aboard ship when Winston Churchill made his famous "Iron Curtain" speech. He could very possibly have been the last of the 181$^{ST}$ men to arrive home and the last out of Calcutta.

Another, who could also have held that unenviable record, was Kermit Clark from Asheboro, N.C. As mentioned earlier, the staging of the troops for shipment home via Calcutta was accomplished at Camp Kanchrapara, just north of the city. It was reported that he, for who knows what plausible reason, remained behind to aid in its cleanup . . . . a report that we have no way of confirming.

As one would expect, First Sergeant Harold Hess (Kankakee, IL) was the last to leave Kunming, staying to help clean up the paperwork. He also flew to Calcutta, where he caught a "Liberty Ship" to New York. From there he entrained to Chicago and received his discharge from Camp Grant, IL.

. . . .

Records show that the first ship to leave Calcutta was the USS General Greeley, on September 29, 1945. The earliest one, to our knowledge, that carried some of the 181$^{ST}$ was the USS General C. H. Muir, which sailed from Calcutta on October 3,

1945. Among its happy throng were Hugh Gibson, Hampton Mc
Bride and Clarence Webster from North Carolina; John J. Mc
Dermott and Ludwig "Luke" Strass from the New York City area;
and George A. Henze from Iowa. The long-awaited view of the
Statue of Liberty occurred on November 3, 1945. Mc Bride
reported that the Muir was confronted with bad storms in the
Atlantic, a last effort by Mother Nature to delay the final
homecoming for our heroes. Processed at Camp Kilmer, N.J., he,
Webster and Gibson were discharged from Ft. Bragg, NC on
November 5, 1945. Gibson could not wait to get home and took
off on the 4TH returning just in time on the 5TH to get that precious
piece of paper.

Six days and four ships later the most important vessel, the
one carrying this writer, upped anchor in the Hooghly river. The
USS General Ballou, which we were told had been originally
supposed to be a Navy tanker, but was, instead fitted as a personnel
transport, became our happy home for twenty-six long days. Ten
o'clock, on the night of October 3, 1945, I, along with several
scores of men from the old 181ST, boarded a C54 at the Kunming
airfield and at 3AM the following morning, after flying over the
entire country of Burma, set down in Calcutta. As so many others
had done before us, we were assigned to bunks at Camp
Kanchrapara, where we languished for six days. Some took
advantage of the time to make a last visit to Calcutta. By this
time, I had lost all interest in anything on the Asiatic continent
and limited my Indian activity to getting a much-needed haircut
and reading the local MORNING NEWS, a copy of which I had
the good sense to bring home with me.

We boarded ship at 3PM on October 9TH, weighed anchor at
5:30PM of the 10TH and after two days, of navigating our way
down the river, reached the Bay of Bengal. Our route took us
around the southern end of India and an overnight stop at
Colombo, on the island of Ceylon (now Sri Lanka). By 9:45AM
we were off again, this time in heavy rain and strong winds, to
take on the Indian Ocean.

In contemplating this voyage, some of us, particularly Charlie Martenson (from White Plains, N.Y) and I, remembered the thirty-two days on the Mariposa, which had brought us to this part of the world. Of paramount concern to us was the prospect of having to again endure the Spartan fare we had received during that infamous excursion. What we had learned, however, was that working parties were not subject to the two-a-day meal limitation. Charlie, a very large man, was more concerned over a repetition of that painful experience than I. Nevertheless, before sailing time, we had both promptly volunteered for what can be referred to as the "Spud Detail". In the depths of the Ballou was a refrigerated locker, in which potatoes were stored. Since it could not hold enough for the twenty-one days still ahead of us, the remainder that had been brought aboard at Colombo, was loaded on a top deck and covered with canvas. The function of the "Spud Detail" was the daily replenishing of the "locker" from the upper deck. This was not a lengthy task but did involve the negotiation of several very steep and narrow stairways (ladders) in order to reach an elevator somewhere in the bowels of the vessel. Weighing about fifty pounds apiece, the crates were a real challenge. The three-meals-a-day reward was well worth it, however, and we received a bonus of sorts when, upon rounding a corner of one of the corridors (companionways), we came upon a sailor, whose sole job was the converting of powdered milk for the officers mess. A really compassionate individual, after hearing our heart-tearing renditions of life in China, he was more than generous with his finished product.

Once we had left sight of Ceylon, the voyage was a mirror of those that had originated in Karachi and which have already been described. On the twenty-eighth of October 1945 we passed the Rock of Gibraltar and witnessed the monstrous, mountainous waves of the Atlantic, still storm-swept, and a school of gray whales, spouting with relish among the blowing white-caps. Of course the climax of this odyssey was the first sight of our gracious lady in New York harbor, followed by the docking at Pier 88 at 9:30PM on November 5[TH]. It took until 2:10AM of the 6[TH] before we could debark, followed by a ferry ride across the Hudson River to Exchange Place in Jersey City, N.J., where I ordered my North Carolina cohorts to get down on their knees and kiss that hallowed ground.

A short train ride and we were at Camp Kilmer, now part of the campus of Rutgers University. As soon as we had been fed and found places to sleep, a group of men from the 181[ST] met outside of one of the barracks for a final photo. It was taken by a fellow named Dave Thorn from Louisiana and who, after taking all of our names and addresses, promised to send each of us a copy. Of course he did no such thing, since it would have only been an unpleasant reminder of where he had just spent three forgettable years. There is no record, of course, of who was in that photo. We do know that, besides Thorn, Martenson and myself, the following were passengers on the Ballou:

| | |
|---|---|
| Pierson Roe | Phillipsburg, NJ |
| William Friedman | New York City |
| Raymond Fichter | Palmyra, NJ |
| Mickey Zace | Kankakee, IL |
| Forrest Brown | Kansas City, KS |
| Paul Mrogenski | Brookfield, MO |
| Willis Dengler | Waterloo, IA |
| Alvin Paul Wagler | Burlington, IA |
| Lloyd Teske | Scranton, ND |
| Millard Sturgell | Cherokee, KY |
| Lois "Luke" Orman | Thomasville, NC |
| Alton Croom | Robersonville, NC |

Following the contingent that left on the Ballou, on October 10, 1945, Lt. Robert Finkel, (the busbody bandit) received orders to leave Kunming for Calcutta and Replacement Depot 494. His flight to India was on the 24TH and on the 29TH he was on his way aboard the USS General M. B. Stewart, a Kaiser Liberty Ship. Because of his background in entertainment in civilian life, he was appointed editor of the ship newspaper the TROOPER and assigned to the ship's staff. The voyage was singular in that it was subjected to twelve successive days of rain. His arrival at New York was on November 26TH and his discharge was received the 28TH at the camp at Indiantown Gap in central Pennsylvania. He was placed on the inactive reserve and given a thirty-day leave of absence.

. . . .

Subsequent reports have described, in more detail, the dangers and even fatalities inflicted by Indian Nationalist mobs on unarmed Americans in truck convoys as they traveled through Calcutta, en-route to the docks. While my memory vaguely recalls the urgency demonstrated by the folks that carried me to the Ballou, I was unaware of the political climate and dangers that existed.

The bottom line, as far as I know, is that all of the men who left their homes in 1941 and 1942 to form and serve as the 181 ST Signal Repair Company finally made it back to the USA. To my knowledge, there were no fatalities among them . . . not surprising, since we were considered service forces, in contrast to the ground forces, although some of the repair teams accompanied those units that carried the fight to the enemy. As reported, in the campaigns in the Salween in China and in Burma, however, some exposure to combat situations by several of the men earned them citations in which they were awarded bronze star medals. In the case of Jim Hoff, from Palmyra, NJ, his citation included a commendation for his role in the battle of Tengchung in Southwestern China, during which he killed a Japanese soldier.

U.S.S. General Brooks

Hoogly River—U.S.S. General Ballou

Shirley (NC), Wingler (IL), Thompson (PA)
(sitting)—Wagler (IA)

New York Harbor

# EPILOGUE

Historical accounts and assessments of the Allied efforts in China, Burma and India vary widely, reflecting the personal opinions of the people who have compiled them. There are some, especially the British, who contended throughout the war that the Chinese should have been left to their own devices, and that they could contribute very little to the final victory. General Chennault, bypassing the theater commander, General Joseph Stilwell, lobbied Washington that air power alone could defeat the Japanese. Articulating the Ground Forces viewpoint, General Stilwell insisted that both the British and Chennault opinions were inaccurate and that the huge Chinese Army could serve the Allied cause if a greater emphasis was placed on feeding, equipping and training it.

One final analysis could conclude that each of these viewpoints had a smattering of truth in it. The reluctance of Chiang in releasing his divisions to the allied campaigns and the countermanding of Stilwell's orders to the Chinese did, indeed, inhibit their ability to perform as well as they probably could have . . . . thereby substantiating the British contentions. The records of the Air Transport Command, the Flying Tigers and their successor, the Fourteenth Air Force rival the accomplishments of any comparable units and if it had been feasible to give them the materiel they asked for (which it certainly was not) who knows to what degree they could have contributed to Japan's defeat? Finally, the ground campaign in Burma, conducted in large part by the American-equipped and trained

Chinese divisions, confirmed Stilwell's position that, with the right support, they could definitely perform effectively. Who knows what could have been wrought if Chiang had put as much effort into defeating the Japanese as he did in holding the Chinese Communists at bay in the north all during the war? There is even an opinion that the entire China, Burma, India Theater was unnecessary.

Historians will argue these points as long as there are historians. Those who take the time to research, in depth, the events that transpired during the war, and who come up with new facts are instantly labeled "revisionists". A tragic example of this, in my opinion, is the decision by the United States, at the end of the war, to support France's claim to Indo-China, especially after Ho Chih Minh had been our ally near it's end. But then, again, this is only one man's opinion!

. . . .

As far as the 181 ST and the men who remained loyal to it, despite all of the seemingly illogical demands it made of them, they have demonstrated all during the twenty-plus years it has taken to unearth their stories, that they are proud of what they had to do, even if it was mostly months on end of poor food, miserable living conditions and unfriendly natural elements. As we have discovered, however, several of them contributed much more than passive endurance of the deprivations that greeted them in that Godforsaken part of the globe.

. . . .

The decision to attempt to write the 181 ST story after what started out as a simple case of curiosity, has been one of the most satisfying events of my life. Not only because it had to be done, but because of the resulting re-uniting with so many of my old friends and comrades. The adventure of finding them, although too many had already been called to that repair shop in the sky, could by itself provide enough material for a second manuscript.

As the search proceeded, I discovered a bank president, a television producer, successful farmers, college professors, telephone company employees, several postal workers, a former gold miner from Alaska and bush pilot, several employees in the electronic field, automobile salesmen, a prominent New York lawyer, a department store owner, an official with the former discount giant "2 Guys From Harrison", a real estate broker, a forester and landscaper . . . . a list that includes just about every facet of American endeavor.

If the other military units that conducted World War 2 were comprised of men of the caliber of those I was privileged to spend time with, it is no wonder that we bested the Axis. Another fact that speaks favorably of the type of men they were is that they attracted an exceptional class of women as wives, mothers, grandmothers and great-grandmothers.

At this writing, 134 of the 187 men, who left California in 1943 on the "mystery ride" that landed them in Bombay, India, are known to have passed on to their eternal rewards. Another dozen or so were never found. Seventy or more, however, who were able to answer the latent call, have, by their enthusiastic responses to it, successfully reversed the relentless momentum that divided and scattered them throughout India, Burma and China . . . . and . . . . during the last quarter of the twentieth century did indeed stand together once again.

As father time does his thing, they will join the millions, who answered our nation's call and have since passed from the American scene. I beg the reader to remember all of them and should the call ever go out again, succeeding generations will do well to follow the examples that were set by men such as those who, for about four years called themselves "The 181 ST Signal Repair Company."

# BIBLIOGRAPHY

Anders, Leslie. THE LEDO ROAD. Univ. of Oklahoma Press, 1965.

Belden, Jack. RETREAT WITH STILWELL. New York: Alfred A. Knopf, 1943.

Bidwell, Shelford. THE CHINDIT WAR. New York: Macmillan Pub. Co. 1979.

Caldwell, Oliver J. A SECRET WAR. Carbondale and Edwardsville: Southern Illinois Press, 1972.

Camp, La Vonne Telshaw. LINGERING FEVER. Jefferson, NC: Mc Farland & Co. Inc.

Davies, John Paton, Jr. DRAGON BY THE TAIL. New York: W. W. Norton & Co., Inc. 1974.

Duiker, William J. HO CHI MINH. (a life) New York: Hyperion, 2000

Dunlop, Richard. BEHIND JAPANESE LINES. Chicago, New York, San Francisco: Rand Mc Nally & Co., 1979.

Eldridge, Fred, WRATH IN BURMA. Garden City, New York: Doubleday & Company, Inc., 1946.

Hunter, Colonel Charles N. (retired). GALAHAD. San Antonio, Texas: The Naylor Company, 1963.

Liu, F. F. A MILITARY HISTORY OF MODERN CHINA. Princeton: Princeton University Press, 1956.

Moon, Tom. THIS GRIM AND SAVAGE GAME. Los Angeles: Burning Gate Press, 1991.

Ogburn, Charlton Jr.. THE MARAUDERS. New York: Harper & Bros. 1956, 1959.

Peers, William R. & Brelis, Dean. BEHIND THE BURMA ROAD. Boston, Toronto: Brown & Co., 1963

Peterkin, Colonel W. J.. INSIDE CHINA. Baltimore: Gateway Press, 1992.

Romanus, Chas. F. & Sunderland, Riley. U.S.ARMY IN WWII STILWELL'S MISSION TO CHINA. Washington, D.C.: Office of the Chief of Military History, Department of the Army, 1953.

Romanus, Chas. F. & Sunderland, Riley. U.S. ARMY IN WWII— STILWELL'S COMMAND PROBLEMS. Washington, D.C: Office of the Chief of Military History, Department of the Army, 1956.

Romanus, Chas. F. & Sunderland, Riley. U.S. ARMY IN WWII— TIME RUNS OUT IN THE CBI. Washington, D.C: Center of Military History, United States Army, 1985.

Rooney, D.D.. STILWELL. New York: Ballantine Books Inc., 1971.

Seagrave, Gordon S.. BURMA SURGEON. New York: W. W. Norton & Co., 1943.

Seagrave, Gordon S.. BURMA SURGEON RETURNS. New York: W.W. Norton, 1946.

Service, John S.. LOST CHANCE IN CHINA. New York: Random House, 1974.

Scott, Robert Lee, Jr. FLYING TIGER. New York: Berkeley Publishing Co., 1960

Shaller, Michael. THE U.S. CRUSADE IN CHINA, 1938-1945. New York: Columbia University Press, 1979.

Slim, Sir William..DEFEAT INTO VICTORY. London: Landsborough Publications Ltd., 1958.

Smith, R. Harris. OSS The Secret History of America's First Central Intelligence Agency. Berkeley, Lo;s Angeles, London: U:niversit;y of California Press, 1972

Stilwell, Joseph W. (arranged and Edited by Theodore H. White). THE STILWELL PAPERS. New York: William Sloane Associates, 1948.

Stone, James H.. CRISIS FLEETING. Washington, D.C.: Office of the Surgeon General, Dept. of The Army, 1969.

Thomas, Lowell. BACK TO MANDALAY. New York: The Greystone Press, 1951.

Thompson, George Raynor & Harris, Dixie R. U.S.ARMY IN WWII—THE SIGNAL CORPS: THE OUTCOME. Washington, D.C.: Office of the Chief of Military History, U.S.Army, 1966.

Tuchman, Barbara W.. NOTES FROM CHINA. New York: Collier Books. 1972.

Tuchman, Barbara W.. STILWELL & THE AMERICAN EXPERIENCE IN CHINA, 1911-1945. New York: The Macmillan Company, 1971.

Wedemeyer, Albert C.. WEDEMEYER REPORTS!. New YOrk: The Devin-Adair Company, 1958.

White, Theodore H. & Jacoby, Annalee. THUNDER OUT OF CHINA. New York: William Sloane Associates, Inc., 1946.

White, Theodore H.. IN SEARCH OF HISTORY. New York: Warner Books. 1978.

Williams, Mary H.. U.S.ARMY IN WWII—CHRONOLOGY 1941-1945. Washington, D.C.: Office of the Chief of Military History, Department of the Army, 1960.

Y Force Operations Staff, Public Relations Officer. RECONSTRUCTION OF THE BURMA ROAD. APO 627 c/o PM, New York: October 24, 1944.

# INDEX